China and the Internet

China and the Internet

Using New Media for Development and Social Change

SONG SHI

Rutgers University Press

New Brunswick, Camden, and Newark, New Jersey

London and Oxford

Rutgers University Press is a department of Rutgers, The State University of New Jersey, one of the leading public research universities in the nation. By publishing worldwide, it furthers the University's mission of dedication to excellence in teaching, scholarship, research, and clinical care.

Library of Congress Cataloging-in-Publication Data
Names: Shi, Song, author.
Title: China and the Internet : using new media for development and social
    change / Song Shi.
Description: New Brunswick, New Jersey : Rutgers University Press, [2023] |
    Includes bibliographical references and index.
Identifiers: LCCN 2023014662 | ISBN 9781978834736 (paperback) |
    ISBN 9781978834743 (hardcover) | ISBN 9781978834750 (epub) |
    ISBN 9781978834774 (pdf)
Subjects: LCSH: Internet—Social aspects—China. | Internet—Political
    aspects—China. | Social change—China. | China—Social conditions—
    21st century.
Classification: LCC HN740.Z9 I56845 2023 | DDC
    302.23/10951—dc23/eng/20230706
LC record available at https://lccn.loc.gov/2023014662

A British Cataloging-in-Publication record for this book is available from the British Library.

References to internet websites (URLs) were accurate at the time of writing. Neither the author nor Rutgers University Press is responsible for URLs that may have expired or changed since the manuscript was prepared.

∞ The paper used in this publication meets the requirements of the American National Standard for Information Sciences—Permanence of Paper for Printed Library Materials, ANSI Z39.48–1992.

rutgersuniversitypress.org

For the activists, friends, NGOs, and other research participants with whom I have been working over the past twelve years

Contents

China and the Internet

1

Introduction

China now has the largest internet user base in the world, with upward of 1,051,000,000 internet users as of June 2022 (China Internet Network Information Center [CNNIC], 2022), over three times the population of the United States. This means that 19.8 percent of internet users worldwide, or nearly one in five, live in China (International Telecommunication Union, 2022). The Chinese internet and related phenomena have become globally significant among policymakers and the general public. Nevertheless, global news of China's internet is dominated by two oversimplified storylines. One celebrates it as an example of the success of consumerism in a postsocialist country, a market with huge potential, and an example of how the internet can boost commerce. For example, every year since 2010, the Chinese e-commerce giant Alibaba has broken the record for the world's biggest online shopping day on November 11.[1] This is China's Singles' Day, an obscure "anti–Valentine's Day" celebration launched by unmarried individuals in China in the 1990s.[2] Global media outlets have zealously touted these record-breaking sales with headlines like "Alibaba's Singles' Day Obliterates Cyber Monday's Sales Total in Less Than Two Hours" (2016) and "Alibaba, JD Smash Singles Day Record with $139 Billion of Sales" (Kharpal, 2021). The other storyline depicts the Chinese internet as a dismal space where every corner is controlled by the government. This was the gist of a piece on NBC News: "China's Internet Crackdown Is Another Step toward 'Digital Totalitarian State'" (I. Williams, 2017). Comprehensive reviews of previous research reveal a similar pattern among academic studies of China's internet (Hockx, 2005; Kluver & Yang, 2005; Qiu & Bu, 2013; Qiu & Chan, 2004).[3] These two storylines expose two important facets of the Chinese internet, yet the exclusive focus on them has tended to obscure the complexity and diversity of the Chinese internet and the vast richness of internet-related phenomena in Chinese society.

In December 2019, an outbreak of a novel coronavirus was first identified in Wuhan, China. By January 2020, the COVID-19 epidemic had spread to all the provinces, municipalities, and autonomous regions of China ("Most Updated Nationwide Data," 2020; National Health Commission of PRC, 2020a; *Real-time National COVID-19 Data*, 2020). On January 23, the Chinese government imposed a lockdown on Wuhan and other parts of Hubei, which quarantined almost 57,000,000 people. A week later, on January 30, the World Health Organization (WHO) declared the outbreak a public health emergency of international concern. On March 11, the WHO declared it a global pandemic. As of April 21, 2020, the Chinese government had reported 83,853 confirmed COVID-19 cases and 4,636 deaths due the outbreak (Johns Hopkins University, 2020).[4] By July 20, the pandemic had spread to 188 countries and territories and resulted in 665,581 total deaths globally (Johns Hopkins University, 2020). The cover-up of the outbreak and delayed response to this massive public health crisis by the Chinese government, especially in its early stages, have been documented and criticized extensively by journalists, international organizations, and political leaders (e.g., Associated Press, 2020; Buckley, 2020; *Coronavirus*, 2020; "COVID-19 and China," 2020; Faulconbridge & Holton, 2020; "He Warned of Coronavirus," 2020; *Li Wenliang*, 2020). The aggressive response and overreactions to the outbreak by the Chinese government in the later stages of the crisis have also been extensively reported and debated by journalists, scholars, medical experts, and international organizations (e.g., Beaubien, 2020; "COVID-19 and China," 2020; Johnson, 2020; Mailk, 2020; McNeil, 2020; "Sustaining Containment," 2020; van Elsland & O'Hare, 2020; World Health Organization [WHO], 2020a). Yet the response of China's grassroots organizations, activists, and volunteers to China's biggest public health crisis has barely been covered by mainstream media.

On January 25, two days after the Wuhan lockdown and the first day of Chinese New Year, NGO 2.0 Project trainee Wang Jun posted a WeChat message to the NGO 2.0 Trainee Group: "We initiated a grassroots organization focusing on donating PPEs and other medical supplies to frontline healthcare workers in Hubei. In our group, we have mask producers, healthcare workers, and individual donors. We are committed to the principle of transparency, openness, and volunteerism. We wish to contribute [to the response to COVID-19 in] Hubei. We wish to hold-on together in this crisis!"[5] Within a day, more than 130 NGO activists, volunteers, hospital health-care professionals, and personal protective equipment (PPE) producers joined the WeChat group—the Group for Medical Supply Donations to Hubei. On January 27, this group, along with activists and volunteers from other grassroots organizations, such as the Zhuoming Disaster Information Service Center, joined the Novel Coronavirus

Pneumonia (NCP) Life Support Network, a network of grassroots organizations that responded to this unprecedented public health crisis.[6] The major communication platform of the network, a WeChat group, incorporated five hundred members. The network launched countless other WeChat groups that connected thousands of activists, volunteers, community workers, media professionals, and PPE makers; thousands of people infected with COVID-19; and health-care workers. During the peak of the pandemic in China (mid-January to early April), the NCP Life Support Network conducted and coordinated more than twenty-eight projects, each consisting of hundreds of actions, to provide badly needed support to various groups that were vulnerable to numerous health and/or social problems caused by the COVID-19 crisis.

In April 2011, Deng Fei, a journalist turned activist, founded the Free Lunch Project, a nationwide online grassroots action to provide free lunches to schoolchildren in China's underdeveloped rural regions. As of December 2022, the project had received more than 979,570,000 yuan ($144,434,657) in donations from millions of participants and had provided free lunches to more than 410,000 children in 1,679 schools in twenty-six provinces and autonomous regions in China (Free Lunch Project, 2022).

In 2009, researcher-activists launched the NGO 2.0 Project in collaboration with numerous NGOs in China to redress the disparity between grassroots NGOs and government-organized NGOs (GONGOs) in communications across Chinese society. It has aimed to empower grassroots NGOs by enhancing their capacity to use new media and information and communication technologies (ICTs) and has provided new media training workshops to roughly four thousand NGOs in China over the past twelve years.

In the first ten years of the Chinese internet (1995 to 2004), internet use was purely an urban phenomenon. As of 2003, less than 0.2 percent of China's 780,000,000 rural population used the internet, roughly one-fortieth of the internet use rate in the cities (Qiang, 2007). Then in 2004, the Chinese government launched the Connecting Every Village Project to promote the use of the internet in rural China. By 2011, 89 percent of administrative villages had attained broadband access (Ministry of Industry and Information Technology [MIIT], 2011b). As of December 2019, 135,000,000 rural households had used broadband internet (MIIT, 2020).

There are many other cases of using new media and the internet for development and social change in contemporary China. The preceding examples are only the tip of the iceberg. China's activists, NGOs, and government offices have used the internet extensively to target deep-seated development problems and urgent social concerns affecting millions of people's lives. Yet this facet of internet use has attracted little attention in mainstream discourse about the Chinese internet. This book will help rectify this shortcoming by analyzing, through theoretically informed empirical investigations, the impact of new media on development and social change in contemporary China. It will look at new media interventions for development and social change carried out by activists, NGOs, and the government. These initiatives have used communication research, theories, processes, and technologies to bring about development and social change (Rogers, 1976; Servaes, 1999) or, in other words, to "advance socially beneficial goals" (Wilkins, 2009; Wilkins & Mody; 2001). These include actions, projects, and policies that aim to use new media and ICTs to promote development and social change.

This book will analyze the impact of new media and ICTs using a communication for development approach. Communication for development (also known as development communication or communication for development and social change) is the study of development and social change brought about through the application of communication research, theory, and technologies (McAnany, 2012; Melkote & Steeves, 2015a; Rogers, 1976; Servaes, 1999, 2008; Wilkins, 2015; Wilkins & Mody, 2001). Since the 1980s, mainstream theories in communication for development (e.g., Huesca, 2001; Kleine, 2013; Melkote & Steeves, 2001; Ogan et al., 2009; Servaes, 1999; Wilkins, 2015) have propelled the conceptualization of development beyond pure economic development and economic growth. New theories in the field have come to envision development as a form of social change (e.g., Dagron, 2001; Dagron & Tufte, 2006; Wilkins, 2000). However, the more established phrase "development and social change" (e.g., Enghel, 2013; McAnany, 2012; Servaes, 2008, 2011; Tacchi & Lennie, 2014) is more useful for the task of this book, examining projects that target conventional development problems, such as hunger and malnutrition, as well as actions that attack the lack of government accountability and other social problems.

In communication for development and related fields, "social change" refers to a significant change in social structure, social relationships, or culture in a given society, community, or context (Dagron and Tufte, 2006; Harper and Leicht, 2015; Hemer & Tufte, 2005; Rogers, 1971; Rogers & Svenning, 1969; Servaes, 2011; Shah, 2010; Wilkins, 2000).[7] Social change may be initiated through grassroots actions, government entities, or a combination of both. Most research on communication for development focuses on using communication to promote positive social change or to "advance socially beneficial goals," such as gender equality, racial equality, and the empowerment of marginalized groups (Wilkins, 2005; Wilkins & Mody, 2001), yet some research reveals how communication has been used for negative social change, such as inciting ethnic hatred (e.g., Cammaerts, 2016; Costa, 2012; Kellow & Steeves, 1998; Myers, 2008). In line with mainstream scholarship in communication for development, social change in the narrative that follows refers to positive social change led by various stakeholders, including activists/NGOs and/or governments. Although communication for development is widely used in studies of the internet and ICTs internationally (e.g., Donner, 2015; James, 2005; Kleine, 2013; Ogan et al., 2009; Torero & von Braun, 2006; Unwin, 2009), it has not been rigorously applied in studies of China's internet, which is surprising given China's stature as the largest developing country with the biggest population and largest internet user base in the world. By employing this approach, this book will offer a new perspective to examine the internet and related phenomena in Chinese society.

Most of the previous research on new media's impact in Chinese society does not consider the government's use of new media for development and social change. In contrast, this book looks at the government as one of several potential stakeholders that may generate development and social change in China. Using a communication for development approach, it analyzes state policies, NGO projects, and activist actions as three types of interventions that intersect and interact with one another. In so doing, this book offers a more comprehensive and complex view of how new media and ICTs have been used for development and social change in Chinese society. Drawing on media coverage, online interactions between activists, NGO project records, government policy documents, and my own experiences working with NGOs and activists over the past twelve years, this book investigates how activists, NGOs, and the government have engaged in new media interventions to empower NGOs, promote government accountability, bridge the digital divide, help alleviate hunger and malnutrition, and battle the COVID-19 outbreak. Second, it explores the complex, multidimensional, and dynamic relations among activists, NGOs, and the government in new media interventions in the social, political, and technological contexts of contemporary China. Third, it examines the role and effects of new media, ICTs, and traditional media in promoting development and social change in China.

The Internet in China: Exploring the Landscape

In China, the internet is huge and fast growing. In the twenty-five years between 1995 and 2020, China's internet penetration rate increased from nearly 0 percent to 67 percent, with the number of internet users increasing over a thousandfold, from roughly 620,000 to 940,000,000 (CNNIC, 1997, 2020b). Yet China's overall internet development level and internet use rate continues to lag behind those of developed countries, such as the United States (see figure 1.1). China's internet use rate in 2020 (67.0%) was still 0.97% below that of the United States in 2005—a decade and a half earlier. To address the internet in China, we must realize that in terms of internet development level and internet adoption rate, China remains a developing country in which 463 million citizens—or almost 33 percent of its population—have never used the internet. Therefore, our investigation of the Chinese internet needs to pay attention to not only the huge number of internet users but also the equally huge number of nonusers. Of course, if the present pattern continues, internet users and the internet adoption rate in China will continue to increase for the foreseeable future. And with more and more people going online, the internet will continue to have increasing influence in China. Another characteristic of China's internet is unbalanced development,

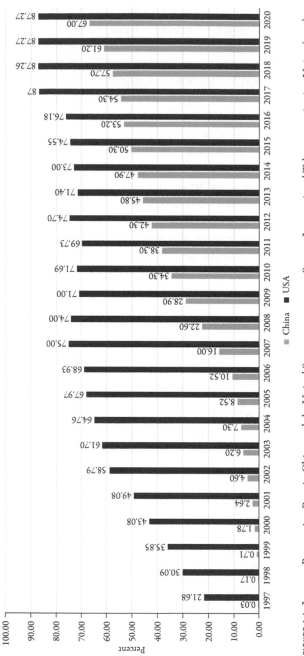

FIGURE 1.1 Internet Penetration Rate in China and the United States, 1997 to 2020. Source: International Telecommunication Union (2017); China Internet Network Information Center (CNNIC) (2020b)

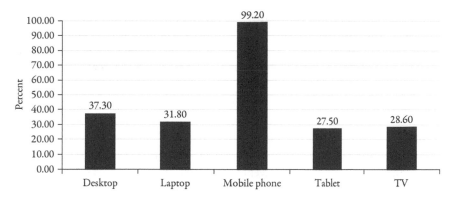

FIGURE 1.2 Internet Access Devices of Chinese Internet Users in 2020. Source: CNNIC (2020b)

with significant disparities in the adoption rate and availability of the internet among different regions and social groups. The digital divide, or digital inequality, within the country is an urgent social problem that merits serious attention. For example, in rural areas, the internet use rate has barely reached 52.3 percent, which is 24.1 percent lower than in urban areas (76.4%). Among nonusers, 56.2 percent are rural residents and 43.8 percent are urban residents (CNNIC, 2020b). The difference in use rates is but one aspect of rural China's disadvantaged position in internet and new media use, however. Chapter 2 will detail this digital divide.

Mobile devices, such as smartphones, and the mobile internet are changing internet use in China, as in most other countries (Donner, 2015). As of June 2020, 99.2 percent of Chinese internet users (932,000,000) used mobile phones to access the internet. Overall, mobile phones have surpassed desktops and laptops as the most widely used internet access devices in China (see figure 1.2). In other developing countries around the globe, mobile apps and the internet have been widely used to solve development problems and to promote social change (e.g., Aker, 2011; Chib, 2013; Chib et al., 2015; Donner, 2015, p. 9; Ekine, 2010). In this book, I will therefore pay special attention to the use of the mobile internet and smartphones in new media interventions in China. Chapter 3 will examine the use of mobile apps in grassroots NGO communications, chapter 5 will examine the use of smartphones in NGO fundraising, and chapter 7 will investigate the use of mobile apps in the response of grassroots organizations to the COVID-19 crisis.

As for education levels among users, college graduates are not the largest group of internet users in China. People with a medium level of education (62% of total internet users) and people with a lower level of education (19.2% of total internet users) outnumber those with a high level of education (18.8% of total internet users) (CNNIC, 2020b).[8] This indicates that the internet is not a luxury service for elite groups in China, as Qiu (2009) and Wallis (2013) point out. Huge numbers of people with medium—or even lower levels of education—use the internet. Indeed, the internet has become a communication channel for a wide range of social groups. Accordingly, it has also become a potential tool for people from different social groups or classes, including the lower class, to pursue social change for their own interests.

It must be noted that the Chinese government heavily regulates, censors, and controls the internet. Its restrictive internet policies and systematic censorship of online expression have been documented, analyzed, and criticized extensively by scholars and journalists, as well as by international organizations and politicians (e.g., Branigan, 2009; "China invents," 2016; Clayton et al., 2006; Delisle et al., 2016; King et al., 2013; Mozur, 2017; Roberts, 2018; Wacker, 2003; G. Yang, 2009; Zittrain & Edelman, 2003). Yet these restrictive internet policies have not stopped online actions for social and political change (Delisle et al., 2016; Qiu, 2009; Yang, 2009). As will be demonstrated in chapter 4, the development of new ICTs has enhanced the resilience of activist resistance to government crackdowns. Under current internet policy, China's "Great Firewall" blocks access to global internet platforms and services, such as Google, Facebook, YouTube, and Twitter, for most Chinese internet users.[9] Domestic counterparts to these international internet platforms, such as Baidu, Renren, Youku, and Weibo, dominate China's internet.[10] However, the two most used internet services in China are rather unique: instant messaging (IM)[11] and mobile messaging apps.[12] As of 2020, 99 percent and 99.8 percent of Chinese internet users utilize IM and mobile messaging apps, respectively (CNNIC, 2020b), whereas in the United States, only 29 percent of online adults use mobile messaging apps (Pew Research Center, 2015).

Studying the Chinese Internet: Three Limitations of Previous Research

As the Chinese internet has grown and continues to expand, so has the field of Chinese internet studies.[13] Herold and de Seta (2015) found that more than 590 academic works on the Chinese internet were published between 1990 and 2013 by scholars representing more than thirty disciplines. Detailed reviews of Chinese internet studies have been presented in various substantial academic works by other scholars (Herold & de Seta, 2015; Kluver & Yang, 2005; Qiu & Bu, 2013; Qiu & Chan, 2004). Offering yet another here would be redundant and exceed the scope of this introduction. This brief review is confined to three core themes regarding the limitations of the dominant perspectives and discourse of previous research about China's internet. It lays the groundwork for the discussion of how the case studies presented in subsequent chapters redress these limitations and how my work contributes to the scholarly debates regarding China's internet. These three themes include previous topics of scholarly research on the Chinese internet, the role of state policies in social change, and the relationship between activists/NGOs and the government in the use of new media for development and social change.

Topics of Research

Scholars have provided insightful examinations of various aspects of China's internet from several perspectives, such as internet censorship and control (e.g., King et al., 2013; L. Li,2019; Roberts, 2018; Wacker, 2003), cybernationalism and the link between social media and China's foreign relations (DeLisle et al.; 2016; Jiang, 2012, 2017; Schneider, 2018; S. Wang, 2017; X. Wu, 2007), cyberspace and civil society (Tai, 2006), online activism and political contention (G. Yang, 2009), ICTs and the formation of the working class (Qiu, 2009), the political economy of China's ICT sector (H. Yu, 2017), the social and cultural implications of mobile communication for migrant women (Wallis, 2013), social media use among rural residents (McDonald, 2016), nonconfrontational activism, "maker culture," and the internet (J. Wang, 2019b),[14] and so on.

Most recent scholarship on the impact of the internet in Chinese society privileges conventional topics that Herold and de Seta (2015), among others (Kluver & Yang, 2005; Qiu & Bu, 2013; Qiu & Chan, 2004), categorize as "political issues."[15] Yang's groundbreaking contribution (2009) to our knowledge of online activism, political contentions, and internet-related struggles in contemporary Chinese society sheds light on the ongoing debate over the potential of new media to promote democratization in contemporary China. Qiu (2009) presents a theoretically guided empirical investigation of the role of ICTs in the formation of a new working class in urban China. DeLisle et al.'s (2016) edited volume offers an in-depth examination of the relationship between social media and China's civil society, politics, legal system, and foreign relations, arguing that social media and China's politics and society exist in a diverse and dynamic relationship. It insightfully points out that simple dichotomies, such as "freedom versus control," are insufficient to understand the impact of new media in contemporary China (p. 3). Using a political economy approach, H. Yu (2017) uncovers the crucial role of the ICT sector in Chinese-style capitalism and how the state, the global market, and class interests have constructed China's ICT industry. S. Wang (2017) offers a quantitative analysis of the relationship between internet exposure and issues such as political beliefs and nationalism in China, based on a survey of 1,200 college students. Using large social media data sets, online experiments, and surveys, Roberts (2018) provides an empirically grounded and theoretically rich investigation of internet censorship in Chinese cyberspace. Rather than focusing on the subject matter that is censored, Roberts emphasizes the influence of censorship on individuals in authoritarian regimes and its political implications. She argues that censorship works not because the whole society is completely denied access to the censored information but because the majority of the public is minimally inconvenienced in accessing that censored information (2018). Schneider (2018) offered an insightful addition to the growing literature on the political impact of ICTs and the internet in China. Using anti-Japanese nationalism as a case study, Schneider explores online networks and their nationalist discourses on the Chinese internet. L. Li (2019) examines why the Chinese state's regulation on online video is more lenient than its regulation on television, situating the Chinese Communist Party's (CCP) regulation of online video in a long history of the party's regulation of cultural production and consumption from the 1930s to the present. She notes that the state's increased management of the internet since 2014 is very likely to unify the online and offline censorship standards and reduce freedom online.

In contrast to the mainstay of the previous research, Wallis (2013) and McDonald (2016) have examined the social and cultural impacts of ICTs in China. Using cultural and feminist theories, Wallis (2013) presents an empirically grounded ethnographic investigation of the use of mobile communication among young migrant women. Examining migrant women's mobile phone use in the shifting social structures and practices of contemporary China, she explores how using mobile phones enables young migrant women to "participate in and create culture, allowing them to perform a modern, rural-urban identity." McDonald (2016) presents an in-depth ethnographic study of the use of social media among residents in a rural town in eastern China. His findings suggest that rural people use social media primarily to extend and transform their social relationships by deepening already existing social networks among friends and coworkers. McDonald argues that social media allows rural users to understand, capitalize on, and challenge normative morality in rural towns.

J. Wang's (2019b) book on nonconfrontational activism exemplifies the rise of a new wave of scholarship on the Chinese internet that questions conventional paradigms, conventional concepts, and mainstream topics. Through a detailed investigation of the "digital gray zone" (p. 59) lurking between the lawful and the illegitimate, she reveals a phenomenon of nonconfrontational activism in Chinese society. She conceptualizes this digital gray zone as a critique of the conventional binary paradigm of "state versus society" found in previous research (p. 62). She examines this phenomenon by showing how actors such as NGOs, millennial college students, digital makers, and the corporate social responsibility (CSR) sector in IT companies "make their social mark" (p. 62) in this gray zone and how the CCP, as the powerful actor, defines the boundaries of "the social" in nonconfrontational politics in China (p. 69).[16]

A brief review of recent research on the impact of the internet in China (above) illustrates the overwhelming corpus of studies on government control of the internet, confrontational activism, possibilities for political transformation, and other political issues in relation to all forms of internet use. This pattern pervades the entire field of Chinese internet studies. Five comprehensive reviews of the field (Herold & de Seta, 2015; Hockx, 2005; Kluver & Yang, 2005; Qiu & Bu, 2013; Qiu & Chan, 2004) all support this finding. In their 2005 metareview of academic articles on the Chinese internet published between 1990 to 2003,

Kluver and Yang (2005) revealed significant gaps in Chinese internet studies due to the excessive attention paid to the politics of the internet in China and the inadequate focus on cultural and social aspects of internet use. They criticized the fact that current research in the field did not seek to create a fuller understanding of the various ways that the internet might affect Chinese life. After almost ten years, Qiu and Bu (2013) revealed a similar pattern. In a review of research on Chinese ICTs published between 1989 and 2012, Qiu and Bu noted that most Western scholarship on the Chinese internet emphasizes the political influence of the internet more than everything else: political issues are the focus in 55.1 percent (276 out of 501) of academic publications, economic issues in 35.7 percent (179 out of 501), and social issues in 19.6 percent (98 out of 501). This same pattern is found in a 2004 review by Qiu & Chan and a 2005 review by Hockx. Indeed, research on the political aspects of the Chinese internet over the past three decades has generated many scholarly works that have had a long-lasting impact on our understanding of China and the internet.[17] Yet recently, this long-standing convention of giving priority to political issues has been contested (e.g., Damm, 2007; Guo, 2020; Herold, 2014; Herold & de Seta, 2015; Kluver & Yang, 2005; McDonald, 2016; Meng, 2010; Qiu & Bu, 2013, J. Wang 2019b).

At the beginning of her book *The Other Digital China* (2019), J. Wang moves beyond the conventional focus on political issues such as online surveillance, censorship, and confrontational political activism. By focusing on the "digital gray zone," her book spotlights the digital practices of invisible change agents such as NGOs, millennials, digital makers, and the CSR sector, which have been overlooked in previous research. Guo (2020) shows how the dominant storylines miss the complex reality of the Chinese internet. Guo sees the Chinese internet not as a dismal space tightly controlled by the government but as "one of the most creative digital cultures in the world." Instead of staying in line with conventional scholarship and focusing on what does not appear on China's internet due to state control, Guo examines the complex mechanisms that give visibility to content on four ICT platforms: the bulletin board system, the blog, the microblog, and WeChat. In a similar vein, Meng (2010) challenges the dominance of what she calls "the pre-formed lens of democratization" in Chinese internet studies. From a critical and postcolonial perspective, she questions the fundamental conceptualization of the "democratization framework." Empirically, she argues that the exclusive focus on conventional political issues such as democratization may oversimplify the diverse activities in Chinese cyberspace, "many of which contribute to a more inclusive communication environment without pursuing overt political agendas." Damm (2007) argues that political issues such as censorship, democratization, and the use of new media by dissidents have been overemphasized in Chinese internet studies. He argues that the dominance of this approach overlooks the fragmentation and diversification of Chinese society and the rise of urban lifestyles, which has diminished public interest in conventional politics. In their comprehensive review of 590 academic publications regarding the Chinese internet, Herold and de Seta (2015) have concluded that the lopsided prioritization of political issues in Chinese internet studies may reduce Chinese internet research to a subset of the field of Chinese politics. To enrich our knowledge of China's internet, they argue, more studies are needed that go beyond Western society's interest in China's political transformation to look at how people in China actually use the internet to achieve their own goals. In concluding their review of Chinese internet and ICT studies, Qiu and Bu (2013) also caution against the lack of diversity in the field and call for more research on how ICTs are used in development and meeting other social goals.

This book is a timely response to these emerging critical voices in Chinese internet studies. To comprehend the immense diversity and richness of internet-related phenomena in Chinese society, we must move beyond excessive concern with conventional issues, such as internet control and confrontational activism. This is not meant to downplay the significance of this concern but to underscore the need to investigate numerous other aspects of China's internet.

Eschewing the conventional overemphasis on the political impact of new media on Chinese society, my work considers other impacts shown through a communication for development approach. It focuses on the use of the internet and ICTs for development as well as the use of new media for social change. Development is a major concern for many Chinese communities as well as for the nation as a whole, as they struggle to overcome the conditions of a developing country with a huge population. New media and ICTs have significantly affected China's development needs but have not yet been acknowledged in the established literature. By analyzing this impact, this book offers a more comprehensive knowledge of China and the internet.

The Role of State Policies

China's internet policy is one of the most examined topics in the prevailing research on the Chinese internet.[18] Yet most of this research is only really concerned with those state policies that function as part of the apparatus to control and contain resistance and obstruct change, such as policies on internet censorship, internet control, and surveillance (Damm, 2007; Herold & de Seta, 2015; Meng, 2010; J. Wang, 2019b; Zhao, 2009). This is a natural result of the long-standing prioritization of possibilities for political transformation in Chinese internet studies. As Meng (2010) and Qiu and Bu (2013) note, Western policymakers and scholars view the internet as the most likely tool for bringing about political transformation in China. So when this new tool is subjected to state censorship, control policies, and other countermeasures, those countermeasures and questions over which side prevails naturally become the most significant issues for research in Chinese internet studies. Chinese state policies on internet censorship and control are certainly worthy of significant attention from scholars, given that this affects every corner of Chinese cyberspace and the internet practices of 940,000,000 online users (Roberts, 2018). Yet like the long-standing prioritization of political issues discussed in the previous section, the exclusive focus on state policies regarding information control may obscure policies on other equally significant issues in Chinese society. In contrast, my work advocates incorporating state policies for development and social change and various other policies into research in Chinese internet studies. This book illustrates the important impact of state policies for development and social change on deep-seated development problems and concerns in many communities in China. The powerful influences of such state policies, as well as their weaknesses, demand consideration and critical analysis. Additionally, this book considers the government as one of several potential stakeholders that may generate development and social change in China. Informed by previous research in communication for development (e.g., Dagron & Tufte, 2006; Huesca, 2001; Kleine, 2013; Melkote & Steeves, 2015b; Pieterse, 2010; Servaes, 1999; Servaes et al., 2012; Wilkins, 2009; Wilkins & Mody, 2001), it analyzes state policies, NGO projects, and activist actions as three types of new media interventions that intersect and interact with one another. As such, it offers a more complex, context-specific, and comprehensive view of the role of state policies in development and social change in China. Moreover, this approach provides a unique opportunity to expose the interactions between state policies and new media interventions initiated by activists and NGOs, and helps illustrate the complex web of influence extending between state policies and initiatives of activists and NGOs, overlooked in Chinese internet studies and communication for development research.

Relations between Activists and NGOs and the Government

Activism, activists, and NGOs are also broadly examined topics in the current literature on Chinese internet studies (e.g., Chase & Mulvenon, 2002; J. Liu, 2016; MacKinnon, 2008; Mina, 2014; Qiu, 2009; Sullivan, 2012; G. Yang, 2009). According to Qiu and Bu (2013), 9.2 percent of the research on the Chinese internet published between 1989 and 2012 examined the use of ICTs among NGOs and activists. In analyzing the relations between the government and activists/NGOs, most extant research, however, has focused almost exclusively on contentiousness and confrontation. Numerous scholars have over-simplistically characterized the relationship between the government and activists as "a cat and mouse game," a canonical portrayal that can be found in much of the previous research (Herold & de Seta 2015). This approach rightly addresses one important facet of the relationship between activists and the government in using new media for social change in China, yet it oversimplifies broader issues. In contrast, this book—by using a context-based approach—is able to convey the complexity, multidimensionality, and dynamic nature of that relationship and how it is shaped by the interests of different governmental agencies, corporations, and beneficiary communities, as well as the context of any given new media intervention. Moreover, research in political science and government (e.g., Brødsgaard, 2017; Koesel et al., 2020; Lieberthal & Lampton, 1992; Lin, 2006; Mertha, 2009; Yu & Guo, 2012) has elucidated the fragmented nature of the Chinese government. Among others, Brødsgaard (2017) holds that the concept of fragmented authoritarianism is key to understanding the political process, policymaking, and policy implementation in China. These scholars have argued that bureaucratic bargaining is central to understanding policymaking in China; in China's fragmented bureaucratic system, policies have to incorporate the goals and interests of the implementing agencies if implementation is to be achieved (Brødsgaard, 2017). In the reform era, the fragmented nature of the government has enabled three stakeholders (officials opposed to a given policy, media and journalists, and NGOs and activists) to engage in the policymaking process (Mertha 2009a, 2009b) as "tentative participants adopting the rule of the game previously only open to bureaucrats" (Mertha & Brødsgaard, 2017, p. 4). In line with works on the fragmented nature of the Chinese government (e.g., Brødsgaard, 2017; Lieberthal & Lampton, 1992; Mertha, 2009a, 2009b; Schlæger, 2013; Yu & Guo, 2012), this book looks at the Chinese government as a huge bureaucracy in which various government entities, through the influence of different social forces, compete and interact with one another in the policymaking and implementation processes. In so doing, it reveals that different government entities have divergent policies on and attitudes toward development and social change initiatives. Therefore, activists' relations with those government entities may vary significantly. Furthermore, activists and NGOs are readily adaptable in their relationship with the government in actions for social change, making that relationship very dynamic, as will be demonstrated in this book.

My approach to this issue has also been influenced by my experiences working with NGOs and activists in the New Media Action Lab at MIT over the past twelve years. A year after the Sichuan earthquake of 2008, which caused 69,180 confirmed deaths, I was conducting fieldwork in China for a pilot project of MIT's New Media Action Lab to examine the use of new media and the internet among Chinese NGOs. I attended a sideline event on NGO-government relations at the 16th Congress of the International Union of Anthropological and Ethnological Sciences in Kunming, China. At this event, I was surprised and amazed by the heated yet friendly debates among the roughly fifty leading Chinese NGOs on their relations with the government. As leading figures in China's nonprofit sector, these NGO practitioners know one another by reputation, if not as friends. Some of them collaborated in actions related to Sichuan earthquake relief and reconstruction. Yet their views on NGO-government relations diverged greatly. Some considered the government to be the major cause of the social problems that they target in their actions. Some emphasized the independence of the NGOs from the government. Others believed that the government should be engaged as a stakeholder to bring about changes in Chinese society. The most impressive aspect of the debate was that it was based more on their rational understandings of Chinese society than on emotional attitudes toward the government. A government crackdown had just dismantled several NGOs headed by conference attendees leading Sichuan earthquake relief actions. Yet even after their organizations had been shut down, these leaders argued that NGOs must cooperate with the government to generate large-scale social change and respond quickly to disasters such as the earthquake. Again and again over the past twelve years, I witnessed very similar debates regarding the relations between NGOs and activists and the government in my work with Chinese NGOs. These experiences and the voices of NGOs working to generate change on the ground convinced me that binary questions, such as whether activists and NGOs are working with or against the government, are oversimplifications. The relations between activists, NGOs, and the government in new media interventions are very complex and multidimensional, and they can only be examined and understood in relation to specific sociopolitical contexts.

Communication, Development, and Social Change as Approaches

Modernization theory (e.g., Almond & Coleman, 1960; Lerner, 1958; Lerner & Schramm, 1967; Rogers, 1962; Rostow, 1953) is the dominant paradigm in communication for development, and it significantly shaped the definition, understanding, and practice of development among scholars, policymakers, and practitioners between the 1950s and the 1960s (Servaes, 1999, 2008; Sparks, 2007). It defined development and underdevelopment in terms of observable quantitative differences between rich (developed) and poor (developing) countries (Servaes, 1999), and it used a number of quantitative economic growth indicators—income, per capita GDP, savings and investment rates—to measure different stages of development. In the late 1950s and early 1960s, modernization theory incorporated noneconomic indicators, such as attitudes toward change, education levels, institutional reforms, and rates of adopting mass media, to measure development (e.g., Almond & Coleman, 1960; Lerner, 1958). Modernization theorists have contended that underdevelopment in developing countries and less developed communities was fostered by internal forces in these societies and communities, such as traditional social, cultural, and political structures; traditional mindsets; and passive attitudes toward change. This implies that the stimulus for change or the solution to underdevelopment in developing countries must come from the outside (Western) world (Servaes, 1999). Accordingly, in development projects guided by modernization theory, less developed communities—the intended beneficiaries of development projects—are viewed as passive agents. Moreover, they have been excluded from policymaking and the process of designing these projects and developing a base of knowledge to solve underdevelopment. With regard to the role and effects of communication in development projects, the modernization paradigm fostered a "diffusion model" (Inagaki, 2007; Morris, 2003; Rogers & Shoemaker, 1983; Servaes, 1999) in which communication is considered to flow one way: from the "sender" (development experts) to the "receiver" (less developed communities).

On an international level, the modernization paradigm asserts that the transfer of technology, capital, values, and sociopolitical structure from developed (Western) countries to developing countries will solve conditions of underdevelopment and "modernize" its targets. The modernization paradigm was extensively criticized by other theories in communication for development from the 1970s to the present (Melkote & Steeves, 2001; Servaes, 1999, 2008; Sparks, 2007). Yet it remains a popular discourse among policymakers and a dominant approach in many development contexts, especially in projects related to ICTs (Inagaki, 2007; Ogan et al., 2009). Chapter 2 shows how the Chinese government's rural internet development policy relies on the Western modernization paradigm.

In the 1960s, the modernization paradigm came under attack via a new paradigm in development studies—the dependency paradigm—for being Eurocentric and ignoring the consequences of macro- and international economic and sociopolitical factors in local development (Fair, 1989; Pieterse, 2010; Servaes, 1999, 2008; Sparks, 2007). Most dependency paradigm researchers agreed that dependency is a conditional situation in which the economies of one group of countries are conditioned by the development of others. Dependency theories argued that the relationship of dependency between developing and developed countries causes underdevelopment in developing countries. Thus, the solution to underdevelopment in developing countries was to eliminate this dependency. In other words, developing countries should disassociate themselves from the world market and opt for a self-reliant development strategy. Although the dependency paradigm is the opposite of the modernization paradigm as a solution to underdevelopment in developing countries, they share the same definition of development and underdevelopment: the observable quantitative differences between rich (developed) and poor (developing) countries.

Since the 1980s, a new paradigm has emerged among academic theories and approaches—the participatory paradigm, or multiplicity paradigm—which has completely transformed the field of communication for development. By incorporating social issues such as freedom and justice, marginalization, and empowerment, these new theories have challenged the limited and biased understanding of development within the modernization and dependency paradigms (e.g., Dagron & Tufte, 2006; Friedmann, 1992; Hemer & Tufte, 2005; Jacobson, 2003; Kleine, 2013; Lennie & Tacchi, 2013; Melkote & Steeves, 2001; Servaes, 1999; Servaes et al., 1996; Sparks, 2007; Wilkins, 2000). Moving away from the focus on economic development in and of itself, scholars have argued for a broader conceptualization of development that includes social change (e.g., Black, 2007; Kleine, 2013; Servaes, 1999; Shah, 2010). Others have come to envision development as a form of social change (e.g., Dagron, 2001; Dagron & Tufte, 2006; Melkote & Steeves, 2001; Servaes et al., 1996; Wilkins, 2000). Although there is contestation over whether to change the name of the field from communication for development to communication for social change or communication for development and social change (Enghel, 2013; Wilkins, 2009), social change and related issues have become a core component in the field. Early research on social change in communication for development—for example, Rogers (1971)—overwhelmingly focused on social structure. Since the 1980s, the role of communication in changes to social structure and culture has attracted significant attention in communication for development and development studies (Dagron & Tufte, 2006; Hemer & Tufte, 2005; Jacobson, 2003; Melkote & Steeves, 2001; Pieterse, 2010; Servaes, 2008).

In practice, since the 1980s various development organizations, international organizations, and NGOs have incorporated social change into the goals of their development agendas. In 2015, the 193 countries of the UN General Assembly adopted a development agenda titled "Transforming Our World: The 2030 Agenda for Sustainable Development." A core component of the agenda is seventeen sustainable development goals (SDGs) (United Nations [U.N.], 2015). At least three of these SDGs focus on social change issues: gender equality (SDG 5); climate action (SDG 13); and peace, justice, and strong institutions (SDG 16). Specifically, social change issues, such as inclusion, justice, human rights, and government accountability, are considered parts of SDG 16, which aims to "Promote peaceful and inclusive societies for sustainable development, provide access to justice for all and build effective, accountable and inclusive institutions at all levels" (U.N., 2015, p. 16). On a more practical level, goals related to social change issues, such as stimulating participation, changing media policies, increasing access to media, expanding opportunities for getting information, and promoting cultural diversity, have all been proposed as goals for interventions initiated by development organizations, NGOs, activists, and governments (Waisbord, 2005).

Since the rise of the participatory paradigm in academia, new topics and problems related to social change, such as social actions and social movements, have significantly broadened the scope of the communication for development field (Dagron & Tufte, 2006; Hemer & Tufte, 2005; Huesca, 2001; Melkote & Steeves, 2001; Servaes, 2007; Wilkins et al., 2014). In the modernization paradigm, conventional research in communication for development primarily focused on the state, various levels of government, development agencies, international NGOs, and other formal development institutions. The modernization paradigm rarely considered actions initiated by activists and grassroots organizations to be legitimate topics of research. The emergence of new theories in the participatory, or multiplicity, paradigm has extensively changed this conventional yet narrow focus of the field. Servaes (1999), for example, asserts that social actions and social movements are important foci in communication for development research in the multiplicity paradigm. Wilkins and Mody (2001) reconceptualized the field "by affirming the intentional use of communication technologies and processes to advance socially beneficial goals" (p. 385). They stated, "Development communication theory also needs to expand its focus beyond the work of development institutions" to incorporate actions and social movements (p. 386). Huesca (2001), among others (Wilkins, 2015; Melkote & Steeves, 2015a), insightfully identifies social movements as an important direction for future research in development communication. In line with this new trend in communication for development, this book analyzes activist actions, NGO projects, and state policies as three forms of interacting and intersecting new media interventions. Three of the five cases presented in the book's chapters are actions or projects launched by activists.

Moreover, emerging theories, approaches, and practices since the 1980s have advocated the use of a participatory communication model in development practice. They consider communication in development initiatives to be a dialogue (e.g., Dagron & Tufte, 2006; Jacobson, 2003; Servaes et al., 1996). This means that the hierarchy between "sender" and "receiver" in the modernization paradigm should be leveled and all participants treated as equals. The meaning and knowledge of development and social change should be constructed through the interactions among different participants, including development experts, local communities, and other stakeholders. Chapter 3 explores how the NGO 2.0 Project was influenced by the principles and assumptions of participatory communication.

By focusing on the use of new media and ICTs in addressing conventional development problems and the use of new media in bringing about social change, this book embraces these new theories and approaches with a conceptual emphasis on social change. The chapters that follow will investigate five cases of new media interventions: the Connecting Every Village Project, the NGO 2.0 Project, Tiger Gate, the Free Lunch Project, and the NCP Life Support Network against COVID-19. The goals of Tiger Gate and the NGO 2.0 Project were more in line with social change initiatives: bringing about changes in social structure or social relationships in Chinese society. The targets of the Connecting Every Village Project, the Free Lunch Project, and the NCP Life Support Network— the rural–urban digital divide, hunger and malnutrition, and public health crises—were more in line with conventional development initiatives. In the cases of the Free Lunch Project and the NCP Life Support Network, I will explore the differences in the conceptualization of the problems that the government and activists aimed to change and the effectiveness of the activists' social change–based approach over the government's approach, which primarily relied on observable quantitative indicators.

Within the field of communication for development lies ICT for development, a subcategory that more closely reflects my research. A multidisciplinary field at the intersection of communication for development studies and other fields, such as ICT studies and information sciences, ICT for development (ICT4D) is generally understood as an approach that uses ICTs to bring about development and social change. The rise of ICT4D as an academic field and the large number of ICT4D projects in different countries are indications of the strong interest among scholars and practitioners in the effects of ICTs on development and social change (e.g., Donner, 2015; Heeks, 2008; Hudson, 2013; Kleine, 2013; Mansell & Wehn, 1998; Ogan et al., 2009; Torero & von Braun, 2006). Using meta-analysis and content analysis to examine publications on communication and development in peer-reviewed journals between 1998 and 2007, Ogan et al. (2009) found that ICT4D had become the most dominant approach employed by researchers concerned with the relationship between communication and development at that time, with 42.3 percent of the articles (85 out of 201) using ICT4D as their primary approach.[19] Yet rarely has this approach been comprehensively applied to studies of China's internet. This book aims to address this deficiency.

The research of Ogan et al. (2009) also reveals that a substantial number of researchers in ICT4D embraced the technological deterministic view of the modernization paradigm, believing that technology is the primary driver of development and that ICTs, such as the internet and mobile phones, are new magic solutions to development problems. Yet their research and that of others (e.g., Kleine, 2013; Servaes & Carpentier, 2006; Slater & Tacchi, 2004; Torero & von Braun, 2006) also indicate that an increasing amount of ICT4D scholarship considers ICTs to be tools for development and social change. For example, Torero and von Braun (2006) state that "ICT is an opportunity for development, but not a panacea. For the potential benefits of ICT to be realized in developing countries, many prerequisites need to be put in place" (p. 343). Servaes and Carpentier (2006) assert that ICTs provide "a new potential for combining the information embedded in ICT systems with the creative potential and knowledge embodied in people" (p. 5). The second group of scholars therefore believes that research on ICT4D should focus on how people use ICTs within specific sociopolitical, economic, and cultural contexts, as well as on the characteristics of ICTs. This book is more in line with the second wave of scholarship on ICT4D. It contributes to ICT4D and communication for development by offering context-based empirical case analyses of new media interventions in contemporary China.

Informed by the literature on communication for development (e.g., Dagron & Tufte, 2006; Hemer & Tufte, 2005; Jacobson, 2003; Kleine, 2013; McAnany, 2012; Melkote & Steeves, 2015a; Najam, 2000; Servaes, 1999, 2008; Servaes et al., 2012; Wilkins, 2015; Wilkins & Mody, 2001; Young, 2000), I devised a framework for analyzing new media interventions in China, which I use throughout the book (see figure 1.3). There are three basic components to this framework: development and social change, stakeholders, and communication channels. The communication for development approach helps to illustrate the

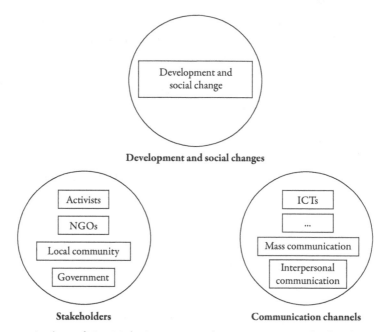

FIGURE 1.3 Analyses of New Media Interventions (Actions, Projects, and Policies)

development and/or social change that new media interventions aim to bring about. Over the past half century, communication processes, communication technologies, and communication channels have consistently been core issues in research on communication for development and ICT4D (e.g., Donner, 2015; Kleine, 2013; Melkote & Steeves, 2015a; Ogan et al., 2009; Rogers & Shoemajer, 1983; Schramm, 1964; Servaes, 1999, 2008). Following this long-standing legacy, my research on new media interventions also concentrates on communication channels and communication interactions. Another focus of my investigation is stakeholders. In communication for development, stakeholders are the public and interest groups that may strongly affect or be affected by development initiatives (Colle, 2008; Food and Agriculture Organization [FAO], 2006; Hemer & Tufte, 2005; Lie, 2008; Servaes, 1999; Servaes et al., 2012; United Nations Development Programme [UNDP], 2017). Works by academics (e.g., Brinkerhoff & Brinkerhoff, 2002; Colle, 2008; Hemer & Tufte, 2005; Lie, 2008; Melkote & Steeves, 2015a; Servaes, 1999; Servaes et al., 2012; Young, 2000) and development practitioners (e.g., FAO, 2006; UNDP, 2017) have both shown that analyzing how stakeholders engage in development initiatives and how those stakeholders are interrelated is crucial to understanding any given initiative. Servaes (1999) identified potential stakeholders in development initiatives, which included political parties, governments, corporations, lobbies, NGOs, activists, and local beneficiary communities. My research mainly focuses on the participation of three kinds of stakeholders—activists,

NGOs, and the government—in new media interventions and the relationships between these stakeholders in using new media for development and social change. Specifically, this book addresses several research questions in connection with the three basic components: What social problem does the intervention aim to resolve? What stakeholders have participated in the intervention? What are the relationships between them in such interventions? How are ICTs and other communication channels used in interventions, and to what effect? I apply this framework to five cases of new media interventions carried out by the government, NGOs, activists, and multi-stakeholders in China.

These new media interventions addressed several issues in contemporary China: the digital divide, NGO empowerment, government accountability and transparency, hunger and malnutrition, and the COVID-19 crisis. Rather than focusing purely on ICTs and new media, I join researchers in ICT4D (e.g., Costanza-Chock, 2014; Inagaki, 2007; James, 2005; Kleine, 2013; Servaes & Carpentier, 2006; Tacchi, 2007) who advocate using a multichannel perspective to examine and understand new media interventions. I investigate ICT use, online communications, and the interactions between ICT channels and other communication channels in the five separate case studies. I assess the effects of ICTs in new media interventions in a media environment in which various communication channels—including ICTs, mass media, and interpersonal communication—coexist with and are even interdependent on one another.

Structure of the Book

In the six substantive chapters and conclusion that follow, five case studies will illustrate my arguments.

In contrast to the impressive record of internet development reported by the Chinese government, China's vast rural hinterland lags far behind. Chapter 2 offers a critical analysis of the Connecting Every Village Project, through which the government has aimed to redress the rural–urban digital divide. Using van Dijk's (2005) definition of the digital divide, it shows how the Chinese government's conceptualization of the divide, as seen in its policy documents, is oversimplified. It exposes the weakness of the Connecting Every Village Project due to this oversimplification and analyzes the theories and assumptions that underpin the project.

Chapter 3 explores how the NGO 2.0 Project used new media and ICTs to empower grassroots NGOs and advocate for information equality in China's nonprofit sectors. It explores the problems that the project has tried to resolve over the past twelve years and examines how the project's workshops on Web 2.0 technologies empowered grassroots NGOs by enhancing their capacity to get their message out to the public through China's internet.[20] It analyzes how the theories and assumptions of participatory communication influenced the project, and examines the communication strategy and ICTs used in the project's advocacy for information equality and empowerment of the grassroots. Using the INfrastructure, EXperience, Skills, Knowledge (INEXSK) model (Mansell & Wehn, 1998) and the digital divide model, it shows how the NGO 2.0 Project and the Connecting Every Village Project are complementary.

Chapter 4 explores how activists use new media for social change through a case study of Tiger Gate, a nationwide grassroots new media action that challenged the authenticity of government-published wild tiger photos and opposed state plans to set up a wild tiger natural reserve. It addresses the following questions: How did ICTs contribute to the mobilization of activists and the construction of collective knowledge among activists in this action? How did activists use multiple communication channels in contesting the government's claims about the tiger photos? What social problem did this action aim to resolve? To what extent did this action increase government accountability? What are the limits of this new media action in promoting government accountability in China? Using Roland's (2004) theoretical discussion on institutional change, I will also reveal why Tiger Gate remains an important case in terms of the potential for bringing about social change in China, even despite its limits. In contrast to conventional portrayals, this chapter will illustrate the multidimensional nature of the relationship between activists and the government in new media actions.

Chapter 5 explores how multiple stakeholders—including NGOs, activists, individual new media users, and the Chinese government—collaborated on the Free Lunch Project to promote development and social change in China. It investigates how the project recruited a massive network of hundreds of thousands of contributors to provide daily free lunch to hundreds of thousands of rural children through an intensive internet blitz to solicit micro-donations of three yuan (30 to 45 cents), and how the project used what organizers called "strategic philanthropy" to influence, guide, and change state policy on child hunger, which affected tens of millions of rural children. It explores why different stakeholders, including NGOs and activists around the country, all got involved in the Free Lunch Project. The chapter also examines the communication channels that were used in this action, the interactions of these channels, and how these channels were used in monitoring, evaluating, and mobilizing this project and the fundraising behind it.

Chapter 6 analyzes the complex, dynamic, and multidimensional relations between activists, NGOs, and the government in the Free Lunch Project. It explores the reciprocal relations between activists and the government and how this grassroots project influenced the National Nutrition Subsidies Policy of the Chinese government. It then investigates the contentiousness Free Lunch Project activists faced over the previous ten years and how activists' efforts to bring about development and social change were met with constant resistance and obstruction by corporations and the government. It argues that the multidimensional relationship between activists and the government in the Free Lunch

Project is a sign of a new activism in China, and analyzes the strengths and weaknesses of this new activism in making social change in Chinese society.

Chapter 7 examines how grassroots organizations and activists responded to the COVID-19 crisis in Wuhan, China, through a case study of the NCP Life Support Network. It exposes this grassroots network's tremendous capacity to quickly and effectively respond to the constant barrage of wide-ranging and rapidly emerging problems in the crisis. It then examines how those in this network took action using ICTs in a city under lockdown. It shows how a transnational network of activists and volunteers connected by ICTs provided a transnational bridge first for PPE donations and purchases from five continents to frontline hospitals in Wuhan in February and then for PPE purchases and transport from Chinese PPE makers to international buyers from the United States, the European Union, and South America the very next month. The chapter then analyzes the interactions between activists and the government in response to COVID-19 and the multidimensional and dynamic relationship between activists and the government. It shows that activists exhibited a more effective response to COVID-19 than the government in many respects, such as distributing donated PPEs and addressing the urgent needs of pregnant women in Wuhan.

Based on the case studies in chapters 2 through 7, the conclusion addresses the broader implications of these cases for Chinese internet studies and communication for development research and lays out what these cases tell us about the internet and development and social change in contemporary China. It also addresses China's particularity and universality and how my findings might contribute to communication for development research and practice in other countries. I synthesize my findings in the case studies based on the conceptualization of the targeted problems (in new media interventions), the role of state policies in promoting development and social change, the relationship between stakeholders in development and social change initiatives, and the role of ICTs and communication channels in development and social change.

2

Connecting Every Village
Project

Government Engagement in
ICT for Development

On November 11, 2019, CNN, CNBC, the BBC, and other global media, as well as Chinese domestic mainstream media, enthusiastically announced that Alibaba had set a new sales record of $38 billion (USD) on Singles' Day, surpassing the previous record the year before by $7.5 billion (*Alibaba Sees Strong Sales*, 2019; *11th Singles' Day Sale*, 2019; Kharpal, 2019; Pham, 2019). On the eve of Singles' Day, Alibaba founder Jack Ma and celebrities such as Taylor Swift were featured in the Tmall Double 11 Gala to kick off Alibaba's Global Shopping Festival. As spectacular as these events and developments in e-commerce may seem, however, the expansion of the internet into the vast interiors of rural China has been equally, if not more, stunning.[1] Unfortunately, however, it has received scant coverage in the mainstream media. This chapter will address this important yet underexamined issue through a case study of the Connecting Every Village Project, a state initiative to promote telecommunication and internet services in China's rural regions.

Overview of the Connecting Every Village Project

The Connecting Every Village Project is a nationwide project launched by China's Ministry of Industry and Information Technology (MIIT) in 2004 to promote universal access to basic telecommunication and internet services in the nation's rural regions. The policymakers behind this project used the concept of universal access proposed by the International Telecommunication Union (ITU) in its 1998 World Telecommunication Development Report: "A telephone should be within a reasonable distance for everyone. The distance depends upon the coverage of the telephone network, the geography of the country, the density of the population and the spread of habitations in the urban or rural environment" (ITU, 1998). The ITU considered universal access to be a transitional goal toward universal service for developing countries and defined universal service as a group of goals for developed countries, including nationwide availability, nondiscriminatory access, and widespread affordability. In ITU's 1998 report, China's universal access policy was cited as "one family, one telephone in urban areas and telephone service for every administrative village in rural areas." The policy goal for rural areas, "telephone service for every administrative village," later became part of the official goal for the Connecting Every Village Project.

In 2004, MIIT declared the goal that "by 2007, every administrative village has access to telecommunications (cell phone or landline)" under the Connecting Every Village Project. In 2008, the goal was extended so that "by 2010, every *xiang* has access to the Internet" (MIIT, 2008).[2] And in 2011, the goal was further extended so that "by 2015, every administrative village has access to broadband Internet and every natural village has access to telecommunication" (MIIT, 2012).[3] Based on MIIT's policy regarding the implementation of this project, the six state-owned companies, including China Mobile, China Unicom, and China Telecom (the main service providers of telecommunication and internet services in China), would directly carry out the project around the country; and MIIT's provincial and local branches would evaluate the project's progress and the efficiency of the six state-owned companies carrying it out (MIIT, 2004). This required that those six companies build the telecommunications infrastructure independently and support the project financially. According to MIIT's 2009 report, the result was that "as of 2008, the six [state run] companies have invested 12.2 billion yuan (roughly $1.8 billion) in the project . . . the percentage of administrative villages with phones reached 99.7%. . . . Currently 98% of *xiang* have access to the Internet, and 95% of the *xiang* have broadband access. Moreover, 89% of administrative villages have access to the internet." And by 2011, 99 percent of *xiang* and 89 percent of administrative villages had already attained broadband access (MIIT, 2011b). As of December 2019, 135,000,000 rural households had used broadband Internet (MIIT, 2020). Data from MIIT's reports indicate that the Connecting Every Village Project effectively extended internet infrastructure in rural China and promoted the development of the internet in rural regions. But this is only part of the story. The data on internet development and use in China overall indicates that the internet remains underdeveloped in vast rural regions of China, and that a huge and ever-increasing gap exists between

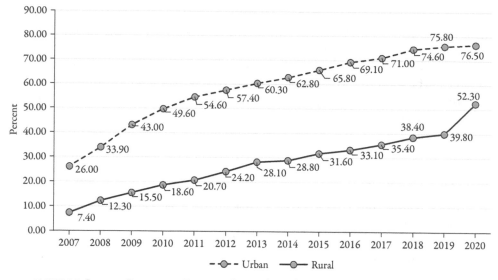

FIGURE 2.1 Internet Penetration Rate in Urban and Rural Regions, 2007 to 2020.
Source: CNNIC (2016b); CNNIC (2020b)

urban regions and rural regions. For example, data from the China Internet Network Information Center as of 2019 show that the internet penetration rates within the urban and rural populations were 75.8 percent and 39.8 percent respectively. In other words, the rural population trails in internet adoption by 36 percent (CNNIC, 2020a). More importantly, CNNIC reports over the past twelve years give no indication that this gap has narrowed between 2007 and 2019 (see figure 2.1).[4]

Connecting Every Village: A State Project to Narrow the Digital Divide

In the analytical framework that I proposed in chapter 1, I noted that understanding the social concerns of any new media intervention is indispensable to analyzing that intervention. By analyzing MIIT's policy documents used in the design and management of the project, this section shows how the Connecting Every Village Project aims to narrow the urban–rural digital divide in China.

The Digital Divide

Before analyzing the Connecting Every Village Project, let us first look at the digital divide and how it is defined.[5] Scholars, policymakers, and development organizations overwhelmingly consider the digital divide to be an important issue in international development (Federal Communications Commission [FCC], 2010; United Nations Development Programme [UNDP], 2001, 2016; van Dijk, 2005). This is conventionally understood to mean the gap between

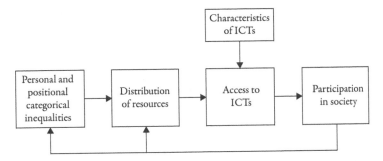

FIGURE 2.2 Van Dijk's "Causal Model of the Core Argument" of the Digital Divide.
Source: van Dijk (2005, p. 15)

those who have and those who do not have access to information and communication technologies (ICTs), such as computers, telephones, and the internet
(Gunkel, 2003; TELEC & TIO, 1999; van Dijk, 2005). In other words, access
connotes physical access: having a computer, a phone, an internet connection,
or a telecommunications connection. And although this definition remains very
popular among policymakers and the public, it has received widespread criticism
for being limited, oversimplified, and technologically deterministic (e.g., DiMaggio & Hargittai, 2001; Gunkel, 2003; Norris, 2001; Qiu, 2009; Shapiro & Richard, 1999; van Dijk, 2000, 2005; Warschauer; 2004). Van Dijk (2005) has
proposed a new model to redefine and conceptualize the digital divide, focusing on the sociopolitical and economic causes and consequences of unbalanced
access to ICTs (see figure 2.2). I will use van Dijk's digital divide model in my
critical analysis of the Connecting Every Village Project in this chapter and in
my investigation of other new media interventions in the chapters that follow.

Van Dijk's core argument is that personal and positional categorical inequalities and unequal resource distribution cause unequal access to ICTs; the unequal
access to ICTs gives rise to unequal participation in the economy, culture, politics, social networks, social institutions, human geography, and other social fields;
and unequal participation in society feeds back into and reinforces personal and
positional categorical inequalities and unequal resource distribution (van Dijk,
2005, p. 15). Van Dijk's model sets itself apart from the conventional definition
by breaking "access" down into four successive stages, or kinds, of access to ICTs:

1. Motivational access (motivation to use digital technology)
2. Material or physical access (possession of computers and internet
   connections or permission to use them and their contents)
3. Skills access (possession of operational, informational, and strategic
   digital skills)
4. Usage access (usage time and range of diverse applications)
   (van Dijk, 2005, p. 20)

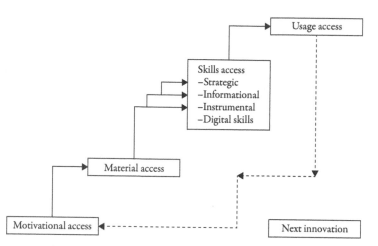

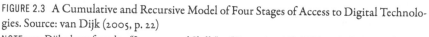

FIGURE 2.3 A Cumulative and Recursive Model of Four Stages of Access to Digital Technologies. Source: van Dijk (2005, p. 22)
NOTE: van Dijk also referred to "Instrumental Skills" as "Operational Skills" (van Dijk, 2005, 21).

Van Dijk also developed a cumulative and recursive model to explain the relations and interactions between the four successive stages or kinds of access. Van Dijk (2005) explains the model in figure 2.3 as follows: "The four successive stages or kinds of access are supposed to be cumulative. The first, motivation, is conditional to this. Trying to gain physical access might be successful. When this happens, appropriation of the new technology tends to lead to the development of digital skills of all kinds. Both physical access and adequate digital skills are requirements for a satisfactory use of the potential applications of the new media" (p. 22).

The Connecting Every Village Project

Statements by leading MIIT officials and MIIT policy documents all indicate that the Connecting Every Village Project aims to narrow the digital divide. On December 5, 2006, the Xinhua News Agency reported the following: "On December 5, 2005, the Deputy Minister of the Ministry of Information Industry, Jiang Jianping, stated that the unbalanced development of telecommunication infrastructure between urban and rural China is still a serious problem. The Chinese government is advancing ICT development in rural China to narrow the digital divide.... In the past several years, through implementing the Connecting Every Village Project, the Chinese government has largely promoted informationization and telecommunications development in rural regions. Currently, 98.9% of administrative villages already have access to telephone" (Wang & Yang, 2006). Jiang asserts that the Chinese government launched the Connecting Every Village Project to narrow the urban–rural digital divide. At an April 25, 2011, national plenary assembly of MIIT and its thirty-one provincial branches to summarize the work of the Connecting Every

Village Project at the time of the Eleventh Five-Year Plan,[6] Xi Guohua, deputy minister of MIIT, stated that the Connecting Every Village Project is fundamental to universal access and informationization in rural regions and that "the implementation of the Connecting Every Village Project greatly improved telecommunications development in rural regions [and] narrowed the digital divide" (MIIT, 2011f). Xi asserted that through the implementation of the Connecting Every Village Project, MIIT aimed to narrow the urban–rural digital divide and promote universal access in rural China.

MIIT officially announced that it had achieved the goals it had set for the project in the Eleventh Five-Year Plan, as follows:

> To change the underdevelopment of telecommunication infrastructure in rural China, MIIT set the following goals for the Connecting Every Village Project at the time of the 11th Five-Year Plan: every administrative village should have access to phone and every Xiang should have access to the Internet. . . . In the past five years, MIIT actively promoted telecommunications development in rural regions. . . . Service providers have invested 48 billion Yuan [in the project]. . . . The goals of the Connecting Every Village Project in the 11th Five-Year Plan have been successfully achieved ahead of schedule, which greatly narrowed the digital divide. (MIIT, 2011a)

This announcement also indicates MIIT's intention to narrow the urban–rural digital divide through the Connecting Every Village Project. Moreover, MIIT reconfirmed this idea in the announcement of its overall goals for the project in the Twelfth Five-Year Plan: "The Connecting Every Village Project has greatly improved telecommunications development [and] narrowed the digital divide . . . and was widely welcomed by the rural population. . . . Service providers . . . must continue to commit to the Project [over the next five years]" (MIIT, 2011f). Documents from major service providers that helped implement the project also indicate that the project aimed to narrow the urban–rural digital divide. For example, China Mobile (2012) asserted: "To narrow the digital divide and to advance the informationalization in rural regions, since 2004, China Mobile has directed the Connecting Every Village Project to increase telecommunications development in rural regions in . . . 15 provinces. As of 2011, China Mobile has . . . built 42,000 telecommunication base stations, and connected 98,000 villages [that did not have access to telecommunication services previously] with mobile phone networks."[7] In its 2010 report on sustainable development, China Mobile claimed: "2010 is a milestone year for reducing the digital divide in China. With the active participation of China Mobile, China has achieved its goal of connecting 100% of administrative villages with telecommunications networks. . . . Since 2004, China Mobile was actively engaged in the Connecting Every Village Project and took 51% of the overall assignments" (China Mobile, 2011). Moreover, comparing MIIT's statements and documents on the digital divide with van Dijk's definition of the digital divide illustrates that MIIT's perception of the problem conforms with the conventional, oversimplified, and limited notion of the digital divide that primarily focused on physical access to the internet and telecommunications infrastructure. For example, Jiang's statement indicates that MIIT equated the urban–rural digital divide with the imbalance in urban and rural development of telecommunications infrastructure. It assumed that it could effectively narrow the digital divide by extending telecommunications networks to reach more villages. MIIT's two official pronouncements and China Mobile's claims share this same logic. For example, in its report on sustainable development, China Mobile demonstrated its belief that by extending the telecommunications network to every administrative village, China had reached a milestone in closing the digital divide.

The overwhelming focus on physical access—especially extending telecommunications networks, internet infrastructure, and broadband infrastructure—can also be seen in MIIT's strategy for implementing the project and its goals. For example, MIIT (2011c) said of its strategy: "In the implementation of the Connecting Every Village Project, we employed the following strategy. . . . First, in terms of network coverage . . . first cover *xiang*, then administrative villages, then natural villages; second, in terms of technologies . . . start with phones, then the Internet, then broadband. . . . Third, in terms of services, first build telecommunication infrastructure, then build information platforms, then promote services." As indicated earlier in this chapter, MIIT's goals for the project focus only on the percentage of *xiang*, administrative villages, and natural villages with access to telecommunications networks and internet connections. The other equally important forms of access identified in the van Dijk model, such as skills access and motivational access, are never considered.

Various factors may contribute to MIIT's oversimplification of the digital divide. A significant contributing factor in this is the Chinese government's past experience with similar projects promoting communication for development to foster rural mass media, such as TV and radio broadcasting. Actually, the project that MIIT launched in 2004 is not the first Connecting Every Village project in China. In 1998, the PRC's State Administration of Radio, Film, and Television (SARFT) launched the Connecting Every Village with TV and Radio Project to increase the reach of radio and TV broadcasting in rural China. SARFT's first goal was to extend the reach of radio and TV broadcasting to every administrative village by 2003. Then by 2010, radio and TV broadcasting was to extend to almost every natural village. Last, by 2020, TV and radio broadcasting was to extend to every household in rural China. In the implementation of the project, SARFT designed and set the goals, then the local branches of SARFT and the local governments got the assignments from SARFT and carried out the project directly (SARFT, 2008). The MIIT project not only shares the name of the SARFT project but has very similar goals and implementation processes. It employed the same strategy of first reaching *xiang*, then administrative villages, then natural villages. Its implementation process was also very similar: MIIT designed and set the goals; MIIT managed six state-owned service providers and gave them their assignments; and the local branches of the service providers directly carried out the project. The only real difference between the two projects is that the first focused on connecting every village with TVs and radios, whereas the second focuses on connecting every village with the internet and broadband. This strongly suggests that the SARFT project and the mindset associated with it significantly shaped MIIT's understanding of the digital divide problem and how to solve it.

Due to this influence, MIIT's current policy of narrowing the urban–rural digital divide through a national effort of expanding the reach of ICTs has a weakness: it overlooks the fundamental and significant differences between the internet and TV or radio broadcasting in terms of access and use. The first characteristic of the internet is that it is a two-way communication channel, whereas TV and radio broadcasting are one-way communication channels. Compared with conventional media broadcasting, the internet's real value and function is not so much to deliver information to rural communities but to promote communication with the outside world and between other rural communities. MIIT's Connecting Every Village Project does not give this difference enough attention. It follows the same two-step strategy as the Connecting Every Village with TV and Radio Project: first, by almost exclusively focusing on extending network reach, and second, by creating stations and programs to deliver content to rural communities. For MIIT's Connecting Every Village Project, the second step of the strategy is referred to as "sending information to rural regions," the language of which conveys its underlying mindset. The pages on MIIT's website outlining this step discuss how the local branches of the six state-owned companies developed platforms and created content to send to the rural communities. In other words, the rural communities were considered passive receivers of information created or collected by local service providers. By doing this, MIIT treated this two-way communication channel as a one-way channel solely for delivering information, a strategy that limits the internet's potential in rural China. And given the threshold of new skills required to access needed information on a computer and the internet, relative to the effortlessness of receiving information through radio and TV broadcasting, MIIT's current strategy of using the internet as a new channel to deliver information to rural communities is inefficient and not likely to be sustainable. The second characteristic of the internet, overlooked by MIIT, is that it requires considerable new skills for effective use compared with TV and radio. The project does not have a component to address the issue of skills access. It also falsely assumes that the urban–rural digital divide can be remedied solely by extending telecommunications networks and internet infrastructure to more and more villages in rural China. We will discuss this in detail in the section on sustainability risks later in this chapter.

The Connecting Every Village Project and the Modernization Paradigm

Though widely criticized by scholars, the modernization paradigm remains the dominant discourse on development, especially in ICT for development projects, as noted in chapter 1. This section will explore the influence of the modernization paradigm on the Connecting Every Village Project.

The modernization paradigm portrays the dual economy, dual society, and dualistic development as problematic characteristics of developing countries and so-called backward societies (Boeke, 1953; Brookfield, 2012; Servaes, 1999). These are characteristics of countries divided by different stages of development and different levels of technology, wherein an advanced or modern sector may coexist with an underdeveloped or traditional sector. Proponents of the modernization paradigm, therefore, argue that development projects should aim to remove obstacles or barriers in an underdeveloped traditional sector in order to reduce the differences between the sectors and ultimately transform and integrate the traditional sector into a modern sector. The Connecting Every Village Project is informed by theories and practices related to the "dual society" problem in the modernization paradigm.[8] The concepts of "dual society" and "dual structure" are fundamental elements in China's state policy discourse on rural development. For example, the Decision on Major Issues Concerning Comprehensively Deepening Reforms is a key policy document on the direction of the Xi Jinping administration reforms that was adopted at the close of the Third Plenary Session of the 18th CPC Central Committee in December 2013. In the section on "urban–rural development," the decision declared, "The existing urban–rural dual structure is the main obstacle to integrated development. Efforts must be made to allow rural residents to participate in China's modernization" ("Highlights of the Decision," 2013). To explain the decision at the session, President Xi Jinping stated in his plenary speech that although tremendous development has been achieved in rural regions, "the urban–rural dual structure hasn't changed fundamentally, and the widening gap between urban and rural development has not been reversed. To solve these problems, urban–rural integration must be advanced" (Xi, 2013). MIIT's Connecting Every Village Project is among a series of projects and policies launched by the Chinese government to "advance urban–rural integration." And the specific barrier that the project aims to overcome is the lack of access to the internet and telecommunications networks in rural areas. For example, in the introduction to the Connecting Every Village Project on its official website, MIIT (2011d) states: "Promoting telecommunication infrastructure development in rural regions and providing access to telecommunications networks to rural residents, who previously did not have access to it, are [MIIT's] specific measures . . . to solve the underdevelopment problems of rural regions and to advance urban–rural integration." Also, on achieving the goals of the Connecting Every Village

Project in the Eleventh Five-Year Plan, MIIT (2011a) stated in an official announcement: "To implement the strategy of ... urban–rural integration of the CPC Central Committee and the State Council ... and to change the underdevelopment of telecommunication infrastructure in rural regions, MIIT set the following goals for the Connecting Every Village Project at the time of the 11th Five-Year Plan: every administrative village should have phone access and every *xiang* should have Internet access." In an interview with China Central Television in March 2017, MIIT minister Miao Yu reaffirmed the discourse presented in the preceding statements: "In pursuing economic development, we must prevent the rise of a new urban–rural dual structure [in the telecommunications sector] and we must close the digital divide. Therefore, from last year, we carried out the Connecting Every Village with a Broadband Project in 10,000 administrative villages.... We have also set the goal that every village should have access to broadband internet by 2020" (Miao, 2017). Moreover, according to MIIT's 2009 report on the Connecting Every Village Project, it began conducting a pilot project on urban–rural integration in Chongqing, a municipality in central China, in 2008. Aiming to reduce the gap in the spread of telecommunications and the internet in urban and rural areas, it focused on increasing the penetration rate of phones, broadband, and the internet in rural areas so that they could catch up with urban areas.

Modernization paradigm proponents also insist that the successful transformation and integration of the traditional sector into the modern sector requires the transfer of capital, knowledge, values, technologies, and expertise from the modern sector to the traditional sector. We see this logic in the implementation of the Connecting Every Village Project. Policymakers, MIIT, and the six state-owned companies who carried out the project directly are all from the urban sector. To achieve urban–rural integration, they transferred capital, expertise, technology, and techniques from advanced urban regions to disadvantaged rural regions. Project officials assumed that doing this would effectively close the urban–rural digital divide, or the gap between rural and urban regions in the digital age.

Moreover, in the modernization paradigm, policymaking and implementation of development projects is generally a top-down process (Apter & Rosberg, 1994; Melkote & Steeves, 2001; Servaes, 2008). The design and implementation of the Connecting Every Village Project were likewise top down, as the central government through the MIIT office set the policy, defined the phases in the project, and established the goals for each phase. For example, MIIT proclaimed that 95 percent of administrative villages would have access to phones in the first phase of the project (2004–2005), 100 percent of administrative villages would have access to phones in the second phase (2006–2010), and 100 percent of *xiang* would have access to the internet in the third phase (2011–2015) (MIIT, 2012). In the implementation of the project, MIIT designated assignments to the six state-owned nationwide companies. The provincial and local branches of the

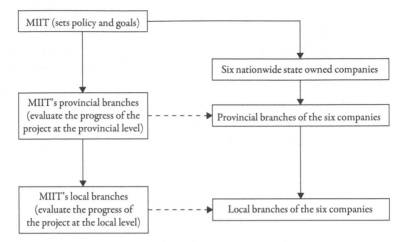

FIGURE 2.4 The Top-Down Organization of the Connecting Every Village Project

companies received assignments from their head offices and directly carried out the project. MIIT's provincial and local branches evaluated the progress. Figure 2.4 depicts the top-down process of policymaking and implementation in the Connecting Every Village Project.

The Sustainability Risks in the Connecting Every Village Project

Scholars in communication for development studies have argued that the stakeholders involved in development projects are an important indicator of the projects' sustainability (e.g., Ogan et al., 2009; Servaes, 2009; Servaes & Liu, 2007; Servaes et al., 2012). From a communications perspective, development projects should engage all important stakeholders through their participation to achieve sustainable development (e.g., Estrella, 2000; Ogan et al., 2009; Servaes et al., 2012). Earlier in this chapter I identified MIIT and its provincial and local branches, the six state-owned telecommunication companies and their provincial and local branches, and local communities in rural areas as the major stakeholders in the Connecting Every Village Project. Government agencies and state-owned companies dominate all processes of the Project: MIIT designed the policy and the project as well as the goals to evaluate its implementation; the six state-owned companies and their local branches provided the capital, technology, and human resources for the project and implemented the project; and MIIT's provincial and local branches evaluated the implementation of the project. Local communities in rural areas were not effectively engaged in any of the phases of the Connecting Every Village Project except as passive recipients. As in most development projects operating from the modernization paradigm, the local beneficiaries of the Connecting Every

Village Project (and their communities) were excluded from the policymaking, implementation, and evaluation processes of the project. From the perspective of communication for development, this lack of involvement and participation by rural communities poses a risk to the sustainability of the project. To further expose the project's sustainability risks, I will use van Dijk's digital divide model in the discussion that follows.

Motivational Access and Sustainability Risk in the Connecting Every Village Project

Motivational access is the first stage in van Dijk's model of the four successive stages through which local communities gain "full" access to ICTs (pp. 16, 22) (see figure 2.3). The motivation of those in rural communities to use the internet cannot be taken for granted. And lack of motivation should not simply be attributed to the reluctant mindset of less developed communities. This relates to many complex social, economic, and cultural factors. Van Dijk's (2005) study demonstrates that "as with all other kinds of access, motivational access is primarily explained by particular resources people have or lack" (p. 35). Two of those resources are particularly relevant to the analysis of the Connecting Every Village Project. First, material resources, such as the funds a person or a family possesses, are an important part of people's motivation for acquiring ICTs. Van Dijk (2005) notes that "those with sufficient material resources will have less difficulty in reaching the decision" to acquire ICTs, whereas many lower-income people consider purchasing a PC and maintaining an internet connection too expensive (p. 36). Scholarly research and Chinese government data indicate that the income disparity between China's urban and rural areas is among the greatest in the world (e.g., Kanbur & Zhang, 1999; National Bureau of Statistics of China [NBSC], 2011; Xie & Zhou, 2014; Xue & Gao, 2012). Most importantly, this income gap has increased significantly since the 1980s (e.g., Kanbur & Zhang, 1999; UNICEF, 2018; Xie & Zhou, 2014; Xue & Gao, 2012). According to data published by the Chinese government, the per capita annual income in urban and rural regions in 2010 was 19,109.4 yuan and 5,919 yuan, respectively. In other words, per capita income for urban residents was 3.23 times higher than it was for rural residents (NBSC, 2011). The data from UNICEF (2018) indicated that the urban–rural income inequities in China stood at 2.7 to 1 as of 2017. Moreover, research based on independent data sources indicates that China's income inequality is actually much worse than what the Chinese government has reported. For example, Xie and Zhou's (2014) research shows that the Gini coefficient in China reached 0.53 in 2010, which is considerably greater than that in the United States (0.469) (U.S. Census Bureau, 2011). The widening urban–rural income gap suggests that rural residents are less likely to overcome the motivational access barrier to ICT acquisition than are urban residents. Moreover, relative to rural incomes, the cost of acquiring a computer and maintaining an internet connection to access the internet was very high for non-urban residents.

For example, according to a market report by ZOL, a new entry-level PC (including a monitor) in the Chinese market cost between 3,000 and 4,000 yuan in 2010—or 50 to 68 percent of the average annual per capita income for rural residents; a usable secondhand PC was about 1,000 yuan (ZOL Center for Internet Consumption Research, 2011).[9] For members of rural communities, lack of money is thus a primary reason for the lack of motivation to acquire ICTs and gain access to the internet.

The second factor is the extent of social resources among potential users. Van Dijk (2005) points out that "social resources may be one of the most important background explanations for (the lack of) motivation" (p. 36): "People become aware of the importance and applications of the new media via social contacts with family, friends, . . . teachers, neighbors and acquaintances. . . . Thus having a large social network consisting of relatively many computer and Internet users is vital if a user is to cross the motivational access barrier" (pp. 36–37). Due to the low adoption rate of computers and the internet in rural areas, many rural community members would lack this kind of social network and, consequently, would not recognize the importance of the internet. Unfortunately, the social and economic factors of rural communities that underlie motivational access were not sufficiently addressed, so the Connecting Every Village Project on the whole could not effectively enable rural communities to overcome this motivational access barrier. CNNIC surveys from 2007 and 2016 also indicate that motivational access among internet nonusers in rural areas over the past ten years has consistently been a significant barrier to internet adoption for a considerable portion of rural residents (see tables 2.1 and 2.2).

Moreover, comparing tables 2.1 and 2.2, 39.5 percent of rural residents indicate "I have no device to access the internet" in 2007, whereas only 9.5 percent cite that reason in 2016. This means that by 2016, motivational access exceeded physical access in terms of reasons for not using the Internet among rural residents. If rural residents cannot overcome the motivational access barrier—the first phase of access to ICTs, according to van Dijk's cumulative model—the extension of infrastructure to rural areas, which is the goal of the Connecting Every Village Project, will not effectively increase the rural population's ICT capacity. So even if the Connecting Every Village Project extends telecommunication infrastructure to rural areas, it will not effectively and sustainably reduce the digital divide between urban and rural China.

Physical Access

In the cumulative model (van Dijk, 2005, p. 22), material (or physical) access is the second phase of access to ICTs and the internet (see figure 2.3). Van Dijk distinguished two kinds of physical access: access to internet connections and access to computers. Earlier in the chapter, I indicated that the Connecting Every Village Project primarily focused on access to the internet. The major goal of the project has been to extend telecommunications and internet infrastructure

Table 2.1

Reasons for Not Using the Internet among Rural Nonusers in 2007

Category of reason (stage of access)	Reason for not using the internet among rural nonusers	Percentage
Physical access	I have no device to access the internet.	39.5
Skills access	I have no knowledge of computers and the internet.	28.3
Motivational access	I have no interest in using the internet.	13.7
Motivational access	I'm worried about harms and bad effects of the internet.	12.2
Motivational access	I don't have time to use the internet.	12.0
Motivational access	My parents or teachers don't allow me to use the internet.	10.9
Motivational access and/or physical access	It is too expensive.	8.4
Motivational access	I'm too young or too old to use the internet.	3.3
Motivational access	I don't need to use the internet.	2.2

SOURCE: Statistical Report on Internet Development in Rural Regions (CNNIC, 2007).

Table 2.2

Reasons for Not Using the Internet among Rural Nonusers in 2016

Category of reason (stage of access)	Reason for not using the internet among rural nonusers	Percentage
Skills access	I have no knowledge of computers and the internet.	68.0
Motivational access	I'm too young or too old to use the internet.	14.8
Motivational access	I don't have time to use the internet.	13.5
Motivational access	I don't need to use the internet/I have no interest in using the internet.	10.9
Physical access	I have no device to access the internet.	9.5
Physical access	The local region doesn't have an internet connection.	5.3

SOURCE: Statistical Report on Internet Development in China (CNNIC, 2016b). The CNNIC survey in July 2016 is currently the latest one that provided data regarding rural nonusers (as of 2020). The CNNIC surveys in 2017, 2018, 2019, and 2020 did not report any data regarding rural nonusers.

to increase the availability of internet connections in rural areas. In late 2009, building telecenters in rural regions was added as a component of the Connecting Every Village Project, focusing on access to the internet as well as the acquisition of computers as policy goals. MIIT encouraged the six state-owned companies to build telecenters in the regions where the Connecting Every

Village Project was being carried out. Every telecenter was to have at least one computer, one phone, and an internet connection. By 2011, roughly ninety thousand telecenters had been built in rural China.

However, the project did not sufficiently address many factors related to physical access that significantly affect internet use and the extent of inequality among users. One of these factors is points of access—the places where users have access to the internet. Scholarly research and the work of international organizations have highlighted the significance of providing public access points to ICTs in less developed regions in order to reduce the digital divide (e.g., Kleine, 2013; Proenza, 2015; van Dijk, 2005; World Summit on Information Society Geneva Declaration of Principles, 2003). For example, at the 2003 World Summit on the Information Society in Geneva, organized by the U.N., leaders and representatives from 175 countries came to the following consensus: "In disadvantaged areas, the establishment of ICT public access points in places such as post offices, schools, libraries and archives, can provide effective means for ensuring universal access to the infrastructure and services of the Information Society" (art. 23). Data published by the CNNIC in July 2016, however, indicate that public places in China's rural areas lag far behind urban regions in providing access to the internet (see figure 2.5). The significant difference between urban and rural users in accessing the internet in public places and schools suggests that ICT public access points are less developed in rural regions than in urban regions in China. This means that the Chinese government and the Connecting Every Village Project have probably not paid enough attention to establishing ICT public access points in less developed rural regions, which would help narrow the urban–rural digital divide.

Skills Access and Sustainability Risk in the Connecting Every Village Project

The third stage of access in the cumulative model (see figure 2.3) is skills access, which comprises three substages: operational skills, informational skills, and strategic skills (van Dijk, 2005, p. 75). These substages encompass a range of digital skills, from operational skills, such as using a mouse and keyboard, searching, selecting, and navigating in cyberspace, to more complex skills, such as using and processing information for the specific goals of shopping, business, employment, education, and other contexts (van Dijk, 2005).

Van Dijk (2005, p. 71) notes that these skills must be learned through either formal education or practice by prospective users themselves. These digital skills, like other embodied cultural capital, can only be acquired through engagement and the investment of personal time and energy by potential users. Earlier in the chapter I noted that the Connecting Every Village Project never seriously considered the issue of improving skills access or removing skills barriers to the internet, which requires the engagement of members of rural communities. No

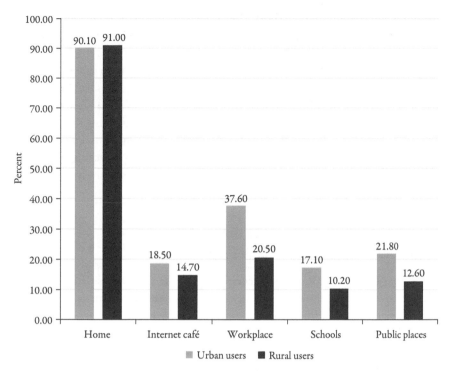

FIGURE 2.5 Access Points of Urban Internet Users and Rural Internet Users.
Source: CNNIC (2016b)

component of the project has addressed the need to enhance the rural population's skills to effectively use the internet to voice their own concerns or participate in social activities related to their interests. Van Dijk's cumulative model of access to ICTs (see figure 2.3) makes clear that even if members of rural communities overcome the motivational barrier and the material (physical) barrier—without overcoming the skills barrier—they will not be able to effectively use the internet to participate in society and thus cannot change the distribution of resources in society (see figure 2.2). Consequently, the digital divide between urban and rural regions cannot be effectively closed. This poses another risk to the sustainability of the Connective Every Village Project.

The data from CNNIC surveys indicate that between 2007 and 2016, the skills access barrier became the greatest barrier to adopting the internet among rural residents, rising from 28.3 percent in 2007 to 68 percent in 2016, whereas the significance of the physical access barrier largely declined over time, having gone from most important to least important (see tables 2.1 and 2.2). This highlights how overlooking skills access has been a significant sustainability risk in the Connecting Every Village Project. Moreover, it must be noted that only 5.3 percent of rural nonusers cited no internet connection as their reason for not using the internet. In short, the overwhelming focus on extending tele-communications and internet coverage of the Connecting Every Village Project has overlooked the major barriers to internet adoption and ICT capacity enhancement for rural residences. Overall, lack of consideration of motivational access and lack of a policy component to address the skills access barrier are two significant weaknesses of the project. As astute observers of rural China pointed out, "Internet connectivity is mainly a showcase by local officials, and the farm-ers either don't have the know-how in obtaining useful information from the internet or totally lack the incentive to be online."[10] The Connecting Every Vil-lage Project must therefore change its current policy to effectively achieve its goal of narrowing the urban–rural digital divide.

Recommendations to Promote the Sustainability of the Connecting Every Village Project

To address both the motivational access risk and the skills access risk, the Con-necting Every Village Project needs to change its predominant focus on physical access, especially extending telecommunication and internet infrastructure. And rather than solely focusing on extending the internet to more villages, the project should also establish goals and evaluation criteria that focus on motivational access and skills access in local rural communities. For example, rather than upgrading internet connections to broadband connections or 5G connections, the project should give more priority to increasing and sustaining motivational access and skills access in rural communities. Specifically, the project should incorporate and give considerable priority to ICT training in order to help rural communities overcome motivational and skills barriers.

The rural-urban digital divide is a universal problem among developing coun-tries. The project should learn from the experiences of national ICT policies to narrow this divide in other countries. For example, the Chilean government established the Agenda Digital to provide free public access to the internet at points of use, as well as free ICT training for all Chilean citizens, which has sig-nificantly enhanced ICT use in less developed regions of Chile (Kleine, 2013). As part of the program, public funding was systematically invested in telecom-munication and internet infrastructure; in telecenters and other free public inter-net access points, especially in less developed regions; and in free ICT training across the nation. As the Connecting Every Village Project has significantly extended the coverage of telecommunication networks and the internet in rural regions of China and has begun to build telecenters in rural regions around the country, a new component to provide public-funded free ICT training at these telecenters should be an effective method to address the motivational and skills access barriers. Data from a CNNIC report (2018b) also indicates that for non-users, being given free ICT training was their most effective motivation to use the internet (see figure 2.6).

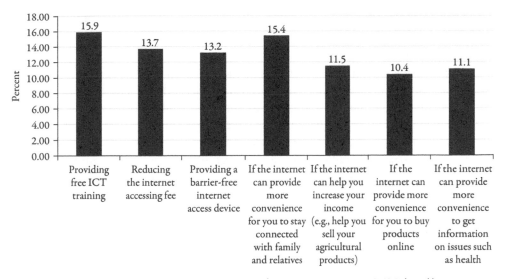

FIGURE 2.6 Factors to Motivate Nonusers to Use the Internet. Source: CNNIC (2018b)

Moreover, to address the underdevelopment of ICT public access points in rural areas, the Connecting Every Village Project should establish public access points not only in telecenters but in schools, post offices, rural libraries, rural community centers, and rural cultural centers in *xiang* and administrative villages.[11] Internet access at these public places should be free to help poorer families and individuals in these communities overcome the barriers of motivational access, material access, and skills access. Furthermore, the Connecting Every Village Project should learn from the example of other countries (e.g., Kleine, 2013; Servaes et al., 2006; Servaes & Liu, 2007) and enhance the capacity of telecenters in rural regions. Rather than providing hardware access to computers and internet connections, telecenters should operate as free community centers for training, sharing, and learning how to use ICTs and as open spaces for information sharing among different stakeholders involved in the effort to reduce the rural urban digital divide, including NGOs, local branches of the six companies, and local government entities, as well as residents of the local community. Given the increasing significance of the skills access barrier, a considerable part of the work of telecenters should focus on ICT training. MIIT's current criterion for standard telecenters (a computer, a phone, and an internet connection) is to serve as places where users can overcome the physical access barrier, not as places to organize ICT trainings to target motivational and skills access barriers. MIIT should therefore design pilot projects to explore new criteria for telecenters. MIIT should also advise telecenters to collaborate with other stakeholders, such as local government entities, to organize free ICT trainings in schools, rural cultural centers, and other places with ICT public access points.

A Fundamental Change

Lack of participation in rural communities and lack of consideration of skills access and motivational access illustrate sustainability risks in the Connecting Every Village Project. These two problems are related to the assumptions and theories of the modernization paradigm that undergirds the project. Through the prism of the modernization paradigm, the members of less developed communities—those who benefit from development projects—are considered to be passive targets and pure receivers in communications. Projects that follow the modernization paradigm thus tend to exclude less developed communities from the policymaking process. Based on the notion of technological determinism—a core component in the philosophy of the modernization paradigm (Servaes, 1999, 2014)—extending internet infrastructure and making computers available should provide a quick fix for the digital divide. As a result, motivational access and skills access were overlooked. To address these two problems, the Connecting Every Village Project should make fundamental changes by incorporating the philosophy and methods of the participatory communication model into its process. Rather than passive targets or receivers in the project, local rural communities should be considered active participants. And as important stakeholders, local communities and NGOs must be encouraged to participate in designing, evaluating, and implementing the project.

Specifically, the current oversimplified one-size-fits-all goals of the project need to become more contextualized, local community-based goals. Rather than setting up a single nationwide goal for all rural regions in the country, goals should match local needs, such as the motivation of the local community to use ICTs, the economic base, and related skill levels in the local community. For example, the project should listen to the voices of local community members and consider the motivations and skills of local communities in prioritizing phones, the internet, and broadband services. Local community members should also be engaged in the evaluation of the project, rather than relying solely on MIIT's local branches. This will give the project a more effective method of evaluating the performance of telecenters and the efficacy of the ICT training in targeting motivational access and skills access barriers. And rather than focusing exclusively on nonusers, the project should recruit those in rural communities who were early adopters of computers, the internet, and smartphones to participate in ICT training. This will encourage rural community members to learn from one another during the training. Rather than having development workers lecture the rural community on how ICT can help them, letting early ICT adopters in the community demonstrate how ICTs benefit them would make the project more participatory and effective. This will also help foster informal learning about ICTs between peers in the rural community after the training. Consequently, this may also increase the self-learning capacity of the community regarding ICTs.

Moreover, NGOs should play an active role in ICT training in rural communities. As I will discuss in chapter 3, NGOs are already engaged in ICT training in less developed areas of China. Cooperation among NGOs, local governments, and local branches of the six companies that are carrying out the Connecting Every Village Project to provide community-level ICT trainings in rural regions will generate a win-win situation. As I will discuss in chapter 6, NGOs could also play an active role in increasing government transparency and accountability. Therefore, NGOs can serve an important role in monitoring and evaluating the Connecting Every Village Project to increase its accountability and transparency. Rather than using oversimplified criterion measuring only the percentage of villages connected to the internet, more complex criteria evaluating the real change in different forms of access (motivational, material, skills, and usage) in rural communities should be developed and carried out by rural communities together with NGOs and local governmental agencies.

3

The NGO 2.0 Project

Using New Media for the Empowerment of NGOs

Launched by researcher-activists of the New Media Action Lab at the Massachusetts Institute of Technology (MIT NMAL) in collaboration with numerous NGOs in China, the NGO 2.0 Project is dedicated to changing inequality in communications and resource distribution between grassroots NGOs and GONGOs (governmental-affiliated NGOs) in Chinese society. To generate this change, an important aim of the project is to enhance the capacity of Chinese grassroots NGOs to use digital and social media effectively in their communications and projects. Between 2009 and 2022, it has provided new media training workshops to roughly four thousand NGOs in China. The project was formally registered in 2014 as a nonprofit organization (NPO) in China and has become the most influential NGO advocating "information equality, ICT-4Good, and empowerment of the grassroots" in the nonprofit sector in China (NGO 2.0 Project, 2019).

Introduction: Chinese NGOs and the NGO 2.0 Project

Before going into the NGO 2.0 Project, I will briefly introduce the beneficiary community of the project, which is Chinese NGOs, and problems that have hampered their development. Despite political, regulatory, and fundraising difficulties, China's NGOs have developed rapidly over the past three decades (e.g., Howell, 2007; Pei, 1998; Saich, 2000; Yang, 2009; K. Yu, 2002a). According to the official report from China's Ministry of Civil Affairs (MCA, 2020), the number of officially registered NGOs and NPOs in 2019 reached 866,000, with 10,731,000 NGO practitioners. However, most researchers believe that the true number, including unregistered grassroots NGOs, is much higher than that published by the government. For example, according to the U.S. Congressional-Executive Commission on China (2009), "Chinese sources estimate there are roughly 3 million NGOs in China." The activities of Chinese NGOs extend to education, women rights, environmental protection, rural inequality, community development, information networks, health, HIV/AIDS, gay and lesbian rights, and almost every other sector of social life (Shi, 2013).

Previous research has long established that grassroots NGOs are different from government-operated NGOs in the Chinese context (e.g., NPO Development Center Shanghai, 2014; Schwartz, 2004; F. Wu, 2002; G. Yang, 2005; J. Zhu, 2004). According to J. Zhu (2004), "Those operated by the government are called GONGOs. They are initiated by the government or are directed by government officials. . . . Those created through a bottom-up process are called grassroots NGOs. They are started by individuals and focus on nonprofit activities to promote social good and community development directly." Due to their lack of connection with the government, grassroots NGOs generally face more challenges than GONGOs with respect to policies, regulations, fundraising, and human resources (NPO Development Center Shanghai, 2014; J. Wang, 2019b; K. Yu, 2002a). The policy and regulation challenges of grassroots NGOs primarily involve registration regulations. Researchers maintain that under current regulations, most NGOs that are not affiliated with government institutions face great difficulties becoming registered. In other words, they lack legal status in the current regulatory environment (e.g., Huang, 2012; Kostka & Zhang, 2018; J. Wang, 2019b; K. Yu, 2002a). This is a serious problem that impedes the development of grassroots NGOs in China. For example, Jing Wang (2016) asserts that this lack of legal status and the dominance of GONGOs "has left grassroots organizations across China often struggling to get resources, qualify for funding for essential projects, and recruit new members and volunteers." First, many grassroots NGOs face fundraising difficulties due to this lack of legal status. According to a report on funders in China's nonprofit sector published by the Non-Profit Incubator and the Swedish International Development Agency in 2011, for example, most funding agencies, including international and domestic foundations, provide funding only to officially registered NGOs. The report indicates that from 2006 to 2011, unregistered NGOs made up only 7.8 percent of the NGOs that received support. Second, in the current policy context, China's NGOs, including both grassroots NGOs and GONGOs, are not legally allowed to accept donations directly from the public. By law, only foundations that are affiliated with the government, such as the Chinese Red Cross Foundation or the China Green Foundation, are permitted to accept such donations.[1]

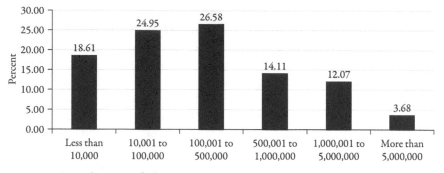

FIGURE 3.1 Annual Income of Chinese NGOs in 2018

Furthermore, except for a few newly established foundations, most of the foundations in China do not accept funding applications from grassroots NGOs. A report from the NPO Development Center Shanghai (2014) shows that among the 3,600 foundations in China, only about one or two percent provide funding to NGOs, including both GONGOs and grassroots NGOs. This means that the foundations that actually provide funding to grassroots NGOs will be even lower than this. This situation has forced grassroots NGOs across the country to compete with one another and against GONGOs for the very limited funding resources provided by international organizations like Oxfam and the Ford Foundation, and funding opportunities provided by the few newly established relative independent foundations, such as the Narada Foundation. In 2016, China passed its Foreign NGO Law, which tightened control and regulations over funding by foreign foundations and foreign NGOs and increased restrictions on the activities of these organizations in China (Hsu & Teets, 2016; Kostka & Zhang, 2018; Shieh, 2018). This significantly reduced the opportunities of grassroots Chinese NGOs to get funding from international organizations. Since 2013, the government simultaneously started to "support the development of NGOs" through "purchasing social services" from Chinese NGOs (Ministry of Finance of PRC, 2016). This, in fact, did little to reduce the inequality of financial resources between grassroots NGOs and GONGOs. GONGOs that are under the direction of the government and whose leaders are either officials or high-level retirees are much more likely to get funding from the central and local governments than grassroots NGOs due to the fact that "the government has more trust in them" or the social networks of their leaders (NPO Development Center Shanghai, 2014). A series of national surveys conducted by the NGO 2.0 Project also indicate that the lack of financial resources is a persistent challenge for Chinese NGOs. For example, according to a 2018 nationwide survey of 489 NGOs, 18.61 percent reported that their 2018 annual income was less than 10,000 yuan ($1,493), and 24.95 percent reported annual incomes between 10,001 yuan and 100,000 yuan ($14,930) (see figure 3.1), meaning that roughly 44 percent of the NGOs in the survey had incomes of 100,000 yuan or less as of 2018.

According to survey data from 327 NGOs in 2009, the problem was even more severe nine years before. In this survey, 38 percent of the NGOs reported less than 10,000 yuan annual income, and 29.36 percent reported annual incomes between 10,001 and 100,000 yuan, with 67 percent of the NGOs having an annual income of 100,000 yuan or less. Lack of legal status and money are the two primary impediments to NGO development in China (e.g., NGOCN, 2018; J. Wang, 2019b; K. Yu, 2002a; Zhu, 2004). These two problems have contributed to a third problem, which is the lack of human resources and high employee turnover. Based on interviews with 474 NGOs in a nationwide survey conducted by the Horizon Research Consultancy Group in 2014, 80.3 percent of the NGOs found it very hard to recruit qualified employees. Nearly half of the NGOs cited their inability to provide competitive salaries and attractive benefits packages as the most important reason for this difficulty. And for those participating in the survey, average NGO salaries in most regions were much lower than other salaries in the same locale. In Beijing, for example, where the average monthly salary is 8,067 yuan, the average among NGO practitioners is only 5,191 yuan. Moreover, only 31.6 percent of NGOs provided their employees with the requisite benefits packages required by the Chinese government, such as health insurance and unemployment insurance. In addition, over a third of the NGOs did not provide any benefits package to their employees. A survey of 1,076 NGO practitioners from 295 NGOs in 2019 indicated little improvement. Nearly two-thirds of the practitioners reported monthly salaries of less than 4,000 yuan, 1,000 yuan lower than the national average monthly salary. In addition, only 38.75 percent of NGOs offered the government-requisite benefits packages to their employees. And nearly 20 percent of the NGOs did not provide any benefits package (Yibao, 2019). These factors all contribute to high employee turnover among grassroots NGOs in China.

The New Media Action Lab (NMAL) at MIT launched the NGO 2.0 Project in 2009 in collaboration with five partners: the Institute of Knowledge Management at the University of Science and Technology of China, the NGO Development and Communication Network (NGOCN), the Institute of Civil Society at Sun Yat-sen University, Friends of Nature (FON), and Ogilvy & Mather. For the first two years of the project, almost all its members came from academic backgrounds. Over time, more NGO practitioners gradually joined the project. In 2014, the NGO 2.0 Project registered in Shenzhen as an NPO aiming to advocate for and practice ICT4Good. As of 2020, its core team had seven full-time NGO practitioners, three volunteers with academic backgrounds, and two volunteers with nonprofit backgrounds. In 2019, the project ran more than five programs to serve the communication, resource, and technology needs of Chinese NGOs (NGO 2.0 Project, 2019). The oldest and most important of these programs is the NGO ICT Training Workshops. Over the past twelve years, the program has offered nearly fifty-one ICT and new media training workshops to Chinese NGOs. The training materials for the workshops have been constantly updated and expanded based on trainee feedback, workshop effectiveness, changing technology within Chinese cyberspace, and data from its surveys of NGO ICT use and needs. Through workshops and other forms of collaboration over a span of twelve years, the project has built a network of more than four thousand NGOs across the country and become the leading NGO providing ICTs and new media services to Chinese NGOs. Meanwhile, the project has conducted six nationwide surveys of Chinese NGOs concerning their ICT and communication capacity and needs and has assembled the largest dataset on ICT and new media use among Chinese NGOs.

NGO 2.0: Empower NGOs through ICTs

The NGO 2.0 Project is informed by the principles and philosophy of the participatory paradigm in communication for development. It assumes that the solution to the problem the project aims to resolve, as well as its goals and mission, should be defined, continually clarified, and refined in dialogue with all participants involved, especially the grassroots NGOs. "Adaptation according to the needs [of grassroots NGOs]" (J. Wang, 2016), which is the project's guiding principle in terms of its project management, particularly reveals this tenet of the project. From 2009 to the present, the mission and visions of the project have been constantly adapted to the needs of the grassroots NGOs (J. Wang, 2016). The training materials of the new media workshops, the programs that the NGO 2.0 Project has conducted, and even the targeted beneficiary community have all been significantly changed over the past twelve years. Yet there is one thing that has not changed: the project's commitment to empowering grassroots NGOs in China. In a 2019 interview, project director and MIT professor Jing Wang was asked, "Is the ten year development of the NGO 2.0 Project similar to what you expected ten years ago?" She answered, "[It is] very different indeed. . . . Yet, our core and initial motivation has not changed. It is to empower grassroots NGOs and to facilitate their development" (Wen, 2019). Through an examination of the policy documents of the project and the interviews and statements of its leaders over the past twelve years, this section will explore the changes and continuity in the goals of the project and the problems that the project has aimed to resolve. It will also show how the project has been committed to empowering grassroots NGOs since its initiation in 2009.

Broadly, empowerment is concerned with the process by which marginalized communities, organizations, and individuals gain control over social and economic conditions and equality of participation in various social fields in a society, a community, or a given context, as well as over their communications and stories (Hamel, 2010; Jacobson, 2003; Melkote & Steeves, 2015a; U.N., 2012; U.N., 2015). Empowerment-oriented approaches to development and social change are also among the most extensively examined in research and the most widely employed in development practice (Melkote & Steeves, 2001). For example, the United Nations considers the promotion of social empowerment to be a key concept in its initiatives for development and social change (U.N., 2012).

In the modernization paradigm, communication is considered only as an instrument facilitating development initiatives to achieve specific goals, such as changing behavior in beneficiary communities through disseminating information (Hemer & Tufte, 2005). Changes in communication have rarely been considered a primary goal of development initiatives. However, newer theories and practices that are more in line with the participatory paradigm have recognized changes in the realm of communication to be an important goal in initiatives for development and social change (Communication for Social Change Consortium, 2018; Dagron & Tufte, 2006; Gumucio-Dagron, 2001; Hemer & Tufte, 2005; Jacobson, 2003; Obregon & Mosquera, 2005; Servaes, 1999; UNICEF, 2011; United Nations Development Programme [UNDP], 2006; Wilkins, Tufte, & Obregon, 2014). Wilkins (2014) asserts that communication for development builds on the definition of communication as "a socio-cultural process of symbolic exchange, rooted in material artifacts and grounded in political and economic structures that guide access to key resources." Therefore, the interests of those groups who have more power than others to assert their perspectives will dominate public agendas and policies. Consequently, the inequality in the realm of communication deserves significant attention from scholars as well as practitioners of communication for development. Due to the increasing impact of these new theories, empowerment in the realm of communication or communication for empowerment has, since the 2000s, become a new focus among scholars and international organizations engaged in communication for development work (e.g., Cadiz, 2005; Hamel, 2010; Jacobson, 2003; Kwapong, 2007; Madanda et al., 2007; Melkote & Steeves, 2015b; Mujahid, 2002; Servaes, 2007; UNDP, 2006). For example, according to the UNDP (2006): "Communication for Empowerment is an approach that puts the information and communication needs and interests of disempowered and marginalized groups at the centre of media support. The aim of Communication for Empowerment is to ensure that the media have the capacity to generate and provide the information that marginalized groups want and need and to provide a channel for marginalized groups to discuss and voice their perspectives on the issues that most concern them" (2006). UNDP stressed that the rapidly changing media and communication environment brought about by media liberalization and new ICTs has "led to a growing information and communication gap between the better off who are able to take advantage of these changes and the disadvantaged and marginalised groups who cannot" (UNDP and Communication for Social Change Consortium, 2010). Therefore, the communication for empowerment framework has become an important component in its efforts for development.

The NGO 2.0 Project started out as a communication for empowerment project focusing on grassroots NGOs that are marginalized in China's media sphere, aiming to give voice to grassroots NGOs that have traditionally been silenced in Chinese society. Through enhancing their communication capacity and ICT capacity, the project has worked to expand the participation of grassroots Chinese NGOs in various fields of Chinese society. In reference to the beginning of the NGO 2.0 Project, Jing Wang (2014) has asserted, "Grassroots NGOs cannot compete with GONGOs for the attention of mainstream media, making it difficult to increase social awareness in the causes they are promoting. Digital media provided an alternative way for those NGOs to communicate with the outside world and the communities they serve" (see also Wang and Whitacre, 2013). Therefore, the project launched the new media training workshops to enhance the capacity of grassroots NGOs to effectively use social and digital media to reach the public and to increase the control of grassroots NGOs over their communications.

As mentioned previously, the lack of legal status, money, and human resources are three main challenges for NGOs, especially grassroots NGOs in China. Because many grassroots NGOs lack legal status in the current sociopolitical context, mainstream media outlets (which are still subject to government control) generally do not feel comfortable reporting information from grassroots NGOs. And due to insufficient funds, most grassroots NGOs cannot afford to use mainstream media. Furthermore, because of lack of resources, networks, and connections with media outlets, grassroots NGOs cannot compete with GONGOs for mainstream media attention. Thus, grassroots NGOs—especially NGOs in underdeveloped regions and those without legal status—remain marginalized in China's mainstream media. According to its 2011 project description, the initial aim of the NGO 2.0 Project was to help enhance grassroots NGOs' ICT capacity in order to take full advantage of new ICTs such as Web 2.0 and thus break the bottleneck in communication and have their voices heard by the public. By empowering the NGOs—many of which focus on disadvantaged or marginalized groups, such as HIV/AIDS patients and their families—the project also indirectly helps those groups voice their needs and concerns. The project's initial beneficiaries were grassroots NGOs in western or central China, the less developed regions in China. Its initial two-year goals included offering four training workshops on ICTs and Web 2.0 technology for about a hundred grassroots NGOs in western and central China, and designing a set of training materials on social media and Web 2.0 for Chinese NGOs (NMAL, 2009). Before 2015, all participants in the workshops were NGOs from western or central China.

Moreover, its policy documents indicated that among NGOs in western and central China, the project prioritized the more disadvantaged NGOs—those with fewer resources and less ICT capacity to voice their needs and concerns. For example, its selection criteria for workshop participants from 2009 to 2011 stated, "Workshops are open to grassroots NGOs in Western and Central China, including NGOs with an interest in and demand for the Internet, but without sufficient ICT capacity and related resources and opportunities. . . . Our selection criteria are: first, NGOs that are the appropriate size. . . . Relatively bigger NGOs with relatively more resources are ineligible. . . . Third, NGOs with relatively less ICT capacity." As of 2011, the mission of the project is threefold:

1. Facilitate grassroots NGOs to increase their capacity to use the internet and social media
2. Use ICTs to promote new philanthropy
3. Enhance grassroots NGOs' capacity for social innovation using the internet

These goals indicate that the mission of the project is to empower grassroots NGOs through enhancing their capacity to use the internet and social media, although concepts such as "using ICTs to promote new philanthropy" have not been clearly defined.

In 2012, the *Southern Metropolis Daily* published a long interview with Jing Wang under the title, "The NGO 2.0 Project: Facilitate the Dreams of the Grassroots" (Ma, 2013). In this interview, she detailed the goals of the project, the value of the project, and the contents of the project's workshops. She stated that the goal of the NGO 2.0 Project is to provide grassroots NGOs in western and central China with new ideas on communication and practical new media tools. Regarding the contents of the workshops, she stated, "We don't need a cutting edge or a cool project. What we shall provide depends on what the grassroots NGOs need" (Ma, 2013). Of herself and the value of the NGO 2.0 Project, Wang said, "I'm not an evangelist of Web 2.0. Rather I'm an evangelist of information equality. To let marginalized communities have equal access and control of information, Web 2.0 is an important tool" (Ma, 2013). The title of that interview and the statements of its director demonstrate the clarity of the goal of the project: to empower grassroots NGOs in the field of communication and information. The project aimed to solve the problem of the marginalization of grassroots NGOs in communications—in other words, the unbalanced relationship between grassroots NGOs and GONGOs in accessing and controlling communications and information. The project's solution to that problem has been to enhance grassroots NGOs' capacity to use Web 2.0 technologies and social media so that they can have more control over and better access to communications and information. The interview also showed that empowerment of grassroots NGOs and information equality have become core values of the project since 2012. Moreover, the project has also begun to pay attention to other dimensions of the disadvantages and marginalization of grassroots NGOs, such as resource acquisition. To address these various dimensions, the project began to build networks between grassroots NGOs and other stakeholders in the nonprofit sector, such as foundations and communities that are outside the conventional nonprofit sector yet are critical for their efforts to promote ICTs to empower grassroots NGOs, such as communities of IT developers. For example, Wang stressed in the interview, "Besides the Web 2.0 training workshops, the project needs to generate networks between grassroots NGOs and other stakeholders in the non-profit sector . . . promote paying more attention to grassroots NGOs among foundations . . . build a bridge between grassroots NGOs and the community of IT developers" (Ma, 2013).

The project's 2018 documents offer a clear description of the most recent mission, vision, and values of the NGO 2.0 Project as of the present:

Mission:
   Promoting information equality among NGOs; facilitating the equality and balance of the ecosphere of the nonprofit sector.
Vision:
   Using the internet and social media to promote the communication capacity of NGOs
   Satisfying the communication needs, resource needs, and technology needs of NGOs
   Building the ICT4Good ecosphere in China through cross-sector collaborations with other partners
Values:
   Information equality
   ICT4Good
   Empowerment of the grassroots

(NGO 2.0 Project, 2018a)

The first item in the mission statement ("Promoting information equality among NGOs") and the third item in the value statement ("Empowerment of the grassroots") indicate that the problem targeted for change by the project remains the unbalanced social relationship between grassroots NGOs and GONGOs. Yet compared with nine years ago, the beneficiary community has expanded from grassroots NGOs in western and central China to grassroots NGOs all over China. The first item in the mission statement, the first item in the vision statement ("Using the internet and social media to promote the communication capacity of NGOs"), and the first item in the value statement ("Information equality") clearly indicate that first and foremost, the NGO 2.0 Project targets inequality in the realm of communications and information between grassroots NGOs and GONGOs, just as it did nine years ago. The project states its position on ICT4Good—a new concept in the vision and value statements—as follows: "Our definition of ICT4Good is very broad. It includes: ICTs serve the social good; ICTs facilitate the social good; ICTs empower organizations working for the social good. It also means that ICTs provide infrastructure for NGO projects; ICTs improve the efficiency of the projects for social good [of NGOs]; ICTs increase public participation in actions and projects for the social good

(2018)." This shows that the project's definition of "ICT4Good" is very much in line with the concept of ICT for development and social change in communication for development studies. Therefore, the first and third items in the vision statement and the second item in the value statement indicate that the NGO 2.0 Project's solution to inequality in communications and information between grassroots NGOs and GONGOs is still increasing the communication and ICT capacity of grassroots NGOs.

"The ecosphere of the nonprofit sector" in the second element of the mission statement is a phrase that the NGO 2.0 Project, as well as other NGO practitioners, researchers, and media in China, use to describe all the people, organizations, and institutions involved in the nonprofit sector, with an emphasis on the complex relationships, interactions, and interdependency between them (e.g., H. Li, 2018; Z. Li, 2017; Wang, 2019b; Yan et al., 2017). The imbalance of this ecosphere refers to the disadvantaged position of grassroots NGOs in various relationships with other organizations and institutions (H. Li, 2018; Wang, 2019b). Therefore, the second item in the mission statement ("Facilitating the equality and balance of the ecosphere of the nonprofit sector") indicates that, as of 2018, the NGO 2.0 Project has formally extended its goals to target the overall unequal relationship between grassroots NGOs and GONGOs in various fields. Through years of practice and interactions with grassroots NGOs, the project realized that in order to change the marginalized position of grassroots NGOs comprehensively and sustainably—in addition to improving the various capacities of NGOs—it must also target aspects of the wider environment that influence and contribute to the marginalization. This means that the project's understanding of how to effectively generate change is now more in line with the "communication for structural and sustainable social change" approach identified by Servaes & Malikhao (2010), which gives special attention to the complex influences of social and structural factors in sustainable social change. The second item in the vision statement identifies financial recourse and the potential to gain support to satisfy technology needs as two aspects of the wider environment that the NGO 2.0 Project aims to target in order to transform the state of disadvantage and marginalization among grassroots NGOs in China's nonprofit sector and in Chinese society in general. This conceptualization of the change targeted by the project stemmed from 2012 and was eventually formalized in the form of the project's mission, vision, and value statements in 2018.

In 2019, the *China Philanthropy Times* published a long interview with Jing Wang on the NGO 2.0 Project. In the interview, Wang reaffirmed the project's commitment to empowering grassroots NGOs in the realm of communications but articulated her concern about the overall unequal relationship between grassroots NGOs and GONGOs: "In any field, to maintain healthy development, the big as well as the small must exist. I always quote what Chen Yueguang, Director of the Dunhe Foundation, said: 'To maintain development in the nonprofit sector, we must have "big trees" as well as "small grasses."' The initial goal of our

[NGO 2.0] training workshops for NGOs in Western and Central China is to help the most disadvantaged NGOs gain social media capacity, gain resources, and empower them" (2019a).

On the scale-up of NGOs and their services, Wang (2019a) has stated, "If we just pursue scale-up of [big] NGOs and their services, then medium and small NGOs will be unable to survive. I think that kind of nonprofit sector ecosphere is unbalanced." She further states, "The core value of the nonprofit sector is social justice and equality. We therefore should help and empower the most disadvantaged [NGOs]. . . . If we think of the nonprofit sector as a sea, it should have big fish, medium sized fish, as well as small fish." The project documents of the NGO 2.0 Project and the statements of its director indicate that over the past twelve years the project has been committed to transforming inequality between grassroots NGOs and GONGOs, especially in the realm of communications and information. The project gradually initiated efforts that targeted the overall inequality between grassroots NGOs and GONGOs through its programs. From the launch of the project in 2009 to the present, its core value has consistently been the empowerment of grassroots NGOs in China. Empowerment first focused on communications but then extended to other fields.

The following section explains how the NGO 2.0 Project achieved its goal of promoting equality in the realm of communication and information among NGOs and how it helped grassroots NGOs eliminate bottlenecks in communications. Specifically, it analyzes how Web 2.0 technologies have empowered Chinese NGOs in general and how the project's workshops on Web 2.0 have empowered grassroots NGOs in particular.

Why Web 2.0?

Before discussing how Web 2.0 has helped NGOs eliminate bottlenecks in communications and how the adoption of Web 2.0 technologies empowered China's NGOs, I will discuss why websites did little to help grassroots NGOs project their message to the public. In the Web 1.0 era, websites were the conventional platform for any organization to publish content online.[2] Therefore, any NGO that wanted to express its voice in cyberspace or publish its information for the public on the internet had to have its own website, often called the NGO's official website. This was not easy for most of China's grassroots NGOs because of their lack of legal status, financial resources, and human resources. First, internet regulations issued by the State Council in 2000 mandated that any NGO wanting to launch a website had to register as an Internet Content Provider (ICP) with the Ministry of Industry and Information Technology (MIIT, 2000). For this registration, NGOs must submit the following documents for review by the MIIT: detailed information regarding the organization, a detailed description of the contents and services of the website, a photocopy of the photo ID of the NGO director, and a signed agreement to comply with the internet security regulations of the Chinese government.[3] If the NGO hopes to develop an internet forum, a bulletin board system, news, or another service, the NGO must first register and gain approval from related government agencies, such as the MCA, before submitting its ICP registration materials to the MIIT, and it must meet special requirements regarding hardware, registered capital, and internet security. As many grassroots NGOs lack legal status and often work on issues that are sensitive to the government, such as HIV/AIDS and gay and lesbian rights, it is not easy for them to receive this registration. Second, an NGO must develop its own website, which requires IT expertise in such areas as website design, development, and coding, which consequently requires large amounts of money and the involvement of IT professionals. The NGO may either outsource the development of its website to commercial IT companies or hire IT professionals to do the job. Both options are very expensive, given the lack of financial resources of most grassroots NGOs in China. For example, in Beijing in the late 1990s, the cost to design and develop a standard website with a content management system[4] for a small or medium-sized IT company was around 80,000 to 100,000 yuan ($11,598–$14,498). Yet even as late as 2018, 44 percent of NGOs had annual revenues of less than 100,000 yuan, according to NGO 2.0 Project surveys. The salary of an IT professional with expertise in website design and development hit 5,000 yuan in Beijing in the late 1990s, while the average salary for NGO practitioners did not reach 5,000 yuan until 2014. This means that the cost to design and develop a website is a big investment that many grassroots NGOs cannot afford. Third, a website that is updated only several times a year will not attract many visitors and can hardly help an NGO get its message out to the public. Therefore, to effectively project a voice in cyberspace, the NGO must continually update and maintain its website and develop a strategy to communicate online with the public, which entails a substantial long-term investment. The NGO may rely on technical support from commercial companies, but this means considerable long-term costs, which many grassroots NGOs cannot afford. Alternatively, the NGO can have one of its staff get training in IT expertise, such as website updates and maintenance. But this option is not likely to be sustainable. Due to lack of human resources, relatively lower salaries, poor or no benefits packages, and a high turnover rate, staff members who learn these skills may leave the NGO to pursue a job with higher pay and better benefits in another sector.

The experience and lessons from earlier projects focusing on ICT training for Chinese NGOs also demonstrate that a website is not a sustainable online platform for many grassroots NGOs. From 2004 to 2006, Green-web.org launched a project, funded by Oxfam, on ICT training and technical support for website development, focusing on Chinese NGOs.[5] The project found that without long-term reliable technical support by IT professionals, many NGO practitioners trained in the workshops failed to update and maintain their NGO websites. As a result, many of those NGOs abandoned their websites within six months to a year after the training workshop.[6] In its project findings, Green-web summarized the problems regarding website development and maintenance. First, although urban NGOs may have resources to develop a static website,[7] they do not have the capacity to develop a website that enables visitors to interact with one another and with the NGOs, and they do not have the capacity to develop a content management system to publish and update their web content. Therefore, these NGOs have to rely on volunteers with IT expertise to manually create and publish static web pages. These volunteers were consequently very slow in updating the websites. Because of the slow update rate and lack of interactivity, these websites attracted only a very limited number of visitors. And if their IT volunteers left, the NGOs could no longer update their websites. Second, these grassroots NGOs faced the real challenge of how to develop websites that were compatible with their ICT capacity, how to update and maintain their websites, and how to promote their websites in cyberspace. Many NGOs were unable to solve these problems appropriately. Therefore, they had to abandon websites in which they had invested significant time and resources.

Following substantial previous research on communication for development (e.g., Costanza-Chock, 2014; Kleine, 2013; Servaes & Carpentier, 2006; Slater & Tacchi, 2004; Torero & von Braun, 2005), this book rejects technological determinism. Yet as van Dijk (2005) points out, the characteristics of technology are not irrelevant to the analysis of social change (p. 22). Web 2.0 technologies and platforms offered two new characteristics that fundamentally changed the structure and use of the internet. These characteristics enable Web 2.0 technologies to empower grassroots NGOs within the specific sociopolitical and economic strictures of contemporary China. First, Web 2.0 platforms are free and open to anyone who has access to the internet. In other words, anyone with access to the internet can read content and generate their own content on a Web 2.0 platform without being charged. The second is that Web 2.0 lowered the technical barrier for end users and ordinary internet users who lack the programming and coding expertise to create web content. This has transformed the internet from a read-only medium to a read-write web for ordinary users (e.g., Lessig, 2005; Richardson, 2006; Thompson, 2008; West & West, 2009). In the Web 1.0 era, only users with IT expertise like coding could create web content, and the internet remained a read-only medium for most ordinary users. With the widespread use of Web 2.0 technologies such as blogs, wikis, microblogs, and social networking sites (SNSs), ordinary users gained the capacity to create (to write) web content by themselves. The internet thus became a read-write web for ordinary users.

These two new characteristics of Web 2.0 technologies have enabled grassroots NGOs to break the bottleneck in communication and have their voices heard by the internet public. First, as Web 2.0 platforms are open to anyone with internet access, NGOs need not register with government agencies such as MIIT and MCA to publish web content and to interact with the public on such platforms.[8] This has significantly reduced the influence and effectiveness of gatekeepers. Thus, the lack of legal status is no longer a major obstacle for grassroots NGOs to get their message out. Second, because of the characteristics of Web

2.0 technologies and platforms, rather than hiring IT companies or IT professionals to develop and maintain official websites that may cost significant money, grassroots NGOs can rely on their own staff to generate web content, create online platforms, and interact with the public on free Web 2.0 platforms. This may lower the costs of online communications considerably for these NGOs. Therefore, lack of money is no longer a major obstacle for the NGOs to get their message out to the public on the internet. Third, because Web 2.0 lowered the technical barrier for ordinary users to create web content, grassroots NGOs no longer have to hire someone with IT expertise to update, maintain, and manage their internet platforms. Ordinary staff members with minimal training are able to update, maintain, and manage an NGO's social media platforms, such as SNS profiles, blogs, microblogs, and WeChat. Thus, lack of human resources is no longer an insurmountable obstacle for grassroots NGOs to reach the public in cyberspace.

The Web 2.0 Workshops of the NGO 2.0 Project

Web 2.0 workshops are the cornerstone of the project's efforts to empower grassroots Chinese NGOs by increasing their capacity to use Web 2.0 technologies. The "cumulative and recursive model of successive kinds of access to digital technologies" proposed by van Dijk (2005, p. 22) offers a framework to explore how the workshops increased the capacity of grassroots NGOs in China to use Web 2.0 technologies.[9]

According to van Dijk's model, motivational access is the first phase of full access to digital technology. In the survey of 327 NGOs conducted by the NGO 2.0 Project in 2009, 86.2 percent of NGO practitioners rated the use of the internet and computer "very important," while 12.8 percent rated it "important." The NGO 2.0 Project selected NGOs with interest in and need for the internet but without appropriate ICT capacity and related resources. Yet the ability of NGOs participating in the workshops to overcome the motivational access barrier to Web 2.0 technologies is never guaranteed because Web 2.0 represents a fundamental change in the structure and the use of the internet, and consequently requires that users change their mindset to use it effectively.

During my fieldwork in western China in the summer of 2009 and 2010, many NGOs continued to focus solely on websites when addressing the ICT needs of their organizations. They were not aware of the rising influence of social media, and they did not think they needed to use Web 2.0 technologies such as blogs and SNSs in order to build alternative online platforms for their organization and to interact with the public and other NGOs. For example, some of the NGOs expressed their frustration in relying purely on volunteers in eastern China to update their websites. Yet when asked whether they would like to start their own blog or use WordPress to publish online content by themselves, they did not consider a blog decent enough for an NGO, and they had no idea how to start one anyway.[10]

To address the motivational access barrier of Web 2.0 technologies and platforms, the first unit offered in the NGO 2.0 Project training workshops was "Web 2.0 Mindset and Best Practices." The unit introduced trainees to new characteristics and concepts in internet use brought about by Web 2.0 technologies and platforms, such as openness, sharing, network building, and collaboration.[11] It also introduced best practices in Web 2.0 technology used by NGOs and activists around the world in order to show trainees the potential of these technologies for nonprofits and for bringing about social change. These best practices included successful examples of NGO use of Web 2.0 in China, such as YiNongDai and 1kg.org.[12]

Material access (access to a computer and an internet connection) is the second phase in van Dijk's cumulative model. As mentioned in chapter 2, the Connecting Every Village Project established broadband service for 99 percent of *xiang* and 89 percent of rural villages by 2011 (MIIT, 2011b). The 2009 survey conducted by the NGO 2.0 Project also indicated that 96.3 percent of the 327 NGOs already used the internet. Thus, the vast majority of Chinese NGOs should already have access to the internet. The survey also indicated that 86 percent of the NGOs have their own computers. Given that 96.3 percent of the NGOs were using the internet, lack of computers should no longer be a barrier to NGO use of Web 2.0 technology.[13]

The third phase in the cumulative model is skills access, the primary focus of the Web 2.0 training workshops. Skills access includes three successive substages: operational skills, informational skills, and strategic skills (van Dijk, 2005, p. 75) (see figure 2.3). Operational skills originally referred to skills needed to operate computers and software, such as managing files and using word processing software. In the Web 2.0 environment, operational skills expanded to include the skills needed to operate the growing number of new Web 2.0 platforms, such as blogs, SNSs, microblogs, and WeChat. According to the responses from the 2009 and 2010 project surveys, only 4.6 percent and 2.7 percent of the NGOs indicated that their most significant ICT needs were developing skills to operate computers and software—suggesting that most Chinese NGOs had no difficulty with this set of operational skills. Therefore, the workshops have not focused on the skills needed to use computers and software but on the new skills needed to operate Web 2.0 technologies and platforms. Most notably, the range of operational skills in this Web 2.0 environment are changing rapidly as new technologies and platforms continue to emerge. In order to offer the most appropriate skills to Chinese NGOs, the NGO 2.0 Project is constantly adjusting the units and skills in its workshops according to the technological context and the specific needs of the trainees. From 2009 to the present, workshops have dealt with operational skills related to a large group of Web 2.0 technologies and platforms, such as microblogs, blogs, WeChat, SNSs, wikis, RSS, Google Maps, Baidu Maps, Skype, online survey tools, OneNote, Tower, and cloud storage.[14]

Informational skills are those needed to search, select, process, and evaluate information in computers and in cyberspace, such as searching, editing, assessing information, combining information from different sources, and generalizing from specific pieces of information (van Dijk, 2005, p. 81). The NGO 2.0 Project's training workshops have focused on developing informational skills related to online sources. Although many units in the workshops involve informational skills, trainees have learned these skills most intensively in the second unit on Listen 2.0. This unit has taught NGOs to use search engines, RSS, Baidu News Subscription, and the search functions of social media platforms to effectively "listen" to information—that is, to search, collect, process, and evaluate the most significant and most recent issues in their fields of interest, the most influential authorities in their field, and information about their own organizations and competitors.[15]

Strategic skills are the capacities to use online and computer sources as a means for attaining specific goals and for the general purpose of improving one's position in society (van Dijk, 2005, p. 74). Strategic skills have been crucial to achieving the NGO 2.0 Project's goal of empowering Chinese NGOs and enhancing their capacity to get their message out to the public. Operational skills and informational skills provide the possibility for Chinese NGOs to gain strategic skills, which are the capacities to use Web 2.0 technologies and online sources as a means to achieve their specific goals and to transform their own marginalization and that of the people they serve in Chinese society. The NGO 2.0 Project gives significant emphasis to strategic skills. For example, the unit "Communication Strategy in the Social Media Age" offers a comprehensive introduction to, and concrete empirical cases of, strategic uses of Web 2.0 technologies and social media to transform the status of NGOs in society. The unit on crowdfunding offered a detailed introduction, a solid case analysis, and guidelines on how to use crowdfunding platforms and other Web 2.0 technologies to change the disadvantaged position of grassroots Chinese NGOs in fundraising. Other units on strategic skills include blog marketing, Listen 2.0, and so on.

One unit of the NGO 2.0 Project workshop has generally focused on one specific Web 2.0 technology, such as WeChat or Weibo, or one issue related to the specific needs of NGOs, such as Listen 2.0. To help trainees effectively use the technology and knowledge learned in the unit, the project generally includes operational skills, informational skills, and strategic skills on the technology or the issue in the unit. For example, the unit on Listen 2.0 includes four components: What is Listen 2.0, and why it is important for NGOs? What to listen to? How to listen? And the role of Listen 2.0 in NGO communication strategies. In this unit, the trainees learn operational skills, such as how to set up Baidu News Subscription and RSS, to collect information. They study informational skills, such as designing searches to collect the most updated information regarding significant issues in their fields of interest. And they learn strategic skills,

Table 3.1
The Most Important ICT Needs of Chinese NGOs

Survey date	Training workshop on Internet communication strategy	Training workshop on Web 2.0 skills and tools (IM, SNS, and so on)
December 2014	37.4% (205 out of 547)	19.6% (106 out of 547)
November 2016	53.9% (286 out of 531)	10.6% (56 out of 531)

such as using the tools and strategies in the unit to increase the effectiveness of their communications.

ICTs change constantly in the Web 2.0 environment, as have NGOs' knowledge of Web 2.0 and their ICT needs. To effectively address the needs of NGOs, the workshops of the project have needed to be adaptive. Over the past twelve years, the project has continually adjusted and updated the curriculum of its Web 2.0 workshops. On this, Jing Wang (2016) has stated, "When we started the NGO 2.0 Project, in China's nonprofit sectors, few people had an idea of Web 2.0. We had to begin our project by introducing Web 2.0 concepts and Web 2.0 mindsets to increase the literacy of Web 2.0 among Chinese NGOs. After six years, the context has changed. Social media are now extremely popular. The most urgent [ICT] needs of NGOs are no longer training workshops focusing on Web 2.0 tools but workshops on communication strategies in the social media age" (p. 2). This means that motivational access is no longer a barrier to Web 2.0 for China's NGOs, many of which have acquired considerable operational skills in Web 2.0 technologies and platforms. To address this change, the NGO 2.0 Project workshops gradually focused on skills access and added more components on strategic skills into the curriculum. For example, since its seventh workshop, conducted in July 2012, the first unit of the workshop has changed from "Web 2.0 Mindset and Best Practices," which primarily targeted NGO motivations to adopt Web 2.0 technologies, to "Communication Strategy in the Social Media Age," which has focused on strategic skills. Moreover, the training time dedicated to operational skills, informational skills, and strategic skills also indicates a change in the focus of workshops. For example, in the second workshop conducted in January 2010, roughly 80 percent of the three-day training (13.3 hours out of 16.5 hours) focused on or strongly related to operational skills. In the fifteenth workshop conducted in November 2016, roughly 36 percent of the training time (7.5 hours out of 20.75 hours) focused on strategic skills. In two surveys of NGO internet use in China, conducted by the project in December 2014 and November 2016, an additional option was added to the question about the most important ICT needs of NGOs in order to evaluate whether the changes to the curriculum actually met the needs of Chinese NGOs. This option distinguished training focused on operational skills of Web 2.0 tools and training focused on strategic skills (see table 3.1

for the results of the surveys). These data demonstrate that in the cumulative model of access to digital technologies (van Dijk, 2005, p. 22), the most important ICT needs of Chinese NGOs have further shifted from operational skills of Web 2.0 tools to strategic skills. And curriculum changes in the NGO 2.0 Project training workshops have met the dynamic ICT needs of Chinese NGOs. This analysis of the Web 2.0 workshops demonstrates that the project appropriately addressed or considered each of the first three stages of access to Web 2.0 technologies in van Dijk's (2005) cumulative model. Therefore, it effectively facilitated Chinese NGOs to gain full access to Web 2.0 technologies in order to transform their marginalized status in Chinese society.

The post-workshop surveys and a follow-up survey for self-evaluation indicated that the Web 2.0 workshops effectively enhanced the use of Web 2.0 technologies and the communication of the trained NGOs. A follow-up survey of seventy-eight trained NGOs showed that the workshops positively affected those NGOs' internet communication; enhanced their proficiency of Web 2.0 tools; increased their adoption of various Web 2.0 tools, such as blogs, microblogs, video sharing sites, and Skype; and strengthened the collaborations among them (NMAL, 2011). For example, when asked, "In the past year, were Web 2.0 thought and tools helpful to the internet communication of your organization?" 73.1 percent of the NGOs chose "very helpful," and 23.1 percent chose "somewhat helpful." When asked, "During your organization's practice of Web 2.0 in the past year, did your organization improve its proficiency in internet use?" 61.5 percent of the NGOs chose "improved," and 20.5 percent chose "largely improved." More importantly, the survey showed that 66.6 percent of trainees had organized workshops within their organization to share what they had learned, and 14.1 percent had organized workshops to share with their organization members and other organizations. This indicated that the workshops' trainees could disseminate the skills and knowledge of using Web 2.0 technologies to enhance communication to other NGOs. Therefore, the Web 2.0 workshops benefited not only the trained NGOs but also a broader community of grassroots NGOs.

The NGO 2.0 Project and the Participatory Communication Model

Theory influences practice. Scholars in communication for development believe that development theories that underpin a project influence the design and implementation of that project. This section will reveal the influence of the participatory communication model and related concepts and mindsets on the design and implementation of the NGO 2.0 Project.

In communication for development, scholars have formulated two models to assess the role of communication in development projects: the diffusion model and the participatory model (Servaes, 1999, 2008). In the diffusion model, researchers and development experts believe that they have full knowledge of and solutions to the development problems of the underdeveloped community in question. In the participatory model, however, researchers and development workers see knowledge of and solutions to development problems in a dialogical way. They believe that the knowledge of a development problem and related solutions are constructed in the dialogues, interactions, and participation of all involved, including experts, development workers, and members of the underdeveloped community.

Since 2014, the NGO 2.0 Project began building platforms for change and networks connecting partners committed to transforming China's nonprofit sector. The participants of these networks include NGOs, foundations, IT companies, researchers, and software developers and designers. Project director Jing Wang (2014) has addressed the goals of these networks as follows: "The networks focus less on solutions per se than on a socially constructed approach to change, which means building cross-sector dialogues and giving every participant the opportunity to share problems and propose strategic alternatives." This clearly illustrates that the NGO 2.0 Project shares the philosophy of the participatory communication model in that the knowledge of a development problem, the solutions to that problem, and even the definitions of that problem are constructed in dialogue with all participants involved in bringing about social change. And the role of the experts of the project is not to provide direct solutions but to foster and facilitate cross-sector communications and dialogue. This is why the third vision of the NGO 2.0 Project is "Building the ICT4Good ecosphere in China through cross-sector collaborations with other partners" rather than providing direct ICT solutions for NGOs (NGO 2.0 Project, 2018a).

Lennie & Tacchi (2013) argue that projects using the participatory model encourage adaptation as insights and evidence become available, rather than requiring fidelity to the original project design (p. 37). The NGO 2.0 Project considered "adaptation according to the needs [of grassroots NGOs]" to be the project's guiding principle in project planning and implementation (Wang, 2016). Based on insights and evidence gained through its practice and research and interactions with NGOs over the past twelve years, the project has constantly adapted its mission, visions, projects, and training materials based on the needs of grassroots NGOs, as discussed earlier in the chapter. Surveys are an important channel through which the project has learned about NGOs' needs. From 2009 to 2018, the project has conducted six surveys of NGO internet use and communication capacity in China. Tables 3.2, 3.3, and 3.4 show the most important ICT needs of Chinese NGOs according to those six surveys. The data from these six surveys illustrate that the majority of Chinese NGOs consistently chose training workshops on Web 2.0 skills or training workshops on Internet communication strategies as their biggest ICT need. Yet a substantial number of NGOs cited technology services, such as website development

Table 3.2

The Most Important ICT Needs of Chinese NGOs in 2009 and 2010

The most important ICT needs	2009 (%)	2010 (%)
Training workshop on basic skills to operate computers, such as managing files and using a keyboard (unrelated to internet use)	4.60	2.74
Training workshop on Web 2.0 skills (IM, blog, wiki, SNS, etc.)	38.50	46.63
Using website development services	34.30	35.16
Computer and other equipment donations	22.60	15.46

Table 3.3

The Most Important ICT Needs of Chinese NGOs in 2012

The most important ICT needs	2012 (%)
Training workshop on basic skills to operate computers, such as managing files and using a keyboard (unrelated to internet use)	4.44
Training workshop on skills to use software (video editing software, photo editing tools, knowledge management software)	19.11
Training workshop on internet communication strategies	42.66
Using website development services	38.50
Computer and other equipment donations	10.58
Other	2.05

Table 3.4

The Most Important ICT Needs of Chinese NGOs in 2014, 2016, and 2018

The most important ICT needs	2014 (%)	2016 (%)	2018 (%)
Training workshop on basic skills to operate computers, such as managing files and using a keyboard (unrelated to internet use)	2.71	4.14	3.48
Training workshop on Web 2.0 skills and tools (IM, SNS, etc.)	19.35	10.55	10.20
Training workshop on internet communication strategies	37.43	53.86	44.17
Using website or mobile app development services	27.85	25.80	29.86
Computer and other equipment donations	10.67	4.14	10.63
Other	1.99	1.51	1.84

and app development, as their biggest ICT need. And except for the 2016 survey, more than 10% of NGOs rated "computer and other equipment donations" as their most important ICT need (see figure 3.2).

Direct interactions with NGOs in the workshops and in their communications is another channel through which the project learned about the needs of grassroots NGOs. For example, Jing Wang noted, "At the very beginning, our initial goal is just to offer training workshops for grassroots NGOs in Western

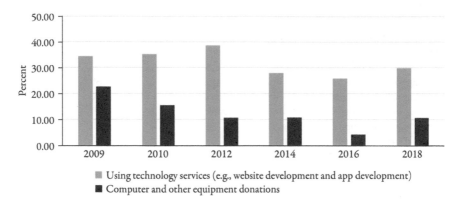

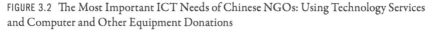

FIGURE 3.2 The Most Important ICT Needs of Chinese NGOs: Using Technology Services and Computer and Other Equipment Donations

and Central China to enhance their ICT capacity. Yet in our workshops and practice, we increasingly realized that one of their most important needs is, in fact, resources. We then gradually extended our projects and made more effort to address their resource needs" (Wen, 2019). Moreover, the project also learned about the urgent resource needs of Chinese NGOs from its own experience as a grassroots NGO in China's nonprofit sector. Over the past twelve years, the project has experienced constant challenges to acquire financial, material, and human resources to support its projects. For example, until it was able to formally register as a nonprofit organization in 2014, it barely had enough funds to hire one full-time staff member. Before then, a team of volunteers had to run the project. In October 2013, the project acquired enough funds to hire a full-time staff for the first time, but could not afford to rent an office. From 2013 to 2016, three full-time members left their paid positions but continued working as volunteers. They left because the project had difficulty securing the finances to support those positions over the long term. Still, they continued to be committed to the project as volunteers because they embraced its mission, values, and vision. Jing Wang stated, "[Over the past ten years,] the most significant difficulties for the project have consistently been financial resources and human resources.... We must have a fundraising capacity strong enough to sustain the development and the operation of the project. These two difficulties are actually interrelated with each other" (Wen, 2019). This direct experience with financial deficits and how they impede an NGO's development was the foundation for the project's position that resources are a vital need for grassroots NGOs in China.

To respond to the needs of grassroots NGOs, the NGO 2.0 Project added two new components to its programs: (1) organizing hackathons and technology salons to build networks connecting NGOs, IT companies, communities of software developers and designers, and software development programs in universities; and (2) developing a crowdsourced map platform, organizing NGO-CSR

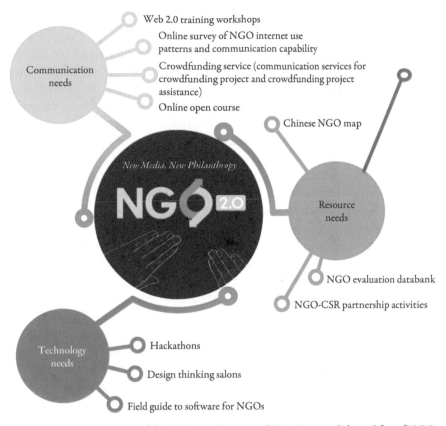

Web 2.0 training workshops

Online survey of NGO internet use patterns and communication capability

Crowdfunding service (communication services for crowdfunding project and crowdfunding project assistance)

Online open course

Communication needs

Chinese NGO map

New Media, New Philanthropy

NGO 2.0

Resource needs

NGO evaluation databank

NGO-CSR partnership activities

Technology needs

Hackathons

Design thinking salons

Field guide to software for NGOs

FIGURE 3.3 Current Projects of the NGO 2.0 Project and Their Focuses (adapted from [NGO 2.0 Project, 2021])

partnership activities to connect NGOs with the corporate social responsibility (CSR) sectors, and providing communication services and one-on-one assistance for crowdfunding projects of NGOs.[16] The first served to target the technology needs of NGOs, such as official website development; the second targeted resource needs, such as financial support and computer donations. Figure 3.3 provides a visual image of the current projects and their focuses (as of 2021). Similarly, the second element in the project's mission statement ("Facilitating the equality and balance of the ecosphere of the nonprofit sector") and the second item in its vision statement ("Satisfying the communication needs, resource needs, and technology needs of NGOs") indicates that the project expanded its mission and vision in 2018 to adapt to the various needs of Chinese NGOs.

Jing Wang (2019a) stresses that the first ten years' work of the NGO 2.0 Project mostly focused on enhancing NGOs' capacity to use information and communication, whereas the hackathon component of the project aimed to address the technology needs of NGOs. The hackathons provided a platform for IT volunteers and NGOs to dialogue with one another in a co-design process to collaboratively identify the technology needs of NGOs and collaboratively find appropriate solutions (Wang, 2019a). From 2013 to 2020, the project organized twenty-two nonprofit hackathons and technology salons in Guangzhou, Shenzhen, Shanghai, and Beijing in collaboration with local NGOs and IT companies, such as ByteDance, Oracle, and Tencent. At the hackathons, NGOs, software developers and designers, development workers from the project, and volunteers from universities co-designed and developed technological solutions and prototypes to address the technology needs of the NGOs, such as app development and online platform development. For example, the project organized four hackathons in 2020 that produced forty prototypes and attracted 120 participants. In December 2017, the project organized an intensive hackathon in which four groups of IT volunteers worked collaboratively with Save Minqin, a grassroots NGO in Western China, to co-design prototypes to address their technology needs in projects combating desertification in Minqin County, Gansu Province. To ensure the sustainability of the collaboration generated during the hackathon, the project has worked with the NGO and the IT volunteer groups as a facilitator and coordinator over the last two years. The first prototype was developed and tested in Minqin in 2019.

In November 2010, the NGO 2.0 Project launched its crowdsourced map platform connecting NGOs with the CSR sector to help provide for their resource needs, such as financial support, volunteers, and equipment donations. Moreover, to promote direct dialogue between NGOs and the CSR sector and to foster potential collaboration between NGOs and corporations, the project since 2012 has begun organizing NGO-CSR partnership forums in collaboration with local NGOs, local governments, and local chambers of commerce. For example, on December 24, 2012, the project organized an NGO-CSR partnership forum at Changsha, Hunan Province, in which at least two NGOs reached preliminary agreements to collaborate with corporations. In October 2015, the NGO 2.0 Project signed a collaboration agreement with Syntao, a leading consultancy company focusing on CSR in Asia, to promote networking, communications, and collaboration between Chinese NGOs and the corporate CSR sector.

Crowdfunding was a popular unit in the Web 2.0 workshops of the project, focusing on how to use crowdfunding platforms, Web 2.0 technologies, and online communications to overcome grassroots NGOs' disadvantages in fundraising. In 2015, the project moved forward to provide one-on-one service to crowdfunding projects of grassroots NGOs. According to a document titled "Examples of the NGO2.0 Crowdfunding Service," this had two components: project assistance and communication services. In project assistance, the staff of the NGO 2.0 Project assisted the grassroots NGOs in designing and optimizing their crowdfunding projects. They also helped the NGOs detail budgets for projects and provided a template and advice for financial transparency reports on crowdfunding projects. The NGO 2.0 Project believed "effective communication to be the key to the success of a crowdfunding project. And Web 2.0

Table 3.5

Total Number of NGOs and Crowdfunding Projects Served by the NGO 2.0 Project and Total Number of Donors and Donations in Those Projects (2015 to 2018)

Year	Total number of NGOs	Total number of crowdfunding projects	Total number of donors participating in crowdfunding projects	Total amount of donations from the crowdfunding projects (RMB)
2015	80	101	111,437	4,463,735.10
2016	46	54	80,585	794,848.00
2017	142	179	183,430	11,391,124.03
2018	145	182	262,910	13,675,278.63
Total	413	516	638,362	30,324,985.76

technologies could largely enhance communications (regarding the crowdfunding project) of a grassroots NGO" (NGO 2.0 Project, 2019). Therefore, in communication services, NGO 2.0 Project staff guided the grassroots NGOs in using Web 2.0 skills and knowledge to design effective communication strategies, identify target audiences, and create effective content for crowdfunding projects. They also advised grassroots NGOs in choosing communication channels and platforms, managing online communities, and servicing donors in the crowdfunding communication campaigns of the NGOs. To introduce crowdfunding to the NGO community, the project redesigned its Web 2.0 workshop crowdfunding unit as a separate workshop, available both online and offline. The project also developed a new crowdfunding training workshop with four stages and thirteen units to serve NGOs contracted for one-on-one crowdfunding services.[17] These units included an introduction to crowdfunding and crowdfunding platforms, preparation for starting a crowdfunding project, project design and planning, and financial transparency in crowdfunding projects. The units dealing with communication services for crowdfunding projects included communication skills for effective content creation, templates for effective content in a crowdfunding project, effective communication strategies (for crowdfunding campaigns), Listen 2.0 (for crowdfunding), maintaining donor relations, building a supportive community, and maintaining relationships with the media. To serve grassroots NGOs effectively in their crowdfunding projects, two of the seven full-time staff members of the NGO 2.0 Project focused on the crowdfunding service (as of 2020). This shows that the project invested considerable resources to target grassroots NGOs' financial resource needs and change the disadvantaged position of grassroots NGOs in acquiring resources. The project's data indicates that it has successfully helped grassroots NGOs acquire financial resources through crowdfunding. It has assisted 413 NGOs in 516 crowdfunding projects, collecting a total of 30,324,958.76 yuan(over USD 4,600,000) in donations between 2015 and 2018 (see table 3.5).

Giving special attention to self-reliance is an important consideration for projects that employ a participatory communication model, compared to projects using a diffusion communication model (Lennie & Tacchi, 2013; Servaes, 1999). According to Servaes (1999), self-reliance implies that in pursuing development and social change, each community primarily relies on its own strength and resources in terms of the energies of its members and its natural and cultural environment. In the Web 1.0 era, as discussed previously, the Internet communications of Chinese NGOs were not self-reliant. NGOs had to rely on outsiders with IT expertise to develop and maintain their websites and on outside financial sources to support their website projects. In the Web 2.0 environment, the two Web 2.0 characteristics mentioned earlier enable NGOs to build their online platforms exclusively with their own money and the skills of their own members. Instead of a website that requires programming skills, they can choose any free Web 2.0 service that does not require technical skills and have their own members create internet content. Thus, their online communications need not rely on any outside human or financial resource. And by increasing the capacity of Chinese NGOs to use Web 2.0, the NGO 2.0 Project expanded NGOs' ability to be self-reliant in their communications.

Self-reliance is also about whether the effects of a project are sustainable after the end of that project (Servaes, 1999, p. 195). A participatory model-based project pays more attention to whether the development process (project effects) in the local community can continue without outside support after the project ends. To ensure that the NGOs could continue to gain new Web 2.0 technologies after the workshops in the context of rapidly changing technology, the NGO 2.0 Project worked to nurture regional NGO-to-NGO ICT collaborations. For example, the fourth goal of the project's workshops is "to promote the collaborations among NGOs" (NGO 2.0 Project, 2019). Specifically, to facilitate networking and collaborations among NGOs, the project fostered QQ and WeChat groups for participants in each workshop and encouraged them to continue communicating and sharing information with co-participants after the workshops. As of 2021, the project had two trainee QQ groups and nine trainee WeChat groups, with as many as 168 members in one group. The WeChat groups and QQ groups have provided a channel and a space for trainees to network and communicate with one another after the Web 2.0 workshops. For example, many NGO practitioners who participated in the workshops as early as 2009 and 2010 continue to post information regarding their projects and to recruit volunteers in the WeChat groups. As noted in chapter 1, for example, on January 25, 2020, project trainee Wang Jun posted information about and the QR code of the Group for Medical Supply Donations to Hubei in the WeChat group to recruit volunteers to respond to the COVID-19 crisis together (see figure 3.4).[18]

The follow-up survey after the 2011 training workshop indicated that 44 percent (34 of 78) of the NGOs that took part in the training later

< **NGO2.0学员大群 (156)**   ···

康，阖家幸福！ 🙏 🙏 🙏

王军友成长沙

@张强-NGO2.0 强哥，打扰哈～
我们发起一个民间组织的专门
为湖北地区各大医院工作的一
线医疗工作人员捐赠物资的群，
内有口罩生产厂家，医疗工作
人员，群众自愿捐赠者，希望
自愿，公开，透明，愿能为湖
北贡献一己之力，愿我们共同
挺过难关！
围观勿进，还望理解～

王军友成长沙

FIGURE 3.4 Screenshot of a Post by Wang Jun to Recruit Volunteers for the Group for Medical Supply Donations to Hubei. See chapter 1 for the translation of the message in the screenshot.

collaborated with their counterparts from the workshop. This demonstrates the effectiveness of training workshops in increasing collaboration between its trainees. In 2018, the NGO 2.0 Project launched its Web 2.0 Mentor Training Program. The program provided workshops to practitioners from local leading NGOs on how to teach Web 2.0 skills and communication strategies and encouraged them to provide ICT training and to foster NGO-to-NGO ICT collaborations at the local level. Ultimately, the project has the potential to nurture NGO-to-NGO collaboration and help build self-reliant networks for Chinese NGOs to achieve their own development.

Channels and Technologies

Communication channels are essential components of new media projects for social change and any scholarly examination of them. This section examines communication channels and strategies that have been used in the NGO 2.0 Project and how these channels and ICTs were used to facilitate the project to achieve its mission.

The Efficacy of ICTs in Advocacy

Early sections in the chapter have revealed how the project's Web 2.0 training workshops have empowered grassroots NGOs and how QQ and WeChat were used by the project to build and sustain NGO communities that may foster NGO-to-NGO collaborations. Yet simply focusing on NGOs and their capacity cannot completely and sustainably change the overall marginalized and disadvantaged position of grassroots NGOs. Servaes (2009) has asserted that social change or structural change can only be achieved when most of the key stakeholders related to the problem are engaged in the change-making process (Servaes et al., 2012) and while aspects of the wider environment that influence the change—such as policies and financial resource—are also addressed. The new focus on the "ecosphere of the nonprofit sector" in the NGO 2.0 Project's mission and vision statements concurs with Servaes's assertion. Through practice, the project realized that to achieve its goal of empowering grassroots NGOs, it must get other key stakeholders in the nonprofit sector, as well as NGOs, engaged in the process. For example, Jing Wang stated, "Our ultimate goal is that all stakeholders [in the nonprofit sector] could take action collaboratively . . . to promote the balance of the ecosphere [of the nonprofit sector]" (2019a). The *Business Presentation*[19] of the NGO 2.0 Project offers more details on the stakeholders whom the project sought to engage:

> To empower [grassroots] NGOs and change the inequality in communication and resource distribution in the ecosphere of the nonprofit sector. . . . The Project is dedicated to promoting ICT4Good, in collaboration with cross-sector partners such as the government, universities, foundations, communities of IT developer and designers, NGOs, and so on. (NGO 2.0 Project, 2018a)

This statement shows that besides NGOs, the key stakeholders that the project aimed to engage include the government, foundations, communities of IT developers and designers, and universities.[20] In the current policy context in China, NGOs are not allowed to accept donations directly from the public; only foundations are permitted to accept such donations. Therefore, foundations are gateways (or gatekeepers) for NGOs to access the financial resources that are vital to the success of their various projects and to their very survival. The preference among domestic foundations to support GONGOs or big NGOs with strong ties to the government is one reason for the marginalization and disadvantages of grassroots NGOs in resource distribution and other fields. The NGO 2.0 Project began to pay attention to this problem as early as 2012. To achieve its mission to "facilitate the equality and balance of the ecosphere of the non-profit sector," the project needs to increase among foundations awareness of the significant role of grassroots NGOs in the "ecosphere" and to foster change in the attitudes of foundations toward grassroots NGOs. In addition, the project needs to promote an understanding of the nonprofit sector as an "ecosphere" in which foundations and grassroots NGOs are viewed as interdependent on each other. To achieve its mission of "promoting information equality among NGOs," the project needs to increase awareness among foundations of the information inequality problem and mobilize them to support efforts promoting information equality among NGOs. To achieve its vision of "building the ICT4Good ecosphere in China through cross-sector collaborations with other partners," the project needs to increase awareness of ICT4Good among foundations, communities of IT developers and designers, and university IT programs, as well as NGOs. Moreover, the project needs to facilitate networking between NGOs and communities of IT professionals and mobilize them to work collaboratively in ICT4Good projects. To engage and influence these various stakeholders, the project has consistently advocated its values of "information equality," "ICT4Good," and "empowerment of the grassroots" in the nonprofit sector over the past twelve years. For example, in its project overview, the project features "constantly advocating for ICT4Good" by using various communication channels as one of its important components, in addition to Web 2.0 workshops (NGO 2.0 Project, 2018a).

The communication strategies employed in the advocacy work of the NGO 2.0 Project share some similarities with the conventional strategies in advocacy communication in communication for development found in the West, though there are also considerable differences (e.g., Servaes & Malikhao, 2012; Wallack, 1994; Wilkins, 2014; World Health Organization [WHO], 1992). According to WHO (1992), "Advocacy for development is a combination of social actions designed to gain political commitment, policy support, social acceptance and systems support for a particular goal or programme. It involves collecting and structuring information into a persuasive case; communicating the case to decision-makers and other potential supporters, including the public, through various interpersonal and media channels; and stimulating actions by social institutions, stakeholders and policy-makers in support of the goal or programme." Like this understanding of advocacy communication in the West, the NGO 2.0 Project also holds that the occurrence of social change is contingent on a supportive environment and that advocacy is an important strategy to facilitate the emergence of such an environment. As in advocacy communication, the project uses communications to gain systems support to achieve its mission. As in advocacy communication, the advocacies of the project also aim to generate policy change. But unlike advocacy communication in the West, which primarily focuses on public policy from the government (Wilkins, 2014; WHO, 1992), the NGO 2.0 Project's advocacies focus on the internal policies of foundations regarding which NGOs and projects should be supported rather than state policies on NGOs. It advocates for more financial support from foundations for grassroots NGOs, projects dedicated to information equality, and ICT4Good projects. Advocacy communication in the West generally targets policymakers and decision-makers (Wilkins, 2014; WHO, 1992). The NGO 2.0 Project's advocacy targets decision-makers as well as ordinary practitioners in foundations and NGOs, and members of communities of IT developers and designers. For example, in its *Communication and Media Plan*, the project stated, "The target audiences are NGO practitioners (including workshop trainees), members of communities of IT developers and designers, foundations, CSR sectors in corporations, and so on" (NGO 2.0 Project, 2018b).

For some scholars, advocacy communication relies heavily on mass media (e.g., Wallack, 1994). Yet others believe that a multichannel approach, incorporating interpersonal communication and mass media, is essential for effective advocacy (Servaes & Malikhao, 2012). The NGO 2.0 Project itself is more like a grassroots NGO. In its first five years, it lacked legal status and funding. Even today (as of 2021), it has not generated strong connections with either the government or mainstream media outlets in China. Like many other grassroots NGOs, the NGO 2.0 Project was disadvantaged in terms of the use of mass media. Therefore, its advocacies primarily used new media. In its *Communication and Media Plan*, the project overwhelmingly focused on new media channels and platforms, such as Weibo, WeChat, other social media platforms, and its official website, where it could speak directly to its audiences. In the four-page document, fewer than four lines address mass media and internet portals (NGO 2.0 Project, 2018b).

Unlike advocacy communication in the West, where pressuring or pushing decision-makers and stakeholders is routine (Wallack, 1994; Wilkins, 2014; WHO, 1992), the communication strategy of the NGO 2.0 Project's advocacy is more like a dialogue in which building networks and communities and generating interactions and mutual trust are far more important. For example, as Jing Wang asserted, "A fundamental component of the strategy of communication and advocacy [of NGOs] in social media is building communities." She further noted that for the NGO 2.0 Project and other grassroots NGOs, "The first step in new media communication and advocacy is to build communities. Once we have built a community, we can then mobilize more people to work collaboratively for the social good. . . . We will not be able to build a community at the last minute. . . . Therefore, we must build our communities intentionally and systemically as early as possible" (J. Wang, 2016). The project holds that in social media, grassroots NGOs need to build a community that trusts their organizations and desires to listen to their voices for effective advocacy and communications. Otherwise, the contents created by a historically marginalized grassroots NGO will most likely be ignored by target audiences, as those audiences are bombarded by a constant barrage of social media content. For example, Jing Wang (2016) told grassroots NGOs, "We are neither Yao Ming nor Yao Chen; [without a community that really cares what we say], who will read the [social media] content created by us?"[21]

Furthermore, the NGO 2.0 Project holds that, in order to build communities in social media, grassroots NGOs must change their conventional understanding of communication that largely focuses on information dissemination.[22] They must embrace a new understanding of communication in which listening to and interacting with others is essential. As Jing Wang stated in 2016, "To build communities on Web 2.0 platforms, we must begin with listening. After listening to others, we can then interact with others. Listening and interaction are two core components of our communication strategy in social media. They can help grassroots NGOs build communities and achieve our communication and advocacy goals. However, the current problem in the nonprofit sector is that NGOs pay little attention to listening. . . . Most NGOs solely focus on disseminating what they want to tell others." Former full-time project member Jianbou Li (2016), who taught workshops on Listen 2.0 in the Web 2.0 workshops, stated, "Listening is the first step of a good communication strategy in social media. . . . An overall communication goal of NGOs is to build communities. To achieve this goal, we must find the right audiences." Effectively listening to others is crucial to finding the right people, and continuous interactions with others is key to building and sustaining a community (Li, 2016). Project CEO Zhang Qiang (2019) stated: "To effectively use social media in communication and advocacy, NGOs need to interact with the public in real-time. Do not focus only on disseminating your own information. . . . Interactions (such as replying to comments) are crucial for building communities and for communications with the public."

Weibo and WeChat. The NGO 2.0 Project primarily used Weibo and WeChat for building communities and networks and for interacting with others in new media. For example, in its *Communication and Media Plan*, the project tasked WeChat groups and Weibo with community building and interactions. As can be seen in table 3.6 (NGO 2.0 Project, 2018b) from its *Communication and Media Plan*, among all its new media platforms, Weibo and WeChat functioned to build communities, sustain partnerships, and interact with audiences, as well as disseminate information and values. Moreover, its *Communication and Media Plan* stated that WeChat groups "will be used to build core audience groups (using topics to stimulate audience discussions and build communities)," and Weibo "will be used for building networks with audiences and interactions, attracting resources, and disseminating real-time news in the field" (2018b). As

Table 3.6
NGO 2.0 Project Communication and Media Platforms

Platform	Type of platform	Functions	Update frequency	Number of audiences/ users/ subscribers	Comments
ngo20.org	Official website	Introduction of the NGO 2.0 Project	Far behind expectations (once a month)		
Baidu Baike	Wiki	Brand promotion	Entries that have been created: China NGO 2.0 Project		Entries recommended to create: NGO 2.0 and ICT4Good
Sina Weibo	Social media platform	Disseminating information, interactions with users	Once a week	29,489	Zhang Qiang operates and manages Weibo
WeChat (including WeChat group and WeChat public account)	We Media, WeChat subscription account	Disseminating information and values, partnership maintenance	Once a week	3,345	Zhang Qiang and Zhang Qian operate and manage together
Jinri Toutiao[a] and other We Media and social media	We Media, social media	Disseminating information and values	Low		Registered, but currently no one operates or manages the account
Video	Video sharing websites, streaming sites	Brand promotion, class demonstration	Low	Small	The project has registered accounts on several video sharing websites

SOURCE: NGO 2.0 Project (2018b).

[a] "Jinri Toutiao is a Chinese news and information content platform. . . . The company's algorithm models generate a tailored feed list of content for each user" (Toutiao, 2023).

Table 3.7
Data from the NGO 2.0 Project's Weibo, January 1 to December 31, 2016

Year	Total reads	Reads per message	Forwards	Comments	Likes
2016	682,772	1,895	285	127	272

discussed earlier in the chapter, WeChat groups have been used successfully to build and sustain communities of trained NGOs, in which the NGO 2.0 Project is a key member. Weibo has been used as a platform to engage with various stakeholders in the nonprofit sector as well as the general public. It is also a major channel through which the project can build a broader community, including NGOs, NGO practitioners, foundations, CSR sectors, and members of communities of IT developers and designers, in order to advocate for information equality among NGOs, and equality and balance in the "ecosphere of the nonprofit sector."

The project initiated its Weibo account in 2010. As of October 2019, the project had generated 29,354 followers, published 6,573 messages, and followed 961 Weibo users. The management page of its Weibo account shows that the project has developed categories—such as foundations, NGOs, CSRs, and IT Geeks—to manage the Weibo users it has followed. This categorization indicates that the project has listened to several potential target audiences listed in its *Communication and Media Plan* in order to network with them in Weibo. The project followed 61 foundations, of which 82 percent (50 out of 61) followed its Weibo in return, and 180 NGOs, of which 89 percent (161 out of 180) reciprocated. This suggests that the NGO 2.0 Project has successfully networked with foundations and NGOs in Weibo.

Data from 2016 indicate that the project messages posted on Weibo are being read by a considerable number of people, with total reads at 682,772 and reads per message at 1,895 (see table 3.7). Similarly, the number of people who forwarded (285), commented (127), and/or liked (272) messages posted by the project indicate significant interaction between the project and other Weibo users. Jing Wang (2016) stated that for generating interactions in Weibo, comments to other Weibo users and retweets of other's posts are more effective than original posts published by NGOs. Therefore, comments and retweets would constitute a considerable number of the messages published by an NGO. From January 1 to December 31, 2016, the project's Weibo account published 344 messages, including 158 original posts and 186 comments to posts of other Weibo users. The percentage of comments in the Weibo messages of the project (54%) indicates that the project used Weibo as a channel to interact with other Weibo users rather than a channel solely for information dissemination. Another key method to increase interactions and facilitate community building in Weibo and other social media is posting messages often and responding to others' comments, liking, or forwarding posts quickly. The project has paid special attention to this in its communications and advocacy in Weibo. For example, in its *Communication and Media Plan* regarding the communication strategy of Weibo, the project stated: "Post at least one message every weekday. Forward and comment on popular Weibo messages [relevant to the field] at all times; reply to users' interactions quickly." In the plan, the project also specified the best time to post various forms of content: "Post messages with positive energy (9:00). Post messages with real stuff in the field (13:00). Post messages on popular topics (20:00 or at any time). Use # and @ as needed." These carefully planned communications contributed to the increase in the NGO 2.0 Project's influence in Weibo. For example, from January 1, 2017, to October 2019, its Weibo followers increased nearly 160 percent from 11,352 to 29,355.

The project's *Communication and Media Plan* indicated that its WeChat public account is another channel that the project held to be most important and invested heavily in (see table 3.6). It assigned two full-time members to manage and operate the public account. The reason for its significance to the project is that since 2011, WeChat has been China's dominant social media app in the increasingly populated world of the mobile internet. As of 2018, 93.5 percent of Chinese Internet users used WeChat. The specific reason is that in the nonprofit sector, NGOs have widely subscribed to WeChat public accounts to get information about the field. For example, 97.9 percent of NGOs subscribed to WeChat public accounts of other NGOs or foundations to get information about the field, according to its fifth survey on internet use and communications among Chinese NGOs conducted by the project in 2016. To address the increasing popularity of WeChat public accounts within the nonprofit sector, the NGO 2.0 Project opened a WeChat public account in 2014. WeChat public accounts enable users to push feeds to the WeChat accounts of their subscribers, offering a new and efficient channel to reach the public on the mobile internet. Yet due to regulations from Tencent and technical constraints, without further development using programming languages, WeChat public accounts lack interaction capabilities. The NGO 2.0 Project was aware of this limitation. For example, project board member and Web 2.0 workshop instructor Xiao Ruifeng stated, "A significant weakness [of WeChat public account] is that it cannot be used for community building. Because a WeChat public account cannot conveniently forward messages from other WeChat accounts. It cannot follow WeChat individual accounts and WeChat individual accounts can only subscribe to a WeChat public account. WeChat public accounts are more like a Web1.0-age mini-media. It does not have the features of Web2.0 tools, such as opening and interactions" (Xiao, 2016). Thus, the project used its WeChat public account primarily to disseminate its information and values through social media, as presented in table 3.6. In its *Communication and Media Plan*, the project also stated that the goal of the WeChat public account is "to advocate for ICT4Good through disseminating contents [created by the project]" (2018b). As table 3.6 indicates,

Table 3.8
Content Creation Plan

Original posts	Comments on popular topics, news from mainstream media, big events in the field, messages to promote the values of the project, news of the project
Information from the internet and other WeChat accounts	Explore the internet, develop good relations with related WeChat users (Zhang Qiang and Zhang Qian)
Translation	Collect and translate firsthand relevant information and news from other countries (Song Shi, student volunteers)
Cases on ICT4Good and information equality	Collect cases and post them in WeChat (New full-time member)

SOURCE: NGO 2.0 Project (2018b)

among all new media platforms used by the project, the WeChat public account has become the channel with the highest update frequency, along with Weibo. Moreover, according to the plan, the project has planned to dramatically increase its update frequency: "After a newly recruited member joins the Project . . . we expect to increase the update frequency to three new messages per week. Messages regarding important events of the Project or the field should be posted the same day. Zhang Qian shall select the topics for WeChat messages. Zhang Qiang and other team members should review the contents to be posted." The project also developed a detailed content creation plan and assigned specific personnel to implement the plan (see table 3.8).

To promote the WeChat public account, the project developed a specific strategy in its *Communication and Media Plan*: "Staff and volunteers forward and like the messages." Moreover, the project also set up a benchmark to evaluate the performance of its WeChat public account:

> Evaluation of the performance of WeChat Public Account: First, ensure the quality and quantity of the contents (from once a month to once a week, and to once a day). Then aim to increase the number of subscribers.
> In the first stage: increase 30 subscribers per month. In the second stage: increase 50 subscribers per month. Then, sustain the increase, improve the percentage of messages that are forwarded [by others], and increase the engagement of subscribers and other users.

All of this indicates the important position of the project's WeChat public account for its communications and advocacy.

A detailed analysis of the account's performance is beyond the focus of this chapter. The data in table 3.9, however, provide a brief overview of this

Table 3.9
Data from NGO 2.0 WeChat Public Account, 2016 and 2018

	2016	2018
Total reads	21,290	39,244
Total number of visitors	10,569	23,676
Total number of subscribers	1,599	3,131
Total reads by subscribers	2,990	3,981
Percentage of total reads by subscribers among total reads	14%	10.10%
Percentage of total reads by nonsubscribers among total reads	86%	89.90%
Total number of forwarded or shared messages from WeChat public account[a]	1,081	2,085
Total reads of forwarded or shared messages	7,937	16,819
Reads per forwarded or shared message	7.34	8.07
Total number of WeChat public account messages that were added to favorites (by other users)	165	442

[a] This indicates how many times the messages published by the WeChat public account were forwarded or shared by other WeChat users.

performance in 2016 and 2018 and generally indicate that the carefully designed communications of the project's WeChat public account have been effective. The impact of the public account has significantly increased between 2016 and 2018. The total reads increased 84.3 percent, from 21,290 to 39,244; the total number of visitors increased 124 percent, from 10,569 to 23,676; and the total number of subscribers increased 96 percent, from 1,599 to 3,131. The project also met its benchmark goal from the *Communication and Media Plan* regarding number of subscribers. From January 1 to December 31, 2016, the number increased from 1,173 to 1,599, with an average increase of 35.5 subscribers per month. In 2018, the number of subscribers increased from 2,205 to 3,131, with an average increase of 77.2 subscribers per month. The percentage of total reads from nonsubscribers among total reads increased from 86 percent to nearly 90 percent. This indicates that the project has successfully attracted an increasing number of reads from communities beyond its direct subscribers. The data in table 3.9 also show that the total times the messages from the public account were forwarded or shared by other users increased 93 percent, from 1,081 to 2,085. And the total times the messages from the account were added to favorites increased 168 percent, from 165 to 442. This indicates that an increasing number of people consider the project's content not only worth reading but also worth sharing with others and collecting. This suggests an increase in the perceived quality of the content on the NGO 2.0 Project's WeChat public account. It also means that the project successfully mobilized its readers to participate in the dissemination of its information. The data in table 3.9 also illustrates that the participation of readers in the dissemination process made up a significant portion of the total reads on the account. In 2016, it contributed to 37.3 percent (7,937 out of 21,290) of the total reads. In 2018, that percentage increased to 42.9 percent (16,819 out of 39,244). Another indication of the increase in the perceived quality of the content on the NGO 2.0 Project's WeChat public account is that the average 7.34 new reads for every forwarded/shared message in 2016 increased to 8.07 in 2018.

Official Website. The *Communication and Media Plan* clearly indicated that Weibo and WeChat were considered the most important channels for the project's communication and advocacy. Table 3.6 shows that Weibo and WeChat have the highest update frequency, with two full-time project staff members designated to manage and operate the two channels. The project's official website, the major online platform of the Web 1.0 era, is considered less important, as it has a lower update frequency and lacks specific personnel to manage or operate it. The preference for Web 2.0 over Web 1.0 platforms (such as websites) is congruent with the project's belief that Web 2.0 technologies and social media can empower grassroots NGOs in their communications. Yet this does not mean that the project's official website has no role in its communications or has been abandoned as a new media channel. Rather, it is considered an important channel in an integrated communication strategy for new media. For example, Jing Wang (2016) stated, "Social media is indeed important, but that does not mean that we should abandon conventional new media channels. . . . For those who are capable of building an official website, around one third of the time and resource should be spent on their official website." The project built its official website very early—in 2010—several months after the launch of the project. As mentioned earlier, NGOs with Web 2.0 skills can choose to use free Web 2.0 services, such as blogs, that do not require any technical skills to create their internet content and platforms, rather than having to rely on conventional websites that require significant programming skills. The project used a WordPress blog as its official website in cyberspace. As with most blogs, no coding or programming or other technical expertise is needed to create or manage the content on the official website of the project. Since WordPress is free, the only cost for the project's official website is about ten dollars to purchase the domain name and seventy dollars per year to rent a virtual space to host the official website on the internet.[23] One weakness of the project's blog-based official website is that the personal diary style of blogs restricts interactions between organizers and those who are interested in the project. Therefore, the project views the function of the official website in its communications to be "disseminating the introduction of the project," including its mission, value, vision, projects, and news, according to its *Communication and Media Plan* (NGO 2.0, 2018b).

Another function of the project's official website is to assemble the contents of the project compiled under various social media platforms in one place. In addition to Weibo and WeChat, the project also uses video sharing websites, as

FIGURE 3.5 Screenshot of the QR Codes and Links on the NGO 2.0 Project's Official Website

presented in table 3.6. It uploads video materials to youku.com, the biggest video sharing website in China. Most video sharing websites, including youku.com, provide a new Web 2.0 function that allows users to embed videos from video sharing websites into a website page or a blog post.[24] By using this function, the project integrates its video materials into its official website. And by using QR codes generated by its WeChat public account and web links to the project's Weibo and other social media platforms, the project integrates its social media into its official website (see figure 3.5).

The first QR code on the left was created by the WeChat public account of the project. Interested users need only scan the QR code to access and subscribe to the public account. The third icon is the link to the project's Weibo. By clicking the link, users can access it directly and follow the Weibo account. Its Weibo profile contains a link to the project's official website. Weibo users who are interested in knowing more about the project can easily access the project's official website. Figure 3.6 illustrates the integrated new media platform of the NGO 2.0 Project, in which official website and social media platforms are all indispensable.

The data regarding the visitors of the project's official website and WeChat public account also indicate the importance of its official website as part of the project's communications. The data in table 3.10 show that as of December 31, 2016, the official website of the project attracted 62,161 reads, 2.92 times more than the WeChat public account. It also attracted 48,304 visitors, 4.57 times more than the WeChat public account. The percentage of visitors coming from mobile terminals such as smartphones indicates that the two channels are actually complementary rather than competing with each other. Only 3 percent of the visitors to its official website were from mobile terminals; in other words, 97 percent (46,896 out of 48,304) are from computers. In contrast, 100 percent of the visitors to the WeChat public account are from mobile terminals. Based on this brief comparison and the information presented in its *Communication and Media Plan*, the project has underinvested in its official website, which is a potential weakness of the project's communication strategy. The official website actually attracted nearly 4.6 times more visitors than the WeChat public account.

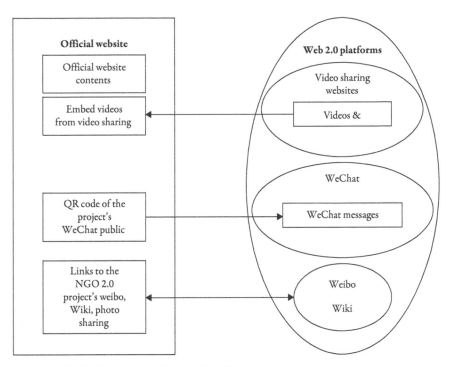

FIGURE 3.6 The Information Platform of the NGO 2.0 Project

Yet its update frequency (of less than once a month) is more than four times lower than that of the WeChat public account (once a week). And the project has not yet assigned specific personnel to operate and manage the official website. The low update frequency means that visitors who only or primarily use computers to access the internet may not be able to acquire the most up-to-date information regarding the project. In other words, the most updated information about the project may fail to reach a substantial number of users who are actually interested in it. Moreover, the bounce rate of its official website is very high, at 96.16 percent, with visitors spending an average of only two minutes on the site.[25] One possibility for this is that although visitors seem to be interested in the project, its official website contains little to read other than a brief sketch of the project. Visitors leave very quickly if they find no update on the website. Thus, the project fails to turn occasional visitors into regular ones.

The project's *Communication and Media Plan* (2018b) shows that the project has begun to recognize its inattention to its official website. The update frequency of the website fell "far behind expectations" (see table 3.6). As part of its to-do list regarding the official website, the project plans to comprehensively update the information on the website and to assign volunteers to update and manage the website. The final goal is to "log in to the management system of the website daily to maintain the website."

Table 3.10

Data from the NGO 2.0 Project's Official Website and WeChat Public Account (January 1 to December 31, 2016)

	Official website	WeChat public account
Total reads	62,161	21,290
Total number of visitors	48,304	10,569
Percentage of visitors from a mobile terminal, such as a smartphone	3% (1,408 out of 48,304)	100%

NOTE: In 2017, the project used Strikingly to upgrade its official website. However, Strikingly's definition of reads and its method of calculating them are dramatically different from those of the WeChat public account; therefore, it is impossible to compare the reads of the official website and those of the WeChat public account using data collected after 2016.

A Multichannel Perspective

Although ICTs such as Weibo, WeChat groups, the WeChat public account, and the official website have served an important role in the NGO 2.0 Project, other communication channels—such as interpersonal communication and mass communication—have also been important for the success of the project. For example, interpersonal communication-based workshops are the core component of the project. They generate the most intensive interaction between the project and the NGOs and enhance the capacity of the trained NGO practitioners to use Web 2.0 technologies. As noted earlier in the chapter, workshops are the most important venue to nurture NGO networks and NGO-to-NGO collaboration in the project. Also, in addition to formal discussions of ICTs and NGOs in the workshops, the project set aside time for participants to introduce their NGOs to one another. The participants also considered communicating with and getting to know other NGOs to be important reasons for taking the workshops. For example, when surveyed regarding their most important goals for coming to the workshop in Changsha, Hunan Province, 74.2 percent (26 out of 35) of participants said "to communicate with other NGOs."

Interpersonal communication also played a vital role in the nonprofit hackathons that the project organized to address the technology needs of the NGOs. Through interpersonal communication during the hackathons, shared knowledge regarding the technology needs of the NGOs as well as the solutions to these needs was collaboratively developed in dialogues among all participants, including the members of the NGO 2.0 Project, NGOs, and software developers and designers. NGO-CSR partnership forums that the project organized to address the resource needs of Chinese NGOs are another example that highlights the significance of interpersonal communication in the project. In 2010, the project launched its crowdsourced map platform connecting NGOs with the corporate CSR sector to address the lack of financial resources among Chinese NGOs.

After two years, the project realized that the map platform and other online communications were insufficient to generate collaborations between NGOs and the CSR sector, although they did facilitate effective information exchanges between them. Therefore, the project began to organize NGO-CSR partnership forums in 2012 to promote direct face-to-face dialogue between NGOs, the corporate CSR sector, and other stakeholders, such as local government entities and local media. The NGO-CSR partnership forums largely increased the potential for NGOs to collaborate directly with the CSR sector and generated numerous successful cases of such collaboration.

Another example of the project's use of interpersonal communication to achieve its mission is its ICT workshops for foundations. To promote information equality among NGOs and to facilitate the equality and balance of the "ecosphere of the nonprofit sector," the project considered foundations to be crucial stakeholders that must be engaged in the change-making process. The project has consistently used new media to advocate for more financial support from foundations to grassroots NGOs and to projects for information equality and projects on ICT4Good. Though important, ICTs are not the only channels that the project has used in its advocacy. In line with past research in communication for development (e.g., Cantrill, 1993; Servaes & Malikhao, 2012; WHO, 1992), the project holds that a multichannel approach incorporating interpersonal communication, mass media, and ICTs could generate more effective advocacy. Besides long-term new media advocacy, the project organized ICT workshops for foundations to advocate for information equality, empowerment of grassroots NGOs, and ICT4Good. In 2012, it organized the first ICT workshops for twenty-seven foundations in Beijing. In its plan for 2018–2020, it began to consider ICT workshops for foundations an important component of its projects. In 2019, it submitted a proposal to the Ford Foundation for support of ICT workshops to train 120 foundations. In the proposal, the project stated why the workshops are needed: "We increasingly realized that foundations, the upstream of the non-profit chain, are the backbone connecting various components of the non-profit sector. If foundations could have a better understanding of ICT4Good and support ICT4Good, through financial support and project collaboration, more and more donors and NGOs will participate in the practice of ICT4Good. . . . And this will eventually improve the balance and equality of the 'ecosphere of the non-profit sector.'" This indicates that the project aimed to use intensive interpersonal communication through workshops and social networks with foundations to increase those foundations' knowledge of and supports for ICT4Good and to promote the balance and equality of the "ecosphere of the non-profit sector."

Before gaining legal status in 2014, the project rarely got coverage from mainstream media. Since then, mass media outlets—especially newspapers that focus on the nonprofit sector, such as the *China Philanthropy Times*—began to pay attention to the project. Yet recognizing that its marginalized position in the mass media has not changed completely, the project's *Communication and Media Plan* (2018b) mentions a brief plan to engage mainstream media amid an extensive mandate on new media, which reads as follows: "Maintain the relationship with media outlets that have reported us. Try to create connections with other media outlets, but focus on attracting media to cover us. For interviews with the founder of the project, we prefer newspapers focusing on the nonprofit sector or newspapers in finance, as they will promote mass dissemination. For news regarding the project, we prefer new media outlets on information technologies as they could generate a quick response in the ICT sector. For events such as the ICT4Good Summit, we prefer to choose major portals." Given the project's limited human and financial resources, it has not assigned specific personnel for mass media relations and has rarely allocated financial resources to pay for mass media reporters but focused on "attracting media to cover us."

The project's communications and advocacy through new media and mass media are, in fact, not separate from each other. The project has employed a strategy of using its mass media communications to energize its new media advocacies and using new media to extend the impact and reach of its mass media communications. For example, in 2016 the project published a book titled *Internet Plus Social Good* (Wang, 2016). Designed as training material on communication strategy in the new media age for NGOs, the book was embedded with the project's core values, such as information equality, empowerment of grassroots NGOs, and ICT4Good. For example, a document laying out why the project edited and published the book stated that its goal was to improve the capacity of NGOs to use social media, enhance NGO practitioners' ability to use ICTs, and facilitate the equality and balance of the nonprofit sectors. An abstract of the book stated that "the readers of the book could be NGO practitioners, NGOs, foundations, university students and faculties, and the general public interested in Web 2.0 communications and cultures" (Wang, 2016). In other words, the readers targeted for the book launch were key stakeholders in its projects and mission. In order to increase the book's reach among these stakeholders in the ecosphere of the nonprofit sector, the project invited leading figures in foundations, the IT industry, universities, and grassroots NGOs to write the preface and endorsements for the book: Dou Ruigang, director of the Tencent Foundation, and Lin Hong, chair of the Ginkgo Foundation, wrote endorsements. Tang Ning, CEO of CreditEase, wrote an endorsement. Deng Fei, funder and leading activist of the Free Lunch Project, and the leaders of two grassroots NGOs who had participated in the project's workshops wrote endorsements. When the book was launched, the project started a new media campaign to promote the book and the project's values simultaneously. The project posted a series of messages about the book in its Weibo that attracted a considerable audience. For example, its May 9, 2016, message has 291,000 reads, was forwarded by 101 users, and was commented on by 38 users. In June 2017, roughly a year after the publication of the book, the project started another new media campaign about

Table 3.11
Rewards for NGO 2.0 Project Donors

Donation	Reward
RMB 1	Get NGO 2.0 Project's newsletter regularly
RMB 49	Get a book signed by authors (including Jing Wang, Zhou Rongting, and other NGO 2.0 team members) and NGO 2.0 Project's newsletter
RMB 99	Get a book signed by authors, an NGO 2.0 T-shirt, and NGO 2.0 Project's newsletter
RMB 199	Get three books signed by authors, an NGO 2.0 T-shirt, and NGO 2.0 Project's newsletter

the book. For example, it started a Weibo topic, "#The First Book on Internet + Social Good#," to encourage readers of the book to post images of the book and their comments about it on Weibo.[26] By June 10, 2017, the Weibo topic had 685,000 reads, and 70 people had participated in the topic.

For the book launch, the project also started an online crowdfunding campaign to raise RMB 50,000 for the publication of the book. In the meeting on this campaign, the NGO 2.0 team reached the consensus that the campaign would be more like a communication campaign to promote the book, communicate the values of the project, and strengthen the communities of NGOs that the project built through its Web 2.0 Workshops. Raising money to cover the cost of the publication of the book was a secondary goal. Therefore, along with the contents of the book, a significant portion of the crowdfunding campaign page focuses on the mission of the project and the project's accomplishments over the past seven years. (Rewards for those who contribute to the crowdfunding campaign appear in table 3.11.) Ultimately, 521 people participated in the crowdfunding campaign, raising a total of RMB 40,961.54. The majority of the donations were between RMB 1 and RMB 49 and came from training workshop participants and other NGOs and practitioners. Through intentionally employing a multichannel approach to enhance and stimulate interactions between its new media communications and its mass media communications, the project used its communications in various channels to reinforce each other. This strategy has been extensively used in projects and actions for development and social change initiated by other NGOs and activists. We will see similar examples in subsequent chapters on Tiger Gate and the Free Lunch Project.

Stakeholder Relationships

Past research in communication for development shows that the government is an important stakeholder in interventions for development and social change (e.g., Kleine, 2013; Melkote and Steeves, 2015a; Servaes, 1999; Servaes et al., 2012).

This is especially true in the nonprofit sector in China, as the government's policies directly impact every aspect of the sector in China. Rather than seeing the government as a negative factor against any positive change, the NGO 2.0 Project sees the government, and specifically government agencies working directly in the nonprofit sector, such as the MCA and the Division on Management of Foundations in the MCA, as stakeholders that should be engaged in the change-making process in the "ecosphere of the nonprofit sector." For example, in the section on "What we want to do?" in its *Business Presentation*, the project stated, "To empower [grassroots] NGOs and change the inequality in communication and resource distribution in the ecosphere of the nonprofit sector . . . the Project is dedicated to promoting ICT4Good, in collaboration with cross-sector partners such as the government, universities, foundations, communities of IT developers and designers, NGOs, and so on" (NGO 2.0 Project, 2018). This indicates that the project believes that to achieve its mission to "change the inequality in communication and in resource distribution in the ecosphere of the nonprofit sector," it must collaborate with related government agencies. It has also actively participated in summits in the nonprofit sector organized by the government to advocate for its values and promote its projects. For example, every year since 2014, the project has participated in the China Charity Fair organized by the MCA, the state-owned Assets Supervision and Administration Commission of the State Council, and local governments in Guangdong. Moreover, as early as 2014, the project considered government relations to be part of its communication strategy, as presented in the document *NGO 2.0 [Project's] Communication Strategy from 2014 to 2015*. For example, in the document, the project lists three categories of government agencies—the MCA, agencies in the MIIT, and GONGOs—as potential targets of its government relations work. In its new media advocacy, the project also considers government officials as its potential audiences. For example, on its Weibo management page, "government [agencies]" and "government official" are two of the groups the project created to categorize and manage the users it followed, along with "foundations," "NGOs," "CSR," "corporations," "individuals," and so on. This shows that the project aims to listen to and interact with government agencies and officials on Weibo. Yet over the past twelve years, the project has had much less success in government relations overall compared with its advocacy and projects concerning other stakeholders in the nonprofit sector, such as NGOs and foundations. For example, on the slide "Self-evaluation [of capacity and performance]" in its *Business Presentation*, government relations is the weakest among nine aspects of capacity. This indicates the difficulties of the NGO 2.0 Project and other grassroots NGOs in influencing government attitudes toward and policies on specific social change issues in China. However, this does not mean that in its efforts to promote information equality among NGOs, the project has not benefited from government policy. The remainder of the chapter explores how the project's efforts to empower grassroots NGOs through

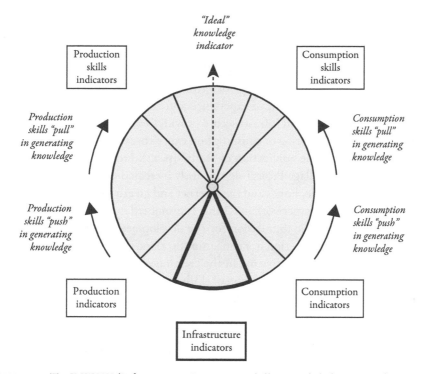

FIGURE 3.7 The INEXSK (Infrastructure, Experience, Skills, Knowledge) Framework.
Source: Mansell & Wehn (1998, p. 22)

enhancing their ICT capacity has benefited from the Connecting Every Village Project, a national program that significantly changed the broader environment of ICT use among Chinese NGOs (see chapter 2).

In 1998, the United Nations Commission on Science and Technology for Development proposed the INEXSK (Infrastructure, Experience, Skills, Knowledge) framework to examine the use of information technology for sustainable development. This framework aims to provide insights into how infrastructure, experience, and skills contribute to knowledge creation and knowledge-based economic development (Mansell & Wehn, 1998, p. 21). Figure 3.7 illustrates most of the key concepts in the INEXSK framework. The first concept related to our analysis is infrastructure indicators, which assess "how broad or narrow the foundation is for the development of experience and skills" (Mansell & Wehn, 1998, p. 22). The second concept is experiences, which includes production experiences and consumption experiences. The INEXSK framework is based on the academic consensus that knowledge is accumulated through production and/or consumption experiences (p. 22).

As discussed in chapter 2, the Connecting Every Village Project was conceived as a state project to promote the development of rural Chinese telecommunication and internet infrastructure. The NGO 2.0 Project is a project to promote the consumption skills of ICTs and internet services among Chinese NGOs. Thus, by examining the relationship between infrastructure and consumption skills and their role in knowledge creation, we are able to expose the relationship between the two projects using the INEXSK framework. The framework indicates that infrastructure development determines how broad or narrow the foundation is for the development of experience and skills. As Mansell and Wehn put it, "A very undeveloped infrastructure provides a narrow base for the development of either production or consumption experiences and a similarly specialized foundation for the application of skills" (p. 22). From 2004 to 2019, the Connecting Every Village Project significantly increased the percentage of villages with access to telephones and the internet and greatly expanded the size of the telecommunication network in China. It promoted infrastructure development and broadened the foundation for the development of skills and experiences. Yet "neither production nor consumption alone will bring infrastructure and experience into productive use in the creation of knowledge. This requires 'pull' influences" from the cultivation of skills (production skills and consumption skills) (Mansell & Wehn, 1998, p. 21). As figure 3.7 shows, "pull" factors based on consumption skills are key to knowledge creation. Mansell and Wehn state that "much of the challenge in harnessing ICTs to development objectives lies in the problems of mobilizing tacit knowledge and organizational capabilities to effectively connect experience with skills in the construction of knowledge based societies" (p. 22). The relatively wider gap between experience indictors and skills indicators in figure 3.8 highlights this problem.

The NGO 2.0 Project has targeted this gap by aiming to enhance the capabilities of Chinese NGOs in applying and using Web 2.0 technologies to promote social change. Mansell and Wehn state that organizational learning is the process through which organizations increase their tacit and organizational capabilities. This "occurs through individuals and their beliefs and actions which shape the organization's view of the world and give rise to particular forms of action" (p. 53). Through its Web 2.0 workshops, practices of participants in and after the workshops, and its advocacies of ICT4Good and "information equality," the NGO 2.0 Project has facilitated the organizational learning process through which NGOs increase their capability of using Web 2.0 technologies for social change. This has changed the viewpoint of Chinese NGOs regarding how to use ICTs and the internet in their communications and led to the adoption of Web 2.0 technologies and strategies in NGO projects and campaigns. In this way, the NGO 2.0 Project has channeled infrastructure assets—which have been enhanced by the Connecting Every Village Project—into productive use in the creation of knowledge among NGOs. This means that the Connecting Every Village Project broadened the infrastructure foundation for the NGO 2.0 Project. At the same time, the NGO 2.0 Project has played a significant role in making the fruits of the Connecting Every Village Project extremely useful for NGOs. In this specific context, the government-led

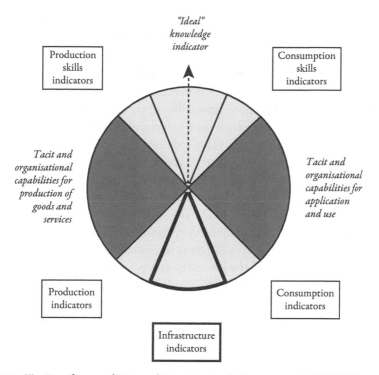

FIGURE 3.8 The Significance of Tacit and Organizational Capacity in the INEXSK Framework. Source: Mansell & Wehn (1998, p. 23)

project (the Connecting Every Village Project) and the NGO-led project (the NGO 2.0 Project) complement each other to enhance the capacity of using new media for social change of NGOs. They are complementary projects that stress different factors for NGOs' online engagement with society.

The complementary relationship between the two projects can also be seen from the perspective of van Dijk's (2005) digital divide model (see chapter 2). In his take on the digital divide, van Dijk identified motivational access, material access, and skills access as the first three of the four successive stages of access (p. 20) (see figure 2.3). Based on my account in chapter 2 and this chapter, the Connecting Every Village Project focuses on the material access stage, whereas the NGO 2.0 Project focuses on the motivational access and skills access stages. The Connecting Every Village Project helps NGOs in rural and less developed regions to overcome the material access barrier; the NGO 2.0 Project facilitates NGOs to overcome the motivational access and skills access barriers. Due to the cumulative relationship among the four stages of access, either of the two projects alone could not have enabled Chinese NGOs in less developed regions gain full access to Web 2.0 technologies. Therefore, in the cumulative model, the Connecting Every Village Project and the NGO 2.0 Project have been complementary projects, enhancing the capacity of NGOs to use Web 2.0 technologies.

NGO 2.0 Project surveys of ICT and the communication capacity of Chinese NGOs also shed light on this complementary relationship between the two projects following van Dijk's model. The third survey conducted in 2012 collected data from 293 NGOs in thirty province-level divisions.[27] It asked NGOs to choose no more than three factors that impeded their use of the internet. Fourteen percent of the NGOs chose "instability of the internet," 14 percent chose "lack of skills in using the internet," and 7.2 percent chose "Our leader does not consider internet use important." This indicates that poor internet infrastructure and other factors related to material access, in addition to factors related to skill access (e.g., "lack of skills in using the Internet") and factors related to motivational access (e.g., "Our leader does not consider Internet use important"), impeded internet use by China's NGOs. The sixth survey conducted in April 2018 collected data from 489 NGOs in thirty province-level divisions. The same task was given, but it generated very different responses. Only 0.16 percent of the NGOs chose "instability of the internet," 2.25 percent chose "lack of skills in using the internet," and 2.04 percent chose "Our leader does not consider internet use important."

It is likely that the Connecting Every Village Project and related policies have contributed to the significant reduction of infrastructure-related impediments to internet use among NGOs between 2012 and 2018. In large part, this is because China began to implement a National Broadband Strategy in August 2013 (State Council of the PRC, 2013), which aimed to increase the speed, quality, and penetration rate of wired broadband and 4G wireless networks in urban and rural China. It planned to boost the wired broadband household penetration rate to 65 percent and 30 percent in urban and rural China, respectively, and to develop 3G and 4G networks covering most urban and rural areas by 2015. It aimed to increase the broadband household penetration rate to 70 percent, the 3G/4G adoption rate to 85 percent, and the percentage of administrative villages with broadband access to 98 percent by 2020. In November 2015, MIIT and the Ministry of Finance launched the Universal Service Pilot Projects in order to "further narrow the rural-urban digital divide . . . and to promote the development of rural and frontier regions" (MIIT, 2018a, 2019). This marked the first time that the central government directly subsidized a national project to reduce the rural-urban digital divide, although the six state-owned companies continued to assume primary roles (MIIT & Ministry of Finance, 2015). For example, its 2018 policy indicated that the central government would subsidize 30 percent of the cost for six years in the rural regions targeted for the pilot projects (MIIT & Ministry of Finance, 2018). By July 2018, such pilot projects have provided RMB 40 billion in rural internet infrastructure and extended or upgraded broadband service in 130,000 administrative villages in twenty-seven provincial divisions. Moreover, as of 2018, 96 percent of administrative villages have been connected by fiber-optic networks, and 95 percent have been covered by 4G networks (MIIT, 2018b). From 2013 to 2018, the percentage of internet users utilizing

FTTH (fiber to the home) increased from 21.8 percent to 86.8 percent, and the number of 4G base-station towers increased from 63,000 to 6,480,000. Average wired internet speed increased from 2.93 Mbit/s to 20.15 Mbit/s (Broadband Development Alliance, 2013, 2018).[28] Average internet speed in eastern, central, and western China reached 20.55 Mbit/s, 20.05 Mbit/s, and 19.29 Mbit/s, respectively. The average download speed in 3G networks and 4G networks reached 8.89 Mbit/s and 19.12 Mbit/s (Broadband Development Alliance, 2018). All of this has significantly enhanced internet infrastructure, boosting the capacity of Chinese NGOs to use the internet and reducing the instability of internet networks and other infrastructure-related impediments for Chinese NGOs.

Aiming to promote information equality among NGOs and ICT4Good, the NGO 2.0 Project has contributed to a significant reduction in both skills-access-related and motivational-access-related impediments to NGO use of the internet between 2012 and 2018. Yet as van Dijk's (2005) cumulative model anticipated, the Web 2.0 training workshops and the constant new media and mass media advocacy of the project alone are insufficient to bring about this change. The project's various efforts to increase ICT capacity for Chinese NGOs, enhanced internet infrastructure, and the growing popularity of the internet—in the nonprofit sector specifically and in Chinese society more generally—all coalesced to contribute to this change in internet use among Chinese NGOs.

4

Tiger Gate

A New Media Action for
Government Accountability

The South China tiger incident, also known as "Tiger Gate," is considered a landmark in Chinese online mobilization among scholars and mainstream Chinese media (Liu, 2008; Wang & Bai, 2008; G. Yang, 2009; Zheng, 2007). This chapter will show how activists used new media and ICTs to promote social change within the sociopolitical and technological structures of contemporary China through a case study of this incident. It will focus on individual activists and the informal online community formed by activists, which Jenkins (2006) has called a "knowledge community" in his study of online communities in convergence culture. In Tiger Gate, individual activists and informal online communities served as engines of action and generators of collective knowledge that came to challenge official government claims. For this achievement, Tiger Gate stands out among the five cases examined in this book. Until recently, however, activists and informal online communities like those in Tiger Gate have not been considered legitimate subjects of research in communication for development due to the myopic focus of modernization-based conventional research on formal development institutions and their initiatives. Yet since the late 1990s, emerging theories and approaches (e.g., Dagron & Tufte, 2006; Huesca, 2001; Melkote & Steeves, 2015b; Melkote & Steeves, 2015a; Servaes, 1999, 2007; Wilkins, 2015; Wilkins & Mody, 2001) have significantly broadened this narrow focus and recognized the legitimate and important role of activists and informal online communities in communication for development (Huesca, 2001; Wilkins & Mody, 2001).

Besides the focus on informal online communities, there are three other reasons why Tiger Gate represents an ideal case to examine using ICTs and new media for social change in China. First, it revealed the role of ICTs in the emergence of an activist network that cuts across geographical barriers and disciplinary boundaries. It demonstrated how ICTs contributed to the real-time coordination of collective knowledge construction among activists and the effective mobilization of their skills. By comparing the use of ICTs in Tiger Gate with the use of ICTs in the Free Lunch Project and the NCP Life Support Network's actions against COVID-19, I will also show the continuities and discontinuities in the ways activists have used ICTs for social change in China. Second, the use of new technologies such as computer vision and 3D photography by grassroots activists in this case demonstrates the new power of ICTs in actions for social change. Third, interactions between activists and the government on the one hand showed how ICTs enhanced activist resilience to the government's crackdowns. On the other hand, they exposed the limitations of new media actions in bringing about social change in contemporary China.

Overview of the South China Tiger Incident

At a press conference on October 12, 2007, the Forestry Department of Shaanxi Province announced that a peasant named Zhou Zhenglong had taken photographs of a wild South China tiger—which was presumed to have gone extinct. It stated that forty digital and thirty-one film photographs taken by Zhou in Zhenping County, Shaanxi Province, on October 3 (nine days earlier) had been authenticated by experts, indicating that at least one wild South China tiger was still alive. Dominant mainstream media outlets, including Xinhuanet.com and China Central Television (CCTV), reported this news.[1]

When eight of the photos were posted online on October 12, however, numerous internet users quickly challenged their authenticity. Photographers and photography fans at leading Chinese online photograph forums, notably xitek .com, were the first to question the photos online. Meanwhile, Fu Dezhi, head botanist at the Institute of Botany at the Chinese Academy of Sciences—who later became a leading figure in the activist community—questioned the authenticity of the photos and the coverage of this story by Xinhuanet.com on his personal blogsite and at emay.com.cn.[2] Hundreds of thousands of internet users at major Chinese forums, such as Tianya.com, kdnet.com, and 163.com, as well as local internet forums in Shaanxi, such as hsw.cn, became involved in the discussions and debate over this incident.

On October 17, as the outcry against the authenticity of the photos quickly proliferated online, the Shaanxi Forestry Department used the mainstream media to refute allegations that the photos were fake. The director of the Shaanxi

Forestry Department's Office of Wild Animal Protection, Wang Wanyun, argued that his office would not be able to provide more photos online to help persuade netizens, due to Zhou's copyright concerns. Yet he insisted that the photos were authentic. He claimed that Zhou also took photos of the tiger's footprints—hard evidence of the authenticity of the photos. He further argued that experts of the National Photographers Association had evaluated the photos and verified their authenticity. Responding to questions, Zhou also claimed to guarantee the authenticity of the photos with his life. However, Zhou's response and official claims did little to appease the increasing contestation over the photos among online activists and the media. On October 23, Shaanxi Forestry Department officials went with Zhou to the National Forestry Administration in Beijing to report the discovery of the wild South China tiger. That office did not comment on the authenticity of the photos. On October 26, Guan Ke, director of the Center of Forestry Information and Propaganda of the Shaanxi Forestry Department, opened a blogsite under his real name to refute the online activists. He later became the leading netizen supporting the official claim of the Shaanxi Forestry Department. In his second blog post on October 26, he disclosed the specifications of the camera Zhou had used to take the seventy-one photos and the exact times (between 4:38:28 P.M. and 5:03:08 P.M.) on October 23 when they were taken. Guan's disclosure of this information provided more ammunition for activists to further discredit the photos and ultimately undermined the official claim.

From November 2 onward, increasing numbers of online activists—using their real names—joined Fu in questioning the authenticity of the photos. This was significant because until this time in China, such charges by netizens had almost always been made anonymously due to fear that citizens would face retaliation by state organs. Meanwhile, anonymous netizens on major forums continued to engage in heated debate over the photos. The media dubbed supporters of official claims "pro-tiger netizens" and opponents "anti-tiger netizens." Later, the two deputy directors of the Shaanxi Forestry Department, Zhu Julong and Sun Chengqian, contested the arguments of the anti-tiger activists in the mainstream and local media in Shaanxi, as well as on their own blogs. In international news, *Science* (Holden, 2007) and *The Wall Street Journal* (Ye, 2008) also reported the incident and the ongoing online debate. On November 16, anti-tiger activists found and published the source of the photos: a New Year's picture printed by a small company in Zhejiang Province.[3] CCTV, *People's Daily*, *The Southern Metropolis Daily*, and other mainstream media outlets, as well as major portals such as 163.com, sina.com, and QQ.com, widely reported this breaking news. Pro-tiger figures, notably Guan Ke, Zhu Julong, and Zhou Zhenglong, as well as some anonymous pro-tiger internet users, nevertheless continued to defend the authenticity of the photos, claiming that the New Year's picture was fake. The debate over the photos continued both online and in the mainstream mass media. On February 4, 2008—without commenting on the authenticity of the photos—the Shaanxi Forestry Department issued a letter of apology to the public for announcing the discovery of a wild South China tiger before investigating it seriously but said it had yet to complete its reevaluation of the photos.

On February 19, 2008, *The Southern Metropolis Daily* reported that Shaanxi Forestry Department officials had revealed that a reevaluation of the photos had not yet begun (R. Tan, 2008). This news triggered a new round of outrage among anti-tiger netizens and criticism by the media over government inaction. On March 7, the South China Tiger forum at hsw.cn, the major forum focusing on the incident, was shut down. Anti-tiger netizens moved to other major public forums to continue their challenges and online actions. On June 29, in the face of increasing media pressure and constant online action, the Shaanxi Forestry Department announced the result of its investigation into Tiger Gate, determining that the photos taken by Zhou Zhenglong were fake. Zhou was arrested by local police. At a press conference held by Shaanxi provincial government authorities, police exhibited the New Year's picture used to fake the South China tiger photos and the implements Zhou used to create the tiger footprints. Thirteen government officials were disciplined for the scandal, and seven of them were removed from office. The only one to face criminal charges was Zhou Zhenglong, who was sentenced to two and a half years in prison for fraud.

In this chapter, I will first address communication channels and processes, then focus on social change and stakeholder relationships. In addition, I will show that despite the significance of Tiger Gate as a landmark for understanding the use of new media for social change in Chinese society, we must recognize that its impact on sustained institutional or policy change was rather limited.

Channels and Technologies

A growing literature has demonstrated that new media and ICTs play an important role in development projects and actions for social change (Donner, 2015; Inagaki, 2007; Kleine, 2013; McKee et al., 2000; Melkote and Steeves, 2015a; Ogan et al., 2009; Qiu, 2009; G. Yang, 2009). Yet as I have noted previously, comprehensive analysis of new media interventions in developing contexts like China requires a multichannel approach. Therefore, I will first focus on new media and ICTs, and then move to mass media and the interactions between mass media and new media.

The Importance of New Media and Technology

Rather than acting as drivers of social change as in modernization paradigms (e.g., Lerner, 1958; Rogers, 1976), technologies in the Tiger Gate case serve as tools that offer new possibilities for combining the capabilities of computer and internet systems with the knowledge of large groups of people (Servaes & Carpentier, 2006).

ICTs as Communication Tools and Platforms to Facilitate the Construction of Collective Knowledge. Researchers in communication for development have argued that communication is fundamental to achieving development and social change by promoting the construction, dissemination, and sharing of knowledge and information (e.g., Lennie & Tacchi, 2013; Melkote & Steeves, 2015b; Servaes et al., 2012). In the South China tiger incident, the collective knowledge that eventually discredited the official clam was constructed by activist communities made up of geographically dispersed individuals working in different fields. ICTs, such as internet forums, blogs, and IM, provided these individual activists with tools and platforms to collectively construct the knowledge that enabled them to contest the authenticity of the South China tiger photos and the official claims. Without these ICTs, those activists would be very unlikely to encounter one another, much less collaborate to challenge state proclamations.

In challenging the authenticity of the photos, activists with various expertise and knowledge collectively developed at least seven perspectives in the incident. For each perspective, various activists developed different methods to show that the photos had been faked. Eventually, the collective knowledge to demonstrate the falsity of the photos extended across a wide array of fields, including botany, wildlife photography, digital photography, math (geometry and linear algebra), computer vision, 3D photography, and so on. The breadth, depth, and wealth of the collective knowledge of the activist community connected by ICTs extended beyond the mastery of any one expert. Table 4.1 provides the perspectives, methods, platforms, places of first publication, and the geographic locations and backgrounds of the activists who developed the various methods used to contest and ultimately discredit the South China tiger photos.

The data presented in table 4.1 indicates that activists, having various levels of expertise and knowledge, developed seven or more methods to contest the tiger photos. ICTs such as internet forums, bulletin board systems (BBSs), and blogs provided the infrastructure and platforms for this large-scale cross-discipline creation of collective knowledge and the accumulation of that knowledge. For example, activists in the xitek.com South China Tiger forum created and published at least six of the methods on the forum. They also created posts to aggregate all the methods they found online that challenged the tiger photos. This made xitek.com a vital platform and space for the creation, accumulation, and communication of collective knowledge contesting the authenticity of the South China tiger photos. During the incident, the forum attracted millions of visitors in cyberspace. For example, in the ten days between November 16 and November 26, 2007, 289,000 viewers read Smallfish's thread at xitek.com, "Result from Human Flesh Search, origin of the tiger has been found!"

Moreover, the ICT-facilitated creation of the collective knowledge of the tiger photos revealed a new form of knowledge construction in social change initiatives, which is quite different from conventional forms within the modernization

Table 4.1

Perspectives and Methods Used to Contest the South China Tiger Photos

Time	Perspective	Methods-based finding	First published	Principal activist	Geographical location	Background of activist
10-14-2007	Botany	The leaves of the plants around the tiger are disproportionately large	Fu's blog and emay.com.cn	Fu Dezhi	Beijing	Head botanist at the Institute of Botany at the Chinese Academy of Sciences
10-15-2007	Zoology	Research-based evidence has established that the wild South China tiger is already extinct	wildchina.cn	Lao Liu	Harbing, Heilongjiang	Professor at Northeastern Forestry University (China)
10-15-2007 9:15 A.M.	**Digital photography**	**Animated GIF of the South China tiger photos indicates that they are fake**	**Tianya.com, xitek.com**	**FirstImpression**	**Shaoxing (Zhejiang Province)**	**Public employee**
10-30-2007 5:16 P.M.	Math (linear algebra)	Linear algebra is used to prove the tiger in the photos is flat[a]	xitek.com	Chimpanzee	Beijing	IT engineer at a government agency
10-31-2007 4:19 P.M.	**Computer vision**	**Matlab software results indicate that the tiger is flat**	**xitek.com**	**Sancho**	**Shanghai**	**Engineer at a computer vision company**
11-1-2007 7:06 A.M.	**Digital photography**	**Increasing the color saturation on the South China tiger photos exposes a layer of optical brightener[b]**	**xitek.com**	**Laobian**	**Shenzhen (Guangdong Province)**	**Professional photographer**
11-14-2007		Video of Zhou returning to the site where he took the photos suggests that the tiger was faked	xitek.com	Ba Mu	(unknown)	(unknown)

(continued)

Table 4.1 (Continued)

Time	Perspective	Methods-based finding	First published	Principal activist	Geographical location	Background of activist
11-16-2007	Wildlife photography	Impossibility of taking several dozen photos of a big cat in the wild in twenty minutes	Bao's blog	Bao Kun	Beijing	Professional photographer
11-16-2007 10:30 A.M.	Human flesh search	Discovery of the original source of the South China tiger photos	Tianya.com, xitek.com	Smallfish, Panzhihua xydz	Weifang (Shandong Province) Panzhihua (Sichuan Province)	Public employee at China Customs
11-23-2007	3D photography	**3D photo pair created with the South China tiger photos show that the tiger is flat**	**bbs.hsw.cn, http://bbs .dpnet.com .cn**	**Cubism**	**(unknown)**	**(unknown)**
12-27-2012	Math (geometry)	Use of geometry proves that the tiger is flat	bbs.hsw.cn and his blog	Wang Yang101	Nanjing	College math teacher

[a] By asserting "the Tiger is flat," activists meant that the tiger photos were not of a living tiger or 3D object, but of a tiger photo.

[b] Optical brighteners are often used to enhance the appearance of color of fabric and paper, causing a "whitening" effect. ("Optical brightener," 2022).

paradigm, wherein experts deliver knowledge to ordinary people and ordinary people are excluded from knowledge production. Instead, it aligns with a participatory model in which the knowledge of ordinary people is valued, and knowledge of social change or specific development problems are considered to be constructed through the dialogue of all concerned, experts and ordinary people alike. Table 4.1 illustrates that knowledge of the South China tiger photos was created through the interactions, participation, and collaboration of activists, including experts and ordinary people. Activists with expertise in fields such as botany, zoology, computer vision, and photography did play an important role in knowledge creation regarding the tiger photos. Yet the most crucial part of the knowledge that questioned the authenticity of the tiger photos was generated by ordinary internet users, such as Smallfish, Panzhihua xydz, and other anonymous internet users—not experts in any specific discipline. Using human flesh search, they discovered the original source of the South China tiger photos: a New Year's picture printed in 2002.

Human flesh search is a Chinese internet phenomenon involving massive research, based on massive human collaboration, using online and offline skills and information to find the information that is of interest to a specific community or group of people. Its goals are very diverse, from addressing entertainment and anti-corruption to humiliating individuals publicly (F.-Y. Wang et al., 2010). In this case, human flesh search served a decisive role in finding the original source of Zhou's tiger photos. Smallfish, who later came to be known as Qiao Yong, a public employee for China Customs in Weifang, Shandong Province, was key in finding the original source of the South China tiger photos.[4] Ever since the photos were published online, he had engaged in the online action to contest the official claim of the Shaanxi Forestry Department and soon became a well-known anti-tiger netizen at Tianya.com, the biggest Chinese online forum. At 6:00 A.M. on November 9, 2007, he started a thread on Tianya.com in which he highlighted the urgent need to search for the original source of Zhou's photos. He posted, "Some anti-tiger activists have mentioned that, because the tiger photos published by the Shaanxi Forestry Department were PSed rather than being drawn by hand . . . , an 'original tiger photo' must exist somewhere.[5] If the original photo cannot be found, we lack the most solid evidence. Therefore, as more evidence comes out, many netizens continue to search for the original photo of the tiger." At 1:10 A.M. on November 16, 2007, Panzhihua xydz replied to Smallfish's post: "Smallfish, add me to your QQ friends.[6] I'll send you some photos. I found a [hard copy of a] New Year's picture in my room that is almost the same as the South China tiger photos, except for the background and the ears." At 10:30 A.M. on November 16, 2007, Smallfish posted the finding and the photos of the New Year's picture he got from Panzhihua xydz on the South China Tiger forum at xitek.com, titled "Result from Human Flesh Search, origin of the tiger has been found!"[7] Within three hours, more than five hundred people had responded to the post. Anti-tiger activists from different fields compared the New Year's picture and the photos taken by Zhou and provided solid evidence that Zhou's photos were taken from the New Year's picture. This was considered the most decisive evidence proving that the South China tiger photos were fake, which marked a turning point for activists and the media in Tiger Gate.[8]

Table 4.1 also indicates that new media and ICTs provided infrastructure and technological potential for an activist network to emerge that cut across geographical barriers. For example, internet forums or BBSs such as Tianya.com, xitek.com, emay.com.cn, and bbs.hsw.cn (the hsw.cn forum) provided activists in Beijing, Shanghai, Shenzhen, Nanjing, Shaoxing (Zhejiang Province), Weifang (Shandong Province), and other parts of China with a space to continuously construct the collective knowledge that challenged the South China tiger photos (see table 4.1 and figure 4.1).

Moreover, the online interactions among activists in Tiger Gate illustrate that the instantaneity of ICTs enabled activists to coordinate their knowledge construction and actions across regions in real time. A specific example of this kind of real-time coordination is the discovery of the producer of the New Year's picture. Just after its discovery, *The Southern Metropolis Daily* broke the news of the methods activists developed to show that the New Year's picture and the South China tiger photos matched.[9] Yet the leading pro-tiger government officer, Guan Ke, continued fiercely defending the authenticity of the South China tiger photos in his interview with a *Southern Metropolis Daily* reporter. He stated that the New Year's picture was badly PSed from the South China tiger photos. To discredit Guan's claim, activists were mobilized to find the producer of the New Year's picture to establish its authenticity (see table 4.2). Actions 2 and 3 came within twenty minutes of Action 1 (Danpier posted the website and the logo of the producer of the New Year's picture): detailed information on the producer was ascertained and posted in the forum, and anonymous activists posted a screenshot confirming that WST Printing produced the New Year's picture. From Action 4 to Action 6 (twenty-one minutes later), anonymous activists collectively explained why WST Printing had to have been the producer of the New Year's picture and suggested two new ways to promote further investigation. Without the internet-based ICTs, such real-time coordinated knowledge creation would not have been possible.

Digital Technologies as Tools in Grassroots Investigations. The last section showed that in Tiger Gate, as in most conventional social change initiatives and development projects, ICTs were used as communication tools to facilitate knowledge construction, information dissemination, and activist coordination. In Tiger Gate, however, digital technologies have surpassed their conventional role as pure communication tools and demonstrated the potential to be tools for grassroots investigations in actions for social change. Jenkins (2006) argued that digital technologies in the hands of ordinary consumers may be used as a strong corrective to traditional power structures, such as the state and capitalist

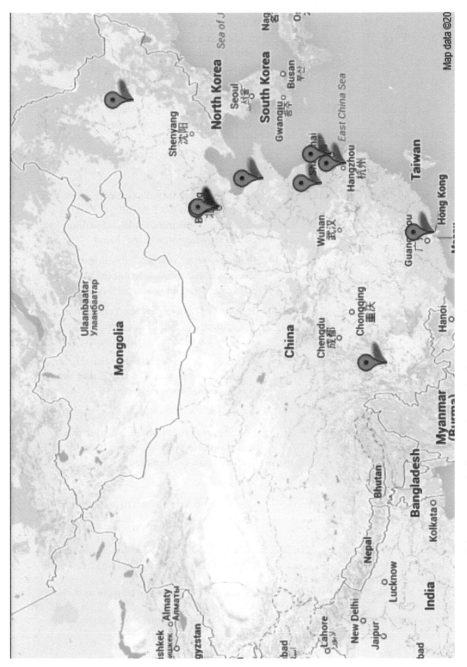

FIGURE 4.1 Locations of the Activists Challenging the South China Tiger Photos

Table 4.2
Finding the Producer of the New Year's Picture

Action	Time	User ID	Content
1	11-16-2007 15:12	Danpier	Danpier, an activist at xitek.com, started a thread at xitek.com titled "The producer of the New Year's picture has been found" and posted the website and the logo of the producer in the post.[a]
			… (Several reply posts omitted)
2	11-16-2007 15:25	Yishifengyun	Posted a detailed introduction and the address, contact information, and name of the CEO of the producer (Yiwu WST Printing & Packing Corporation) on the thread.
			…
3	11-16-2007 15:32	OldSaltedFish	Found a product introduction of the New Year's picture on Yiwu WST Printing & Packing Corporation's website, made a screenshot, and posted the screenshot in the thread.
4	11-16-2007 15:35	Corn	Explained why Yiwu WST Printing & Packing Corporation is the producer of the New Year's picture and gave advice for further investigation:
			"1: On the photo of the New Year's picture (uploaded by Smallfish), there is a logo on the lower left corner. It is this producer's logo.
			2: If the producer is still there, contact the producer to confirm the production and sales of the New Year's picture."
			…
5	11-16-2007 15:40	cs67	Posted part of the New Year's picture that contains the logo of the producer as evidence to support Corn's explanation.[b]
			…
6	11-16-2007 15:56	xiangboo	Can we "find someone at Yiwu to confirm the information about the producer?"[c]
			…

[a] Please refer to http://forum.xitek.com/forum-viewthread-tid-484551-ordertype-1-highlight.html to see Danpier's post and the producer's logo.
[b] Refer to http://i6.xitek.com/forum/200711/4644/464495/464495_1195198818.jpg to see the image posted by cs67.
[c] Yiwu (a city) is the location of the producer. This information was exposed in Action 2, the address of the producer.

corporations. In the specific context of Tiger Gate, when ordinary people had direct use of digital technologies, they successfully used them as communication tools to coordinate their collective knowledge creation and to mobilize a large group of activists to press for a thorough investigation of the incident. In addition to this, however, they creatively used digital technologies to conduct grassroots investigations in order to generate knowledge and evidence that challenged official claims. This means that going forward, they no longer have to wait for the government to investigate such incidents for them. Rather, they can use new technologies to investigate an incident by themselves and use the collective knowledge and evidence created in grassroots investigations to lead public opinion on the incident and pressure the government to hold those officials involved in the incident accountable. The data on different perspectives and methods that challenged the authenticity of the South China tiger photos in table 4.1 show how digital technologies were widely used in investigations on the South China tiger photos by grassroots activists.

Among the eleven methods used to investigate the South China tiger photos, four employed digital technologies as tools of investigation, including GIF animation, digital photography, computer vision, and 3D photography (identified in bold in Table 4.1) The most impressive and widely cited among activists and in the media was the computer vision method developed by Sancho, a thirty-six-year-old, who worked for a computer vision company in Shanghai and was reported to have a PhD in mechanical engineering and automation from Shanghai Jiao Tong University. At 4:19 p.m. on October 31, 2007, Sancho posted a thread titled "Game over—Let's see who is the real tiger" on the South China Tiger forum at xitek.com. In it, he presented how he used the computer vision software Matlab to prove that the tiger in the South China tiger photos was flat.[10] He first introduced the image-processing principles in his analysis: "If several points are on the same plane, then they can be aligned through perspective transformation.[11] If they are not on the same plane, then they cannot be aligned through perspective transformation."[12] He then selected two photos obviously shot from different perspectives from the South China tiger photos supposedly taken by Zhou, Photo A and Photo B, and imported them into Matlab software (see figure 4.2). Then he used a Matlab tool to develop a short program to perform a perspective transformation on Photo A, through which a new photo, named Photo A-transformed, was created. Finally, to display the result, he used Photoshop to adjust the transparency of Photo B to 50 percent and superimposed it onto Photo A-transformed. He argued that because the tiger in Photo B aligns with the tiger in Photo A-transformed, the tiger is flat—whereas the grass and branches around the tiger cannot be aligned and thus are real.[13]

Sancho's computer vision method at xitek.com was read by 79,315 people between October 31 and November 23, 2007. Activists at xitek.com and hsw.cn widely considered it to be the most persuasive of all the methods used to challenge the South China tiger photos. In the report from *Southern Metropolis Weekly*

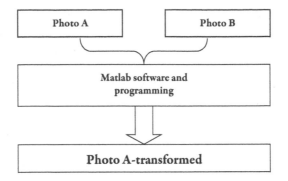

FIGURE 4.2 Computer Vision Method to Challenge the Authenticity of the South China Tiger Photos

titled "Best Anti-Tiger Activists," Sancho was named the "Best Detective" in "using Matlab software to find a breakthrough to prove that the tiger in the South China Tiger photos is flat" (R. Hu, 2007). Sancho's method has also been widely reported by mainstream media and major Chinese portals, including *Southern Metropolis Weekly*, *The Southern Metropolis Daily*, QQ.com, and 163.com.

A New Multichannel Perspective

In his study of collective knowledge construction in cyberspace, Lévy rightly points out that the internet and ICTs enable community members to coordinate their knowledge construction in real time (Lévy, 1999, p. 14). Yet he overlooks the significant role that mainstream media and other communication channels play in a multichannel media environment. By analyzing the data from the discovery of the New Year's picture, this section highlights the importance of mainstream media in the construction of the collective knowledge that contested the authenticity of the South China tiger photos. For the specific data, please see table 4.3.

The "Media" column in Table 4.3 indicates the extent to which the mainstream mass media, such as *Beijing News*, CCTV, and *The Southern Metropolis Daily*, as well as major online portals, such as 163.com, have been deeply involved in this incident. Specifically, the breaking news reported in *The Southern Metropolis Daily* of the discovery of the New Year's picture and the methods activists developed to show that the New Year's picture and the South China tiger photos were identical (Action 4) catapulted this incident beyond the boundaries of cyberspace. When the mainstream media and major portals, such as *The Southern Metropolis Daily* (Actions 4 and 5, for example), *Beijing News* (Action 10), CCTV (Action 13), and 163.com (Actions 6 and 8, for example) became actively involved, the discovery of the New Year's picture became a public incident in convergence culture—that is, a public incident that cut across the boundaries of different media channels. Also, the activist community proposed two urgent needs regarding the authenticity of the New Year's picture (Action 3): to

Table 4.3

Discovery of the Original Source of the Tiger Photos

Action	Time	Content	Media
1	11-16-2007 01:10	Smallfish started a thread to promote the urgency of finding the original source of the South China tiger photos.	Tianya.com
		Panzhihua xydz replied in the thread: "I found a [hard copy of a] New Year's picture in my room that is almost the same as the South China tiger photos, except for the background and the ears," and sent four digital photos of the New Year's picture to Smallfish.	
2	11-16-2007 10:30	Smallfish uploaded the four photos he got from Panzhihua xydz on xitek.com and asked xitek.com users for help comparing the New Year's picture to the South China tiger photos.	xitek.com
3	11-16-2007 10:30 to 12:00	Activists at xitek.com developed various methods to show that the tiger in the New Year's picture and the tiger in the photos were identical. To determine the authenticity of the New Year's picture, they stressed the urgency of (1) continuing to search around the country for copies of the New Year's picture, and (2) finding the producer of the New Year's picture.	xitek.com
4	11-16-2007 12:30	*The Southern Metropolis Daily* reported the breaking news of the discovery of the New Year's picture and the methods activists developed to show that the New Year's picture and the South China tiger photos were identical.	*The Southern Metropolis Daily*
5	11-16-2007 12:30	The leading pro-tiger government officer, Guan Ke, told a *Southern Metropolis Daily* reporter that the New Year's picture was badly PSed from the South China tiger photos.	*The Southern Metropolis Daily*
6	11-16-2007 12:54:33	Major portals, such as 163.com, sohu.com, and xinhuanet.com, and mainstream media began to report the breaking news of the discovery of the New Year's picture.	163.com, sohu.com, xinhuanet.com, etc.
7	11-16-2007 15:12	Danpier, an activist at xitek.com, started a thread titled "The producer of the New Year's picture has been found." By analyzing the logo on the New Year's picture, Danpier determined that the producer of the New Year's picture was Yiwu WST Printing & Packing Corporation in Yiwu, Zhejiang Province. Danpier also found the website of the producer and posted the link in the thread.	xitek.com

(continued)

Table 4.3 (Continued)

Action	Time	Content	Media
8	11-16-2007 15:23:02	163.com reported that it consulted Hu Huijian, a zoologist at the South China Institute of Endangered Animals. From the stripes of the tiger, Hu said that he is sure that the tiger in the New Year's picture is the same as that in Zhou's photos.	163.com
9	11-16-2007 16:28	*The Southern Metropolis Daily* reported that the activists at xitek.com found the producer of the New Year's picture and its official website. Luo Guanglin, CEO of the Yiwu Corp., confirmed to a *Southern Metropolis Daily* reporter that his company produced the New Year's picture.	*The Southern Metropolis Daily*
10	11-17-2007	163.com, *The Southern Metropolis Daily*, and other media, including *Beijing News*, continued to search for copies of the New Year's picture around the country.	163.com, *The Southern Metropolis Daily*, *Beijing News*
11	11-17-2007 09:20	A user at 163.com, Mr. Huang, texted 163.com that he had in his possession a New Year's picture identical to the one found by the activist at xitek.com. At 12:50 pm, a staff member of 163.com visited Mr. Huang in his apartment in Dongwan, Guangdong Province, and took photos of the New Year's picture, which he had purchased two years earlier.	163.com
12	11-17-2007 afternoon	After reading the report on the New Year's picture in *The Southern Metropolis Daily*, Mr. Xu, the manager of the Xinglong Picture Store in Guangzhou, called the newspaper to say that the store had a large number of hard copies of a picture that was identical to the one discovered by activists.	*The Southern Metropolis Daily*
13	11-17-2007 afternoon	Kena, an activist at xitek.com in Beijing, along with reporters from CCTV, found many copies of the New Year's picture at a retail store in Beijing. He then posted that information at xitek.com.	xitek.com, CCTV
14	11-17-2007 14:14	An hsw.cn user found another copy of the New Year's picture in a bookstore in Jinan, Shandong Province.	hsw.cn

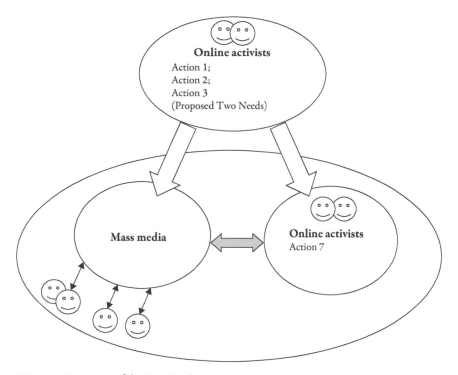

FIGURE 4.3 Discovery of the New Year's Picture

continue searching for copies of the New Year's picture around the country, and to find the producer of the New Year's picture. The first need was met through the involvement of the mainstream mass media (Actions 12 and 13) and online portals (Action 11). The second was solved by the online activist community (Action 7) and was confirmed by the mainstream media (Action 9). Figure 4.3 provides a vivid depiction of this episode.

The data in table 4.3 also indicates that the mainstream media played a significant role in the real-time coordination of the construction of the collective knowledge that challenged the authenticity of the South China tiger photos. For example, in Action 4, two hours after the New Year's picture was uploaded on xitek.com and half an hour after the activists proved that the New Year's picture and the South China tiger photos were identical, *The Southern Metropolis Daily* reported both the discovery of the New Year's picture and the methods used to show that the New Year's picture and the South China tiger photos were identical. It disseminated the information to the public and facilitated coordination in real time to further construct the collective knowledge that challenged the South China tiger photos. Also, within half an hour of the online disclosure of the New Year's picture as identical to the South China tiger photos by anti-tiger activists, *The Southern Metropolis Daily* reported on the responses of leading pro-tiger officials to that discovery. This provided information for the activist community to create new knowledge to further challenge the denials of pro-tiger figures.

Mainstream media outlets such as *The Southern Metropolis Daily* also played an important role in effectively mobilizing skills, as the data in table 4.3 and figure 4.3 show. Figure 4.3 shows that mainstream media coverage increased the number of the people who became engaged in the incident. It thus was largely responsible for extending the community whose skills and knowledge could be mobilized to construct the collective knowledge to challenge the South China tiger photos. For example, after reading the report in *The Southern Metropolis Daily*, Mr. Xu told newspaper reporters that his store had a large number of hard copies of a picture that was identical to the one discovered by activists (table 4.3, Action 12). And after reading the news reports on the New Year's picture, Mr. Huang sent a text message to 163.com saying he, too, had a New Year's picture identical to the one found by xitek.com activists (table 4.3, Action 11). The data in table 4.3 demonstrate that mainstream media reports contributed to the mobilization of ordinary people like Mr. Xu and Mr. Huang, who became engaged in the construction of collective knowledge that challenged the South China tiger photos.

Interactions between New Media and Mainstream Media. In the media environment of convergence culture, where media contents flow across multiple channels and platforms ever more quickly (Jenkins, 2006), the relationship between ICT channels and other communication channels, such as the mainstream media, are not mutually exclusive in actions for social change. Rather, they interact with and reinforce each other, as table 4.3 indicates. A more detailed depiction that focuses on the interaction and the reinforcement process can be seen in the data in table 4.4.

As depicted in Actions 3 and 5 in table 4.4, the collective knowledge constructed by the online activist community in Actions 1, 2, and 4 reinforced the news reports of *The Southern Metropolis Daily* (a mainstream media outlet). In Action 5, new knowledge about the South China tiger photos (i.e., that the tiger resembles an Indochinese tiger), which was generated based on the online community's original discovery of the New Year's picture, was collaboratively developed by mainstream media reporters and Hu Huijian (an expert who was not part of the online community at xitek.com) and was integrated into a news report by *The Southern Metropolis Daily* (identified in bold in Action 5). In Action 6, the new knowledge in the news report of *The Southern Metropolis Daily* (identified in bold in Action 5) fed back into the online activist community and reinforced the community's collective knowledge challenging the South China tiger photos. Furthermore, based on this new knowledge, online activists proposed a new perspective for future investigation. The pattern of interaction and reinforcement between mainstream media and new media, as seen in the example of *The Southern*

Table 4.4

Interaction and Reinforcement of New Media and Mainstream Media

Action	Time	Content	Media
1	11-16-2007 10:30	Smallfish uploaded the four photos of the New Year's picture acquired from Panzhihua xydz at xitek.com.	xitek.com
2	11-16-2007 10:30 to 12:00	Activists at xitek.com developed various methods to show that the tiger in the New Year's picture and the tiger in the South China tiger photos were identical.	xitek.com
3	11-16-2007 12:30	*The Southern Metropolis Daily* broke the news of the discovery of the New Year's picture and the methods activists at xitek.com developed to show the indistinguishability of the New Year's picture and the South China tiger photos.	*The Southern Metropolis Daily*
4	11-16-2007 15:12	Danpier, an activist at xitek.com, found the producer of the New Year's picture and posted this finding and the website of the producer at xitek.com.	xitek.com
5	11-16-2007 16:28	*The Southern Metropolis Daily* reported the following: (1) Activists at xitek.com found the producer of the New Year's picture. (2) Hu Huijian, a zoologist at the South China Institute of Endangered Animals, confirmed that the tiger in the New Year's picture and the tiger in Zhou's photos are the same tiger and, after carefully studying the New Year's picture, thought **the tiger resembled an Indochinese tiger, not a South China tiger, because of its big ears.**	*The Southern Metropolis Daily*
6	11-16-2007 17:18	Xitek.com activist dcaoyuan cited *The Southern Metropolis Daily*'s report and Hu's words, then argued, "In the photos taken by Zhou, the ears of the tiger are deliberately covered under leaves. This indicates that someone who knows the South China tiger well must be involved in the fraud."	xitek.com

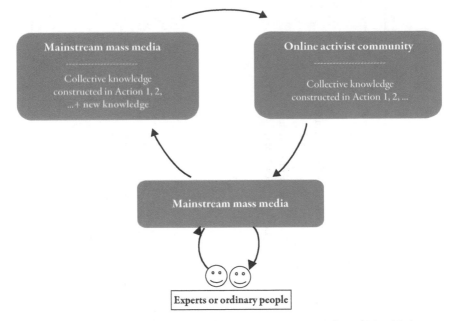

FIGURE 4.4 Interaction and Reinforcement between Mainstream Media and New Media

Metropolis Daily (figure 4.4), is widespread and not exceptional in new media interventions, as we will see in the chapters on the Free Lunch Project and the NCP Life Support Network as well.

Correcting Government Policy and Holding Government Accountable

Having analyzed the channels and ICTs involved in the actions in the last section, I focus on the social change component in this section.

Activists as Correctives in Government Policymaking

Public announcements by the Shaanxi Forestry Department and information provided by mainstream news coverage indicate that the core component of the Shaanxi Forestry Department's official discourse in the South China tiger incident was to advocate and legitimize a proposed policy to set up a wild South China tiger reserve in Shaanxi Province that would bring the province tens of millions of public funds from the central government.

On October 12, nine days after Zhou took the photos, the Shaanxi Forestry Department announced that expert evaluation showed that the photos were real and a small breeding population of wild South China tigers might inhabit an area around Zhenping County, Shaanxi Province. When several methods that challenged the authenticity of the South China tiger photos went viral on the internet (see table 4.1) and were reported by mainstream media and portals, Xu Taoqing (an expert from the evaluation committee of the Shaanxi Forestry Department's Report on the South China Tiger) and Zhu Julong (a deputy director of the Shaanxi Forestry Department) rebutted challenges to the authenticity of the South China tiger photos and told the media that a new South China tiger reserve would be set up very soon (Ding, 2007; Y. Zhang, 2007). By October 30, activists had developed various methods to challenge the South China tiger photos from at least four perspectives. That same day, the Shaanxi Forestry Department showed the photos that were developed from negatives to CCTV and other mainstream media outlets and reconfirmed the authenticity of the South China tiger photos. The department claimed that the first step to set up a national wild South China tiger reserve around Zhenping County had been initiated ("Shaanxi Forestry Department Showed the Negative Films," 2007). On October 31, local media at Shaanxi reported that the Shaanxi Forestry Department was going to submit its policy proposal to set up the South China tiger reserve to the provincial government at Shaanxi (Li et al., 2007). Also, on October 26, the Shaanxi Forestry Department launched a media campaign to counter activist voices that contested the South China tiger photos. On November 3, during the prime-time news program on the Shaanxi Television Network, Guan Ke defended the authenticity of the photos and argued that setting up a South China tiger reserve was extremely important, regardless of the authenticity of the photos (*Officials from Shaanxi Forestry Department*, 2007). In a public announcement on November 22, six days after activists found the New Year's picture that was considered to be the original source of the South China tiger photos, the Shaanxi Forestry Department continued to assert the authenticity of the photos taken by Zhou and the existence of wild South China tigers in Zhenping County. In addition, it issued urgent notifications to the local government of Zhenping County to strengthen regulations protecting wild South China tigers ("Shaanxi Forestry Department's Announcement," 2007). Based on the official discourse of the Shaanxi Forestry Department, the policy to set up a new South China tiger reserve at Zhenping County would certainly have been implemented were it not for the persistence of activists who challenged the authenticity of the photos. Thus, Tiger Gate activists served to correct a wrongheaded policy that was based on false materials put forward by the local government in Shaanxi.

Government Accountability and Transparency in Policymaking

Government accountability, in the context of policy discourse in the United States, is generally understood to mean that public officials are obligated to explain their decisions and actions to their citizens, and the government is answerable to the public for its performance (e.g., Adserà et al., 2003; Johnston & Romzek, 1999; Przeworski et al., 1999; U.S. Department of State, 2005; Wong & Welch, 2004). Some scholars of Chinese government accountability have

Table 4.5
Nine Indicators of Government Accountability

	Indicators
Government accountability	Honesty of officials
	Responsibility of officials for their behavior
	Punishment of officials for illegal activities
	Highlighting incidents of corrupt practices in government
	Communication between officials and citizens
	Respect for the opinions of citizens by officials
	Official mechanisms for accepting and dealing with public opinion
	Public knowledge of government procedures and regulations
	Frequency of elections and changing officials

defined accountability as the obligation of the government to be held accountable for its performance and for the efforts of the government to serve the interests of the people (e.g., Cheung & Leung, 2007; Chien, 2010; Diamond, 2003; Liebman, 2011; W. Pan, 2003). Although government accountability has yet to be clearly defined in China, it has entered public discourse, the official policy discourse of the Chinese government, and the literature of leading scholars of China (Editorial Board, 2011; K. Yu, 2002b; Zhu & Zhou, 2011). A detailed analysis of the various understandings and the translations of the concept of government accountability in Chinese is beyond the scope of the current chapter. Generally, the understanding of government accountability in Chinese combines the previous two definitions and adds one more component: trustworthiness, or honesty of public officials and the government. For example, Yu Keping (2002b)—a leading scholar in political science and governance in China—asserted that nine indicators should be included in the Chinese understanding of government accountability (see table 4.5). Moreover, the three ways to understand government accountability are all consistent in viewing enhancing government accountability as crucial to fight corruption.

From a communication for development and social change perspective, government accountability is about the relationship between activists/the public and the government/officials. Accordingly, increased government accountability means more balance between the public and the government authority, increased government answerability to the public, enhanced participation of activists and the public in policymaking, and assured punishment of officials for wrongdoing. A growing literature and body of practices in the field have shown that increasing government accountability is crucial to achieving sustainable development and social change, and that communication plays a significant role in ensuring government accountability in policymaking (e.g., Servaes, 2009; United Nations Educational, Scientific and Cultural Organization, 2005; U.N., 2018; World Bank, 2006). A system of checks and balances, whose key components are communication and public participation, could generate accountability among and within various government agencies and effectively limit situations that are conducive to corruption (e.g., Servaes, 2009; World Bank, 2006). Communication would be a key component in a system of monitoring to control for government accountability. For example, media coverage, including that in mainstream and new media, creates pressure to promote government accountability, improve government performance, and reduce corruption (e.g., Adserà et al., 2003; Liebman, 2011; Servaes, 2009). Communication can also enhance the potential for activists and NGOs to hold government authorities accountable and to engage in public policy making and thus significantly improve both government performance in public sector work and sustainability in social change and development (Servaes, 2009). By analyzing mainstream media coverage of Tiger Gate and online content created by activists, the following section shows that these actions aimed to address government accountability as a social concern. Media coverage shows how this incident and related actions are presented to the public. Online content by activists reveals how activists themselves think about what social problem they aimed to resolve. Both are vital to understanding the social problem that the actions aimed to address.

Analysis of Online Content Created by Activists. During Tiger Gate, government accountability was a major concern among the activist community, especially after the discovery of the New Year's picture (the original source of the South China tiger photos). I will first analyze Fu Dezhi, a leading anti-tiger activist who engaged in constant action throughout the incident, challenging the authenticity of the South China tiger photos. A high-profile botanist at the Chinese Academy of Sciences and the first activist to challenge the authenticity of the photos using his real name, Fu has been widely quoted online and reported in mainstream media as "the leader" of the anti-tiger activists. On November 26, he blogged, "The Tiger Gate fraud has now been gradually uncovered. It is a fraud . . . designed by officials in the Shaanxi Forestry Department. . . . The victims of the fraud are not only the local people and local government but also the Chinese government." This statement demonstrates that Fu believed that Tiger Gate was not a fraud masterminded by Zhou but a fraud orchestrated by government officials. He argued that Zhou should not assume most of the responsibility for the fraud. Instead, officials at the Shaanxi Forestry Department should be held accountable for it (Fu, 2007b). From this we can see that Fu considered Tiger Gate to be related to Yu's (2002b) second, third, and fourth indictors of Chinese understanding of government accountability (see table 4.5). On February 4, 2008, the Shaanxi Forestry Department issued a letter of apology to the public for announcing the discovery of a wild South China tiger without serious investigation but also said that it had not completed its reevaluation of the photos and had no comment on their authenticity. On March 13, 2008, leading legal scholar Cai Dingjian, a professor at the Chinese

University of Political Science and Law, told the media that he did not think that Tiger Gate was an important incident concerning government accountability. He believed that because the Shaanxi Forestry Department had issued a letter of apology, and the officials involved were suspended from their duties, the media and the public did not need to keep focusing on the incident. Fu (2008d) made a counterargument to Cai's statement in his blog post: "Shouldn't we keep trying to hold those involved in the fraud accountable . . . ?! . . . Plenty of evidence shows that the South China Tiger photos were faked. But the public hopes the government can openly acknowledge that fact. . . . If the government announces that the photos were faked, related governmental agencies would have to take action to investigate the fraud and hold those involved accountable." Here he highlights two points. First, those officials who were involved must be punished. Second, the government must openly respond to the public's question regarding the authenticity of the photos. The first point relates to the first four indicators of government accountability in Yu's (2002b) framework of Chinese understanding of government accountability (see table 4.5). The second relates to the sixth, seventh, and eighth indicators. He further argued that the longer the government takes no action on Tiger Gate, the more the government will be damaged.

In his March 24 special report on Tiger Gate to the Endangered Species Scientific Commission of China, Fu (2008b) titled the fifth part of his presentation "[Tiger Gate] Severely Damaged Honesty in Government." He argued that "the online satire of the Tiger Gate incident about governmental officials show[s] the damage of Tiger Gate to honesty in the government," and the government's inaction in this incident made the public question the policies of local and central governments (Fu, 2008b). This assertion indicates that Tiger Gate relates especially to the first indicator of Chinese understanding of government accountability—the government's honesty and trustworthiness.

Second, I will analyze Smallfish, an ordinary activist who was engaged in the whole process of the action and who played a crucial role by finding and publishing the New Year's picture online. A typical public employee in a middle-sized city in Shandong Province, Smallfish represents a more ordinary grassroots activist—especially compared to Fu. On November 19, 2007, three days after he posted the New Year's picture online, Smallfish posted a thread at Tianya.com and xitek.com titled *I am tired of being coward, about the New Year picture*. He stated, "As a public employee, what I am most concerned about is honesty in government! Prolonged government inaction on this incident has made a simple incident very complex and severe. . . . The result is that when our Premier Wen visited Singapore, the news of his visit and the Tiger Gate scandal were all on the front page of the *Lianhe Zaobao*.[14] The crisis of honesty in our government was created by those irresponsible officials." His post shows that his concern over honesty in government—the first indicator of government accountability (Yu, 2002b)—is his major motivation for his ongoing participation in the action to contest the authenticity of the South China tiger photos. In his November 21, 2007, thread at Tianya.com, Smallfish stated, "I don't want to be in the limelight because, as a public employee, being in the limelight is sometimes a vital mistake and will cost [you] your job. . . . Actually, it has affected mine." At the end of the post, he stated that the reason he created the post was to unite all netizens because "in the crisis of honesty, what we need is to unite together to rebuild honesty for the society" (Smallfish, 2007d). This indicates that his reason for putting his job at risk in order to continue engaging in the social change action was to rebuild honesty in society and government.

On June 28, 2008, after almost eight months of constant online and offline action challenging the authenticity of the photos and the official claims of the Shaanxi Forestry Department—on the eve of the press conference covering the final result of the reevaluation of the photos—Smallfish created a long post at Tianya.com, which offered up his understanding of the Tiger Gate incident and why activists around the country constantly engaged in the social change action:

> What concerns netizens most is honesty in government. . . . This is the fundamental reason why activists constantly engaged in the anti-tiger actions that challenged the South China Tiger photos. . . . Why could so many people continue to engage in the action for eight months? The reason is very simple. The Tiger Gate incident involved all kinds of corruption in our government including illegal behavior such as bribery, as well as malfeasance such as disrespecting citizens' opinions. . . . The ultimate goal for citizens engaging in the anti-tiger action is to reduce these corrupt behaviors and . . . give honesty more space and a better environment to thrive.

First, this indicates that Smallfish associated Tiger Gate with government corruption, which is widely understood to be connected to lack of government accountability (e.g., Servaes, 2009; U.S. Department of State, 2005; World Bank, 2006). Second, he believed that the Tiger Gate incident concerned many components of the Chinese understanding of government accountability, such as honesty of officials and the government, highlighting the incidence of corrupt practices, and respect for the opinions of citizen by officials (see table 4.5). Third, he argued that the reason that activists engaged in the action was that they wanted to make real changes regarding these various components of government accountability.

Last, I will analyze the most ordinary activists, those grouped as anonymous activists who never had a significant role in any specific events in the incident. At the very beginning of the incident, even before the discovery of the New Year's picture, anonymous activists began to assert that Tiger Gate was about government accountability. On November 3, 2007, Fu Dezhi started a thread on emay .com.cn in which he disclosed a conversation he had with a high-level government official (see table 4.6).

Table 4.6
Online Content Regarding Government Accountability Created by Anonymous Activists

Activists ID	Content
Ssb (quoted Fu)	"The major argument of the government official is that the debate over Tiger Gate represents democracy in academic research in China, and the government need not rashly intervene in such debate." (Fu, 2007d)
Truth Wei	"I . . . can't agree with some of the points in his [the high-level official's] argument. . . . This incident is not about academic debate, rather, it is about honesty in government. . . . The local government is using this photo to steal [a] huge amount [of] public funding. . . . We urge related government agencies to investigate it and take it as an example to rebuild honesty in our society. Government must be honest . . . officials must be honest."
Sechs	"You are absolutely right. I support you."
tianxing2008	"I support you!"
TaoGe	"The current debate represents democracy and freedom in academic research in our country?! Exposing fraud to the light of public scrutiny is an academic issue??"
tianxing2008	"If this is an academic issue, there wouldn't be so many people engaged in it. From the evidence currently exposed, it is an astounding fraud. . . . We urge relevant government agencies to take serious action to investigate it."

The posts in table 4.6 show that anonymous activists such as Truth Wei, TaoGe, and tianxing2008 did not accept the claim of the high-level official that Tiger Gate was about academic debate and academic freedom. Rather, they took Tiger Gate to be about aspects of government accountability, including the honesty of government and government officials and the incidence of corruption. Also, the goal or the reason they and the public engaged in the action questioning the South China tiger photos was to make changes regarding these aspects of government accountability. The posts in table 4.6 are not isolated cases in the Tiger Gate incident. Large numbers of anonymous activists at Tianya.com, xitek.com, emay.com.cn, and hsw.cn asserted that the Tiger Gate incident was about government accountability.

This shows that the activist community—including leading activists such as Fu; ordinary activists such as Smallfish, who assumed important roles in the online actions; and the most anonymous ordinary activists, such as Truth Wei and TaoGe—considered Tiger Gate to be about different aspects of government accountability.

Analysis of Mainstream Media. Being exposed to what online activists think about the social problem they seek to resolve is central to understanding the very change they seek to bring about. Yet because almost 80 percent of the population did not have access to the internet during the South China Tiger incident,[15] the voices of citizen actors were barely heard by the majority of the society. Most members of society got their information about Tiger Gate from mainstream media coverage. Media portrayals of the intended changes behind citizen actions in Tiger Gate therefore deserve rigorous investigation. At the time of the incident, Tiger Gate was widely reported on by the regional and national mainstream media. From October 12, 2007 (when the Shaanxi Forestry Department held a press conference to announce the discovery of the South China tiger) to July 7, 2008 (one week after the Shaanxi Forestry Department announced that the photos were faked), the number of news reports and comments on the Tiger Gate incident in the national and regional newspapers peaked at 315, according to the data collected for this research.

The first newspaper I will examine is *The Southern Metropolis Daily*, a leading commercial newspaper in south China that has been involved in the reporting and investigation of a variety of social incidents, such as the cover-up of SARS in Guangdong Province and the death of Sun Zhigang, which had a broad impact on Chinese journalism (e.g., Qiu, 2009 G. Yang, 2009; Zhao, 2007).[16] Reports in *The Southern Metropolis Daily* on Tiger Gate played a significant role in the construction of the mainstream media environment and public opinion during Tiger Gate. Among the 315 newspaper reports, 67 of them were printed in *The Southern Metropolis Daily*. At a very early stage of Tiger Gate, *The Southern Metropolis Daily* asserted that the incident concerned government accountability. On October 21, nine days after the Shaanxi Forestry Department announced the alleged discovery of the South China tiger and when activists had just begun to question the authenticity of the photos online (see table 4.1), *The Southern Metropolis Daily* published an editorial titled "To Clarify Public's Doubt on the Tiger Gate Incident, Government Must Face Questions from the Public," which stated: "The focus of the Tiger Gate incident is whether the tiger in the photos taken by Zhou is real or not.... The evidence from the anti-tiger activists questioning the authenticity of the photos is increasing every day, the pro-tiger officials, however, can't rebut any of these questions but tried to distract people's attention from the focus.... The performance of the officials in the Shaanxi Forestry Department is disappointing. They neither started to reevaluate the photos nor did they properly respond to the increasing questions from the public." As the title and the content of the editorial indicate, for *The Southern Metropolis Daily*, Tiger Gate was about the obligation of public officials to be answerable to citizens and public opinion, which is an important aspect of government accountability.

On November 16, *The Southern Metropolis Daily* broke the news of the discovery of the New Year's picture. The same day, it published an editorial titled "It Is Shameful to Cover Up or Manipulate Truth," which stated: "Facing the overwhelming voices questioning the authenticity of the photos from the public, the Shaanxi Forestry Department not only denied the fraud but also ... used the photos as evidence to set up a natural reserve ... while the higher level government, including the State Forestry Administration, responded to the increasing questions from the public coldly ... and refused to take administrative responsibility to evaluate the authenticity of the photos, which further increased the public's disappointment." In the editorial, *The Southern Metropolis Daily* extended its criticism of the lack of government accountability to higher levels of administration and raised questions as to how officials could be held accountable by the public and how to ensure that they would answer to citizens and public opinion.

Four days later, on November 20, *The Southern Metropolis Daily* published an editorial titled "Government Against Public Opinion, the Tiger Gate Incident Falls Into Stalemate Again," which stated: "Contrary to public expectations, the Shaanxi Forestry Department reaffirmed their previous claim that 'the tiger photos are real, regardless of newly emerged solid evidence that questions the authenticity of the photos.' ... Leaders in the Shaanxi Provincial Government also claimed that whether the tiger photos are real is not important. ... Government credibility and the honesty of officials are all [being] used as bargaining chips against public opinion." This passage highlights the question of how the public could hold officials accountable again. The editorial went on: "The goal of the public [in this incident] is to urge the government not to be manipulated by interest groups within its own system and to reinforce exposure to the truth ("Government Against Public Opinion," 2007). The point of this passage is that the goal of activists engaged in contesting the South China tiger photos should be to hold the government accountable to the public and increase government transparency.

On November 21, *The Southern Metropolis Daily* published an editorial titled "Facing the Tiger Gate: What to Do Except Wait?" in which it not only outlined three possible ways for the public to hold the officials involved in the fraud accountable but highlighted the irony that although the public had successfully exposed the South China tiger photos as fake, they lacked ways to hold officials further accountable:

> In the current context, the public only has three ways to hold those involved in the fraud accountable. First, the higher-level administration or officials clearly order the local government to be held accountable. This means that the public has to wait for the higher level administration to hear the voice of public opinion ... and to take action. Second, the Deputies to the People's Congress use their right to officially question the government on the Tiger Gate incident. This means the public has to wait for enough numbers of Deputies to the People's Congress to express their concern over the issue. ... Third, through legal process; but the current legal system doesn't grant individual citizens the right to file public interest litigation. ... After the success of the public

[in exposing the fraud of the tiger photos], the public lacks ways to hold government officials involved in the fraud accountable and has to rely on the self-regulation of the government.

My analysis of the contents of the four editorials published by *The Southern Metropolis Daily* show that the newspaper argued, first, that Tiger Gate was about various aspects of government accountability. Second, the reason the public and activists engaged in the action that questioned the South China tiger photos and official claims was to increase government accountability. On December 5 and 20, 2007, and February 6, March 9, and April 6, 2008, *The Southern Metropolis Daily* published an article by its deputy editor in chief and another four editorials on the Tiger Gate incident, reinforcing these arguments.

The second newspaper I will examine is *People's Daily*, the official newspaper of the Central Committee of the Communist Party of China. *People's Daily* and its online news platform people.com.cn are considered to be the most official voices within the context of Chinese media. To some extent, *People's Daily* is on the opposite end of *The Southern Metropolis Daily* within the spectrum of China's media. Compared with *The Southern Metropolis Daily*, the official response to the Tiger Gate incident by *People's Daily* was much slower. On November 21, five days after the discovery of the New Year's picture, *People's Daily* published the first article on the Tiger Gate incident in a people.com.cn opinion column by Su Xianlong, deputy editor in chief of politics for *People's Daily* (Su, 2007). Although it acknowledged the facts exposed by activists and other media outlets that the local government in Shaanxi tried to use the fake tiger photos to acquire a huge amount of money illegally from the central government, it did not address the issue of government accountability. On November 22, people.com.cn published an article in its opinion column titled "It Is Time to Tell the Public the Truth Behind the Tiger Gate Incident" by Cheng Jiaxing (2007), a *People's Daily* commentator.[17] Cheng wrote: "Currently, it is meaningless to discuss whether there is any wild tiger in Zhenping County without considering whether the photos are real or not. . . . If the photos are fake, all the investigation and debate based on the photos are not reliable. . . . It is time for the local officials to tell the public the truth behind the Tiger Gate incident. Any other attempts of cover-up, of distraction . . . will further diminish the credibility of the local government and experts." The title and text of this article indicate, first, that Cheng acknowledged the importance of whether the photos Zhou took were real or fake. Second, he argued that the Tiger Gate incident is about government transparency (to inform the public of the truth behind the incident) and various aspects of government accountability, such as the honesty and credibility of government and its officials.

On November 30, *People's Daily* published an article titled "Tiger Gate, Another Disappointing Result?" by Lu Xinning (2007a), the director of the paper's editorial department. In it, Lu highlighted that Tiger Gate is a significant public incident about government accountability and transparency in government policymaking. Lu first rebutted the claim by local officials that the debate over whether the tiger photos are real is meaningless and irresponsible: "For the citizens who engaged in the incident, whether there are wild tigers in Zhenping is important; however, the truth of the tiger photos is even more important. . . . The first is about wild animal protection, the second is about government accountability. . . . The protection of the South China tiger demands immediate attention; but the protection of government accountability and ensuring citizens' rights to know are even more important" (Lu, 2007a). To reinforce her argument, she employed the official discourse of the "Report to the Seventeenth National Congress of the Communist Party": "The 'Report to the Seventeenth National Congress' states that government must ensure the people's right to know, the right of participation, the right of expression. . . . When Tiger Gate became a public incident, facing the question from the public, government has no right to keep silent. It has the obligation to explain the whole incident to the public" (Lu, 2007a).

On December 4, four days after this article, people.com.cn published a second piece on Tiger Gate by Lu (2007b), in which she reaffirmed her argument and stated that the Tiger Gate incident may weaken government accountability and hurt the whole society: "When Tiger Gate became a public incident, the local government in Zhenping and the Shaanxi Forestry Department both became deeply involved. Their honesty and interest are at stake. They have the obligation to clarify the truth to the public. . . . When Tiger Gate caused the situation in which the public began to question the government, experts, and academic institutions . . . we have reason for concern that the trust crisis caused by this incident will not only diminish government accountability but also hurt . . . the entire society." In this passage, Lu asserts that Tiger Gate is about various aspects of government accountability, for example the government's obligation to answer to citizens and for officials to be honest. On December 19, 2007, February 20, 2008, and at 3 A.M. and 9 A.M. on June 30, 2008, *People's Daily* and people.com.cn published another four commentaries on Tiger Gate by editors or commentators that reaffirmed the discourse of the previous articles. These texts in *People's Daily* and people.com.cn, the most official organs of China's media, also portrayed Tiger Gate as a public incident concerned with government accountability and transparency in policymaking—although this response to the incident occurred long after that of *The Southern Metropolis Daily*. Other national and regional newspapers such as *Dongfang Daily* (G. Wang, 2007) and *Beijing News* (J. Hao, 2008) also published large numbers of opinion pieces and news reports on Tiger Gate, stressing that the incident was concerned with government accountability. From what has been discussed here, we can see that *People's Daily*, the most official newspaper; *The Southern Metropolis Daily*, the leading commercial newspaper; and many other newspapers portrayed Tiger Gate as a public incident concerning various aspects of government accountability, and acknowledged that people became engaged in the incident because of their concern over the lack of government accountability and transparency in public policymaking.

The Limits of New Media Action in Achieving Social Change

New media actions effectively contested official claims in Tiger Gate, fostering overwhelming support in the mainstream national media, and activists demonstrated their commitment to such actions. Yet this action had a very limited impact on government accountability: thirteen governmental officials did receive disciplinary punishment, but no changes were made to the governmental structure. Zhou Zhenglong, the peasant who claimed to have taken the tiger photos, was the only one criminally charged with fraud. In court, Zhou claimed that he single-handedly created the seventy-one South China tiger photos. But when asked about the details of how he made those photos, he mostly replied, "I don't know." All thirteen officials were in the Shaanxi Forestry Department. No higher-level officials in the People's Government of Shaanxi Province or the central government were punished. Nor was there any formal institutional or policy change directly related to government accountability. This means that this eight-month nationwide new media action only brought about a limited degree of accountability—in the local government—not significant change in government accountability or in the relationship between activists/public and the government/officials on a national level.

This is due in part to the fact that formal institutional change or policy change in government accountability was not the focus of the majority of activists. The immediate goal of most activists in Tiger Gate was the punishment of local officials for their wrongdoing in this specific scandal, rather than institutional change or policy change in government accountability in the central government or in society as a whole. From the very start of the incident, key activists, such as Fu Dezhi and Smallfish, targeted only the wrongdoing of specific officials in the Shaanxi Forestry Department.

For example, on October 22, ten days after the Shaanxi Forestry Department's press conference to announce the discovery of the South China tiger, Fu stated in his blog: "It is so obvious [that the tiger photos are fake because] the leaves of the plants around the 'tiger' are much larger than the 'tiger.' Yet, some people [in the Shaanxi Forestry Department] continue using the fake photos to cheat that peasant . . . cheat the people, and cheat our country. Enough! It is time to stop this" (Fu, 2007a).

On November 27, after *People's Daily* published a series of official comments to support the anti-tiger activists' position, Fu cheered in his blog: "I discovered a big secret! *People's Daily*, the party organ of the Central Committee of the CPC and the State Council, is 100% in line with our anti-tiger activists. . . . This means the Central Committee and the State Council is 100% in line with us. . . . I'm now waiting to see the death of the several [officials involved in Tiger Gate] in the People War led by the Party and the State Council" (Fu, 2007b). He then warned the several officials in the Shaanxi Forestry Department to surrender themselves as soon as possible. Fu's post could well have been a strategic choice of rhetoric to legitimize the action, given the sociopolitical context in China. Yet it also indicates his focus on the wrongdoing of the several officials in the specific case, rather than institutional or policy change in Chinese society. On June 29, the Shaanxi Forestry Department announced, "The South China Tiger photos are fake; Zhou Zhenglong has been sentenced; and the thirteen officials involved in the scandal have been disciplinarily punished." Fu commented, "The truth was exposed . . . the mission has been achieved" (Xu, 2008).

Yet in Tiger Gate, not all activists lack interest in or shy away from pressing for institutional change or policy change in government accountability. From June 30 onward, activists at xitek.com expressed extensive disappointment with the so-called official result of Tiger Gate by the Shaanxi government. For example, a thread titled "Punishment with Chinese Characteristics" stated that Zhou was only the scapegoat in Tiger Gate and all the officials who orchestrated or were involved in making the fake tiger photos have been sheltered away from criminal charges in the so-called investigation by Shaanxi authorities. Citing the article "Why Independent Investigation Is Missing in Tiger Gate?" by special columnist Xiao Shu at *The Southern Metropolis Daily*, they advocated introducing "independent investigators," as in the United States, to enhance government accountability in Tiger Gate and similar incidents in China.

Rather than limiting themselves to online advocacy, some activists in Tiger Gate also took actions to use existing channels within the government to promote institutional change in government accountability. Hao Jinsong, a veteran legal activist, sued the National Forestry Administration for its inaction and lack of transparency. Before Tiger Gate, Hao had conducted several cases of public interest litigation against various government agencies, such as the Ministry of Railways for public welfare and government accountability. In 2006, for example, he sued the Ministry of Railways for its lack of transparency on price hikes during Chinese New Year. Hao lost in court in 2006 and then on appeal in 2007. Yet on January 10, 2007, the Ministry of Railways announced that it would abandon its fourteen-year tradition of hiking prices during Chinese New Year.

On November 7, 2007, Hao sued Zhou Zhenglong for making fake South China tiger photos and for cheating the public—and Hao—by creating fake news regarding the discovery of a wild South China tiger. Hao requested the court to punish Zhou by having him first apologize for cheating Hao in using the fake tiger photos, then clarify the whole process of making the fake photos in written form to Hao. In his complaint, Hao stated that what Zhou had done had not only harmed him but also harmed the trust among citizens, the honesty of the government, and the honesty of society. Hao initiated the legal case for this reason (Hao, 2007). Hao's two demands and his reason for initiating the case indicate that his goal was not to punish Zhou Zhenglong but to expose the truth of the tiger photos and to increase government accountability. His case was rejected by a first instance court and an appeals court in Shanxi Province.

On November 11, 2007, Hao submitted an application for administrative reconsideration regarding administrative decisions on the discovery of a wild South China tiger by the Shaanxi Forestry Department to the National Forestry Administration. In his application, Hao stated that he refused to accept the two administrative decisions by the Shaanxi Forestry Department: (1) that a wild South China tiger was discovered in Shaanxi Zhenping, based on the tiger photos ostensibly taken by Zhou Zhenglong, and (2) that the department should announce that finding to the media and the public in a press conference. According to the Administrative Reconsideration Law, he applied to the National Forestry Administration for administrative reconsideration and required the administration to organize an evaluation of the tiger photos and report the result to the public (Cui, 2007).

On November 26, the National Forestry Administration rejected Hao's application citing this reason: "The applicant is not the subject of Shaanxi Forestry Department's decisions. And his interests and rights have not been affected by the decisions" (Y. Yang, 2007). On December 10, 2007, Hao sued the National Forestry Administration for its rejection of his application for administrative reconsideration in Beijing. Rather than suing Zhou Zhenglong, Hao took further legal action to directly target the central government agency in charge of the tiger issue for its inaction in Tiger Gate in order to enforce government accountability. His case was rejected by a first instance court and the Higher People's Court of Beijing Municipality on December 17 and May 10, 2008, respectively. The court decisions reaffirmed the statement of the National Forestry Administration—"the applicant is not the subject of Shaanxi Forestry Department's decisions"—rejecting the case based on the Administrative Reconsideration Law. Yet Hao's legal actions were extensively supported by activists in major forums on Tiger Gate, including xitek.com, Huashang.net, and Tianya .com, as well as by leading anti-tiger activists such as Fu Dezhi and Smallfish. Hao's legal actions in Tiger Gate were also widely reported by the mainstream media (e.g., *Beijing News* and *Beijing Times*) and major portals, as well as party organs such as Xinhua News Agency and people.com.cn.

In Tiger Gate, besides the four legal actions, Hao also used other existing channels to enforce government accountability. On May 12, two days after receiving the final rejection of his application for administrative reconsideration from the court, he applied to the National Forestry Administration and the Shaanxi Forestry Department for documentation related to the investigation of Tiger Gate, according to the PRC Regulations on Open Government Information newly passed in 2007. In December 2008, Hao applied to the National Forestry

Administration for reports on the follow-up investigation of the South China tiger in Zhenping. Yet those applications failed to yield any more information regarding Tiger Gate.

The four rejections of Hao's two legal cases in two regions and the lack of results from the three applications for government information regarding Tiger Gate indicated the failure of activist attempts to use existing institutional channels to promote government accountability in the aftermath of Tiger Gate. Overall, the various actions in Tiger Gate, including mainstream anti-tiger actions and legal actions, indicate that activists lack the capacity and institutional channels to bring about formal institutional change or policy change in government accountability in China's current authoritarian context.

The Stakeholder Relationship

Although official discourse, as seen in the "Report to the Seventeenth National Congress of the Communist Party," states that different levels of government are obligated to improve government accountability and transparency in public policymaking (J. Hu, 2007), relations between the government and activists in Tiger Gate were far from harmonious. Rather, this is a multidimensional relationship in which contentiousness is a significant dimension.

Contentiousness between the Government and Activists

A growing literature has addressed the contentiousness between activists and the government in Chinese cyberspace (Hughes & Wacker, 2003; King et al., 2013; Roberts, 2018; G. Yang, 2009). The crackdown of activists' online forums, the contestation of activists by officials in various new media campaigns, and the judicial rejection of activists' cases regarding government accountability by Chinese courts illustrate the contentious relationship between the government and activists in Tiger Gate.

The act of shutting down websites or closing the online forums that activists rely on to communicate, share knowledge, and coordinate actions is the most extreme example of the contentious relationship between the government and activists in this case, wherein one side (government agencies) uses its political power to try to silence the other side (activists). The bbs.hsw.cn website is a forum at hsw.cn (Huashang.net), the biggest regional portal in Shaanxi Province. The website's South China Tiger forum became the leading forum for anti-tiger activism, especially after the discovery of the New Year's picture on November 16, 2007. The last two methods that challenged the South China tiger photos after the discovery of the New Year's picture—the 3D photography used by Cubism and geometry used by Wang Yang101 (see table 4.1)—were both published on the bbs.hsw.cn South China Tiger forum. Without any prior notification, the bbs.hsw.cn South China Tiger forum was suddenly shut down on March 7, 2008. All contents formerly posted on the forum were no longer available. Although hsw.cn denied that political pressure was involved in its decision to close the forum, media reports and activists asserted that hsw.cn was forced to close the forum because of intervention by government agencies ("South China Tiger Forum Was Shut Down," 2008; Langziya, 2008).

By analyzing the history of website closings in Tiger Gate and activist responses to the shutdown of the forum, this section shows that in China's current technological, media, and political context, the Shaanxi government's extreme response of trying to silence activists who questioned the official claims about the South China tiger photos failed.

First, the history of the Tiger Gate incident demonstrates that in convergence culture, where information flows ever faster across different channels and platforms and where internet users have control of different ICTs in their own hands, closing major forums or major channels of an online activist community is insufficient to silence or purge that community. Actually, during the eight-month time frame of the Tiger Gate incident, three major forums—emay.com.cn, the xitek.com South China Tiger forum, and the bbs.hsw.cn South China Tiger forum—were all closed for various reasons. However, the activist community was not purged, and as I have shown in previous analyses, the collective knowledge that challenged the South China tiger photos was constantly enhanced.

The emay.com.cn website is a botany internet forum initiated by leading anti-tiger activist Fu and other researchers at the Institute of Botany. It played a significant role in the very early stages of the Tiger Gate incident. On November 6, 2007, Fu announced that emay.com.cn would withdraw from the debate over Tiger Gate and the forum would be silenced at 12 P.M. on November 7.[18] Fu stated that as an academic forum focusing on botany research, emay.com.cn had fulfilled its responsibility to question the authenticity of the South China tiger photos from a botanical perspective and the time had come for the forum to resume its normal focus. However, the closing of emay.com.cn did not silence or purge the activists who had contributed to the discussion on this forum. Fu later stated that the forum's activists never withdrew from questioning the South China tiger photos; rather, they moved to Fu's blog (blog.sina.com.cn/emaycomcn). In addition to his blog activity, Fu actively engaged in discussions and debates over Tiger Gate in other major forums, including xitek.com and the bbs.hsw.cn South China Tiger forum, as well as in QQ groups of anti-tiger activists.

Xitek.com opened a temporary forum for the Tiger Gate incident on October 30, which soon became the leading forum for anti-tiger activism to challenge the South China tiger photos, especially after emay.com.cn was silenced. As shown in table 4.1, six methods (nos. 3–7 and no. 9) were developed at this forum. On November 21, xitek.com announced that the temporary forum for the Tiger Gate incident would be closing that day. The announcement declared that the temporary forum would be closed because the discovery of the New Year's picture on November 16, 2007, meant that Tiger Gate would likely end very soon. In table 4.1 we can see that the closure of the xitek.com forum did not hinder the construction of the collective knowledge that challenged the South China tiger photos. New methods questioning the photos continued to emerge at other major forums, including the hsw.cn South China Tiger forum. In addition, leading activists such as Smallfish moved to the hsw.cn South China Tiger forum and continued taking part in actions.

A similar pattern could be observed when the hsw.cn South China Tiger forum was suddenly shut down. Leading activists and the activist community as a whole quickly moved to and regrouped at other forums or platforms to continue their actions. At least three forums quickly emerged as new leading online spaces for anti-tiger activists to continue actions that challenged official claims. The first was the South China Tiger forum at www.shunyi.cc, a new forum launched by anti-tiger activist LittleRabbit (or Fishing Little Rabbit), later known as Wang Ling—a small business owner who ran the website www.shunyi.cc.[19] After the hsw.cn South China Tiger forum was shut down, LittleRabbit opened a new forum on his own website and invited anti-tiger activists to move to the new forum, which would be managed by the activists themselves. Within a day (by March 8, 2008), more than 226 activists from the hsw.cn South China Tiger forum had registered on the new forum, including leading anti-tiger activists Smallfish and FromPeasant, who later volunteered to be forum administrators.[20] According to LittleRabbit, more than ten thousand people visited the new forum within the first several days (*Anti-tiger activists are voted*, 2008).

Activists quickly moved to a second new web forum at hsw.cn: Huashang General Topics. After the hsw.cn South China Tiger forum was shut down, activists first used Huashang General Topics to protest the shutdown. Later, the website imposed heavy-handed censorship to delete any comments pertaining to Tiger Gate. Eventually, a form of compromise seems to have been reached between the website and activists. Activists continued to communicate information about Tiger Gate and what to do next, while the website exercised the right to delete any content it considered problematic. Within the same day of the shutdown of the South China Tiger forum, a large group of anti-tiger activists moved to Huashang General Topics. At 22:30 on March 9, the simultaneous online users of Huashang General Topics increased tenfold to 120. Also on March 9, Li Xue Fei and Netizen_B, leading activists at the previous hsw.cn South China Tiger forum volunteered to be assistant administrators for Huashang General Topics.

Anti-tiger activists moved to a third new virtual space at the xici.net South China Tiger forum, which was also started by an anti-tiger activist. Influential activists, such as Wang Yang101, who developed a mathematical method to challenge the South China tiger photos, moved to the new forum. In addition to these three forums, leading Chinese portals, such as Tianya.com and tieba.baidu .com, also opened forums focusing on Tiger Gate. Moreover, these newly emerging Tiger Gate forums were not disconnected from one another. Wang Yang101 and many other activists, for example, registered at more than one South China Tiger forum and forwarded posts from one forum to another. And to avoid the prospect of having their contents deleted by websites later, many activists posted their contents on multiple forums as a defensive tactic. This tactic enabled them to continue connecting with other anti-tiger activists on different forums as a community.

Second, activist responses to the shutdown of the hsw.cn South China Tiger forum indicated that the desperate attempt to silence activists failed. At 12:48 on March 7, two hours after the shutdown, Fu Dezhi created a post on his blog titled "On the closing of the South China Tiger forum," in which he stated: "Many activists already foresaw this result and even reminded me to be careful of my words. I herein promised that as long as the blog is not shut down, I welcome all activists to comment, discuss, and communicate any information regarding the Tiger Gate incident in the blog. . . . Meanwhile, the emay.com.cn Red Alter forum will be open for all activists to post new information and developments of the Tiger Gate incident." This post indicates that instead of being more careful with his words, Fu became more actively engaged in the online action contesting the South China tiger photos. He not only used his blog as a platform to assemble information on Tiger Gate but reopened emay.com.cn as a virtual space for all anti-tiger activists.

Also, after the hsw.cn South China Tiger forum was shut down, activists quickly created lots of new content regarding the Tiger Gate incident on new forums. On March 9, two days after the shutdown of the forum, 616 new posts were created on Huashang General Topics, most of which addressed the Tiger Gate incident. Within two months, 10,960 new threads had been created on the new South China Tiger forum started by LittleRabbit. On April 28, anti-tiger activists at that forum began publishing their own newsletter. In July 2008, the forum also organized offline activities to strengthen the community in Beijing and Xian, the capital of Shaanxi Province. In the convergence culture and the technological, social, and political context of contemporary China, this discussion shows that after the close of major activist forums, activists were able to quickly move into or regroup in new online spaces. New technologies and the commitment of activists to actions for social change have turned desperate attempts to silence and purge the activist community into failures.

In addition to government agencies shutting down activist forums, contention between government agencies and activists can also be seen in online debates. At a very early stage in the Tiger Gate incident, governmental officials in the Shaanxi Forestry Department, notably Guan Ke, opened blogs to dispute anti-tiger activists and propagate disinformation among the public. From October 2007 to June 2008, Guan posted thirty articles on his blog and became the leading pro-tiger figure in cyberspace. On October 26, when the South China tiger photos had already become widely challenged by netizens (see table 4.1),

Guan posted a blog article rebutting Fu's allegation that the leaves of the plants on and around the tiger were too big. He argued that based on his own experience, leaves big enough to cover the head of a tiger are very common in the mountain area where Zhou took the photos. Two days later, he posted another blog article titled "What Changed a Real Tiger into a Paper Tiger," in which he used his social capital as an established wildlife photographer to rebut Fu and First-Impression for challenging the authenticity of the South China tiger photos using botany and GIF animation methodology, respectively. He called online actions that questioned the authenticity of Zhou's photos "bullying the poor through the Internet" (Guan, 2007a). On November 26, 163.com published the forty digital photos Zhou took without gaining Zhou's permission. This provided more material for grassroots investigation. On November 30, Guan posted a blog titled "Tiger Gate Is a War to Protect Human Rights," in which he alleged that 163.com had violated Zhou's copyright and human rights (Guan, 2007b). Then on April 20, 2008, five months after the discovery of the New Year's picture, Guan created a blog post titled "The Astonishing False News in the Tiger Gate Incident," in which he argued that the New Year's picture is PSed from the South China tiger photos taken by Zhou (Guan, 2008). Other government officials, such as Zhu Julong (a deputy director of the Shaanxi Forestry Department), and academic researchers such as Liu Liyuan, associate professor at Beijing Normal University, aggressively participated in new media campaigns to defend the South China tiger photos. The pro-tiger posts and comments from government officials and academic researchers triggered fierce online debates between anti-tiger activists and pro-tiger internet users.[21]

On another front in Tiger Gate, concerted efforts by legal activists to hold the Shaanxi Forestry Department and the National Forestry Administration accountable and the obstruction of those efforts by various government bodies demonstrated the contentiousness between activists and the government. From November 7, 2007, to December 22 of the following year, Hao Jinsong and other legal activists launched a series of legal actions to hold the two government agencies accountable. These included two legal cases in Beijing and Shanxi Province, one application for administrative reconsideration of Tiger Gate according to the Administrative Reconsideration Law, and three applications to release government information regarding Tiger Gate based on the Regulations on Open Government Information. These actions demonstrated that legal activists tried to use existing institutional channels, one after another, to hold the two agencies accountable. Yet one after another, their actions were blocked by various units in the government, including four courts in Beijing and Shanxi Province, the National Forestry Administration, and the Shaanxi Forestry Department.

A Multidimensional Relationship between Activists and the Government

Although contentiousness is a significant dimension of the relationship between activists and the government in Tiger Gate, other aspects of this relationship make it multidimensional. Most importantly, the Chinese government should be seen not as a unitary entity but as a huge bureaucracy in which various institutions are influenced by the interests of different social groups that compete with one another in policymaking and implementation processes. While the local government in Shaanxi tried to silence activists and continuously used various channels to contest the activists over the eight-month span of the incident, party organs of the central government, such as *People's Daily* and CCTV, supported the activists' position and pressured the local government to address the activists' concerns. From November 22, 2007, to June 30, 2008, the day after the Shaanxi Forestry Department was forced to announce that the tiger photos had been faked, *People's Daily* and its online platform published eleven official commentaries by its editors or *People's Daily* commentators supporting the activists' position. For example, Lu Xinning, the editorial director for *People's Daily*, stated that the local government in Shaanxi had the obligation to clarify the truth about Tiger Gate for the public and warned that "the crisis of trust caused by this incident will not only diminish government accountability but hurt . . . the entire society" (Lu, 2007a). Lu's comments and other official commentaries in *People's Daily* were often cited by activists as central government support for their request to hold the local government accountable in Tiger Gate. Leading activist Fu Dezhi, for example, cited Lu's three editorial commentaries on Tiger Gate forty times in blog posts against the Shaanxi government's claims concerning the South China tiger photos. Referring to her as "the anti-tiger hero Lu Xinning" (Fu, 2008e), he clearly identified Lu as one of "us"—anti-tiger activists. On November 24, he published a post on his blog titled "Tiger Gate: The *People's Daily* Is 'Surprisingly' 100% in Line With the People"(2007c): "[In Tiger Gate,] to the surprise [of those officials who supported the fake tiger photos], the party organ of the central government *the People's Daily* is 100% in line with the people, who the supporters and makers of the fake tiger photos called 'online mobs.' . . . [Therefore] I am very confident that the truth of Tiger Gate will soon be exposed by the people."

The *People's Daily* also portrayed itself as an ally for activists in Tiger Gate. For example, vice director of *People's Daily* Zhu Huaxin (2009) called Fu Dezhi, Smallfish, Lu Xinning, and CCTV's Chai Jing the "top four anti-tiger heroes" in Tiger Gate. On November 30, *People's Daily* published Lu's commentary "Tiger Gate, Another Disappointing Result?" in which Lu rebutted the claim by local officials and supported the position of activists. By noon the same day, anti-tiger activists had circulated her article widely on online forums such as Tianya.com and xitek.com. Anonymous anti-tiger activists cheered for the article and asserted that the central government seemed to be calling for the Shaanxi government to hold accountable the local officials who had been involved in Tiger Gate. Following Lu's article, the anonymous anti-tiger user reno1983 on Tianya.com commented, "Look! A party organ is going after [those involved in the fake tiger photos]!" The anonymous anti-tiger user BuYuGuiLiLuangSheng

(2007) commented, "It is the first time that I have a good impression of *People's Daily*!!! It seems that even the boss [the central government] of those officials can't stand what they've done in Tiger Gate!"

Rather than comply with the increasing pressure from *People's Daily*, CCTV, and other party organs, and constant online action, the local government in Shaanxi used the provincial media to defend its own claims and rebuff activists and party organs of the central government. On November 28, 2007, the *Nanjing Morning Post*, a local newspaper in Jiangsu Province, published an "investigative" news report based on interviews with residents in Xian, the capital of Shaanxi Province, titled "Most Xian Residents Believe That the South China Tiger Photos Are Real" (Pan, 2007a). On December 2, the *Nanjing Morning Post* ran a story titled "Zhou Zhenglong Is Looking Forward to Searching for Tigers After the First Snow," in which Zhou stated that the South China tiger photos are real; the New Year's picture is fake; and Fu Dezhi, the botanist who questioned his tiger photos, must openly apologize to him (Pan & Bian, 2007). On December 12, Shaanxi's ranking provincial newspaper *Three Qin Daily* published "Wildlife in a Camera," a long article on Guan Ke, the leading pro-tiger official, portraying him as a veteran wildlife photographer, a committed environmentalist, and an expert on wild animals in the mountain region where Zhou took the tiger photos (Yang & Sun, 2007).

On December 30, the *Nanjing Morning Post* featured a story titled "Breaking News on the Tiger from Zhenping: Tiger Footprints and Tiger Cub Skeleton Are Found" (Pan, 2007b). On December 31, *Ta Kung Pao*, a leading Hong Kong newspaper with the longest history of any Chinese newspaper, published a piece titled "News on Tiger Cub Skeleton Is Fake News," pointing out that reports of the discovery of tiger footprints and a tiger cub skeleton were false, based on their investigation (L. Cheng, 2007). On December 8, a leading investigative news program, CCTV's *News Probe*, aired a report highlighting the many methods developed by activists and featuring its own investigation into the authenticity of the South China tiger photos and the official claims of the Shaanxi Forestry Department. In an investigative report published by the *Nanjing Morning Post* on January 4, 2008, the Shaanxi Forestry Department reaffirmed its claim that the South China tiger photos were real, and a *Post* reporter questioned the reliability of CCTV's investigation in Zhenping County (Pan, 2008). In response, anonymous "pro-tiger" bloggers on major online forums such as Tianya.com and other internet sites fiercely attacked CCTV's investigative report out of support for the Shaanxi government's claims, accusing CCTV of "bias," "lack of neutrality," and "cherry picking" (e.g., Shou Xi Ya Tou, 2007; YiTiaoBan Hanzi, 2007; Zhang San, 2007).[22] Meanwhile, anti-tiger activists celebrated the report and contested those supporting the Shaanxi government (e.g., haw561, 2007; Shou Xi Ya Tou, 2007). After grassroots investigations by activists led to the discovery of the New Year's picture as the original source of the South China tiger photos, party organs of the central government, such as *People's Daily* and CCTV, and other mainstream media outlets began reporting Tiger Gate as a fraud. Yet coverage by some provincial media outlets, such as the *Nanjing Morning Post* and *Three Qin Daily*, continued to support the pro-tiger discourse of the local government.

The relationship between activists and the government that was evident in Tiger Gate stands in stark contrast to the relationship between activists and the government reported in previous research. Until now, scholars in Chinese internet studies have tend to depict the relationship between activists and the government in new media actions as singularly contentious and confrontational. Yet in Tiger Gate, activists and party organs of the central government allied against the local government in Shaanxi, while the local government, with the support of the local media, contested the forces of activists, the mainstream media, and, to some extent, the central government.

This raises other questions: Why was the response of government agencies in Shaanxi (shutdowns of major activist forums) so extreme in the context of the overwhelming media support for activists by the mainstream media and party organs of the central government, and why did local officials constantly engage in fierce debates with activists and use lower-profile provincial media to defend their own claims and oppose party organs such as CCTV and *People's Daily*? The conventional wisdom might have us believe that this represents the contentiousness between local government and the central government. Along this line, O'Brien and Li (2006), among others (Verran, 2009), have argued that online resistance and online discontent serve to alert the central government to public opinion and cases of local malfeasance and civil unrest. In Tiger Gate, the new media actions led by activists served to report malfeasance by the Shaanxi Forestry Department to the central government. However, the long delay in holding officials at the local level responsible for fraud illustrates the contentiousness between the local government and the central government and the inability of the central government to effectively address local malfeasance.

On the front of grassroots actions in Tiger Gate, although legal activist Hao Jinsong's cases were rejected by various courts, they received positive coverage in party media organs of the central government, such as the *Procuratorate Daily*, *New Legal Report*, CCTV, people.com.cn, and Xinhua News Agency. The fact that these organs tolerated and even encouraged Hao to continue voicing to the public the imperative of holding accountable the Shaanxi Forestry Department and the National Forestry Administration through legal actions, even while his cases were rejected by the courts, indicates the complex and multidimensional relationship between legal activists and the government in Tiger Gate. For example, after Hao sued Zhou Zhenglong in court in Shanxi, Xinhuanet.com, the online platform of the Xinhua News Agency (the national news agency of the government), strongly praised Hao's legal action, proclaiming, "We really need people . . . who take [incidents like] Tiger Gate seriously. They demonstrated an engaged citizenry. Their actions exemplified citizens' practicing their rights entitled by law. . . . Law should protect the rights of this kind of person to take legal action. The law should offer them unconditional support" (Liu, 2007). The *Procuratorate Daily*, the official organ of the Supreme People's Procuratorate, published at least seven articles in support of activists during the incident.[23] On December 11, 2007, it published an article titled "New Progress in Tiger Gate: Lawyer Hao Jinsong Sued the National Forestry Administration" (Jia, 2007). This article reported on Hao's legal action against the National Forestry Administration for its rejection of his application for administrative reconsideration, Hao's criticism of the administration for its inaction in Tiger Gate, and Hao's goal to improve legal awareness on government accountability in this legal action. It quoted Hao as saying, "I just want to tell people around us that we can use the law to improve government accountability" (Jia, 2007). After the Shaanxi authority announced the result of the so-called second official evaluation of Tiger Gate on July 3, 2008, the *Procuratorate Daily*'s online platform broadcast an intensive live interview with Hao Jinsong. ("Crazy Lower Hao Jinsong Talking About Tiger Gate," 2008) In it, Hao continued his sharp criticism of the Shaanxi Forestry Department and the National Forestry Administration for their lack of government accountability in Tiger Gate and advocated for further investigation of the scandal. He stated:

> It is impossible that Zhou Zhenglong could have single-handedly masterminded the fraud. . . . This is a group crime. . . . The local government in Zhenping and the Shaanxi Forestry Department wanted the central government to establish a wild tiger reserve in Zhenping. . . . Once this was approved, the Shaanxi Forestry Department would get ten million [yuan] in public funds from the National Forestry Administration. This huge amount of money is the target of the group crime. . . . Therefore, we must further the investigation to hold those officials involved in the group crime accountable for the fraud.

In the interview, Hao announced that he would continue his legal actions against the Shaanxi Forestry Department. He said that although his most recent legal case against the department was rejected by a first instance court, he would appeal to an appeals court very soon. Near the end of the interview, he lauded the participation of activists in Tiger Gate, citing it as an example of the "rise of civil society" in China: "Until now, we have achieved partial success. Netizens extensively cheered for the success of justice. I believe that in the future we will see more netizens voice their concerns in similar public events during China's transition period. The participation of netizens in public events and the rise of civil society complement with each other in Chinese society."

The Implications of Tiger Gate

Although the efforts of countless activists in Tiger Gate may have failed to bring about formal structural change or policy change in government accountability, they are not without significance. So what are the implications of Tiger Gate for understanding the use of new media for social change? And why does it remain an important case regarding the potentials for bringing about social change in China? Roland's (2004) theoretical discussion on institutional change helps shed light on these questions. In his comparative research on economic development, Roland proposed a new framework for understanding institutional change. Following North (1990, p. 3), he defines institution as "constraints on behaviors imposed by the rules of the game in society," and he stated, "Institutions include in particular social norms and all other constraints" (Roland, 2004). He then distinguishes two sets of institutions: "slow-moving institutions" and "fast moving institutions." Slow-moving institutions are institutions changing slowly and continuously, such as culture, values, beliefs, and social norms. Fast-moving institutions are institutions changing rapidly and irregularly, such as political institutions and legal institutions.

From Roland's (2004) perspective, Tiger Gate brought about significant change on "slow-moving institutions" regarding government accountability. Over nearly one year of nationwide online actions during the incident, the participation of millions of people in online forums and the wide coverage by the mainstream media made issues of government accountability (such as honesty in government, punishment of officials for wrongdoing, and government answerability to public opinion) the most read issues on Chinese internet portals and in newspapers. This alone could significantly increase public awareness of government accountability. Mainstream anti-tiger actions, in which Fu Dezhi and Smallfish took part, showed the public that by using online actions and collective knowledge creation facilitated by the internet, activists could challenge the claims of local officials. Using the internet and new media, the public could increase the limited accountability of government, at least at the local level, and could change wrongheaded policies on specific issues. Similar new media actions to change specific policies or punish wrongdoing by local officials were not uncommon following Tiger Gate, in public events such as the Free Lunch Project and the COVID-19 crisis, which will be examined in subsequent chapters.

Moreover, despite the lack of success of legal actions brought by activists such as Hao Jinsong, their actions received extensive support among activists and in mainstream media coverage. This result may change the knowledge, experiences, and beliefs of activists and the public regarding the relationship between the public and the government and activist approaches to increase government accountability. For example, as someone who only engaged in conventional actions to use online opinion to pressure the government to investigate the tiger photos, Fu Dezhi told Hao he believed Hao's legal action is important: "Whether they accept your case is not so important; the fact that you sued [the government] is of great importance" (*Anti-tiger Hero Hao Jinsong*, 2008).

Hao himself intended his legal cases to not only increase the limited account-ability of government in Tiger Gate but promote a means for more activists to use legal actions for government accountability more broadly. For example, he stated, "When anti-tiger activists felt they could do nothing but desperately curse those tiger supporters online, we need to use legal action to encourage them.... Some of them may imitate us [to use legal actions to enhance government accountability] in the future, as we have demonstrated a mode or channel" (*Anti-tiger Hero Hao Jinsong*, 2008). More broadly, Hao believed that his legal actions serve to change people's values, beliefs, and norms regarding their relationship with the government in Chinese society. He asserted:

> Why are there abundant cases where accountability is seriously lacking, but no one really cares? Because many people are spiritually kneeling down before the government, like slaves before their masters. When someone stands up against the government saying "I object!" they feel uncomfortable: "Everyone is kneeling down, why do you stand up?!" "Everyone is happily sleeping in the 'iron house,' why do you cry out?" ... But of course, there are also people who understand [what I'm doing], even imitate what I'm doing. In the future I believe more people will stand up, using similar ways [of increasing government accountability] (*Anti-tiger Hero Hao Jinsong*, 2008).

The use of the "iron house" metaphor especially indicated Hao's aim to change the values, beliefs, mindset, and culture regarding the relationship between the government and individuals in Chinese society. The "iron house" metaphor is from Lu Xun (1881–1936), the most famous intellectual writer in China of the twentieth century and a leading figure of the New Culture movement, which was extremely critical of "traditional Chinese culture" and advocated for a "New Culture." It is a metaphor of the "traditional society," "traditional culture," and traditional values and norms that Lu Xun desperately struggled against (Lee, 1987). In the preface to his famous short-story collection *Call to Arms*, Lu Xun recorded a conversation between him and his friend Qian Xuantong, another leading figure in the New Culture movement, while Qian invited him to write for the magazine *New Youth*:[24]

QIAN: "I think you might write something. . . ."
LU: "Imagine an iron house without windows, absolutely indestructible, with many people fast asleep inside who will soon die of suffocation. But you know since they will die in their sleep, they will not feel the pain of death. Now if you cry aloud to wake a few of the lighter sleepers, making those unfortunate few suffer the agony of irrevocable death, do you think you are doing them a good turn?"

QIAN: "But if a few awake, you can't say there is no hope of destroying the iron house."
(Lu, 1922)

Lu Xun eventually chose to write for the hope that he "could not blot out" (Lu, 1922). Lu Xun's "iron house" metaphor is widely known to the public in contemporary China. The use of this metaphor in Hao's statement indicates that Hao self-identified as one of the few "lighter sleepers" that cried aloud to wake up the "fast asleep" masses in order to change the culture, values, and social norms regarding government accountability.

Mainstream media and major portals also portrayed Hao's legal actions in Tiger Gate as actions that could change the values, experiences, and beliefs of individuals and their relationship to government. For example, *New Legal Report*'s article on Hao's legal actions in Tiger Gate was titled "Hao Jinsong: I Wanted to Foster the Rule of Law in China Using This Case" (H. Cheng, 2008). Sohu.com titled its interview with Hao, "Hao Jinsong: Individual Could Change the Times; [Individual] Rights Need to Be Acquired Through Actions" (2011). *The Southern People Weekly* titled its article on Hao and Tiger Gate "Hao Jinsong, the Citizen Who Disobeys." In it, Hao was portrayed as a pioneer who would attract many others in the long fight for a more open and just society (Kuai, 2009).

After Tiger Gate, Hao continued conducting his legal actions for government accountability in various high-profile public incidents and public interest litigation. For example, in November 2009 he represented two victims of entrapment in their legal cases against a local law enforcement agency in Shanghai (Hao, 2009). Hao believed his public interest litigation could increase awareness of government accountability and the rule of law in China. In fact, he was not waging a one-person war against the lack of government accountability using public interest litigation. Other activists and NGOs, especially in fields such as environmental protection, have also engaged in legal actions for government accountability at the local level. Since 2011, environmental activists and NGOs have conducted hundreds of public interest litigation cases to hold local governments and state and private corporations accountable for environmental problems (Chu, 2018; de Boer & Whitehead, 2016). For example, in November 2011, the All China Environment Federation sued a local government and a corporation in Qingzhen, Guizhou for water pollution. FON, a partner of the NGO 2.0 Project examined in chapter 3, conducted forty public interest litigation cases between 2014 and 2018 against local governments and corporations, thirty-four of which were accepted by the courts. In 2014, FON and the Center for Legal Assistance to Pollution Victims collaboratively launched a legal assistance network to provide training, legal assistance, and funds to activists and NGOs engaged in public interest litigation (FON, 2019).

This indicates how Tiger Gate contributed to the change in "slow-moving institutions," such as culture, values, beliefs, and social norms, which shape notions of government accountability, although it may not have changed "fast-moving institutions," such as legal and political institutions in Chinese society (Roland 2004). Yet as Roland (2004) has pointed out, "slow-moving institutions are good candidates to influence fast-moving institutions." Changes in people's awareness, experiences, and values regarding government accountability may influence potential changes in policy and other "fast-moving institutions" related to government accountability in the future. This kind of change is not certain to happen, nor is it likely to occur within a short period of time, as the interactions between "slow-moving institutions" and "fast-moving institutions" are complex and multidirectional (Roland, 2004). It requires a long and tedious nurturing process, and as a social change action, Tiger Gate represents a milestone in this process.

5

Free Lunches

Activist, NGO, and State
Collaboration in Development
and Social Change

"Besides generating angry public opinion to pressure policy makers to change this country, are there any new possibilities?" This is the question journalist turned activist and founder of the Free Lunch Project, Deng Fei, posed in his book on the project (Deng, 2014, p. 15). The project he inspired, to provide free lunches for schoolchildren in underdeveloped regions of China, was a heartfelt effort to find new possibilities for change in China.

The Free Lunch Project is a nationwide grassroots new media action started by activists, run by a grassroots NGO, and funded mainly through online micro-donations by individuals.[1] As of November 2022, the project had received more than 979,570,000 yuan ($144,434,657) in donations from millions of participants and had provided free lunches for more than 410,000 children in 1,679 schools (Free Lunch Project, 2022). More importantly, this grassroots action indirectly prompted the central government in Beijing to launch a National Nutrition Subsidies Policy, aiming to provide 16 billion yuan ($2.32 billion) per year for 26 million primary and junior high school students in rural areas (State Council of the People's Republic of China, 2011). This chapter will explore how multiple stakeholders, including NGOs, activists, individual users of new media, and the government, collaborated to promote development and social change through the Free Lunch Project.

In March 2011, Deng Fei, then a journalist for the *Phoenix Weekly Magazine*, initiated the Free Lunch Project on Weibo with the support of other journalists and media practitioners. On April 2, 2011, the project launched its official microblog on Sina Weibo. In the same month, with the support of the China Social Welfare Foundation, it began to accept donations from the public.[2] Using the slogan "Three yuan [approximately fifty cents] enables schoolchildren in underdeveloped regions to get a free lunch" (Free Lunch Project, 2012c), the project promoted three yuan donations for free lunches for children in underdeveloped areas.[3] On July 13, 2011, the Free Lunch Project opened its online store at Taobao.com, the biggest online shopping website in Chinese cyberspace, which gave the project a new fundraising platform and significantly increased its fundraising capability. Between April 2011 and December 2014, the Free Lunch Project had received roughly 100 million yuan in donations from millions of people. In 2014 alone it received 41 million yuan in donations, 67 percent of which (27.47 million) came from microdonations by individuals (Free Lunch Project, 2015a). This is significant in that the Free Lunch Project has always been a grassroots action supported and funded by millions of small donors, rather than a charity that relies on a few big national or international corporate donors. This also indicates that millions of ordinary people in China have been engaged and mobilized in the project by new media actions.

The basic procedure is for the public to donate any amount of money to the Free Lunch Fund, which the project then uses to fund its programs at schools in underdeveloped areas around the country. To qualify for free lunches, schools in these places must submit email applications to the project, publicly publish their proposals and budgets on their Weibo accounts, and candidly answer questions from the public on Weibo. The Free Lunch Project team evaluates the proposals and budgets submitted by the schools that apply. If they are accepted, schools receive full financial support for the free lunch service based on the proposed budgets. The schools are to provide free lunches to their students directly and publish detailed reports of their daily costs to the public and to the Free Lunch Project team on their official Weibo accounts.

New media and ICTs, such as microblogs, websites, online shopping services, and mobile payment apps, have been used extensively to increase transparency and accountability and public awareness of the project. Mass media, including newspapers and commercial websites such as Taobao.com, have also had a significant role in the project. By October 26, 2011, six months after grassroots activists started the Free Lunch Project, the central government in Beijing inaugurated a National Nutrition Subsidies Policy (State Council of the People's Republic of China, 2011). The standard of support under this state policy is the same as that of the Free Lunch Project—three yuan per student per meal. After the central government launched the National Nutrition Subsidies Project,[4] the Free Lunch Project gained momentum to extend its free lunch service, especially in schools beyond the scope of the governmental project, and coordinated with the National Nutrition Subsidies Project in various ways (Free Lunch Project, 2013b; L. Gu, 2015; Liu, 2017). Between 2012 and 2019, its annual income from donations almost quintupled (from 25,438,705.59 yuan to 123,580,740.03 yuan), 7.26 times more rural schools were covered by the project's free lunch service (from 175 to 1,271), and 9 times more children benefited from the project (from 36,467 to 332,044) (Free Lunch Project, 2013a, 2020a).

The Free Lunch Project: Grassroots Action to Fight Hunger and Malnutrition

Understanding the targeted social concerns of any new media action is crucial for analyzing that action. Drawing from Free Lunch Project documents, online posts by leading activists, and mainstream news coverage of the Free Lunch Project, this section illustrates that the Free Lunch Project has aimed to eliminate hunger and malnutrition in China's underdeveloped regions. It also indicates that activists took part in this action to change the state policy on this issue as well as to provide free lunch services directly.

The Hunger and Malnutrition Problem in Contemporary China

A growing literature indicates that hunger and malnutrition are urgent global problems (Fan, 2017, Food and Agriculture Organization [FAO], 2017; Servaes, 2008; Tacchi, 2007; United Nations [U.N.], 2000a; U.N., 2011; U.N., 2016). In its *Millennium Declaration*, the U.N. asserted that hunger and malnutrition are among the most urgent development problems faced in the world today (2000b). In its 2011 report on its Millennium Declaration Goals (MDGs), the U.N. stated, "The proportion of people in the developing world who went hungry in 2005–2007 remained stable at 16 percent. . . . Based on this trend, and in light of the economic crisis and rising food prices, it will be difficult to meet the hunger-reduction target in many regions of the developing world. . . . Nutrition must be given higher priority in national development if the MDGs are to be achieved" (U.N., 2011). In 2016, the Sustainable Development Goals adopted by 150 world leaders at the U.N. Sustainable Development Summit reaffirmed the significance of hunger and malnutrition reduction to achieve global sustainable development (U.N., 2016). However, hunger is not only a conventional development problem but a human rights issue. In the international human rights system of the U.N., the right to be free from hunger or the right to food has been consistently presented as a basic human right (Convention on the Rights of the Child, 1989; International Covenant on Economic, Social and Cultural Rights [ICESCR], 1966; Universal Declaration of Human Rights [UDHR], 1948). For example, the UDHR (1948) states, "Everyone has the right to a standard of living adequate for the health and well-being of himself and of his family, including food, clothing, housing" (art. 25). The ICESCR (1966), an international human rights treaty adopted by the United Nations General Assembly in 1966 and signed by 166 countries, states, "The States Parties to the present Covenant, recogniz[es] the fundamental right of everyone to be free from hunger" (art 11). Regarding the right of children to be free from hunger, the Convention on the Rights of the Child (1989), a human rights treaty signed by 196 members of the U.N., states, "States Parties recognize the right of every child to a standard of living adequate for the child's physical, mental, spiritual, moral and social development" and "States Parties . . . shall take appropriate measures to assist parents . . . to implement this right and shall in case of need provide material assistance and support programmes, particularly with regard to nutrition, clothing and housing" (art. 27). The right to food and nutrition is especially important for children because it is the basis for achieving all other rights, and the effects of childhood hunger and malnutrition are lifelong and extend across several generations (UNICEF, 2016).

Hunger and malnutrition continue to remain significant problems in China, the second biggest economy in the world. In the past three decades, China has experienced tremendous economic development. Yet hunger and malnutrition are still significant social concerns for contemporary Chinese society. For example, between 1990 and 1992, 23.9 percent of the Chinese population (289 million) was undernourished according to FAO (2015). Between 1992 and 2008, the proportion of the undernourished population gradually decreased to 11.5 percent. Yet since 2008, hunger reduction in China has shown little improvement. Between 2016 and 2018, the proportion of the undernourished population remained at roughly 8 percent. This means that as of 2018, 108.2 million people were undernourished in China (FAO et al., 2019). More importantly, urban and rural China are sharply divided in terms of hunger and malnutrition. For example, whereas only 2 percent of children in urban China were underweight in 2011, as many as 9 percent of rural children were underweight (FAO, 2011). In fact, there is a higher proportion of underweight children in rural China than in many less developed countries in Asia. For example, according to the FAO, only 7 percent of children in rural Mongolia are underweight (FAO, 2011).

Chinese researchers and official reports also acknowledge the significance of hunger and malnutrition, especially hunger and malnutrition among children in China's rural and less developed regions (Lu, 2009; Ministry of Health of the People's Republic of China, 2012; National Health and Family Planning Commission & Ministry of Health of the People's Republic of China, 2015; Zhao & Wang, 2017). For example, in its *2015 Nutrition and Chronic Disease Report on Chinese Residents*, the PRC's National Health and Family Planning Commission and Ministry of Health documented that the nutrition divide between children in urban and rural China persisted between 2002 and 2012. The prevalence of underweight children in China's rural regions is two to three times higher than it is in urban regions. Moreover, the prevalence of underweight children in less developed parts of rural areas is 1.5 times higher than in rural areas as a whole (National Health and Family Planning Commission of the

People's Republic of China & Ministry of Health of the People's Republic of China, 2015). Lu's (2009) case study of hunger and malnutrition among students in four primary schools in less developed areas of Guangxi Province also demonstrates that malnutrition among schoolchildren remains a serious concern. For male students in the four schools, for example, the daily caloric intake is only 75 percent of the recommended amount; for female students, it is only 67 percent. Vitamin A intake is only at 4 to 6 percent of the recommended daily amount, and vitamin C intake is almost zero (Lu, 2009). More recently, Zhao and Wang (2017) found that 12.15 percent of 142,632 schoolchildren in less developed rural areas of Shaanxi Province were undernourished.

The Chinese government frequently touts its success in reducing poverty and hunger in China's rural regions in both its official media (e.g., B. Gu, 2016) and global media (e.g., Ministry of Foreign Affairs of PRC, 2015; United Nations Development Programme, 2015). For example, *People's Daily* has claimed that as a result of governmental poverty reduction projects, the population living in extreme poverty in rural China between 1978 and 2015 has decreased by 92.8 percent, from 770,000,000 to 55,750,000 (Gu, 2016). Organizations within the U.N. also praised the Chinese government for its success in achieving its MDGs and in reducing poverty and hunger (UNICEF, 2015). Yet the persistent hunger problem in rural China is ultimately the result of China's state policy. It is one facet of urban–rural inequality that has resulted from unjust pro-urban state policies dating from the early development of the PRC in the 1950s and exacerbated by the launch of economic reforms in the 1980s (e.g., Chen et al., 2016; Li et al., 2014; Tsai, 2007; Whyte, 2010; D. T. Yang, 1999, H. Yu, 2017). The Free Lunch Project thus came about as a grassroots action to target this inequality and to redress the unjust pro-urban policies of the state. More specifically, it is an action to protect the right of rural children to be free of hunger, a basic human right that has been overlooked by state policy.

The Mission of the Free Lunch Project

The section titled "Background of the Project" on the Free Lunch Project website quotes a 2011 report from the China Development Research Foundation to substantiate the severity of hunger and malnutrition among schoolchildren in less developed regions of China:[5] "[The report] shows … that malnutrition is a serious problem among children in less developed regions. 12% of the students in the research suffer from growth retardation; 72% feel hungry in class. . . . The report asserts that poverty among Chinese children will result in a severe loss of human capital" (Free Lunch Project, 2018a). It then introduces the Free Lunch Project as an initiative to solve hunger and malnutrition among schoolchildren: "In April 2011, Deng Fei, along with several hundred other volunteers … advocated donating three yuan per day to provide free lunches for school children in less developed regions" (Free Lunch Project, 2018a). The project's mission statement and vision follow: "Our mission is to help Chinese children avoid hunger and grow up healthy and strong"; "Our vision is, through years of work, to ultimately make free lunches a basic social welfare benefit for Chinese children" (Free Lunch Project, 2018a). In its strategy statement, the project states: "Our strategy is to explore the safe, transparent, high-efficient, and replicable free lunch model to provide a professional [free lunch] service to the government, corporations, NGOs, and individual donors, and to promote public policy through 'strategic philanthropy'"[6] (Free Lunch Project, 2018a). The mission statement and vision of the project illustrate that hunger and malnutrition among children in China's less-developed regions are social problems that the Free Lunch Project wants to change. The vision ("ultimately to make free lunches a basic social welfare benefit") and the strategy ("to explore a replicable model" and "to promote public policy through 'strategic philanthropy'") show that the Free Lunch Project aims to change state policy on this problem, in addition to directly providing free lunch services.

Founder Deng Fei, a veteran investigative journalist, was actively involved in several new media actions before initiating the Free Lunch Project (Deng, 2011a). In an interview with ifeng.com, Deng stated the following regarding his initial motivation for starting the project:

> In March 2011, in the annual convention of Tianya.com . . . a teacher from a rural primary school in Guizhou Province told me that most of her students don't have anything to eat for lunch. . . . We went to her school and several nearby schools, and found that this is the common situation in most rural schools in Guizhou: children don't have anything for lunch. . . . We were astonished. . . . We thought this situation must be changed. . . . We then started the Free Lunch Project to provide free lunches for these schoolchildren. (Deng, 2011c)

On March 24, 2011, Deng posted on his Weibo page: "Tomorrow, I'll go to a rural school in a mountain area in Guizhou. Students there do not have lunch and have to fill their stomachs with cold water. I . . . and Liang Shuxin want to build a communal kitchen at the school and promote a free lunch program in underdeveloped mountainous parts of China" (Deng, 2011a).[7] Deng's post and interview indicate that he started the Free Lunch Project to solve the hunger and malnutrition problem of children in several specific schools in a mountainous area in Guizhou Province. Yet in addition to small-scale changes in several schools, Deng aimed to bring about change at the national level from the very beginning of the project by transforming the state policy on hunger and malnutrition: "At the very beginning of the project, we began to think about how to influence the government at the national level. So, after we started the Free Lunch Project in several schools in one province, we immediately moved to another province. In so doing, we hope that more media and more people could be engaged in the project and eventually influence the government's public policy" (Deng, 2011c).

The objective of activists to transform state policy can also be seen in the concept of "strategic philanthropy," a term that leading activists of the Free Lunch Project constantly used to describe the project (e.g., Deng, 2014; Free Lunch Project, 2017d; Zhao, 2011). By "strategic philanthropy," activists meant using bottom-up grassroots philanthropy actions to influence, guide, and promote public policy, and eventually, through legislation, to make free lunches for schoolchildren a basic right and hold the government responsible for that obligation. In this connection, the Free Lunch Fund's vice director, Dang Jun, stated: "From the beginning, what we want to do is 'strategic philanthropy': the first step is to promote public policy, like what we have achieved now; the second step, through legislation, is to make free lunches for school children a government obligation, like compulsory education" (Zhao, 2011). Activists and the Free Lunch Project considered the problem of hunger—although it is not specifically highlighted in the mission or strategy statements—to be a facet of inequality between urban and rural populations resulting from long-standing unjust policies to extract resources from rural China for so-called development in urban regions. Activists aimed to take actions to redress this injustice and protect the basic rights of rural children. For example, Deng Fei (2014) stated: "[The reason for the hunger problem among rural children is that] the Chinese state employed a long-standing policy to scarify rural population for the development in big cities. State policies have been systemically extracting resources, capital, and human capital from rural regions. The result of these unjust policies is that the 61 million left-behind children [in rural China] have to pay the price."[8] In addressing the goal of the Free Lunch Project, Deng Fei (2014) stated that he and other activists initiated the project on Weibo to "take actions to help rural children be free from hunger and fight for their basic right to nutrition justice."

Moreover, activists and the Free Lunch Project believe that hunger is just one of the many social problems related to inequality between rural and urban populations that need to be redressed. Free Lunch programs are just the first step toward changing these problems. Over time and in collaboration with other NGOs and other activist communities, they sought to address this multifaceted inequality between rural and urban populations from various perspectives. According to Deng Fei (2014), "Other fellow activists and I are working to organize an alliance of NGOs serving rural children to attract and direct urban resources to feed back to rural schools. We will try our best to serve the 61 million left-behind children from the perspective of nutrition, libraries, critical illness insurance, safety . . . and education. We will give them an equal, healthy, and safe environment for their future development."

On July 18, 2012, Deng Fei, other activists, and several NGOs launched China Rural Kids Care (2017) to provide critical illness insurance to rural children. In its mission statement, the project stated: "In China's underdeveloped regions, the death rate of children affected by critical illness is as high as 54%! More grievously, 50.5% of the children who die of critical illness barely get any treatment [because their rural families have little or no money]. We aimed to provide critical illness insurance to rural children. And we fight for health justice for rural children." Regarding its goals, the project noted, "We aimed to provide an example for how to solve the problem of critical illness of children in underdeveloped regions and we aimed to lend experience to, and advocate for, public policy change on this issue" (2017). As of June 2018, 1,561,089 rural children have benefited from the project's critical illness insurance (China Rural Kids Care).

Due to long-term separation from parents, girls who are left behind in rural regions are much more vulnerable to becoming victims of sexual harassment and assault. To address this problem, in October 2013 women's rights activists and NGOs, with the support of Free Lunch activists such as Deng Fei, started the Protecting Girls Project to provide training workshops on gender and sexual harassment to rural schoolgirls and to advocate for change in the government's outdated law regarding the sexual harassment of minors. As of March 2020, more than ten thousand volunteers have participated in the Protecting Girls Project, offering training workshops for roughly 3.85 million schoolchildren in thirty-one provinces in China (Beijing All in One Foundation, 2020).

The Free Lunch Project in the Mass Media

National and regional mass media have extensively reported on the Free Lunch Project as a grassroots action that fights against hunger and malnutrition among children in China's rural and less developed regions (e.g., W. Liu, 2017; Liu et al., 2012; Tian, 2015; Wu, 2012; T. Zhang, 2011). Moreover, in addition to the immediate benefits of the Free Lunch Project to the children in the schools it serves, mass media coverage has also emphasized the project's influence on state policy regarding hunger and malnutrition in the broader context of Chinese society (e.g., W. Liu, 2017; L. Gu, 2015; *"Free Lunch" Has Become a New Model*, 2012; T. Ye, 2012; T. Zhang, 2011).

On May 11, 2011, five months before the central government announced its National Nutrition Subsidies Policy, *People's Daily* published the following commentary on the Free Lunch Project: "The free lunches [provided by the Free Lunch Project] represent the right to nutrition, a basic right directly related with rights of health. It is also about social equality and social justice, and sustainable development. The government has the responsibility to provide material and economic support, and to provide policies and laws to ensure this right. Thus, to ensure that the 'Free Lunch' can cover more schools and benefit more children, the government must take action" (T. Zhang, 2011). This commentary asserts that the goal of the Free Lunch Project—providing free lunches to children in less developed regions—is strongly linked to protecting children's rights to nutrition, social justice, and sustainable development. It also urges the government to take action to change state policy on these significant issues in order to bring about large-scale changes in hunger and malnutrition.

On October 30, 2012, almost a year after the central government announced the National Nutrition Subsidies Policy, Xinhuanet published an article titled *Free Lunch Has Become a New Model for Grassroots Philanthropy Projects* (2012). It asserted, "The new model advocated by the Free Lunch Project, including promoting public policy through grassroots actions, transparency in project monitoring, and the use of new media in actions for social change, has gradually become a new example for grassroots philanthropy projects." First, the article argued that in addition to bringing benefits to the children in the schools that were served, the Free Lunch Project contributed to the creation of the National Nutrition Subsidies Policy ("to promote public policy through grassroots actions"), which may significantly change the structural factors of hunger and malnutrition on a much larger scale. Second, the Free Lunch Project provided a new model for grassroots actions to influence state policy, which may have a long and lasting impact on how these actions contribute to development and social change in Chinese society.

On December 28, 2012, the *China Youth Daily* published an article by Ye Tieqiao titled "Public Policy on Rural Education Is Getting Back on the Right Track." In it, Ye called the Free Lunch Project a grassroots action that contributed to positive change in the central government's implementation of the National Nutrition Subsidies Policy for school students in rural areas: "After a year of implementation, the mode and the transparency policy of the National Nutrition Subsidies Project gradually moved toward those of the Free Lunch Project. . . . Projects supported by the National Nutrition Subsidies fund now conventionally employ the same method to publish their cost reports on Weibo to enhance project transparency" (Ye, 2012). This passage asserts that the Free Lunch Project influenced the implementation of the National Nutrition Subsidies Policy and increased the transparency of the Nationwide Nutrition Subsidies Project launched by the central government. L. Gu (2015) and W. Liu (2017) both hold that the Free Lunch Project complemented the weakness of the National Nutrition Subsidies Policy by offering a model emphasizing project transparency and by providing extra funds to cover the operational costs of the National Nutrition Project.

My analysis of the Free Lunch Project's policy documents, Deng's online postings, published and broadcast interviews with him, and news coverage of the Free Lunch Project indicate that the Free Lunch Project is not only a conventional development project to provide food to rural children but also a grassroots action to fight inequality between rural China and urban China. Moreover, the analysis also illustrates that this action has brought about society-wide change—as well as immediate and individual level change—through its programs and its influence on public policy related to this issue.

Channels and Technologies

As my analytic framework illustrates, communication channels and technologies are an important component of new media actions. This section explores the communication channels used in the Free Lunch Project, the interactions between these channels, and how these channels and ICTs are used in the fundraising, monitoring, evaluation, and mobilization process of the project.

The Importance of New Media and ICTs

In my earlier analysis of Tiger Gate (chapter 4)—a landmark of online actions from 2007—I showed how ICTs such as internet forums, blogs, and IMs played a significant role in that action for social change. ICTs such as forums and bulletin boards, blogs, and IMs have played a very important role in various aspects of the Free Lunch Project. In this case, however, my analysis of new media and ICTs will focus on new ICTs and new phenomena that make the Free Lunch Project different from past online actions like Tiger Gate. The Free Lunch Project strategy statement asserts, "Our strategy is to explore the safe, transparent, highly efficient, and replicable free lunch model, to provide professional (free lunch) service to the government, corporations, NGOs, and individual donors, and to promote public policy through strategic philanthropy" (Free Lunch Project, 2018a). Thus, in my analysis, I will emphasize how ICTs and new media have helped achieve the strategic goals of the Free Lunch Project.

Microblogs as a Tool to Promote Transparency in the Free Lunch Project. Since 2009, microblogs, or *weibo* in Chinese, have gradually become one of the most widely used internet services in Chinese cyberspace.[9] Chapter 3 examined how the Weibo microblogging website is used by the NGO 2.0 Project in its advocacy. For the Free Lunch Project, Weibo played the important role of increasing transparency.

Since the very beginning of the project, transparency has been one of the core concerns, as Deng and other leading activists in the action have repeatedly emphasized (Deng, 2011, 2014; L. Gu, 2015; Tian, 2015; F. Zhang, 2012). Deng stated, "Because of our background as investigative journalists, we know that transparency of information is crucial for the project and is the fundamental qualification for us to conduct the project" (Deng, 2011c). In his book, Deng (2014) further explained: "This is simple logic: To make the project sustainable, we must have donations. To attract donations, we need to persuade donors to trust us. To gain the trust of the donors, we need to keep the project open and transparent. We must tell the public what we are doing, the effects of the project, and how each donation is used." Xiao Xinglong, chair of the Free Lunch foundation steering committee, asserted that after a year of implementation, the Free Lunch Project had won the trust of the public through openness and transparency (F. Zhang, 2012). In 2015, after four years of practice and hard work,

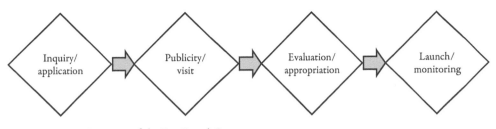

FIGURE 5.1 Processes of the Free Lunch Program

Deng and the leadership of the Free Lunch Project attributed the success of the project to openness and transparency (L. Gu, 2015; Tian, 2015).

Weibo is the major platform and tool being used to increase the transparency of various processes of the Free Lunch Project. According to the project's guidelines, four processes are involved in the free lunch program at every school that participates (see figure 5.1) (Free Lunch Project, 2020b).

During the publicity and visit process, a school must open an official Weibo account, publish all its application materials—especially a detailed lunch budget—and answer all the questions raised by activists and ordinary netizens on Weibo, as well as those of the Free Lunch Project team. The school also needs to be endorsed by at least two volunteers who have visited the school within the last six months. These volunteers must fill out a report verifying all the information that the school has provided in its application materials, then post it to their Weibo pages. Participating schools also need to forward these endorsement posts to their own Weibo accounts (Free Lunch Project, 2020b).

As part of the monitoring process, schools must update their Weibo every business day and post at least four pieces of data regarding the lunches: estimated cost, real cost, balance, and the number of students who ate those lunches (Free Lunch Project, 2020b). Thus, anyone with an interest can monitor the program's implementation through the information published on Weibo and can share posts from the school with other Weibo users. On Weibo, they can post any question requiring further clarification from the school. To increase the transparency of their programs, many rural schools post detailed lunch menus and photos of the lunches in their Weibo posts. As shown in figure 5.2, the Weibo of the Furong Primary School in Mati Xiang indicates that as of June 30, 2020, 191 people were monitoring the school's free lunch program. On that day, the school published on its Weibo detailed information regarding the lunch menu, the cost of the lunch, the total number of students who ate the lunch, and photos of the lunch.

To effectively achieve transparency in its programs, the Free Lunch Project must consider the digital divide between participating schools, which are located in underdeveloped rural regions, and concerned activists and donors, who live in relatively developed urban regions. Many of the participating schools do not have access to the internet and computers. To facilitate internet communications

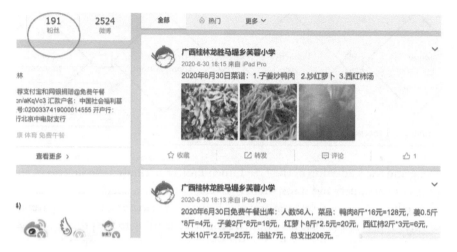

FIGURE 5.2 Weibo Post of Furong Primary School in Mati Xiang, Longsheng County, Guilin Prefecture, Guangxi Province (2020)

between rural schools without internet access and Free Lunch Project activists and donors on Weibo represents a significant hurdle. Fortunately, Weibo has a new feature that can help bridge the urban–rural divide. Weibo accounts can be tied to specific cell phone numbers to send and receive Weibo posts via text messages and multimedia messaging services (MMSs) through mobile phone networks, without having to access the internet.[10] To link a cell phone number to a Weibo account, a user need only log in to a personal Weibo account and input a cell phone number there. The user can then upload posts to the Weibo account by sending text messages to the number 1069 009 009.[11] Those posts will automatically appear in the Weibo account in real time. Any replies or comments to those Weibo posts will be automatically sent to the user's cell phone by text message as well (Weibo.com, 2020).[12]

After the implementation of the Connecting Every Village Project (discussed in chapter 2), a nationwide mobile phone network was established that penetrated almost every corner of rural China. According to China's Ministry of Industry and Information Technology, 98 percent of China's population was linked to a mobile phone network by 2011 (MIIT, 2011a), indicating that schools in underdeveloped regions would have already attained mobile network access. Moreover, because the link feature is based on text messaging and MMS technology, a basic $20 non-smartphone device is sufficient to support all the needed functions to communicate by text and MMS with other users on Weibo. Moreover, the service fees for text messaging and MMS in China are very low. For example, sending a text message costs only about a penny, and receiving limitless numbers of text messages is generally free. By linking school Weibo accounts to cell phones through this Weibo feature, teachers and volunteers at disadvantaged rural schools without computers and internet access can communicate with Free Lunch Project activists and donors on Weibo for a very low cost.

Because Weibo is used as its primary communication platform, the Free Lunch Project must also consider the length limits of posts for most microblog services. Like Twitter, the maximum length of a Weibo post is 140 Chinese characters. This length limit becomes a problem for any communications longer than 140 characters. For example, the application forms and detailed budgets of school free lunch programs, which schools are required to publish on their Weibo account during the inquiry/application process (see Figure 5.1), are generally much longer than 140 characters. Activists have developed an innovative way to overcome these length limits. Weibo allows users to attach images to their posts. Thus, by converting any texts that are longer than 140 characters, such as budgets, into images that can be posted, Free Lunch Project activists, school volunteers, and donors have successfully overcome the length limits of microblogging.[13] In its application guidelines, the Free Lunch Project includes a detailed introduction on how to overcome the length-limit problem (Free Lunch Project, 2020b).

Online Shopping and Mobile Payment Platforms as Safe and Efficient Channels for Microdonations. Since 2003, online shopping and online payment platforms have gradually become important online services in China. According to the China Internet Network Information Center, 79.7 percent of Chinese internet users (749 million in total) have used online shopping services as of June 2020 (CNNIC, 2020b). Online shopping platforms such as Taobao.com and Tmall.com, and online payment platforms such as Alipay have been important tools and platforms in increasing the safety, transparency, and efficiency of microdonations for the Free Lunch Project.[14]

By December 2014, the Free Lunch Project (2015a) had received roughly 100 million yuan in donations from millions of people, with microdonations by individuals amounting to almost 70 percent of its 41-million-yuan revenue from donations in 2014 alone. To ensure the safety and efficiency of the donation process for this huge number of donors, the Free Lunch Project used the online shopping platform Taobao.com as a new donation platform, in addition to traditional bank transfers. On July 13, 2011, with the support of Taobao.com and the China Social Welfare Foundation, the Free Lunch Project opened an online store at Taobao.com (Free Lunch Online Store, 2016). Donators could donate three yuan to the Free Lunch Project simply by purchasing a three-yuan virtual product from this online store.[15] In 2018, the online store of the Free Lunch Project migrated to Tmall.com, Alibaba's business-to-consumer platform, where it is now called the Free Lunch Project Online Store at Tmall. As of 2019, 23.9 million yuan (or 19.33% of its 123.6-million-yuan revenue) has come from this online store, increasing 49.4 percent over the year before (Free Lunch Project, 2020a).

Compared with traditional donation channels such as bank transfers, Taobao.com/Tmall.com provides a free, safe, transparent, and efficient donation platform for donors. First, all donations can be made for free at the Free Lunch store through the Taobao.com/Tmall.com online shopping service, whereas bank transfers usually entail a 1 percent service fee.[16] Second, all donations made to the Free Lunch store at Taobao.com/Tmall.com, like all other online commercial transactions on the platforms, are protected by the payment system used by Taobao.com/Tmaill.com, thereby enhancing the security of the donation process. Third, donors can check the history of their online donations by visiting their user accounts on the online shopping platforms, where a history of all their online transactions is recorded. Donors can also check how many people have bought the virtual products (i.e., donated to the Free Lunch Project) and read their comments on the donation process, thereby increasing the transparency of the Free Lunch Project.[17] Fourth, Taobao.com and Tmall.com have reached almost 880 million users as of 2020 (Alibaba, 2020). The online donation service of the Free Lunch store at Taobao.com/Tmall.com thus provides an efficient and convenient way for a huge number of Taobao.com/Tmall.com users to donate to the Free Lunch Project. In 2018, the Alibaba Group—the owner of Taobao.com and Tmall.com—launched its Goods for Good program to facilitate NGOs and other public welfare organizations raising funds from online sellers. Participating sellers in the Goods for Good program pledged to donate a certain percentage of the price of their products to their designated NGOs and other public welfare organizations. When customers purchase products with a Goods for Good label on Taobao or Tmall, the system transfers the donations directly to the chosen organizations. The Goods for Good program became a new means of raising funds for the Free Lunch Project on these online shopping platforms. As of 2019, the Free Lunch Project had brought in 16.1 million yuan (or 13.02% of its 123.6 million revenue) from this new channel (Free Lunch Project, 2020a).

Alipay, China's leading third-party online payment solution, overtook PayPal in 2013 to become the world's largest mobile payment system. In 2014, as mobile payments and smartphones became increasingly popular among Chinese urban residents—the Free Lunch Project's primary donor group—the Free Lunch Project began collaborating with Alipay and employing new technologies such as QR codes to streamline the donation process via smartphone and mobile internet.[18] In order to donate to the Free Lunch Project, anyone with an Alipay application installed on a smartphone need only scan the QR code using the application's QR code scanner and then confirm the donation amount.[19] One need not access the internet in any part of this process, as the payment is completed through a mobile phone network. In Alipay, users can also scan the QR code to set up a monthly donation, invite their friends to donate to the Free Lunch Project together, and check the real-time information of online donations of the Free Lunch Project and their own history of donations. Online

Table 5.1

Free Lunch Project Donations from Different Channels

Year	Bank transfers (%)	Online donations (Alipay and 51give)[a](%)	Tenpay	Free Lunch Project Online Store (Taobao/ T mall) (%)	Alibaba Goods for Good program	Other (%)	Total in donations (yuan)
2011	65.23	13.89		20.39		0.47	11,964,632.88
2012	55.12	13.89		22.53		8.46	25,438,705.59
2013	65.99	8.77		14.68		10.56	33,010,916.89
2014	50.78	28.28		13.79		7.17	41,382,915.50
2015	46.12	33.39		16.49		3.57	59,329,896.52
2016	48.84	28.77		18.88		3.50	75,727,696.33
2017	14.22	41.18	33.42%	10.72		0.46	115,367,329.38
2018	8.92	41.35	28.69%	13.97	5.84%	1.23	114,389,759.02
2019	7.91	35.16	23.22%	19.33	13.20%	1.18	123,580,740.03

SOURCE: Financial Reports of the Free Lunch Project (from 2011 to 2019).

[a] The Free Lunch Project's financial report does not disaggregate Alipay donations from those coming through 51give in its final reports from 2011 to 2016. Since 2017, the proportion of donations in the column are all from Alipay. 51give was no longer listed as a donation channel in the project's financial reports since 2017.

promotions, as well as newspaper and magazine advertisements, subway posters, and other offline promotions for the Free Lunch Project, use this QR code extensively. According to the annual financial report of the Free Lunch Project, donations made through Alipay and 51give online donation platforms increased 304.1% in 2014 over the previous year.[20] Alipay and 51give were responsible for 11.7 million yuan (or 28.28% of its total revenue of 41.38 million yuan) (2015a). The Free Lunch Project attributed this huge increase to its collaboration with Alipay and the increasing popularity of mobile payments in China. By November 2017, 18,702,043 people had donated 91,782,850 yuan to the Free Lunch Project through Alipay (Alipay, 2017). In the mid-2010s, WeChat rose to be the most used social media app in the increasingly saturated Chinese mobile internet. As of 2017, 84.3 percent of Chinese internet users used WeChat (CNNIC, 2017b). Accordingly, WeChat's mobile payment system, Tenpay, became a strong rival to Alipay, gaining 37 percent of China's mobile payment market as of 2016 ("Race for China's $5.5tn Mobile Payment Market," 2017). To adapt to this new context, the Free Lunch Project also worked with Tenpay and designed a second QR code to facilitate WeChat users donating to the project through Tenpay.

The data in table 5.1 highlight the success of fundraising for the Free Lunch Project. From 2011 to 2019, its annual revenue from donations increased tenfold (from 11,964,632.88 to 123,580,740.03 yuan).

The data in the table reveal dramatic shifts in the fundraising platforms and channels used for donations—that is, the rise of mobile payment platforms and online shopping platforms, and the rapid decline of traditional channels such as bank transfers. Between 2011 and 2019, the proportion of donations from mobile payment platforms (Alipay and Tenpay) quadrupled (from 13.89% to 58.38%), making them the dominant channel for the project's fundraising since 2017. Meanwhile, donations through bank transfers rapidly declined, from 65.23 percent to 7.91 percent. The proportion of donations from online shopping platforms, including the project's online store at Taobao.com/Tmall .com and Alibaba's Goods for Good program, fluctuated each year yet consistently made up a substantial part of the project's fundraising. The data also indicate that the project's collaborations with mobile payment platforms and effective use of mobile internet technologies (such as QR codes) in fundraising and promotion have likely contributed to this enormous success.

A Multichannel Perspective

Since the very beginning of the Free Lunch Project, activists have considered mass media to be an important part of their communication strategy. For example, Deng (2011c) stated: "[In our previous new media actions], we found that Weibo can be used to mobilize people. . . . We can mobilize and organize thousands of netizens to find a solution for a problem. . . . When the free lunch issue is proposed, the first step of our action is to show the suffering of children [on Weibo]. The second step is using the hot discussions of the suffering of children on Weibo to attract the mass media to report this issue in depth. Then, we could further mobilize millions of urban residents." Based on this comment, Deng views mass media and the interactions between new media and conventional mass media (using hot online discussions to attract mass media coverage, for example) as important components in the Free Lunch Project's communication strategy. Deng's description illustrates how the Free Lunch Project's communication strategy used a multichannel approach to mobilize the public.

The Free Lunch Project also employed a multichannel approach to increasing the transparency of its programs. Mass media, interpersonal communication, and other communication channels, as well as ICT channels such as Weibo, have been used to promote the transparency of free lunch programs. For example, Deng (2011c) noted: "Every school must open its own Weibo account. The free lunch programs in schools must be monitored through Weibo every day, otherwise, monthly cost reports may have problems. . . . Every school posts its daily cost reports on Weibo, we then forward their Weibo posts to other netizens. People around the country are watching, thus there is very little chance that costs [of free lunches] might be manipulated." This indicates how Weibo had a very significant role in increasing the transparency of the free lunch programs in rural schools. Deng went on to say: "We also give our phone numbers to the students' parents. If they discover that their kids don't have lunch . . .

they can report to us at any time. Besides, we have also recruited local volunteers. Once there is some problem, we will have our local volunteers come to the school to investigate. . . . Local media also play an important role to ensure the transparency of the projects." This illustrates that interpersonal communication channels, such as phone calls and visits by local volunteers, as well as mass media coverage, have also been used to increase the transparency of the free lunch programs in rural schools.

In-depth analysis of the communication channels used in all the processes of a free lunch program in a rural school will further reveal the importance of different communication channels and the interactions between those channels in specific free lunch programs. By analyzing the application guidelines and other documents from the Free Lunch Project and observing the interactions on two schools' Weibo pages with details of their free lunch programs, I identified five processes that operated in each program within the Free Lunch Project (see table 5.2).

The third column in table 5.2 illustrates the different communication channels operating in the five processes of a school's free lunch program, including ICT-based communication channels such as email and Weibo, interpersonal communication, and mass media. In the inquiry/application process and the evaluation/appropriation process, email plays the most important role. In the publicity process and the implementation/monitoring process, Weibo plays a very important role. In the implementation/monitoring process, local mass media also play a role. In the visit process, face-to-face interpersonal communication plays the most important role. Face-to-face communication with local community members, including teachers, students, and local residents, is the only way that Free Lunch Project volunteers can gain information about a school, the food prices at nearby farmers markets, and the current status of student lunches, which are crucial for evaluating each program. Only through face-to-face communication with the local community of the school can volunteers verify the information in the school's application materials, which are submitted through email. Thus, interpersonal communication plays a vital role in ensuring the success of the free lunch program in each school.

In my analysis of Tiger Gate (chapter 4), I showed that mass media and new media interact with and reinforce each other in new media actions. Similarly, the processes of free lunch programs in table 5.2 demonstrate how ICT-based communication and interpersonal communication interact with and reinforce each other (see figure 5.3).

In the publicity process, the school posts its application materials for its free lunch program, including school information, detailed budgets, and a student roster on Weibo. Free Lunch Project activists may ask questions regarding the school's application materials. The application materials and the interaction between school and activists on Weibo provide the preliminary information about the school and its free lunch program for the volunteers who visit the

Table 5.2
Processes of a School Free Lunch Program

Process	Content	Main communication channel
Inquiry/ application	The school completes the application materials, including application form, introduction of the school, detailed budget of its free lunch program, and student roster, and sends the e-version of all application materials to the Free Lunch Project.	Email
Publicity	The school must open its official Weibo account and publish all application materials, especially a detailed budget of its free lunch program, and answer all questions from activists, ordinary netizens on Weibo, and the Free Lunch Project team.	Weibo
Visit	At least two volunteers visit the school to communicate with teachers, students, and other local community members. They verify the information in the school's application materials, learn about information about the students, the quality of infrastructure, the current status of lunches at the school, and so on.	Interpersonal communication
	Volunteers then fill out a Free Lunch Project Field Visit Report, detailing the status of the power and water supply at the school, the status of telecommunications, the prices of food at nearby farmers markets, and so on, and include a recommendation as to whether free lunches are needed at the school.	
	The volunteers publish the Free Lunch Project Field Visit Report on Weibo and endorse the school's application for free lunches.	Weibo
Evaluation/ appropriation	The Committee of School Management of the Free Lunch Project sends all the materials to the Free Lunch Project team.	Email
	The team members vote in the email list to decide whether to support a free lunch program at the school. If it passes, the Free Lunch Project will provide the funding for the first month of free lunches.	
Implementation/ monitoring	The school is required to update its Weibo every business day and post at least four pieces of data regarding the lunch: estimated cost, real cost, balance, and number of students at lunch. Activists, ordinary netizens, and the Free Lunch Project team monitor the implementation of the program on Weibo.	Weibo, phone, interpersonal communication, mass media
	The parents of students report to the Free Lunch Project by phone if they suspect anything is wrong with the implementation of the program.	
	Local volunteers around the school and inspectors from the Free Lunch Project visit the school and inquire about the implementation of the program.	
	Local mass media outlets report any misconduct regarding the implementation of the program.	

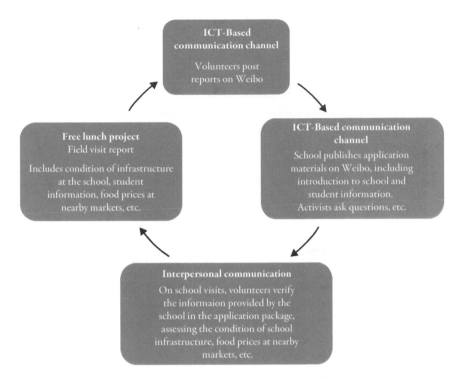

FIGURE 5.3 Interactions between ICT-Based Communication and Interpersonal Communication

school. Through face-to-face interpersonal communication during the visit process, volunteers verify the information regarding the school and its free lunch program and learn more detailed information about the school and its local community. Then volunteers construct more detailed and verified information about the school and its free lunch program in their Field Visit Report. Through posting these reports, more detailed and verified information about the school and its free lunch program is fed back into Weibo, the major online communication space of the Free Lunch Project, thus reinforcing the collective knowledge of the school and its free lunch program and helping to prepare that knowledge for the evaluation/appropriation process and the implementation/monitoring process.

Interpersonal communication plays a very important role in inspections, as well as visits, in ensuring transparency, accountability, and effective monitoring in free lunch programs at rural schools. According to inspection reports, through systematic and purposeful observation during inspections, interviews with members of the rural school community, surveys of students, and reviews of accounting information, inspectors from the Free Lunch Project effectively evaluate the sanitation status of school kitchens and dining rooms, the quality and nutrition of the lunches, the management and accounting of the programs, and student satisfaction, as well as other significant issues related to free lunch programs at rural schools (Supervision Center of the Free Lunch Project, 2017b, 2020). Inspectors also need to verify the number of students submitted by the schools and investigate potential discrepancies between the prices of lunch foods posted on Weibo and those at local markets, the possible outsourcing of lunches to individuals or corporations, and other issues related to free lunches. To facilitate the inspection process, the project developed a fifty-item evaluation form covering four categories of issues related to free lunches: sanitation, quality of lunches, program implementation and management, and accounting. Project inspectors are full-time members of the project or trained volunteers from different parts of the country.

Weibo and aspects of the Free Lunch Project model, such as requiring schools to publish the cost, account balance, and number of students at lunch, have increased the transparency of the free lunch programs in rural schools and enhanced the capacity of the public to monitor them. Yet the Free Lunch Project realized early on the limitations of this ICT-mediated program monitoring method, such as the inability to verify the information published by the schools on Weibo. Therefore, they implemented inspections to address the various weaknesses of ICT-mediated program monitoring and to serve as another method for enhancing the transparency and accountability of free lunch programs in rural schools. As the Free Lunch Project stated: "Inspections are the most important method for the Free Lunch Project to evaluate and monitor the implementation of free lunch programs in participating schools. Through irregular spot checks, the project will be able to learn about the real status of free lunch programs in the schools, evaluate the implementation of the programs, and ensure food safety and appropriate use of the funds [from the Free Lunch Project] in the rural schools" (Supervision Center of the Free Lunch Project, 2017a).

The first official inspection report of the project dates back to November 3, 2011. Comparing the first several inspection reports (November 3, 2011, November 24, 2011, and January 10, 2012) with those in 2017 illustrates the significant change that has occurred in the content and form of inspection reports. Early inspection reports did not have an evaluation system and did not address many issues in the fifty-item evaluation form. Yet from the earliest inspection reports to the inspection reports in 2017, the following was highlighted in red at the bottom of each report: "We firmly believe: A system without transparency and accountability inevitably leads to corruption, and a Free Lunch Project without inspections is inevitably unsustainable!" (Free Lunch Project, 2017b). This indicates that the Free Lunch Project has consistently considered inspection-based interpersonal communication to be a crucial component to ensure the transparency of its programs, which activists of the project have called "the fundamental qualification for us to conduct the project" (Deng, 2011c). In 2012, the Free Lunch Project inspected 58 percent (116 of 205) of the participating schools in the project. It withdrew its financial support from four schools due to serious problems related to mismanaging funds or publishing false information about the number of students eating lunches, which were detected during the inspections (Free Lunch Project, 2013a).

In the Free Lunch Project, ICT-mediated program monitoring and interpersonal communication–based inspections complement each other to enhance the transparency of free lunch programs in rural schools. A substantial part of the inspection and inspection report is designed to address the lack of verification in Weibo-based program monitoring. For example, when arriving at a school, the inspector must immediately count the number of students at the school. In the first part of the inspection report, the inspector must provide a detailed breakdown of the number of students at the school by grade and must compare the number of students counted in the inspection with that provided by the school. The inspector also needs to paste a screenshot of the school's Weibo post on the inspection day right behind the breakdown of the number of students. If there are any discrepancies between the posted number of students at lunch and the number in the inspection, the inspector must highlight it as an "important problem," which the school must further clarify. Among the eleven "important problems" that require formal clarification from schools, four are directly related to verification of the information the schools publish on Weibo: (1) discrepancies between the reported number of students at lunch and the number in an inspection exceeding 5 percent; (2) unreliability of the information published on Weibo; (3) unreliability of the information provided by the school regarding the kinds, quantity, and costs of food products; and (4) noticeably higher pricing of the foods used in lunches than is found at local markets. The inspector also needs to examine issues that ICT-mediated monitoring is unable to address, such as the quality and taste of the lunches, the management of free lunch funds at the school, and whether students wash their hands before eating.

Inspection-based interpersonal communication is a good method to address many of the weaknesses of ICT-mediated program monitoring. Yet due to limited human and financial resources, the Free Lunch Project is unable to monitor the daily implementation of its programs in participating schools. For example, most schools that joined the Free Lunch Project in 2011 were inspected only between two and five times from 2011 to 2020 (Free Lunch Project, 2020d). This means that the project could inspect a school only once every two to four years.

The data in table 5.3 indicates that while the number of schools in the project has generally increased every year from 2012 to 2020, the percentage of schools that were inspected has reduced from around 60% to around 36%. For example, in 2012, 56.6 percent (116 of 205) of participating schools were inspected, whereas in 2019, only 36.4 percent of participating schools (308 out of 845) were inspected. Weibo and the model developed by the Free Lunch Project provide a real-time, low-cost method for the public to monitor the free lunch programs in participating schools. By implementing this dual approach, the project increased

Table 5.3
Number of Inspected Schools and Total Number of Schools in the Free Lunch Project (2012 to 2020)

Year	Number of inspected schools	Total number of schools	Percentage
2012	116	205	56.6
2013	216	381	56.7
2014	232	381	60.9
2015	183	420	43.6
2016	211	585	36.1
2017	252	734	34.3
2018	312	848	36.8
2019	308	845	36.4
2020	139	1,079	12.9[a]

[a] Due to the unusual impact of COVID-19, data regarding 2020 was not included in the discussion.

the transparency of its programs and promoted the participation of the public in the project. Eventually, through transparency and efficient use and management of donations, the Free Lunch Project aims to gain sustainable support from the public to "ensure that more and more children [in China] will get free lunches" (Free Lunch Project, 2017d).

The Sustainability of the Free Lunch Project's Communications

Past studies evaluating the sustainability of development projects in communication for development indicate that the compatibility of the chosen channels with the capacities of actors and with structural factors, such as telecommunication infrastructure, is an important factor that must be considered (Servaes et al., 2012). In this case, activists, the NGO (the Free Lunch Project), project donors, government agencies, and the rural school community—including teachers, parents, students, and local volunteers—are all major actors (stakeholders) in the Free Lunch Project. The communication channels used in the project include ICT channels, such as Weibo; newspapers and other mainstream mass media outlets; and interpersonal communication channels. Among these channels, Weibo plays the core role in being the platform and providing the space for the interactions and communication among different stakeholders (actors). The major concern for the project with regard to communication channels is whether Weibo fits the capacity and the structural factors in the rural school communities. Most of the schools in underdeveloped or less developed regions fall on the disadvantaged side of the digital divide. In van Dijk's (2005, p. 22) cumulative model of access to digital technology, material access (or possession of an internet access device and internet access) is a significant structural factor that affects rural school communities' use of Weibo (van Dijk, 2005, p. 21). In the early stages of the Free Lunch Project, many of these rural schools did not have stable

Table 5.4
Fengjia Zheng Primary School's Weibo Posts in November 2015 and November 2016

Date	Number of posts	Posts by computer	Posts by cell phone text message	Total words	Words per post	Posts with images	Total number of images
November 2015	21	0	21	2,615	124.5	0	0
November 2016	21	21	0	3,891	185.2	11	57

access to the internet. As mentioned earlier, in schools without access to the internet, teachers and volunteers could send and get Weibo posts through text messages or an MMS by tying their Weibo accounts to their cell phone numbers. When sending more complex contents, such as application materials in Word files, teachers or program volunteers generally had to go to the nearest internet café, usually in a nearby town, to use a computer with internet access. This significantly limited the capacity of the rural school communities to use Weibo. Due to the increasing popularity of smartphones and mobile internet in rural regions in recent years, following the implementation of the Connecting Every Village Project (see chapter 2), most of the rural schools in the Free Lunch Project had already gained relatively stable access to the internet, which significantly improved their capacity to use Weibo. Fengjia Zheng Primary School in Xinghua County, Hunan Province, was one of the first seven schools supported by the Free Lunch Project. Before January 2016, almost all of its Weibo posts were created as cell phone–based text messages. Around January 2016, it acquired internet access. From February 2016 on, those at the school began using smartphones and computers to create Weibo posts. Comparing this rural school's use of Weibo before and after gaining stable access to the internet, using all the Weibo posts of the school in November 2015 and November 2016, I found that the school made a total of twenty-one Weibo posts in November 2015, all by cell phone–based text message. A year later, the school made twenty-one posts—all by computer.

Table 5.4 shows that the school's Weibo posts in November 2016 contained more detailed textual information about the lunches, with almost 1.5 times as many words per post as a year before. And more than half of the posts in 2016 included photos to convey more vivid information about the lunches. These included high-resolution photos of the lunch dishes and photos of students receiving their lunch trays. The November 2015 posts, however, contained no images. Moreover, each Weibo post published in November 2016 by computer used the @ method to inform the Free Lunch Project and the regional coordinator of the Free Lunch Project that the post for each lunch had been published. The posts created through text messaging never used Weibo's @

feature. This indicates that the expansion of rural internet access and the popularity of computers and smartphones increased the capacity of rural school communities to provide more detailed and vivid information about the free lunches on Weibo and improved the efficiency of coordinating the Free Lunch Project. This also indicates that material access was no longer a major obstacle to using Weibo for rural school communities. Structural factors in rural school communities had become more compatible with the demands of Weibo.

Weibo, a leading social networking service in China, is widely used to construct and sustain social networks. It is also a space for urban activists, the Free Lunch Project, donors, and other urban netizens to communicate, discuss, and debate issues related to the Free Lunch Project and the National Nutrition Project. Yet in November 2015 and November 2016, all the postings by Fengjia Zheng Primary School were required reports about the cost of lunches for a current day. Over those two months, the school never posted any other information, nor did any user retweet any of the posts. Only one user posted a comment in November 2015, and the school never responded to it. In November 2016, there were no user comments on the school's posts. This indicates that gaining physical access to the internet did not increase interactions between the rural school community and urban activists and donors. Weibo, which has the potential to be a two-way social-network-building communication tool, was used almost exclusively as a one-way data reporting tool by the rural schools. In Weibo, rural school communities are almost voiceless in the space where urban activists, the Free Lunch Project, donors, and the urban public discuss the Free Lunch Project and the National Nutrition Project. Their health, their lives, and their futures are directly affected by the Free Lunch Project and the National Nutrition Project; yet the members of these rural communities are voiceless in Weibo online discussions about the two projects. This lack of communication poses a significant risk to the Free Lunch Project. Weibo does enhance information transparency and effective project monitoring among Free Lunch Project organizers, participants, and urban activists. Yet it does not operate as a communication channel that promotes productive participatory communication and interactions between the rural school community and urban activists, the Free Lunch Project team, and donors. From the perspective of communication for development, Weibo is used only to disseminate information, despite its power to promote participatory communication.

The inability of rural schools to use Weibo as a channel to participate in online discussions regarding the Free Lunch Project indicates that technology advancement alone cannot bridge the digital divide. Disparities in the use of ICTs and related unequal participation within society will persist despite the removal of barriers to physical access. This also suggests that motivational access and skills access barriers are the primary sources of this inability, as put forth in van Dijk's (2005) model. As discussed in chapter 3, Weibo and other Web 2.0 technologies represent fundamental changes in the use of the internet and consequently require users to change their mindset in order to use them effectively. Therefore, those in the rural school community may not understand Weibo's potential or be aware of the significance of interacting with activists, donors, and other netizens to develop sustainable support for various activities in their own communities. In turn, they are simply not motivated to use Weibo as a space for communications with the outside world.

Given the low literacy in new media technology among those in underdeveloped regions of China, rural schoolteachers, parents, and students in those areas may also lack the skills and knowledge to effectively use and manage Weibo. For example, on Fengjia Zheng Primary School's Weibo, there is almost no interaction. In a year of Weibo posts, the school posted 142 reports of its lunch costs and one greeting to the Free Lunch Project team members at the end of fall semester 2015. The most used skill is publishing texts and images in a post and including @ the Free Lunch Project and its regional coordinator in Weibo. Other skills have seldom been used by teachers or others at the school. Like many NGOs in underdeveloped regions (discussed in chapter 3), rural school communities may have gained operational skills to use computers, but they lack the skills to fully operate Web 2.0 tools such as Weibo, informational skills in the Web 2.0 age, and especially strategic skills for using online sources as a means of improving their positions in society.

In short, primarily because of skills access barriers and the lack of motivation to use Weibo to interact with the outside world, the limitations of rural school communities and their incompatibility with Weibo may put the Free Lunch Project's communication at risk. However, there are steps the Free Lunch Project could take to mitigate this problem. First, the project could incorporate ICT training workshops and training materials to enhance the ICT capacity of the rural school community and to help them overcome the skills access and motivational access barriers to use Weibo and ICTs to interact and communicate with the outside world. Although the Free Lunch Project already has volunteers who help the schools set up their Weibo account, ICT training workshops to help rural school communities learn how to effectively use Weibo and other ICTs are unfortunately not part of the project. To remedy this, the Free Lunch Project could cooperate with the NGO 2.0 Project and other NGO-led ICT training projects to provide training workshops and materials for rural schoolteachers or local volunteers involved in the Free Lunch Project or the National Nutrition Subsidies Project. These training workshops would focus on motivational issues, skills to effectively operate Web 2.0 technologies, informational skills, and strategic skills. The Free Lunch Project could also encourage local school-to-school or NGO-to-school ICT collaboration and nourish local ICT support networks among schools, the NGO, and local governments.

Second, the Free Lunch Project could change the major channels it uses to communicate with the rural school community. The first approach focuses on changing the capacity of the rural school community to help these schools effectively communicate with urban activists, the NGO, and donors on Weibo. The second approach, a more participatory approach, is to change the channels used by the Free Lunch Project and activists to communicate with the rural school community. Rather than exposing the rural school community to Weibo—the most used communication channel for urban activists and the NGO—the Free Lunch Project would listen to the voices in that rural school community and ask what the most effective ways would be for that community to communicate with activists, the Free Lunch Project, project donors, and the urban public. This approach to enhancing the communication of the project is concerned with a more fundamental change regarding the monitoring of the project's programs. The current model relies heavily on urban activists monitoring the programs remotely through Weibo and urban inspectors traveling to rural schools to conduct program evaluations. This does increase the transparency of the free lunch programs in rural schools; however, without local level engagement, the effectiveness and the sustainability of project monitoring is at risk. Deng Fei also acknowledged this risk in his interview with the media. When asked to name some of his regrets concerning the implementation of the Free Lunch Project, he stated, "The most perfect model for us is to connect the local community with the schools. Let the local community monitor the programs in the schools . . . rather than us. We didn't do very well in this respect" (H. Fu, 2012). Thus, involving local communities in its programs and nourishing local-level monitoring of programs primarily through interpersonal communication in those communities would significantly enhance the effectiveness of the Free Lunch Project.

6

Contention and Reciprocity in the Free Lunch Project

Complex and Multidimensional Relations between Activists, the State, and Corporations

On the relationship between the Free Lunch Project and the government, Deng Fei has said, "We are brave government critics as well as pragmatic action-takers" (Deng, 2014). This illustrates a new, complex, and multidimensional relationship between activists and the government in actions for development and social change in contemporary China. Over the past ten years, activists and the Free Lunch Project have constantly contended with the government as well as big corporations in their efforts to solve the hunger and malnutrition problem among children in underdeveloped rural China. At the same time, however, they have worked in concert with different levels of government and government agencies that are willing to address the problem cooperatively. The complex relationship between various stakeholders in this case demonstrates that bottom-up actions led by activists have the potential to solve deep-seated development problems and foster social change within authoritarian state structures. Yet this entails a difficult process that requires a long-term commitment by activists and NGOs and long-term support by the public. Efforts by activists and NGOs to bring about development and social change may be met with constant resistance and obstruction by the government and corporations, which may even collaborate together in that resistance.

Reciprocal Relations between Activists and the Government

As I have shown in previous chapters, stakeholder relationships are an important component in the analysis of new media actions. This section explores the reciprocal relationships between activists and the government in the Free Lunch Project. And it examines how this grassroots action influenced the National Nutrition Subsidies Policy of the Chinese government and increased transparency in its implementation.

First, the policy documents of the Free Lunch Project illustrate the reciprocal relationship between the Free Lunch Project and the government. In its strategy statement, the Free Lunch Project states: "Our strategy is to explore the safe, transparent, high-efficient, and replicable free lunch model, to provide professional [free lunch] service to the government, corporations, NGOs, and individual donors, and to promote public policy through strategic philanthropy" (Free Lunch Project, 2018a). This demonstrates that from the very beginning, based on its long-term strategy, the Free Lunch Project considers itself to be a service provider for multiple stakeholders, including the government. The government will benefit from the safe, transparent, and efficient free lunch services provided by the Free Lunch Project (the NGO). Moreover, the Free Lunch Project aims to "promote public policy through strategic philanthropy," meaning that the project believes that the government will also benefit from taking the Free Lunch Project as an exemplar and develop a similar policy to eliminate hunger and malnutrition among children in less developed regions.

The Free Lunch Project strategy statement also states: "To ensure that the donations will be effectively used to provide free lunches, volunteers should help the school open its Weibo account and publish the estimated and real costs of the free lunches every day. . . . At the same time we invite local government, media, NGOs, and parents . . . to monitor the implementation of the programs" (Free Lunch Project, 2018a). This indicates that the Free Lunch Project considers the government to be a stakeholder that could effectively help to monitor the implementation of its programs, and that the government's monitoring would benefit its school programs.

Second, the implementation of the project's programs reveals that in many cases, local governments cooperated with the Free Lunch Project to solve the hunger and malnutrition problem together. For example, Deng stated: "First, we have many officials who experienced hunger [when they were young]. . . . So they are very supportive in providing free lunches to our children. . . . Second, many officials are very open-minded. . . . They think the free lunch is a good thing because it solves the hunger problem for our children" (Deng, 2011c). He then gave two positive examples of local government collaboration with the Free

Lunch Project: "[In Xinghua County] we told them that we provide two yuan [per student/per day]; you [the local government] provide one yuan [per student/ per day]. Then you build the kitchen and we'll buy kitchenware and provide the cooks' salaries. . . . They immediately agreed. In Mashan County in Guangxi Province, we reached the same agreement. . . . They provide two and a half yuan [per student/per day]; we provide one yuan [per student/per day]" (Deng, 2011c).

The free lunch programs in Hefeng County, Hubei Province, offer a more detailed example of collaboration between the Free Lunch Project and local government. In December 2011, after two months of communications and negotiations, the Free Lunch Project and the local government in Hefeng signed a cooperative agreement to provide free lunches to 3,937 primary school students in rural Hefeng. The project provided two yuan, and the government provided one yuan per student per lunch. The government provided funding to build a kitchen and dining room for each school. The budget for the first year of free lunch programs in Hefeng was 5.98 million yuan. The local government offered up to 2.19 million yuan, and the project provided the rest. As part of the agreement, the local government was required to organize a special committee to monitor the implementation of free lunch programs in rural schools and maintain transparency and accountability of those programs. The government was also tasked with ensuring that all participating schools follow the Free Lunch Project guidelines by keeping samples of each lunch for forty-eight hours.[1] Deng Fei called this approach to collaboration with local government in Hefeng "the Hefeng Model," which he said could be replicated in other parts of the country (Deng, 2014). As of September 2020, after eight years of collaboration, the Free Lunch Project had provided 47.66 million yuan and the government had provided more than 25 million yuan for free lunch programs in Hefeng, where more than 110,000 students in fifty-five rural schools have benefited from these programs (J. Wang, 2020). With the support of local government, the Free Lunch Project has also introduced other projects for less developed regions in Hefeng, such as critical illness insurance for rural children. Deng Fei stated, "We will continue the strategy of multi-stakeholder collaboration and work for a win-win situation" (J. Hu, 2017). In 2017, the project was working to replicate the Hefeng Model in other less developed regions of Hubei Province.

Data from the inspection reports published by the Free Lunch Project and the Weibo posts of the schools also indicated that local governments collaborated with the Free Lunch Project in various ways. For example, the inspection report of the Ganxi Village Primary School at Hunan Huaihua, Xinhuang County, shows that the school had forty-four students, made up of thirty-one first and second grade students and thirteen preschool students. The National Nutrition Project provided lunches for the thirty-one first and second grade students but not for the thirteen preschool students, since preschool children are not eligible for the subsidies. To remediate this, the Free Lunch Project provided free lunches for the thirteen preschool students, three teachers, and one cook.

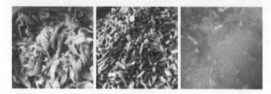

广西桂林龙胜马堤乡芙蓉小学 ∨
11月9日 15:36 来自 微博 weibo.com
芙蓉小学2017年11月9日：菜谱:猪肉炒豆角，猪肉炒莴笋，西红柿瘦肉汤。午餐
支出：猪肉25.3*13=328.9元，豆角20*3.5=70元，莴笋25*4=100元，西红柿
5*2.5=12.5元，红萝卜3*2.5=7.5元，大米32*2.5=80元。合计支出599元。应到人
数143人，实到人数143人，其中营养午餐88人，支出376.5元，免费午餐55人支
出222.5元，人均4.05元，免午结余19699.8元。收起全文 ∧

FIGURE 6.1 Furong Primary School's Weibo (November 9, 2017). The underlined sentence reads, "143 students were actually in the lunch [program]. The National Nutrition Lunch Project supported 88 of them. . . . The Free Lunch Project supported 55 of them."

The project also provided the cook's salary as well as funds to cover other operational costs related to school lunches, such as purchasing a refrigerator and kitchenware (Free Lunch Project, 2015b). The Weibo of the Furong Primary School at Mati Xiang, Longsheng County, Guangxi Province, indicates that the project and the government adopted a new form of collaboration: among the 143 students at the school, the National Nutrition Project supported lunches for 88 students and the Free Lunch Project supported free lunches for the remaining 55 students (Furong Primary School, 2017) (see figure 6.1). The active cooperation of local governments in these free lunch programs in rural schools demonstrates their reciprocal relations with the Free Lunch Project.

Third, statements by leading activists regarding the relationship between the Free Lunch Project and the National Nutrition Subsidies Project indicate the reciprocity of the project and the government at a broader level. On September 26, 2011, the *Jinghua Times* asked Deng about the Free Lunch Project's future plans if the government launched its National Nutrition Subsidies Project:

> From the very beginning, our goal is to promote the government's intervention [to solve the hunger and malnutrition problem]. . . . Large-scale changes can hardly be achieved merely through grassroots donations. They require financial supports from the government. . . . But government's intervention does not mean that we shall sit back and relax. We can play an important role in monitoring projects. . . . We are trying to develop a model for how to use Weibo to achieve transparency, openness, real time disclosure of financial status. . . . If government will take over the schools in the Free Lunch Project . . . they can appropriate our model at the same time. (R. Zhang, 2011)

This statement indicates that Deng took the National Nutrition Subsidies Project and the Free Lunch Project to be reciprocal projects aimed at resolving the same social problem: hunger and malnutrition among children in less developed regions. Likewise, the transparency and openness developed by the Free Lunch Project as well as its monitoring system can serve as a model to the benefit of the National Nutrition Subsidies Project. At the same time, the Free Lunch Project also benefits from the capacity of the National Nutrition Project to take on hunger and malnutrition on a large scale.

After the central government announced its National Nutrition Subsidies Policy on October 26, 2011, Deng outlined three possible ways that the National Nutrition Project could be implemented: "First, local governments and schools will implement the project. Second, the government will encourage any NGO that has an interest in free lunches . . . to bid on implementing the project . . . and the government will supervise the implementation of the project. . . . Third, the government and the Free Lunch Project will cooperate in their projects [to solve the hunger and malnutrition problem together]" (Deng, 2011b). This indicates that Deng viewed the Free Lunch Project as having the potential to be actively engaged in, or cooperate with, the National Nutrition Project of the central government in at least two ways.

Other members of the Free Lunch Project also asserted that the Free Lunch Project would cooperate with the government in the implementation of the National Nutrition Project. For example, Xiao Xinglong, chair of the steering committee of the Free Lunch foundation, stated, "In the schools that already have free lunch programs, the National Nutrition Subsidies Project can . . . provide one yuan [per student per day] to support the lunch and provide two yuan for breakfast. . . . In many underdeveloped regions, because of the lack of related facilities, the National Nutrition Subsidies Project can't be implemented. The Free Lunch foundation will provide financial supports to schools [in these underdeveloped regions] to build kitchens, to buy fridges, disinfection cabinets . . . and so on" (F. Zhang, 2012).

From 2012 to 2020, the Free Lunch Project collaborated in various forms with the National Nutrition Project in at least fifteen counties in eight Chinese provinces, including Hubei, Yunnan, Henan, Hunan, Sichuan, Guangxi, Anhui, and Guizhou (Free Lunch Project, 2019d). On its eighth anniversary, the project featured these collaborations in a high-profile forum called "Promote Free Lunches Through Multi-Stakeholder Collaborations." In a news release about the forum, the Free Lunch Project stated, "Over the past eight years, the Free Lunch Foundation's collaborations with the government have become ever more diversified. . . . We innovatively created various customized modes to adapt to the local conditions in our collaborations with the National Nutrition Subsidies Project in providing safe and nutritious lunches to students" (Free Lunch Project, 2019d).

The Free Lunch Project's Influence on the National Nutrition Subsidies Policy

The reciprocal relationship between the Free Lunch Project and the government can also be seen in the Free Lunch Project's impact on the National Nutrition Subsidies Policy proposed by the central government. First, many media reports portrayed the National Nutrition Subsidies Policy as a public policy guided and promoted by the grassroots action of the Free Lunch Project, although the Chinese government has never directly confirmed this ("Central Government Will Provide," 2011; H. Fu, 2012; N. Shi, 2011; C. Yang, 2012). On October 30, 2011, four days after the official announcement of the National Nutrition Subsidies Policy, major Chinese portals such as People.com.cn, QQ.com, and Chinadaily.com widely disseminated an article by Shi Nianjun printed in the *Qilu Evening Post*, titled "Government Takes Up the Torch from the Free Lunch Project." In it, Shi (2011) noted:

> Half a year ago, the Free Lunch Project was launched by grassroots volunteers such as Deng Fei. It has raised a fund of over 17 million yuan and provided free lunches for more than 10 thousand students. . . . However, its real success is much bigger. On October 26, the State Council announced the National Nutrition Subsidies Policy to provide 16 billion yuan per year for 26 million students in . . . rural areas. From the Free Lunch Project to the National Nutrition Subsidies Policy, it is widely believed that the grassroots action guided the national policy.

The title and content of that article indicate Shi's view that the Free Lunch Project guided and promoted the National Nutrition Subsidies Policy. On March 13, 2012, Yang Chaoqing published a commentary on the Free Lunch Project and the National Nutrition Subsidies Project in the *Southern Metropolis Daily*, which stated, "Initiated on the Internet, the Free Lunch Project is a grassroots action that has achieved amazing success. . . . However, to solve any social problem, the cooperation between government, the market, and civil society is of crucial importance. It is not wise to only rely on one stakeholder or exclude any stakeholder. . . . It is praiseworthy that the government took up the torch from the Free Lunch Project to launch the National Nutrition Subsidies Project within only half a year" (C. Yang, 2012). This illustrates that Yang also viewed the Free Lunch Project as guiding the National Nutrition Subsidies Policy and saw the project and the government as reciprocal stakeholders that should cooperate with each other to pursue a sustainable solution to the hunger and malnutrition problem. On July 14, 2012, almost one year after the announcement of the National Nutrition Subsidies Policy, Xinhua News Agency, the official press agency of the Chinese government, published an article on the Free Lunch Project that made a similar argument on the relationship between the Free Lunch Project and the National Nutrition Subsidies Policy: "The Free Lunch Project is a grassroots action launched in April 2011 to improve the nutrition status of the students in less developed regions. . . . Under the influence of the Free Lunch Project, in October 2011, the State Council announced it would provide 16 billion yuan per year to launch the National Nutrition Subsidies Project which will benefit more than 26 million students" (H. Fu, 2012).

Second, the experience and the model of the Free Lunch Project also guided the implementation of the National Nutrition Subsidies Policy. The National Student Nutrition Commission of the Ministry of Education—the government agency implementing the National Nutrition Subsidies Policy—introduced core components of the Free Lunch Project's model that have proven to be effective for ensuring the success of free lunch programs in rural schools. For example, to ensure the transparency of the implementation of the policy, the commission issued an official notice on June 6, 2012, that requires its local branches to open Weibo accounts and use Weibo as a platform to ensure transparency in the implementation of their programs around the country:

> To improve the communication and transparency of the National Nutrition Subsidies Project . . . the National Student Nutrition Commission will learn to use new media strategy to publish information on the project and respond to the public inquiries. . . . Branches of [the] Student Nutrition Commission at all levels should open their own Weibo accounts. . . . All county-level Student Nutrition Commission [branches] in western China should open their Weibo accounts and the schools involved in the project are also encouraged to open their own accounts.[2] (National Student Nutrition Commission, 2012b)

Furthermore, the commission stated the following in a notice regarding the contents that should be published on Weibo:

> For the provincial level Student Nutrition Commission, the contents that must be published on Weibo include the provincial student nutritional subsidies policy, regulations, dynamic reports of the implementation of the project, emails and phone numbers for inquiry and reports of misconduct in projects. . . . For the county level Student Nutrition Commission, the contents must be published, include the names of schools, the numbers of students benefited, the regulation on the free lunch service providers, the price of the lunch, the menu of the lunch, and the local email and phone number for reports of misconduct. (National Student Nutrition Commission, 2012b)

These excerpts show that the National Student Nutrition Commission introduced the Free Lunch Project's use of Weibo to increase the transparency of the National Nutrition Subsidies Project. Strategies such as publishing the cost and the lunch menu at each school increased the public's capacity to monitor the implementation of the National Nutrition Subsidies Project.

Another bit of evidence that the Free Lunch Project guided or influenced the implementation of the National Nutrition Subsidies Policy is the National Student Nutrition Commission's acknowledgment of the significance of building kitchens in its projects. Following the National Nutrition Subsidies Policy announcement, the Free Lunch Project stated in various media reports that based on its experience, the current subsidies standard of three yuan per student per lunch was insufficient for rural schools to build their own kitchens and dining rooms, a fact that could hinder the effective implementation of the National Nutrition Subsidies Policy. As a result, the Free Lunch Project cooperated with the National Nutrition Subsidies Project to provide money for schools to build their own kitchens (Deng, 2014; H. Fu, 2012; F. Zhang, 2012). After the media exposed several cases concerning the lack of kitchens in the National Nutrition Subsidies Project in 2012,[3] the National Student Nutrition Commission issued an official notice on December 25, 2012, to inform local governmental agencies of eight requirements for the implementation of the National Nutrition Subsidies Policy. Two of those requirements relate to kitchens:

(1) ... The additional costs from the implementation of the National Nutrition Project such as salaries for workers at school kitchens and dining rooms, and the transportation costs to deliver lunches should be provided by the local government. ... The National Nutrition Subsidies cannot be used to pay the additional costs. ...

(2) Complete the proposals regarding the building of school kitchens and dining rooms as soon as possible. Complete the construction of school kitchens and dining rooms for all schools in the pilot experiment projects ... by 2013. (National Student Nutrition Commission, 2012a)

On January 4, 2013, the Ministry of Education and the Ministry of Finance issued a joint official notice on the status of kitchens in the implementation of the National Nutrition Subsidies Policy. The notice stated that the Ministry of Finance would allocate special funds to support the construction of kitchens and dining rooms in all rural schools, which would be covered by the National Nutrition Subsidies Policy. Among the pilot experimental projects, the construction of school kitchens and dining rooms was to be completed in all schools by 2013. Before 2015, most schools in western China were to have their own kitchens and dining rooms (Ministry of Education & Ministry of Finance, 2013).

This indicates how the Free Lunch Project guided or influenced various components of the National Nutrition Subsidies Policy when it was implemented. The analysis of the impact of the Free Lunch Project on the National Nutrition Subsidies Policy in this section reveals that the Free Lunch Project and the government were in a reciprocal relationship in which the Free Lunch Project influenced the government's policy and the implementation of the government's projects They collaborated together to eliminate the hunger and malnutrition problem in less developed regions in China.

Contentions between Activists and the Government

Notwithstanding the reciprocal relationship that emerged between Free Lunch Project activists and the government, contentions also arose between the two parties. In fact, since the very beginning, activists have been challenging various government agencies in the implementation of their programs. In his book on the Free Lunch Project, Deng (2014) describes the contentiousness between activists and local government over the first free lunch program in Guizhou Province:

> Very quickly, we got into trouble. . . . Media coverage of the Shaba Primary School free lunch [program] made the local education bureau very unhappy.[4] Officials from the bureau argued that local people only eat two meals a day. So, there is nothing to complain about if the local kids only eat two meals a day. They seem to believe that this is not a problem at all. . . . Shaba Primary School's principal told us that he was under severe pressure from local officials. They blamed him for bringing a large group of investigative journalists to Guizhou, which [could] expose the underdevelopment and local problems [of Guizhou] to the public. (Deng, 2014, p. 36)

Deng's account of how activists viewed the consequences of this contentiousness and how they handled it further reveals the complex and multidimensional relationship between activists and the government in the Free Lunch Project: "After carefully examining the situation, we thought probably we were not discreet enough. Maybe the response from the local officials could be better if we had communicated with the local education bureau about the free lunch [program] (at Shaba Primary School) in advance. . . . Now we have a troubled relation[ship] with the local education bureau, which may be fatal to the project. If we lose the support of [the] local education bureau, it is impossible to replicate our program in other schools" (Deng, 2014, p. 36).

Deng's account shows that activists believed that good relations with the local government are crucial for the success of the Free Lunch Project. Project activists viewed local government not as an impediment to the project but as a crucial stakeholder that needed to be engaged with in order to eliminate the hunger and malnutrition problem faced by children in rural schools. Even when local governments became an obstacle to their programs, activists did not point their fingers at officials. They even considered whether being more discreet could help avert contention: "[In the current situation] the Free Lunch Project will have to confront more obstacles by local officials to continue to be promoted in Guizhou. If I were still solely an investigative reporter, I would have fiercely contested these local officials in the media until they yielded. But now I am an activist making real change. I have to try to avoid contentiousness. I decided, on the one hand, we should continue mobilizing public opinion online [to support the Free Lunch Project] and, on the other hand, we will try to approach other counties to make breakthroughs" (Deng, 2014, p. 37).

Deng's account of how activists handled contentiousness illustrates that rather than confronting local officials who got in the way of their programs, activists approached other regions to make headway. Rather than generating more contentiousness, activists of the Free Lunch Project tried to minimize contention with the government and focused on "making real change" on the ground. This is significant because it illustrates a new type of activism that deviates from the conventional form of activists and advocacy in Western societies and in earlier internet actions within Chinese cyberspace. Conventional activism focuses on pressuring the state, policymakers, and other institutions through media campaigns, protests, and demonstrations to bring about change (e.g., Cammaerts, 2007; Martin, 2007; G. Yang, 2009). The new activism embodied by Deng and other activists of the Free Lunch Project focuses on bringing about change and solving social problems directly. And rather than confronting the government, it aims to engage the government as a stakeholder to bring about change together. These activists take the lead to solve problems, using the effects of their actions and public opinion (which enthusiastically supports their actions) to guide and encourage the government to develop public policy and national projects to solve similar problems.

Yet for advocates of the new activism, engaging the government absolutely does not mean that activists should or will give up their role as watchdogs and critics of government policies and projects. The following statement from Deng Fei (2014) provides a more vivid depiction of how activists think about their relations with the government within the new activism:

> Historically, in Chinese society, the first kind of people thought the government is superman and completely relied on the government to solve every problem. The second kind blamed the government for all problems in society and thought every governmental policy is ill conceived and counterproductive. The third kind of people is indifferent to the government and its policies. We actually could become the fourth kind of people: we don't believe the government is a superman that can solve every problem and we don't think every problem comes from the government either. . . . On one hand, we monitor the government and hold them accountable for abuses of power. On the other, we take actions to solve the problems directly and guide government to address social concerns that it overlooks. (p. 165)

Specifically, activists of the project have guided and collaborated with local governments in different parts of the country to address the hunger and malnutrition problem among rural children. Simultaneously, however, they have made constant efforts to push government accountability and to criticize and correct government policymaking regarding the implementation of the National Nutrition Subsidies Policy. A most significant example of these efforts is activists' opposition to the Milk+Bread mode of the National Nutrition Project.

The Milk+Bread Incident: Contentions between Activists, the Government, and Corporations

On October 30, 2012, Diaoya—who was later reported to be Liang Xuye, a volunteer teacher at a rural primary school in Fenghuang County, Hunan Province—reported in her Weibo that the lunch her students received from the Fenghuang Education Bureau contained only a small box of milk and a tiny piece of toast.[5] She questioned whether the three yuan per student per lunch in national subsidies was actually being used for lunches for her students. Liang's Weibo post quickly went viral in Chinese cyberspace. Leading Free Lunch Project activists such as Deng Fei called for a thorough investigation of the incident on Weibo. Furthermore, Deng (2014) questioned the Milk+Bread mode of the National Nutrition Project, which was apparently found in many rural schools:

> Most of the schools [in the National Nutrition Project] are in very remote underdeveloped areas, where safe transportation and storage facilities for milk are unavailable or very expensive. Therefore, milk is much more likely to cause food safety problems [than locally purchased food]. And excluding the one yuan spent on bread, only around two yuan could be used to buy the boxed milk. After subtracting the cost of packaging and transportation and the profit of the dairy industry, ultimately perhaps only several dimes would really be used to buy milk [to feed the children].[6]

Deng advocated that rather than purchasing packaged milk and bread from far away, rural schools should directly provide hot lunches, with meat and vegetables purchased locally for all students covered by the National Nutrition Subsidies Policy: "We firmly believed that local food materials are good enough to provide nutrition for local communities. Why should we seek supplies from far away and neglect what lies close at hand?! And force children to eat the same food every day?! In fact, netizens have exposed many cases that children [served by Milk+Bread mode] are fed up with eating milk and bread every day. A substantial amount of milk and bread therefore ended up [being] left over, which is really a waste" (Deng 2014).

Liang's Weibo post and activists' questions regarding the government-subsidized lunch were widely reported in the mainstream media (L. Li, 2012; S. Wang, 2012; Yi & Chu, 2012; Zhuang & Liu, 2012) and raised nationwide concerns over, and discussions on, the implementation of the National Nutrition Subsidies Policy. Lu Mai, the director of the China Development Research Foundation—the major state think tank advising the State Council on the National Nutrition Subsidies Policy—stated that local governments must build school kitchens and dining rooms to effectively implement the National Nutrition Subsidies Policy, and the Milk+X mode could only be used as a temporary transition to a hot meal mode (Wang, 2012).[7] On December 25, 2012, the National Student Nutrition Commission issued an official notice to inform local governmental agencies about eight new requirements for the National Nutrition Project, including the construction of school kitchens and dining rooms and the promotion of project transparency (National Student Nutrition Commission, 2012a). But it did not directly require local governments to implement a hot meal mode and abandon the Milk+X mode. Table 6.1 provides a more detailed illustration of this incident.

The events in table 6.1 first illustrate that the engagement of activists and NGOs, including the Free Lunch Project, Liang, and other anonymous Weibo users, increased the transparency and accountability of the government on its National Nutrition Subsidies Policy. Action 1 (activists exposed the problems in the government-subsidized lunch at Fenghuang County), Action 2 (activists and the NGO questioned the Milk+Bread mode used by Hunan Province), Action 3 (mass media reported the Milk+Bread incident and activists' questions on the implementation of the National Nutrition Subsidies Policy), Action 5 (a state think tank affirmed that the Milk+Bread mode can only be used as a transition to hot meals), and Actions 7 and 8 (government agencies partly changed their policy on the National Nutritional Lunch by highlighting the need to build kitchens and enhance the transparency of their projects but did not acknowledge the public's concern over the Milk+Bread mode directly) indicate that activists and the NGO influenced public policy on the implementation of the National Nutrition Subsidies Policy. And although the activists achieved only part of their goal, the incident demonstrates the potential of new media actions to increase various aspects of government accountability, such as making the government accountable to the public and spreading knowledge of government procedures and regulations.[8]

Second, the data in table 6.1 indicate the significance of the multichannel perspective for researching and understanding new media actions for development and social change. In this incident, as in Tiger Gate (see chapter 4), mass media and the interaction between new media and mass media played a significant role in facilitating real change and correcting government policy. The last column in the table illustrates how the mass media, such as the *Yangcheng Evening Post* and *China Youth Daily*, played important roles in the incident. Mass media's coverage and investigation of the Milk+Bread incident dramatically increased public awareness of the problems in the implementation of the National Nutrition Subsidies Policy, both online and offline. For example, the *Yangcheng Evening*

Table 6.1

The Milk+Bread Incident

Action	Content	Media
1	On October 30, 2012, Liang reported on her Weibo that the government-subsidized lunch her students received from the Fenghuang Education Bureau was only a small box of milk and a tiny piece of toast, and she questioned whether the three yuan national subsidies were actually being used to provide lunches for the students. Activists and ordinary internet users widely disseminated and commented on Liang's post on Weibo and questioned the implementation of the National Nutrition Subsidies Policy in Fenghuang County and the Milk+Bread mode of the National Nutrition Lunch in many rural schools.	Weibo
2	Deng forwarded Liang's post and questioned the Milk+Bread mode used by the Education Bureau of Hunan Province. He called for all volunteer teachers in Hunan to expose the problems of the Milk+Bread mode and urged local governments to change the current policy regarding the implementation of the National Nutrition Subsidies Policy.	Weibo
3	On November 25, the *Yangcheng Evening Post* covered Liang's post, activist questions, and its own investigation of the implementation of the National Nutrition Subsidies Policy in Fenghuang County. Its investigation revealed that more than a third of the three-yuan national subsidies became profit for the corporations that provided the milk and bread. Major media and Chinese portals, including *China Youth Daily*, People.com.cn, Xinhuanet.com, and Ifeng News, began to intensively investigate and report on the Milk+Bread incident and activists' questions regarding the implementation of the National Nutrition Subsidies Policy.	Mass media: *Yangcheng Evening Post*, *China Youth Daily*, People.com.cn, Xinhuanet.com, Ifeng News
4	On November 26, 2012, Deng posted on his Weibo that he had been contacted by sixteen media outlets asking him to comment on the Milk+Bread incident. The reports on the investigation into the incident in mass media outlets, such as the *Yangcheng Evening Post* and *China Youth Daily*, were widely forwarded and quoted by activists such as Deng and ordinary users on Weibo.	Weibo
5	Since November 27, 2012, Lu Mai has been widely quoted in several mass media news outlets, such as *China Youth Daily*; in major portals; and by online activists: (1) According to research, the Milk+X mode can only provide 20 percent of the required daily caloric intake, much less than the hot meal mode (2) Local governments must build school kitchens and dining rooms to provide hot meals to students. And the Milk+X mode could only be used as a temporary transition to a hot meals mode.	Mass media and portals: Caixin.com, *China Youth Daily*, People.com.cn

(continued)

Table 6.1 (Continued)

Action	Content	Media
6	On November 30, Deng and Lu participated in a Weibo interview[a] with Weibo users on the Milk+Bread incident and the implementation of the National Nutrition Subsidies Policy. Deng and Lu respectively reiterated their previous arguments on the incident.	Weibo
7	On December 25, 2012, the National Student Nutrition Commission issued an official notice to inform local governmental agencies of eight new requirements under the National Nutrition Subsidies Policy's implementation, including the need to build school kitchens and dining rooms and enhance the transparency of the project. Yet it did not require local governments to implement a hot meal mode or abandon the Milk+X mode.	Widely reported by mass media
8	On January 4, 2013, the Ministry of Education and the Ministry of Finance issued a joint official notice on the issue of building kitchens to implement the National Nutrition Subsidies Policy. The notice stated that the Ministry of Finance would allocate special funds to support building kitchens and dining rooms in all rural schools covered by the National Nutrition Subsidies Project. The construction of school kitchens and dining rooms in all schools in the pilot programs would be completed by 2013.	Widely reported by mass media

[a] A Weibo interview is a text-based online interview hosted by Weibo.com. Weibo users post questions to interviewees through Weibo posts. Interviewees respond to the questions through Weibo posts in real time.

Post's report on the Milk+Bread incident was shared and forwarded by thirty-one thousand people on social network sites such as Weibo.com and QQ.com. Mass media investigation into the incident, such as the *Yangcheng Evening Post*'s investigation of the government-subsidized lunch in Fenghuang County (Yi & Chu, 2012) enhanced people's knowledge of the incident, especially regarding excessive corporate profiteering from the National Nutrition Project in Fenghuang County.

Moreover, in this case, like the Tiger Gate incident, mass media and ICT-based new media, such as Weibo, were not isolated from each other. They interacted with and reinforced each other in an action for social change aimed at correcting government policy and promoting government accountability in the implementation of the National Nutrition Subsidies Policy. As figure 6.2 shows, the pattern of interaction and reinforcement process between mass media and new media in this case is the same as that in Tiger Gate (compare figure 6.2 with figure 4.4).

In Action 3 in table 6.1, the collective knowledge constructed by online activists on Weibo in Actions 1 and 2 reinforced the news report of the *Yangcheng*

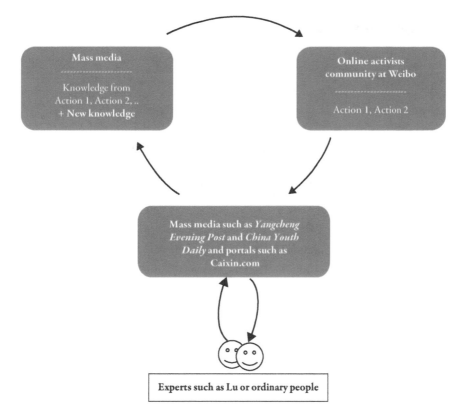

FIGURE 6.2 Interactions and Reinforcement between Mainstream Mass Media and New Media in the Milk+Bread Incident

Evening Post (an organ of mass media). Also in Action 3, new knowledge on the Milk+Bread incident and the implementation of the National Nutrition Subsidies Policy (e.g., the investigation of the Milk+Bread incident at Fenghuang County) was developed by the *Yangcheng Evening Post*'s reporters and was integrated into the news report. In Action 4, the new knowledge in the news report of the *Yangcheng Evening Post* fed back into the online activist community on Weibo and reinforced collective knowledge of the Milk+Bread incident and the implementation of the National Nutrition Subsidies Policy. Similarly, in Action 5, collective knowledge constructed by online activists on Weibo in Actions 1 and 2 reinforced the news report in *China Youth Daily*, and new knowledge on the implementation of the National Nutrition Subsidies Policy was integrated into the coverage. This included research on and recommendations regarding the Milk+X mode and hot meal mode by Lu Mai (the expert who was not an activist on Weibo), which were developed collaboratively by reporters and Lu. Later, the new knowledge from that news coverage was fed back to the activist community on Weibo.

An Eight-Year Struggle

As the Milk+Bread incident shows, it is not easy for NGOs and activists to correct government policy in an authoritative context like China. Holding the government accountable has required that NGOs and activists engage in long-term struggle. Yet ultimately, they may achieve only a fraction of their goals. The Milk+Bread incident in Fenghuang County was only the start of a persistent eight-year contestation (beginning in 2012) over the implementation of the National Nutrition Subsidies Policy between the Free Lunch Project and different corporations and levels of government. The ongoing struggle of NGOs and activists to pressure the government to shift from Milk+X meals and snacks to hot lunches and the obstruction and resistance of the corporations and various levels of government to this change indicate the complexity of relationships between forces seeking to set the agenda for development and social change in China.

Between 2012 and 2020, activists, the Free Lunch Project, and the media have exposed extensive problems with the Milk+X mode of the National Nutrition Project, such as incidents of food poisoning (Cheng, 2020; Lei, 2013; "Problematic School Milk Products in JiangSu," 2019; *65 Primary School Students Were Poisoned*, 2016; "Why Did a Nutritional Meal Become a Problematic Meal?," 2013), mismanagement of national subsidies (e.g., *Corporations Are Profiting*, 2013; Yi & Chu, 2012), lack of culinary variety, and students' dislike of the foods served (Liu & Wu, 2017; *Primary School Students Poured Milk*, 2018). Facing pressure from the media, activists, and the Free Lunch Project, the Ministry of Education reiterated the significance of building school kitchens and dining rooms in key policy documents regarding the National Nutrition Project (L. Liu, 2014; Ministry of Education, 2017). For example, in his report on the implementation of the National Nutrition Project in 2014, Deputy Minister Liu Limin (2014) stated: "By February 2014, 47,698 schools have completed the building of new school kitchens and dining rooms, 69% of the schools that were approved by the Ministry. . . . This provides the condition to foster a shift to a means for schools to provide meals directly through their kitchens and dining rooms. It also laid a good foundation for the National Nutrition Project to enter a more mature phase."

The Ministry of Education's 2017 special report on the National Nutrition Project states: (1) local governments must provide financial supports to build school kitchens as well as cover the operational cost of these kitchens, such as the salaries of the cooks; (2)the Ministry of Education sought to increase the percentage of schools that implemented a hot meal mode(2017). In doing so, the ministry was, at some level, implicitly lending support to the position of the Free Lunch Project that hot meals are the best means to implement the National Nutrition Subsidies Policy. In his report, for example, Liu (2014) stated, "Providing meals directly through school kitchens is currently the safest and most welcomed mode among students. It is also the model we are trying to promote

Table 6.2
Nutrition Levels of the Three Modes in the National Nutrition Project

Nutrition	Recommended level	Lunch mode	Breakfast mode	Snack (recess) mode
Energy intake (kcal)	810	866.80	450.09	298.20
Protein (g)	28	28.90	21.33	12.04
Fat (g)	30	29.80	21.37	10.14
Calcium (mg)	400	193.70	151.40	182.12
Iron (mg)	5.4	10.47	4.60	3.76
Sodium (mg)	530	864.09	405.00	402.61
Vitamin A (mcg)	300	212.82	146.47	64.99
Vitamin B1 (mcg)	0.6	0.78	0.34	0.20
Vitamin B2 (mcg)	0.6	0.78	0.34	0.20
Vitamin C (mcg)	20	25.86	9.51	1.44

Source: China Development Research Foundation, 2017.

[in the National Nutrition Project]." In its 2017 report, the Ministry of Education reaffirmed its support for the hot meal mode and even criticized the Milk+X mode directly: "Some provinces provided milk, eggs, bread, and cakes to the students. The provided foods lack variety and nutrition. Students do not like eating [milk, bread, and cakes every day] and this resulted in large amount of waste." Yet its official policy still remains very ambiguous. It neither required its local branches to use the hot meal mode nor did it require local governments to abandon the Milk+X mode. It even generated a self-contradictory discourse, in that "the Student Nutrition Project does not mean free lunches," as its goal is to improve the nutritional status of schoolchildren (L. Liu, 2014; Ministry of Education, 2017). Its core policy is that the provincial branches and county-level branches of the Ministry of Education and local government choose the best mode, based on local conditions, to implement the National Nutrition Project. Although this approach may sound good, in reality it gives local governments the freedom to choose the Milk+X mode, the very thing that is constantly being criticized from all sides, including by the Ministry of Education itself.

In June 2017, the China Development Research Foundation released a report on the National Nutrition Project based on 10.2 million pieces of data collected from 3.83 million students in 9,200 schools in a hundred counties that participated in the project. This research reaffirmed that hot meals are the best mode for students, while the Milk+X mode is more expensive, less effective, and less safe than hot meals. The report identified three modes used in the project. The lunch mode, which the Free Lunch Project advocates and uses, is where schools directly provide hot lunches with meat and vegetables through their own kitchens. The other two modes, the breakfast mode and the snack (during class recess) mode, are both Milk+X modes. The report shows that the (hot) lunch mode provides much better nutrition than the breakfast or snack modes (see table 6.2).

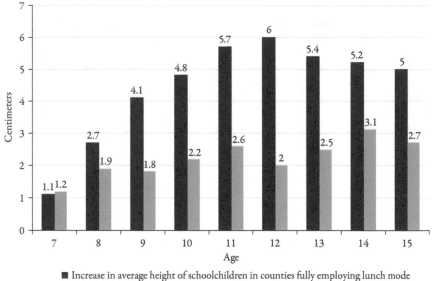

FIGURE 6.3 Increase in Average Height of Schoolchildren in the National Nutrition Project, 2012 to 2016

According to the data in the report, the average height of schoolchildren in less developed rural areas has increased remarkably since the implementation of the National Nutrition Project in 2012 to 2016. To compare the effect of different modes in providing nutrition to students, the report compared the increase in height among schoolchildren in counties fully employing the lunch mode with those employing the snack mode.[9] Figure 6.3 clearly shows that lunch mode is much more effective than snack mode (a typical Milk+X mode) in improving nutrition and growth among schoolchildren in less developed regions. The report also urged that snack mode be removed from the National Nutrition Project as soon as possible because of food safety risks, overpricing, and the limited variety of the packaged foods it provides. In its policy recommendations, the China Development Research Foundation (2017) rearticulated that "[in the National Nutrition Project,] meals should be provided through school kitchens."

Under constant pressure from the media, activists, the Free Lunch Project, and state think tanks such as the China Development Research Foundation, a gradual shift began occurring from the Milk+X mode to the hot meal mode in the National Nutrition Project, but only very slowly. In 2012, only 35.9 percent of the schools (42,000 of 117,000) in the project used school kitchens to provide meals to students, generally in the form of a hot meal (X. Lu, 2012).[10] Two years later, the number had increased to 56.47 percent (L. Liu, 2014). And by 2017, it had reached 71 percent (Ministry of Education, 2017a). Yet even today, nearly 30 percent of the schools receiving national nutrition subsidies continue to use the Milk+X mode. In Hebei Province, for example, 71 percent of schools (1,623 of 2,285) used the snack mode in 2015 (Ministry of Education, 2016b), and the provincial government continued to expand the National Nutrition Project using the Milk+X mode in rural schools in twenty-four counties in the province through 2019 (Education Department of Hebei Province, 2019).

Why did so many local governments continue using and promoting the Milk+X mode after it had been extensively criticized and proven less effective? The explanation offered by the Ministry of Education is that many local governments, due to unbalanced economic development, do not have the financial resources to build school kitchens and dining rooms and cannot afford the operational costs of the hot meal mode. But the lack of financial resources to build school kitchens does not explain this completely and is unlikely to be the most important reason. For example, in 2012 the Ministry of Finance provided 12 billion yuan in funds to promote the construction of kitchens and dining rooms at rural schools in the National Nutrition Project. Yet by May 2012, only five of the twenty-nine provinces in the project had submitted proposals to apply for the funds. Ministry of Finance director Huo Bugang complained to the representatives from the twenty-nine provincial branches of the Ministry of Education: "If you don't submit proposals [to build school kitchens], how can we appropriate funds to you?!" (Deng, 2014). Moreover, many provinces with relatively low GDP per capita have fully implemented the hot meal mode, whereas others with relatively high GDP per capita use the Milk+X mode. For example, Guizhou Province, ranking twenty-ninth in GDP per capita (33,242 yuan as of 2017), has fully implemented the hot meal mode, whereas Hebei Province, ranking nineteenth in GDP per capita (42,866 yuan as of 2017), has been using Milk+X mode as the primary mode of delivery for the National Nutrition Project. Finally, the China Development Research Foundation (2017) reported that according to its data, most schools that employ the snack mode actually have school kitchens.

Deng Fei, other activists, and the China Development Research Foundation have argued that some local governments do not like the hot meal mode, in part because it requires a much greater time commitment by local officials for the National Nutrition Project. Yet in the current sociopolitical system in China, evaluations of the job performance of officials within the higher levels of bureaucracy are based primarily on short-term economic growth, meaning that local officials do not perceive hunger and malnutrition among schoolchildren to be a significant part of their responsibilities. Implementing the hot meal mode benefits schoolchildren greatly but is of little or no benefit to local officials in terms of performance and promotions. Plus, it requires them to assume responsibility for added risks, such as problems with sanitation, food safety, and parents' complaints. Therefore, many local officials adhere to the Milk+X mode because it is the "safest" and most "time-saving" mode for local government (e.g., China Development Research Foundation, 2013, 2017; Deng, 2014).

A more important reason is that different levels of government are influenced by corporate lobbying or may even collaborate with corporations to profit from the national nutrition subsidies. Media and activists have exposed several cases in which corporations have made large amounts of money from the Milk+X mode in the context of National Nutrition Project operations in different areas (e.g., Deng, 2014; Lei, 2013; *Primary School Students Poured Milk*, 2018; Yi & Chu, 2012). For example, an investigation published in the *Yangcheng Evening Post* of the Milk+Bread incident in Fenghuang County revealed that more than 30 percent of the three-yuan national subsidies became the profit of the corporations that provided packaged milk and bread to the National Nutrition Project in that county. This means that corporations would earn more than 6,000,000 yuan profit every year from the project in that county (Yi & Chu, 2012). The huge profit potentials of the National Nutrition Project have motivated a large number of national and local corporations and powerful business associations to lobby different levels of governments to implement whichever mode benefits them most. Among these corporate entities, the most systematic and aggressive is the Chinese dairy industry. Through advice given in the National People's Congress by elite CEOs, promotion of the so-called School Milk of China Project by business associations, and PR campaigns by the mass media, the Chinese dairy industry aimed to get a large share of the National Nutrition Subsidies from 26,000,000 schoolchildren in rural China through the Milk+X mode.

Efforts of Dairy Industry to Promote Milk+X Mode

In the Third Plenary Session of the Twelfth National People's Congress, which is the legislative body of the PRC, about thirty deputies of the National People's Congress recommended "requiring full use of School Milk products in rural schools [receiving National Nutrition Subsidies]" ("Advice on 'A Cup of Milk' Attracted Warm Responses," 2015).[11] This policy advice was initiated by Wang Jinghai, CEO and chairman of the board of the Wondersun Dairy, the third-largest dairy company in China, and Liu Yonghao, CEO and chairman of the board of New Hope Group, China's largest agriculture and food corporation, and was cosigned by CEOs from China's biggest dairy companies, such as the Yili Group.[12] A report from the *Economic Daily* (2015) states: "Through the National Nutrition Project for rural schoolchildren, our government gives millions of children in less developed rural areas who have never drunk milk before the opportunity to drink milk. Yet, since last year, many schools began to build school kitchens and dining rooms and stopped providing [boxed] milk in the National Nutrition Project. As a result, many areas stopped providing School Milk products. . . . The sales of School Milk products in 23 of the 31 provinces have unfortunately declined since then." The report further conveys Wang's concern over this situation: "To give every child in less developed areas a cup of milk, Wang Jinghai proposed the following advice: first, central and local governments should increase the amount of the subsidies [to the National Nutrition Project]; second, [the National Nutrition Project should] make milk a required food for each meal for every student; third, universalize and subsidize the milk-drinking policy in rural schools; fourth, establish the regulation that the National Nutrition Project must use milk products with the School Milk of China logo" (2015).[13] The report clearly indicated that these CEOs from the dairy industry were concerned that the implementation of the hot meal mode was costing them 20 billion yuan in lost market share each year. They required the government to impose the Milk+X mode in the National Nutrition Project, to use the nutritional subsidies to buy their products, and to secure a monopoly for dairy companies affiliated with the Dairy Association of China, which issues the School Mile of China logo, in the National Nutrition Project. Given that each box of official School Milk was priced between 1.5 and 2 yuan, these requirements meant that half of the four yuan per child per day subsidies would be spent on their milk products and that the government would pay a total of roughly 10 billion yuan each year to the dairy industry to support the less nutritional and more costly Milk+X mode. And although recommendations by deputies during the National People's Congress do not have the same power as bills passed by Congress in the United States, they still put pressure on related government agencies. According to *The Provision on the Advice from the Deputies of the National People's Congress* issued by the Standing Committee of the National People's Congress (2005), "By law, related government agencies are obliged to seriously study and consider the advice of deputies and to formally respond to the advice."

On February 26, 2016, the Ministry of Education published its official response to this advice, titled *Response to the No. 8952 Advice from the Third Plenary Session of the 12th National People's Congress*. The ministry first stated:

(1) Regarding the advice to make milk a required food for each meal for every student, the National Nutrition Project focuses on less developed areas, ethnic minority areas, as well as remote mountain areas. . . . The priority is to solve the hunger problem of schoolchildren in the least developed areas. The project's effects demonstrate that using school kitchens to provide meals [is] currently the best mode. On [the] one hand, the "school kitchen mode" is convenient for schools to manage the project. On the other hand, it increases food safety and ensures that "each penny of the subsidies is used to feed the students." Therefore, it has become the most used mode [in the National Nutrition Project] around the country. . . . Every community has its own dietary habits and unique food ingredients. Therefore, the food provided by the National Nutrition Project in different parts of the country need not be the same, like milk and eggs.

This Ministry of Education statement rearticulates the first and foremost goal of the National Nutrition Project, which is to solve the hunger problem among children in less developed rural regions. And the ministry reaffirmed that the hot meal mode (provided directly through school kitchens) is the best mode to safeguard food safety and efficient management and to ensure that "each penny of the subsidies is used to feed the students." The ministry declined to follow the recommendation to impose milk on all rural schools in different parts of the country, taking a more reasonable, locally oriented, and contextualized approach. Regarding the third recommendation, the ministry stated:

(2) Regarding the advice to universalize and subsidize the milk-drinking policy in rural schools, the School Milk of China Project improved the nutritional status of school children, increased dairy consumption, and promoted the development of the dairy industry in our country. . . . In September 2013, seven ministries co-issued the "Notice on the Implementation of the School Milk Project." The notice clearly stated that the implementation of the School Milk Project has changed from a government guided and policy supported method to a market oriented and NGO supported approach. In 2013, the project has been completely transferred to the Dairy Association of China. The advice you proposed to universalize and subsidize the milk-drinking policy in rural schools is a complex and systematic issue. According to the notice, the Dairy Association must first develop pilot projects. The Ministry of Education will facilitate the Dairy Association and other agencies to design pilot projects and encourage local governments to carry out pilot projects. (Ministry of Education, 2016a).

The ministry's statement that "the implementation of the School Milk Project has changed from a government guided and policy supported method to a market oriented and NGO supported approach" reaffirms the co-issued notice of the government's withdrawal from the School Milk of China Project and the end of state sponsorship, and its transformation into a market-oriented approach run by a business association. In so doing, the ministry declined the recommendation that the government subsidize the School Milk Project. But it acknowledged the health benefits of the School Milk Project for schoolchildren and encouraged local governments to conduct pilot projects to further promote the project. Yet it failed to clarify whether local governments could use the National Nutrition Subsidies to buy School Milk products in their pilot projects in order to promote the School Milk of China Project. This gives the local governments the freedom to use the National Nutrition Subsidies to buy packaged milk products from the dairy industry. The 1.5 to 2 yuan per box cost of School Milk will inevitably lead to the implementation of a Milk+X mode in those schools in the so-called pilot projects. The ministry responded to the last advice as follows:

(3) Regarding the policy to use milk products with the School Milk of China logo, the Ministry of Education will coordinate with the Dairy Association to ensure the promotion of the School Milk Project connected with the National Nutrition Project . . . and to expand the coverage of the School Milk Project. (Ministry of Education, 2016a)

This is probably the most problematic part of the response. The Ministry of Education did not provide any explanation as to the meaning of the phrases "to ensure the promotion of the School Milk Project connected with the National Nutrition Project" and "to expand the coverage of the School Milk Project." It also portrayed the two projects as reciprocal projects and failed to mention that the School Milk of China Project competes with the hot meal mode for the four yuan per student per day National Nutrition Subsidies. The dairy industry later used the ministry's vague terms to continually misinform the public and local governments in mass media campaigns promoting the School Milk of China Project. Although the first initiative to impose milk on the National Nutrition Project and to secure a substantial share of the project's subsidies through making recommendations to the National People's Congress was not very successful, the advice from elite CEOs in the dairy industry got lots of positive coverage on Xinhua.net and other official Chinese media outlets (*Deputy Wang Jinghai stated*, 2015b). Then, galvanized perhaps by the positive media coverage and the Ministry of Education's vague response, Wang and other dairy industry CEOs continued to make similar recommendations during the National People's Congress in 2016, 2017, and 2019.

A powerful business association made up of sixty-eight top dairy companies in China, the Dairy Association of China played a key role in the dairy industry's efforts to acquire a sizable share of the National Nutrition Subsidies. It lobbied different levels of government to use the Milk+X mode in the National Nutrition Project by aggressively promoting its School Milk of China Project. The School Milk of China Project was first initiated by the Ministry of Agriculture and the Ministry of Education in 2000 to encourage schoolchildren to drink milk during recess. The goals of the project were (1) to increase the consumption of dairy products and foster the development of the Chinese dairy industry, and (2) to improve the nutritional status of schoolchildren in China (Ministry of Agriculture, 2013). In 2013, all PRC government agencies, including the Ministry of Education and the Ministry of Agriculture, withdrew from the project, and the Dairy Association of China assumed control, meaning that the project is no longer a state project but a commercial project of a business association. The Dairy Association continues using the same name and the same logo in its promotional campaigns to create the impression that the project is administered or partly funded by the state. From the very beginning of the project, its core principle has been that students and parents voluntarily order milk products registered as School Milk. The government did not subsidize School Milk products

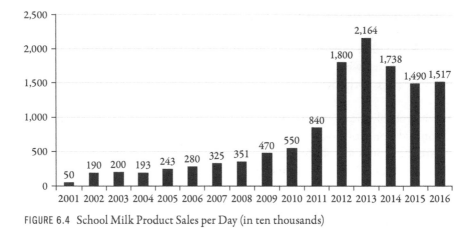

FIGURE 6.4 School Milk Product Sales per Day (in ten thousands)

but gave the dairy companies registered with School Milk a monopoly on this market (Ministry of Education & Ministry of Agriculture, 2002). Between 2005 and 2011, before the implementation of the National Nutrition Project in 2011, the dairy industry persistently claimed that it would barely profit from the School Milk of China Project because the government required School Milk products to be sold at 30 percent below market price.[14] And it has constantly lobbied the government and waged mass media PR campaigns to advocate for government subsidies for the project (e.g., "Because of Lack of Profit," 2005; Ge & Ding, 2006; H. Xu, 2011). The data from the Dairy Association showed that sales of School Milk products increased slowly before 2010 (see figure 6.4). Yet sales between 2011 and 2012 more than doubled, from 8.4 million cartons to 18 million cartons. Sales in 2012 were 3.27 times higher than in 2010, the year before the announcement of the National Nutrition Subsidies Policy (in October 2011). This indicates a strong correlation between the high percentage of Milk+X mode in the early years of the National Nutrition Project and the success of the School Milk of China Project in those years, and the influence of the dairy industry's aggressive promotion of the School Milk Project on the dominance of the Milk+X mode in the National Nutrition Project in 2012 and 2013. Moreover, the decline in sales of School Milk products between 2013 and 2015 is related to the rise of the hot meal mode in the National Nutrition Project. What contributed to the decline of School Milk product sales was criticism of the Milk+X mode by the media, activists, the Free Lunch Project, and the China Development Research Foundation and their advocacy of the hot meal mode. This clearly shows that the School Milk of China Project competed against the hot meal mode for the National Nutrition Subsidies in less developed regions.

Figure 6.4 also indicates that the dairy industry has gained a substantial share of the National Nutrition Subsidies since 2010. The industry's hope that the government would subsidize the School Milk products to increase its profits has been realized through the Milk+X mode in the National Nutrition Project. Yet this has come at a price: in 2012, only 35.9 percent of the schools in the National Nutrition Project employed the hot meal mode, meaning that just over a third of the twenty-six million disadvantaged rural children were provided the best mode for their health. Threatened by the wide application of the hot meal mode from 2015 to the present, the dairy industry has worked to secure the same share of the National Nutrition Subsidies that it had enjoyed earlier. The strategy of the Dairy Association is (1) to advocate for the Milk+X mode directly, and (2) to misinform the public and local governments about the relationship between the National Nutrition Project and the School Milk of China Project in order to increase or sustain the use of School Milk products in the National Nutrition Project.

For example, at the Third Student Nutrition and School Feeding Conference, organized by the National Student Nutrition Committee in 2015, Gu Jicheng, the director of the Dairy Association of China, stated:

> Compared with developed countries, the student nutritional projects in our country started much later. Yet with economic development and growing attention to these projects by the government, we have made remarkable improvement. The effective implementation of the National Nutrition Project and the School Milk Project have benefited an increasing number of children. In most regions, governments organically connected the two projects by promoting Milk+N mode and attained significant success and gained much experience. Consumption of School Milk products in schools has reached 21 million [individual containers] per day. Yet the coverage of the School Milk Project remains very low compared with the real number of students. (J. Gu, 2015)

Here, Gu frames the National Nutrition Project and the School Milk of China Project as similar projects that will improve the nutrition levels of Chinese children while concealing the fact that the latter was also designed to expand the market for the dairy industry. Since 2012, the Ministry of Education and the National Student Nutrition Committee have consistently maintained that the hot meal mode is the best for the National Nutrition Project and that the Milk+X mode should serve only as a temporary transition to a hot meal mode. Yet Gu asserted that "in most regions, governments organically connected the two projects by promoting Milk+N mode and have succeeded significantly and gained much experience." By portraying the two projects as reciprocal, Gu misled the audience and the public regarding the relationship between the two projects.

In his 2015 interview with Xinhuanet (C. Lu, 2015), Gu stated, "Children in less developed rural areas have never drunk milk, therefore their nutritional status is generally much worse than [that of] urban children. . . . The concept of drinking milk to improve the nutrition level of schoolchildren advocated by the School Milk Project has been accepted by the National Nutrition Project. . . . The two projects to improve the nutrition status of schoolchildren have the same goal. And the National Nutrition Project has required including milk [in the food provided to schoolchildren]. Therefore, the two projects have common goals and good connections." Gu has portrayed the hunger and malnutrition problem among rural children as a "milk divide" to make the public believe that School Milk is the best solution to the problem. He has also misinformed the public by saying that "the National Nutrition Project has required including milk [in the food provided to schoolchildren]" to make people believe that the two projects have the same goal. Gu (C. Lu, 2015) further stated: "In this year's National People's Congress . . . some deputies proposed to make milk a required food in the National Nutrition Project. I completely agree with this advice. . . . Regardless [of] whether the school has a school kitchen and dining room, the students should drink milk in lunches or at recess. And the school must ensure that they drink milk every day. School Milk products will make the food provided by the National Nutrition Project more nutritional." Here, Gu shows that the ultimate goal of the dairy industry is to impose packaged milk and the Milk+X mode on the National Nutrition Project to ensure that it can continue benefiting and profiting from the National Nutrition Subsidies. Having promoted the requirement that students drink School Milk at recess, it shifted to advocating that students drink it at lunch in dining rooms, in addition to recess, a strategy to make use of the loopholes in the Ministry of Education's policy. The vague policy from the Ministry of Education never clearly requires the abandonment of the Milk+X mode; it only requires that schools use school kitchens and dining rooms to provide meals to students. Therefore, drinking packaged milk at lunchtime in a dining room supplemented by eating eggs boiled in school kitchens will superficially satisfy the requirement from the ministry. To protect their own interests, the entire dairy industry, including the largest dairy companies and business associations, collaborated to oppose the hot meal mode.

The vagueness of the actual policy, based on the wording of documents from the central government and the Ministry of Education, provided ammunition for dairy industry campaigns to promote the Milk+X mode and oppose the hot meal mode. For example, the official website of the School Milk Project contains a special page about the relationship between the National Nutrition Project and the School Milk Project, citing the vague reply of the Ministry of Education to the recommendation of the CEOs of the dairy industry during the National People's Congress in 2015. This is aimed at giving readers the impression that the Ministry of Education encouraged or even required the National Nutrition Project to buy School Milk products with the National Nutrition Subsidies: "The ministry of Education will coordinate with the Dairy Association to ensure the promotion of the School Milk Project connected with the National Nutrition Project . . . and to expand the coverage of the School Milk Project" (2015).

In June 2016, the State Council organized an inspection of the implementation of the National Nutrition Project in eighteen provinces. The inspection report reconfirmed the significance of building school kitchens as part of the project and specified that the project should implement a hot meal mode using those kitchens. For example, the inspection report stated: "The shift to a school kitchen [meal providing] mode needs to be improved: First, the progress in building school kitchens is very slow in some regions. . . . Second, in some areas, schools have failed to start using these newly built school kitchens in a timely manner. . . . Third, some officials in local governments are waiting passively. They do not do enough to provide students with full lunches using the school kitchens." The report even stated, "For those schools that already completed the building of school kitchens, they must provide hot meals to students as soon as possible" (State Council of the People's Republic of China, 2016). But the inspection report stated the following in the food safety section: "[The schools] must require proof of inspection [from the providers] for livestock products such as meat, chicken, and eggs. . . . [As for milk products], the schools should choose to buy milk products with a School Milk of China logo. . . . These measures will ensure food quality and improve and monitor food safety from the purchasing and distribution process." The statement that "the schools should choose to buy milk products with a School Milk of China logo" almost satisfied the fourth requirement of the recommendation proposed by the elite dairy industry CEOs to the National People's Congress in 2015, which was to "establish the regulation that the National Nutrition Project must use milk products with the School Milk of China logo." This offered the dairy companies affiliated with the Dairy Association of China a monopoly over milk products in the National Nutrition Project. The State Council seems not to have realized the tension between the hot meal mode that it advocated and the packaged-milk-dominated Milk+X mode in the competition for the National Nutrition Subsidies. Moreover, the dairy industry used this statement again and again to misinform the general public and local governments. For example, in her plenary speech at the China Students Nutrition Summit in October 2017, Liu Ling—the vice director of the Dairy Association of China—stated: "The implementation of the National Nutrition Project for rural schoolchildren provided a new opportunity for the School Milk of China Project. In 2016, the inspection report on the National Nutrition Project from the State Council stated that 'the schools should choose to buy milk products with [a] School Milk of China logo.' This indicated that the School Milk of China Project is organically connected with the National Nutrition Project."

On September 13, 2017, several provincial newspapers, such as the *Huashang Newspaper* in Shaanxi Province and the *Sichuan Daily* in Sichuan Province, simultaneously published very similar articles from a dairy industry's public relations campaign, titled "Mengniu's School Milk Products Ensure the Success of the Student Nutrition Project."[15] The article in the *Huashang Newspaper* quoted the same sentence in the inspection report as an endorsement by the State Council of its argument that "milk has become an indispensable food in the National Nutrition Project." The article argued: "In fact, since the start of the National Nutrition Project, different parts of the country have innovatively developed different meal-providing modes in keeping with local conditions, for example Milk+X mode, drinking milk N times a week, and parents voluntarily ordering milk for students to drink during recess. At the same time, these different meal-providing modes demonstrate that the National Nutrition Project is undergoing a shift from 'having something to eat' to 'eating well.' Milk has become an indispensable food in the National Nutrition Project." This shows that the dairy industry continued to promote its elite CEOs' notion that "milk should be listed as a required food in the National Nutrition Project," a notion that was rejected by the Ministry of Education. And the dairy industry continued to advocate the use of the Milk+X mode in the National Nutrition Project, although the central government's policies reiterated the indispensability of the hot meal mode. The article aimed to misinform the public about the relationship between the hot meal mode and the Milk+X mode by creating the impression that the Milk+X mode is more advanced ("eating well") than the hot meal mode ("having something to eat"). Policy documents from the central government have clearly stated that the Milk+X mode should only be used as a temporary transition to a hot meal mode. Yet the article implies just the opposite: that the Milk+X mode (the advanced mode) will replace the hot meal mode (the less advanced mode). Liu's speech and the articles on Mengniu School Milk products demonstrated the dairy industry's constant efforts to inject School Milk products into the National Nutrition Project so as to profit from the project's subsidies.

The various efforts of the dairy industry to influence the policy of the central government on the National Nutrition Project were not very effective, given that both the Ministry of Education and the State Council agreed that the project should use the hot meal mode to provide hot lunches through school kitchens. Yet the Ministry of Education's vague reply to the recommendation of the dairy industry CEOs and its self-contradictory claims that the National Nutrition Project is not intended to provide free lunches suggest that the dairy industry's lobbying efforts succeeded in influencing some high-level officials in the central government. The real "success" of the efforts of the dairy industry has occurred at the provincial level. The Dairy Association is a network of sixty-eight big dairy companies located in twenty-nine provinces, all of which produce School Milk products. Many of these companies are among the biggest corporations in their home province or home county. Therefore, the dairy industry lobby has had more influence on the implementation of the National Nutrition Project at the provincial and county levels. This probably explains why, despite comprehensive scrutiny by the media, activists, and the Free Lunch Project, more than a third of the schools still use the Milk+X mode. For example, on June 11, 2016, the Department of Education of Shandong Province issued the following policy statement, titled *Notice on the Promotion of the School Milk of China Project*:

> Third, the promotion of the School Milk Project must follow the principle that students and parents voluntarily order School Milk products. . . . Schools should not force parents to order the products by any means.
>
> Fourth, the Department of Education encourages local governments to incorporate the School Milk Project into the National Nutrition Project. Currently, some counties in our province have made the School Milk Project a part of the National Nutrition Project and subsidize the School Milk Project. Other counties should learn from this experience and take it as an example.

This statement indicates that the department completely ignored the warning that, for students and parents, purchases of School Milk products must be voluntary, which it even stated in the third point of the notice. Without the approval of either students or parents, the subsidies for the students in the National Nutrition Project were used to buy School Milk products. Second, this provincial policy actually implemented the dairy industry's recommendations, which were rejected by the central government: (1) to make milk a required food for each meal for every student, and (2) to use the National Nutrition Subsidies to fully subsidize the School Milk products. Through incorporating or injecting the School Milk Project into the National Nutrition Project, provincial policies guarantee the dairy industry a substantial share of the National Nutrition Subsidies. Although 95 percent of the schools in Shandong Province already have school kitchens, according to the inspection report on the National Nutrition Project from the State Council, many of those rural schools have to use the Milk+X mode because this provincial policy forced them to use a large proportion of the subsidies to buy School Milk products.

Hebei Province represents another example of how School Milk was incorporated into provincial policy regarding the implementation of the National Nutrition Project. Ranked No. 1 in dairy production among the thirty-one provinces in China as of 2017 (*Report on Chinese Dairy Products*, 2017), Hebei is also the home province of big dairy companies such as Liu Yonghao's New Hope Dairy Corporation, the fourth-largest dairy company in China. This helps explain why Milk+X mode played a major role in the implementation of the National Nutrition Project in Hebei. For example, as of 2015, 71 percent of the schools receiving the National Nutrition Subsidies in Hebei (1,623 of 2,285) used the Milk+X mode (Ministry of Education, 2016b). The report from the province indicated that in 2016, the percentage of schools using the "school kitchen mode" increased to 54.3 percent in 2016 (Ministry of Education, 2017b). Based on this increase (from 30% to 54.3%), it would seem that the implementation of the National Nutrition Project in Hebei has shifted from a Milk+X mode to a hot meal mode. Yet the provincial policy on the National Nutrition Project stated that "schools providing meals through school kitchens must ensure that students drink School Milk more than three times a week." This is actually a variation of the Milk+X mode, requiring students receiving the National Nutrition Subsidies to drink milk N times a week, which is mentioned in the articles on Mengniu School Milk discussed earlier in the chapter. This means that all the schools covered by the National Nutrition Subsidies in Hebei have to use the Milk+X mode three of the five school days a week at least, regardless of whether they use school kitchens and dining rooms or not. This requirement by Hebei's Department of Education will ensure that the dairy industry continues to gain a substantial portion of the National Nutrition Subsidies in Hebei. The Shandong and Hebei examples demonstrate that the Milk+X mode is extending its share in the National Nutrition Project through its various forms being implemented by provincial governments.

The Free Lunch Project's Struggle against the Milk+X Mode

Over the last ten years, the Free Lunch Project and activists have advocated for a hot meal mode and fought against the Milk+X mode. Yet the strategy of the Free Lunch Project has not simply been to confront different levels of government. It has also aimed to engage and collaborate with the government at those different levels to implement a hot meal mode if they shifted away from the Milk+X mode. In his book, Deng Fei (2014) stated, "Some government agencies get the National Nutrition [Project] subsidies but do not provide hot meals to students. We, on [the] one hand, criticize and pressure them. On the other hand, we work on our own free lunch programs to provide an example. Through the two approaches, we try our best to push them in the right direction—abandoning the Milk+Bread mode and providing hot meals to students."

Besides the Milk+Bread incident in Fenghuang County, the Free Lunch Project exposed many other problematic cases related to the Milk+Bread mode in the National Nutrition Project. It played a key role in mobilizing public opinion and putting sustainable pressure on different levels of government to increase transparency of the use of the National Nutrition Subsidies and to investigate misconduct in the implementation of the National Nutrition Project. For example, at 6:29 on June 8, 2013, an activist revealed the following on Weibo: "The alleged milk poison incident in Zhongchuan Middle School in Gansu Lanzhou: The incident caused diarrhea for about 100 students and many of them have gone to local hospitals for treatment. After the incident, the local Bureau of Education was required to replace the milk products in the National Nutrition Project. The informant revealed that the milk products are from Shenghu Dairy." At 7:28, just an hour later, Deng Fei retweeted the activist's post to his five million followers and created the Weibo hashtag "#Let's shout together! Our children need hot meals!#". He then posted the following: "Just after the milk and cake poisoning of 500 students in Qinghai Datong on June 7, an alleged milk poisoning incident broke out in Zhongchuan Middle School in Gansu Lanzhou.... Although the problems of the National Nutrition Project gave more credit to our free lunch programs, we cannot accept the suffering of our children. Therefore, we must continue shouting: Our children need hot meals! Our children need [food] safety!" Within a day, more than 202 Weibo users retweeted Deng Fei's Weibo post to demand that the government thoroughly investigate the incident. This means that Deng Fei's post reached the five million people following his Weibo as well as all the followers of the 202 Weibo users. Just three weeks later, at 3:45 P.M. on June 26, 2013, CCTV featured this breaking news: "A food poisoning incident broke out in Xiandong Middle School in Lianyuan City, Hunan Province.... More than 150 students have been sent to hospitals for examinations.... The incident is suspected to be related to the milk provided by the National Nutrition Project." Fifteen minutes later, Deng Fei posted to his followers on Weibo: "Milk [provided by the National Nutrition Project] caused the food poisoning incident in Qinghai Datong [several days ago] and now the same problem happened again in Lianyuan, Hunan. Yuan Rengui! Yuan Rengui!!" In the post, Deng Fei demanded that Ministry of Education minister Yuan Rengui take action to remove the Milk+X mode from the National Nutrition Project. Eight minutes later, he posted again: "If the Ministry of Education does not stop providing [packaged] milk [in the National Nutrition Project], if the [food] safety of our children cannot be protected, I will call the name of the head of the Ministry of Education of China in Weibo every day [to remind the public who should be held accountable for this]. Until they shut down my Weibo account!" (Deng, 2013b). These posts were retweeted by 2,471 people within a day, reaching hundreds of millions of people.

In his new media advocacy, in addition to posting directly to his five million followers in Weibo, Deng Fei also employed a multichannel strategy to use mass media to mobilize the public and pressure the government to take action. At 9:13 P.M. the same day, Deng Fei posted a Weibo topic with the hashtag "#Most Recent Update on Hunan Lianyuan School Milk Poison Incident 1#": "Email from reporters at Lianyuan: First, more than 200 students were poisoned and the local government began to control information regarding the incident. Second, the school provided hot meals last year but was forced to shift to Milk+Bread this year. Third, the shift from hot meals to Milk+Bread was proposed by a vice mayor of Lianyuan. Fourth, the bread is made in Wuhan and the milk is from Yahua Dairy. Please provide more information to us. For the safety of our children, we must stand out! @Blue Media." He used "@Blue Media" to forward the post to an online community of investigative journalists calling themselves Blue Media Solon to ask them to investigate and report on this incident in the mass media.[16] Similarly, on April 25, 2013, Deng Fei posted a Weibo post with the hashtag

"#When On Earth Could the Milk+Bread Be Removed?#": "Scandal regarding the National Nutrition Project was exposed again in Fuyuan, Yunnan. Students had to eat moldy bread. Ministry of Education, please answer my question: it has been one and a half years [since the start of the National Nutrition Project], why can't children in Yunnan yet eat a hot meal? @Chuncheng Evening Post" (Deng, 2013a). He used "@Chuncheng Evening Post" to forward the post to the *Chuncheng Evening Post*, a leading newspaper in Yunan Province, to encourage them to investigate and report on the incident.

The Free Lunch Project was also aware that one reason for the Milk+Bread mode was that the initial subsidies standard of three yuan per student per lunch was insufficient for some schools to build their own kitchens, and the local government had no capacity to provide financial support to cover the operational cost of the hot meal mode. Therefore, to encourage and facilitate those schools to implement a hot meal mode, the Free Lunch Project provided funds to cover the operational cost of implementation and the cost of including teachers and preschool students in the free lunches. On July 18, 2013, almost three months after the scandal regarding the National Nutrition Project in Fuyuan, Yunnan, Deng Fei posted on Weibo: "We noticed that many less developed counties in Yunnan had to provide Milk+Bread to students and have been consistently criticized for various problems. We are willing to provide funds and a Free Lunch Project model to support Yunnan Province to provide safe lunches to all rural children in Yunnan." The Free Lunch Project even wanted to provide support for local governments that contended with the project previously, as long as they embraced the hot meal mode. For example, in the Milk+Bread incident at Fenghuang, Hunan Province, activists and the Free Lunch Project fiercely struggled against the Department of Education of Hunan Province. In December 2012, the department issued a policy notice stating that it would urge rural schools in the National Nutrition Project to abandon Milk+Bread mode and shift to a hot meal mode in spring semester 2013. About three months later, in March 2013, representatives of the Free Lunch Project met with the director of the Department of Education of Hunan Province to introduce the Free Lunch Project. The two parties decided to launch pilot projects, collaborating to provide free lunches using the model developed by the Free Lunch Project (Deng, 2014).

This does not mean that the Free Lunch Project does not have its own principles in pursuing collaborations with the government to redress hunger and malnutrition among children in less developed areas. Rather, compared with the government's vague policy regarding purchasing packaged milk from the dairy industry using the National Nutrition Subsidies, the Free Lunch Project has maintained a very clear and nonnegotiable policy toward packaged milk. As Deng Fei firmly stated in his book, "The Free Lunch program refuses to co-exist with Milk+X mode. This is our principle" (2014). If a school were to buy packaged milk with the National Nutrition Subsidies or other funds, the Free Lunch Project would be forced to sever its financial support for that school. From the very early stages of the project, an important goal of its inspections is to ensure that the rural schools are not using the National Nutrition Subsidies to buy milk products from the dairy industry. On September 27, 2012, the Free Lunch Project inspected the free lunch program of the Haoyou Primary School in Fenghuang County, Hunan Province. It reported: "The inspector did not see packaged milk products in the school. . . . Yet during the visit to four students' families, the inspector was told 'the kid had lunch yesterday but drank milk the day before yesterday.' The parent also displayed the used milk box to take a picture. The parent also told the inspector that when the school didn't cook lunches, they provided milk or eggs" (Free Lunch Project, 2012d). This indicates that the milk issue is a core concern of the school inspection and that the inspector is required to investigate it from different sources. In October 2012, the regional coordinator of the Free Lunch Project decided that the project had to withdraw from Haoyou Primary School. Lan Xiaowan, a regional coordinator of the Free Lunch Project, stated this decision in the report:

> For the first half of the year, we've been negotiating with the Education Bureau of Fenghuang to cooperate with them and to use the National Nutrition [Project] subsidies to provide hot meals; but [we] failed. Then we communicated with teachers in the school. They were willing to give up the milk and bread from the National Nutrition Project and work with us to provide hot meals. I personally said to them several times not to take the milk and bread; otherwise we have to withdraw from their school. They promised they wouldn't. . . . Given what has happened now, we had to advise that the school be withdrawn from the Free Lunch Project. (Free Lunch Project, 2012b)

This passage illustrates that the Free Lunch Project and the activist worked very hard to negotiate with different levels of government and to persuade the rural schools to shift the Milk+X mode to a hot meal mode. Second, it shows the determination of the activist and the project that the free lunch programs cannot coexist with any form of the Milk+X mode. Since 2015, the project used evaluation forms to systematically assess the free lunch programs in rural schools. To highlight the significance of the milk issue, these evaluation forms included the "milk issue" in a list of "important problems" that schools might have. Inspectors were required to investigate whether schools had any of these problems. If any of these "important problems" were found at a school, the school would have to explain the problem in writing (Free Lunch Project, 2020d). Among the eight "important problems" for which schools might be charged, that of "using the National Nutrition Subsid[ies] or free lunch funds to buy milk and bread" is the most serious, costing twice as much in fines (40 points) as having its students lie to an inspector (Free Lunch Project, 2020d). One question about milk is also part of the student survey in the inspection: "Has the school ever given you milk and bread [for lunch, breakfast or as a snack]?" Over the past eight years, the Free Lunch Project has withdrawn its financial support from many schools because of decisions by local governments to use various modes of Milk+X in the National Nutrition Project. For example, in September 2017, five schools in Qinghai Province were withdrawn from the Free Lunch Project because the local governments used a Milk+X mode to provide National Nutrition Lunch to the schools. Up till then, all five schools had collaborated with the Free Lunch Project for more than three years using the hot meal mode and performed well during inspections (Free Lunch Project, 2017c). Yet due to the decisions of local governments, the students in the five schools had to lose hot meals with meat and vegetables that were cooked in school kitchens. And every day since fall semester 2017, they have to eat packaged milk, bread, and eggs provided by corporations and transported long distances. This is also a waste of the kitchens that were financed by the Free Lunch Project and built by the schools. The Free Lunch Project has also been pressured by media, dairy corporations, and netizens because of its principle not to coexist with the use of packaged milk. Deng Fei (2014) emphasized this as follows: "Because of our principle, some schools left. They changed from hot meals to milk and bread. We were also under significant pressure from the media and dairy corporations. They claimed that we use children as hostages to challenge the government. Netizens also questioned 'Why are children who drink milk provided by the government not allowed to eat your lunches?!'" Deng Fei (2014) responded to this pressure by saying, "I told the Free Lunch team: this is our red line. We will never make any concession on it!" This case illustrates the firm position the project took in contestations with the government and corporations.

Deng Fei (2014) stated, "Any [social] change is a gradual, slow, and complex process. Since becoming an activist, I fully understand that haste makes waste." He predicted that after a substantial period of struggle, by 2014 the large majority of schools in the National Nutrition Project would begin to use a hot meal mode. Yet he was overoptimistic. By 2017, only 71 percent of the schools fully or partly prepared lunches for their students in school kitchens (Ministry of Education, 2017).[17] Given that various versions of Milk+X were imposed on schools that provided lunches through their kitchens, as discussed earlier, the real percentage of schools using a hot meal mode would be even lower. Large-scale change is not easy to achieve. Deng Fei and the Free Lunch Project underestimated the resistance to the hot meal mode by different levels of governments and the dairy industry. During the 2017 National People's Congress, Wang Jinghai, the CEO of China's third-largest dairy company, proposed a new slogan: "Implementing the milk drinking project comprehensively to improve the physical health of the nation." He gave this advice: "Since 2014, many schools have removed milk from the National Nutrition Project. By June 2016, the sales of School Milk products in the National Nutrition Project had dropped to 13 million boxes per day. Yet the total number of schoolchildren in China [both rural and urban] is 140 million, but only 20 million of them drink School Milk" (X. Pan, 2017). This suggests that elite CEOs of the dairy industry continued to use the National People's Congress, the legislative body of the PRC, as well as other channels to pressure and lobby the Ministry of Education to make the policy of the National Nutrition Project more pro-milk. More importantly, the data disclosed in the advice shows that roughly 65 percent (13 million out of 20 million) of School Milk product sales were from the National Nutrition Project. This suggests that sustaining the various Milk+X modes in the National Nutrition Project is crucial to the entire milk industry.

On June 17, 2017, the Dairy Association of China published *White Paper on Promoting the School Milk of China Project in a New Era*. The white paper stated: "The School Milk of China Project started from big cities. . . . Before 2011, the project did not cover any rural regions, especially less developed rural areas. Since the launch of the National Nutrition Project for schoolchildren in less developed rural areas, milk with the School Milk of China logo entered rural schools and the sales of School Milk products have increased rapidly." This suggests that in the so-called new era, the dairy industry planned to continue targeting the National Nutrition Project and the subsidies provided to schoolchildren in underdeveloped rural regions by injecting School Milk products into the National Nutrition Project. The white paper also stated what the strategy in the "new era" is: "We established the following strategy: First, use multiple approaches to enter schools. Develop multiple modes to drink milk. . . . Second . . . drink milk in class recess as well as in dining rooms. Collaborate with governments as well as NGOs. . . . Our goal is very simple: to have school-children drink School Milk" (Dairy Association of China, 2017). In this new strategy, the dairy industry would focus on having students "drink milk in class recess as well as in dining rooms." This would increase the cases of students drinking packaged milk in school dining rooms, as in Hebei Province, as discussed earlier. And local governments and the dairy industry would develop and impose new Milk+X modes as part of the National Nutrition Project. In December 2020, the association published its own five-year plan for the School Milk of China Project from 2020 to 2025. It aimed to increase the number of students covered by the School Milk Project by 34 percent (from 26 million to 35 million) and to increase the daily supply of School Milk products by 50 percent (from 21.3 million boxes to 32 million boxes). In a market that is already crowded with 123 producers, the Dairy Association of China planned to increase the registered producers by 46.3 percent (from 123 to 180) (Dairy Association of China, 2020). It continued to "promote the School Milk of China Project to be deeply connected with the National Nutrition Project" as their strategy to achieve these goals. (Dairy Association of China, 2020). To maintain and increase the huge share of the National Nutrition Subsidies they receive, the dairy industry will continue obstructing the implementation of the hot meal mode in the National Nutrition Project. The long battle will continue between the hot meal mode advocated by activists, the Free Lunch Project, and other NGOs and various Milk+X modes in the National Nutrition Project. What is at stake is the rights and needs of twenty-six million children in underdeveloped regions in China to be free from hunger and malnutrition.

The Rise of New Activism: Strength and Weakness

The multidimensional stakeholder relationship in the Free Lunch Project indicates the emergence of a new form of activism in China that is different from both conventional forms of activism in the West and online activism that has been analyzed in previous research (e.g., Cammaerts, 2007; de Jong et al., 2005; Frey et al., 2006; Martin, 2007; Qiu, 2009 G. Yang, 2009). First, unlike the conventional conception of activism in the West (e.g., de Jong et al., 2005; Martin, 2007), this new activism in China no longer focuses exclusively on advocacy. Activism in China has developed what activists call "strategic philanthropy," which uses effective actions and projects to gain wide public support in order to guide government policymaking. Compared with online Chinese activism that has been examined previously (e.g., Qiu, 2009; Tai, 2006; G. Yang, 2009), this new activism has put more emphasis on fostering collaboration among multiple stakeholders to generate development and large-scale social change, which in its view requires the engagement of different stakeholders (including the government). This new activism collaborates with the government as long as the government addresses the same social problems it has targeted. Yet it also criticizes and attacks problematic government policies and misconduct through actions for social change. It uses long-term online advocacy, public opinion, and mass media reports to constantly pressure different levels of government to redress problematic policies and to steer government accountability and transparency in policymaking and implementation. Like online activism illustrated in previous research, this new activism challenges the authority of the Chinese government but uses a different approach. By showing the public that activists and NGOs are capable of solving social problems in more effective ways, this new activism dispels the old discourse of hegemony generated by long-standing propaganda, which has represented the government and the party as necessary "leaders" for every effort to bring about development and social change in China. Rather than being led by the government, this new activism educates and guides the government to carry out social change and promote development.

The Free Lunch Project is only one of many examples of this new activism that aims to induce development and social change through collaborations with multiple stakeholders. Actions and projects with similar strategies have also emerged in COVID-19 response, as presented in chapter 7, and in other fields, such as poverty reduction, health, education, and environmental protection. For example, the China-Dolls Center for Rare Disorders (CCRD) is an NGO that was initiated by activists and patients with rare disorders to support and empower those in their community and to fight for their equal rights in health, education, and employment. The goal of the center is "removing social stigma, improving social security system, changing public policy, and promoting the equal rights of medication, education, employment, and social integration for the rare disorder population" (CCRD, 2020). Between 2009 and 2018, it has raised more than 25 million yuan in donations. Another notable example is Yi Nong Dai (YND), the largest peer-to-peer lending platform for poverty reduction in China, which aims to reduce poverty among rural women through collaborations between "charitable lenders," NGOs working on poverty reduction and women's empowerment, local governments, and rural women. On the platform, charitable lenders can choose a project of rural women to lend or donate at least 100 yuan ($15.8). Rural NGOs or rural cooperatives help YND select "credible projects" initiated by rural women, assist the implementation of the projects, and monitor the use of microloans. This project also focuses on empowering rural women and women rights in rural communities. YND (2020b) stated that it aims to empower rural women and increase gender equality in decision-making regarding efforts to reduce poverty in their own families and communities. Therefore, the platform gives more priority to projects of rural women. Consequently, the large majority of borrowers on the platform are all rural women. YND also requires cooperating NGOs to offer workshops on gender, women's rights, and women in community development to increase various capacities of rural women in local communities. From 2009 to 2021, 179,429 charitable lenders have lent 379,779,200.63 yuan to support 29,878 projects of rural farmers in more than thirteen provinces in China (YND, 2021). By December 2018, the repayment rate of the projects on YND platform was near 99 percent.

Second, compared with online activism seen in earlier research, this new activism is more patient and focuses more on long-term change. As Deng (2014) states, any efforts to promote social change entail a long, complex, and gradual process wherein "haste makes waste." This activism aims more toward evolutionary change than revolutionary change. Like more conventional forms of activism in the West, the new activism is confident in its own "ability to act and make or change history" (Cammaerts, 2007). Yet this confidence is not manifested as intensive head-to-head direct confrontation with the government as in revolutionary change. In the ongoing efforts of activists to generate change from one rural school to the next, this confidence entails patient negotiations with different levels of government against problematic state and corporate practices, as well as long-term advocacy work by activists to change governmental policy. The new activism believes that large-scale long-term change requires the sustained efforts and commitments of activists, NGOs, and the general public. Therefore, in their actions, they put more emphasis on gaining sustainable support from the public than on attracting intensive media coverage through vigorous campaigns. In their projects, they pay more attention to long-term change in different parts of the country than completely focusing on the success of one region. In the Free Lunch Project, for example, when they faced resistance from the local government in one region, they sought to make headway in other regions. The Free Lunch Project fully understands that large-scale change is never easy, especially in authoritarian contexts like China, and is never achieved overnight. For ten years, it has been committed to the fight against hunger and malnutrition among rural children. And it will continue sticking to its course, knowing that it has a long way to go to achieve its mission. Other projects in the new activism also pay special attention to long-term change. For example, in addressing why it believes a microloan approach is better than pure donations, YND asserted that it is more sustainable. It believes that the microloan approach attracts long-term contributions from charitable lenders, fosters self-reliant poverty reduction projects in rural communities, and provides sustainable long-term supports to rural communities. It stated, "A child suffering long-term hunger needs sustainable supports for three meals a day, rather than a luxurious dinner. A land suffering draught needs sustainable water rather than a flood.... Poverty reduction and supports to rural communities are the same.... We believe in the power of long-term efforts [to generate changes]" (YND, 2017).

This new activism also has weaknesses. It tends to be overly optimistic, as Deng Fei (2014) boldly conveyed in his book: "When the Internet focuses the tiny strength [of ordinary individuals] in huge numbers, everything will change." It overlooks many complex issues related to development and social change in China, as with the resistance to, and obstruction of, change. NGO and activist efforts for development and social change may face constant resistance and obstruction by the government and corporations, which may even collaborate together in that resistance. In this case, for example, due to the stake in profiting from huge National Nutrition Project subsidies for children in underdeveloped regions, state-owned companies such as Wondersun Dairy, private companies such as New Hope Dairy, and other agents of the dairy industry have actively campaigned to obstruct the implementation of a hot meal mode, which has proven to be the most effective means of overcoming hunger and malnutrition among children in disadvantaged areas.[18] The central government is currently unable or unwilling to really hold local governments accountable for the implementation of the National Nutrition Project. For example, in this case, the central government has reiterated in various policy documents that the National Nutrition Project must use the mode that school kitchens provide hot lunches to students, which is the hot meal mode advocated by the Free Lunch Project and activists, and that the Milk+X mode is only a temporary transition to the hot meal mode and must be replaced as soon as possible. It even allocated nearly 20 billion yuan for the rural schools supported by the National Nutrition Subsidies to build kitchens and dining rooms. Yet provincial governments have designed various forms of the Milk+X mode to infiltrate the "school kitchen" mode proposed by the central government and make Milk+X a permanent, major part of the National Nutrition Project. That is why we see the ironic policy from provincial governments that students are required to drink boxed milk in school dining rooms more than three times a week. Moreover, activists, NGOs, and the media pay a lot of attention to scrutinizing policies from the central government but in many cases overlook or are incapable of monitoring the policies and implementation of the policies by local governments. And in underdeveloped regions where activism, NGOs, and relative independent media are less developed, local communities have far less capacity than big cities to hold government accountable. For example, in the Milk+Bread incident, the key activist, Diaoya, is actually a volunteer teacher from an urban region. Without the initiation of this urban-based activist, it is very unlikely that the problems with the National Nutrition Project in Fenghuang County would have been exposed online and attracted nationwide attention. Given the lack of capacity of local communities to hold government accountable, the results of government-led projects for development and social change largely depend on self-regulation and the agenda of local officials. The report based on the data from ten thousand schools in a hundred counties in the National Nutrition Project from the China Development Research Foundation (2017) also acknowledged this problem: "Whether [the National Nutrition] Project would be effectively implemented is first and foremost depending on the leaders [of the local governments]. Whether the project is effective depends on whether the local government has a leader that really cares about children's health. . . . If local leaders think this issue [is] of no significance and focus on economic development and short-term performance, then the project is less effective."

This is a significant problem in government-led policies and projects for development and social change in China. In this sociopolitical context, the new activism is not yet able to fully confront this problem. Nor does this new activism fully account for the unequal power relations in actions for development and social change between the government and corporations and activists and local communities. Prior research in communication for development has shown that long-term social change must address the unequal power relations among different stakeholders in a society or community (e.g., Melkote & Steeves, 2015a; Servaes, 1999, 2008). Melkote and Steeves (2015a) argue, "Real change may not be possible unless we address power inequities between marginalized individuals and groups at the grassroots and those who make policy." The disparity of power between government and corporations and activists and rural communities is a significant problem in this case. For example, the National People's Congress, the legislative body of the PRC that is supposed to hold the government accountable, is closed to activists due to lack of genuine elections. Elite CEOs of the dairy industry, however, can assume positions as deputies of the National People's Congress to constantly lobby and pressure the Ministry of Education to promote policies that benefit their industry. To address this kind of power imbalance, activists have to connect their actions with various forms of advocacy for badly needed political change in Chinese society. Yet activists in the Free Lunch Project have rarely made any effort to engage in such discussions. Moreover, due to the attempt to foster collaborations with multiple stakeholders, including the government, this new activism focuses more on fields such as hunger, rural development, poverty reduction, women's rights, education, and health, where government is more tolerant of grassroots actions led by activists and NGOs. It also therefore pays less attention to, and has less influence on, fields that the Chinese government finds more politically sensitive, such as labor rights, freedom of expression, and anti-corruption. Overall, this emerging activism has mobilized new approaches and new strategies, increasing the diversity and richness of actions generating development and social change in Chinese society.

7

NCP Life Support Network

New Media Actions against
COVID-19

> We used to believe that you have all been well treated and will soon be cured
> [of COVID-19], until thousands of test results and phone numbers appeared
> online in desperate calls for help. We recruited doctors attempting to explain
> to you the meaning of terminology such as "ground glass opacity."[1] Regrettably,
> what we could do for you is extremely limited, as "the distance" between we and
> you is great and insurmountable. What we could do is to reduce our yearning
> to a minimum: getting a simple message that you have been admitted to the
> hospital. HOLD ON, DO NOT GIVE UP! (NCP Life Support Network, 2020c)

On February 5, 2020, this message was headlined on the NCP Life Support Network's Weibo, two weeks after the lockdown of Wuhan, a city of eleven million
people and the epicenter of COVID-19 in China. It documented the hardest
moment of China's COVID-19 crisis. It also illuminated the fundamental reason why thousands of activists, volunteers, and ordinary people were mobilized
to build the NCP Life Support Network, a network of grassroots organizations
that came together to save lives and support the groups that were vulnerable to
various health and social problems resulting from the COVID-19 pandemic.

On January 22, on the eve of the Wuhan lockdown, Hao Nan, a health professional turned activist at the Zhuoming Disaster Information Center, launched a
grassroots organization called New Coronavirus Relief (nCoV Relief) together

with other NGO activists and health professionals. The initial goal of nCoV Relief was to provide those infected with COVID-19 and their families with free telehealth services and mental health assistance in response to the serious overflow of hospital patients in Wuhan, as stated in its Weibo and volunteer recruitment announcement published on January 23. Within several hours, nCoV Relief had received roughly two thousand applications from health professionals in top hospitals outside Wuhan and from other volunteers around the country. At the peak of the pandemic in Wuhan, the grassroots telehealth service had about four hundred doctors and two hundred social workers and mental health professionals serving more than nine hundred individuals infected with COVID-19 and their families (N. Hao, 2020). With the participation of and collaborations with other grassroots organizations, nCoV Relief quickly developed into a network of grassroots organizations that responded to fast-changing problems affecting the lives and well-being of various vulnerable groups in the pandemic. This network was later named the NCP (novel coronavirus pneumonia) Life Support Network.

From mid-January to early April, the NCP Life Support Network conducted and coordinated hundreds of actions to provide badly needed support and assistance to those susceptible to the COVID-19 crisis. This included those with COVID-19 and their families, COVID-19 survivors, non-COVID-19 patients with serious illnesses,[2] elders living alone, migrant workers in Wuhan, Chinese returning from other countries, pregnant women and women in general, and frontline health workers, including Wuhan health workers and those coming to join the fight from other provinces. The problems that the network targeted were broad and cross-disciplinary, including public health problems, such as the difficulty of maintaining and expanding the capacity of hospitals treating COVID-19 patients; lack of testing capacity; shortages of ventilators and PPE; and social problems, such as discrimination toward COVID-19 survivors and increased domestic violence and sexual harassment during the lockdown.

NCP Life Support Network: A Network to Save Lives and Support Vulnerable Groups during the COVID-19 Crisis

In other chapters, my analysis addresses the need to identify the problems targeted by new media interventions in order to understand the social implications of those interventions for social change and development. The fundamental mission of the NCP Life Support Network has been to save lives and to provide supports to various groups that are vulnerable to health and/or social problems associated with COVID-19, which has caused an unprecedented public health crisis. The network needed to overcome two challenges in order to achieve its goals—challenges that set it apart from the cases presented in previous chapters. First, due to the rapidly changing nature of the crisis, new social and/or health problems related to COVID-19 emerged at a tremendous speed during the crisis. Second, the COVID-19 crisis penetrated the whole society, not just the health sector. Those vulnerable to various problems caused by COVID-19 occupied every corner of society. Therefore, the network first had to be adaptive to effectively achieve its goal. It needed to have the capacity to quickly respond and provide solutions to the various problems that emerged at different stages of the crisis. Second, the network needed to be able to attend to the suffering of a wide range of social groups and respond to them quickly. Table 7.1 provides a rough list of the network's projects and actions from January 23 through March 20.

Table 7.1 shows that within the sixty-one days from the start of the Wuhan lockdown on January 23 to March 20, the NCP Life Support Network conducted or coordinated more than twenty-eight actions. These actions quickly responded to various public health and/or social problems that arose in the crisis at tremendous speed. The column "Problem Targeted" illustrates the breadth and depth of these problems. The expertise and knowledge required to effectively respond to these problems was correspondingly vast in breadth. Conducting and coordinating so many projects targeting a broad range of problems in sixty-one days would be impossible for a conventional development initiative led by a few full-time professionals. The NCP Life Support Network's solution to this otherwise impossible task was to attract and organize a large number of volunteers and grassroots organizations through the internet and other ICTs to collectively respond to these problems. This "volunteer principle" was a core principle of the network. On February 17, the network posted on its Weibo: "Since 23, we firmly commit to our 'Volunteer Principle': we do not accept any financial support or material donations [to fund the network]." All participants of the network's projects and actions work as volunteers. For example, the doctors in its free telehealth service are all full-time health professionals in China's top hospitals outside Hubei. They used their spare time to collaboratively provide services and supports to those infected with COVID-19 in Wuhan.

According to Hao Nan, the founder of the network, the NCP Life Support Network employed a "decentralized" structure to attract and mobilize grassroots organizations with expertise on various problems to join the network in order to effectively respond to the crisis collectively. When asked about the most important aspects of coordinating the network, Hao Nan stated that decentralization was the most important:

> The network has so many projects. It would be an impossible mission if I
> managed or directed these projects in a conventional way—however hard
> I worked every day. . . . Therefore, decentralization is crucially important. We
> must give power to grassroots organizations. Let each grassroots organization
> choose and form its own model. Let them run their projects or actions
> independently. As a coordinator of the network, my work is to promote the
> communication between different groups, learn what each group is doing and
> their strengths, and facilitate reciprocal collaborations between different
> groups based on their strengths and expertise.

Table 7.1
The Actions of the NCP Life Support Network

Initiation of action	Project/Action	Description	Problem targeted	Beneficiary community
1/23/2020	Free telehealth and mental health services and other assistance to those with COVID-19 and their families	Provided those with COVID-19 and their families with free telehealth and mental health services in response to the serious hospital overflow in Wuhan; provided one-on-one assistance to help those with severe COVID-19 symptoms secure beds in hospitals	Lack of hospital capacity to treat those with COVID-19 in Wuhan	Those with COVID-19 and their families
1/23/2020	The information project of the network	Collected, documented, organized, managed, and disseminated information for various vulnerable groups seeking help in the crisis and information on available resources from organizations and people who wanted to help	Lack of well-organized, reliable, and public-accessible platforms focusing on the two kinds of information. The gap between help seekers and the people and organizations who aim to help	Vulnerable people seeking help and groups that sought to help them (e.g, donors, activists, and NGOs)
1/23/2020	The communication project of the network	Created and disseminated information regarding COVID-19 to the public	Lack of knowledge about COVID-19; lack of reliable COVID-19 information platforms; infodemic[a]	The public, including those with COVID-19
1/25/2020	The project to donate PPEs and medical equipment to hospitals in Hubei	Jointly collected, organized, and managed PPE needs and requirements for qualified PPEs from hospitals; collected, organized, and managed information on global PPE makers and dealers; collectively created information on the compatibilities of PPE standards used in different countries; coordinated the purchase, donation, and transportation of PPEs and other medical equipment	Shortage of PPEs for frontline health workers in hospitals; shortage of ventilators and other medical equipment	Frontline health workers and people with COVID-19

Date	Project	Action	Problem	Target population
1/26/2020	Wuhan Pregnant Women Group	Recruited obstetricians to provide telehealth services to pregnant women in Wuhan; recruited volunteers to assist families in contacting hospitals to secure beds; and organized local community workers and volunteer drivers to drive pregnant women to hospitals	Health system difficulties in providing obstetrical services to pregnant women and problematic policies that ignored the needs of pregnant women during the COVID-19 crisis	Pregnant women and their families
1/26/2020	The network's real-time portal for information channels and products for identifying COVID-19 close contacts	Created, managed, and published a portal for web links of information channels and products for identifying COVID-19 close contacts	Difficulty in determining whether someone is a close contact of COVID-19	The public; potential COVID-19 close contacts
1/26/2020	Project to provide information on the availability of beds for those with COVID-19 in Wuhan hospitals	Created a real-time, verified, and comprehensive list of available beds for those with COVID-19 in COVID-19 designated hospitals in Wuhan	Lack of hospital capacity to treat those with COVID-19 in Wuhan; lack of timely and accurate information regarding available beds for those with COVID-19 in Wuhan hospitals	Those with COVID-19 and their families
1/27/2020	Project to protect the privacy of people returning from Wuhan	Provided consoling services and legal advice for returnees from Wuhan whose privacy rights were violated	Lack of protection of the privacy of people returning from Wuhan to their hometowns during the COVID-19 crisis	Returnees from Wuhan to their hometowns
1/31/2020	Advocacy project for pregnant women	Advocated to change the public health policy regarding pregnant women during the COVID-19 crisis in Wuhan	Lack of public health policy to take care of pregnant women during the COVID-19 crisis in Wuhan	Pregnant women and their families
2/2/2020	Home Quarantine Guidelines for Those Infected with or Presumptively Infected with COVID-19	Created and published the Home Quarantine Guidelines for Those Infected with or Presumptively Infected with COVID-19, versions 1 and 2	Lack of hospital capacity to treat those with COVID-19 and lack of capacity for COVID-19 testing in Wuhan	Individuals infected with or presumptively infected with COVID-19 and their families

(continued)

Table 7.1 (Continued)

Initiation of action	Project/Action	Description	Problem targeted	Beneficiary community
2/4/2020	Home oxygen generator donation project	Provided free oxygen generators to home quarantined individuals infected with or presumptively infected with COVID-19	Lack of hospital capacity to treat those with COVID-19 and lack of capacity for COVID-19 testing in Wuhan	Individuals infected with or presumptively infected with COVID-19 and their families
2/5/2020	Information collection project on individuals with COVID-19 seeking help	Collaborated with *People's Daily* in collecting information on individuals with COVID-19 seeking help to get hospitalized	Lack of hospital capacity to treat those with COVID-19, lack of capacity for COVID-19 testing, and difficulty of those with COVID-19 in getting beds in hospitals	Individuals infected with or presumptively infected with COVID-19 and their families
2/6/2020	Comprehensive list of Wuhan hospitals admitting and treating COVID-19 patients with preexisting conditions	Created a comprehensive list of Wuhan hospitals admitting and treating COVID-19 patients with preexisting conditions, including pregnant women and patients with renal failure or surgical disease	Lack of hospital capacity to treat COVID-19 patients with preexisting conditions; lack of timely and accurate information regarding that capacity	Those with COVID-19 and with preexisting conditions and their families
2/7/2020	Fangcang hospital project[b]	Investigated the lack of adequate basic provisions, such as heating and warm water, among Fangcang hospitals and makeshift quarantine camps; created and published guidelines and checklists of personal belongings needed for admission to a Fangcang hospital or a makeshift quarantine camp; created and published grassroots videos of Fangcang patients about their lives in Fangcang hospitals	Lack of basic provisions in Fangcang hospitals and makeshift quarantine camps; lack of knowledge about Fangcang hospitals	COVID-19 patients with mild symptoms and their families; the public

Date			
2/11/2020	*Situation report on COVID-19 in Hubei Province*	Created and published six grassroots reports on the COVID-19 situation in Hubei (Feb. 11 to March 8), analyzing the crisis, risks and problems, and potential solutions	Lack of independent firsthand reports and analysis of the situation of the COVID-19 crisis in Hubei	Grassroots organizations, NGOs, activists, and volunteers; the public; the government
2/13/2020	The project to provide information and assistance for non-COVID-19 patients	Collected, organized, verified, and published information on the availability of beds for non-COVID-19 patients with cancer, cardiovascular disease, renal failure, surgical disease, etc., in Wuhan hospitals	Lack of hospital capacity to treat non-COVID-19 patients with severe or chronic diseases; lack of timely and accurate information regarding that capacity; difficulties of non-COVID-19 patients to get hospitalized	Non-COVID-19 patients and their families
2/14/2020	Anti-discrimination new media campaign for COVID-19 survivors	Launched new media campaign: "Please Don't Discriminate against COVID-19 Survivors"	Discrimination of COVID-19 survivors	COVID-19 survivors, their families, and the public
2/18/2020	Telehealth services and assistance for non-COVID-19 patients	Shifted the future focus of telehealth services to non-COVID-19 patients; opened telehealth services and assistance for non-COVID-19 patients	Lack of hospital capacity to treat non-COVID-19 patients; difficulties of non-COVID-19 patients to get hospitalized	Non-COVID-19 patients and their families
2/21/2020	Anti–sexual harassment during the COVID-19 Crisis	Launched an action called Anti–sexual harassment during the COVID-19 Crisis; created and published *Guideline to Anti–sexual harassment during the COVID-19 Crisis: How to Protect Yourself from Sexual Harassment during COVID-19*	Sexual harassment during COVID-19	Women such as female COVID-19 patients and female volunteers

(continued)

Table 7.1 (Continued)

Initiation of action	Project/Action	Description	Problem targeted	Beneficiary community
2/25/2020	The network's information project to support heath workers coming from other parts of the country	Created, managed, and published a portal for web links to projects and activities providing logistical supports for frontline health workers from other parts of the country; these projects/actions aimed to provide health workers with hotel rooms, food, in-city travel, and other daily life needs	Lack of logistical supports and accommodations (lodging, food, in-city travel, and other daily life needs) for frontline health workers coming from other parts of the country; lack of platforms aggregating information on projects/activities that provide those supports	Frontline health workers from other parts of the country who came to Wuhan to aid in the fight against COVID-19
2/26/2020	Project to support those stuck in Wuhan due to the lockdown	Collaborated with the Wuhan Civil Affairs Bureau to provide supports to people who were stuck in Wuhan and had lost their source of income (generally homeless people and migrant workers who had lost their jobs); the supports included free accommodations, potential jobs or volunteer opportunities, and less than RMB 3,000 in cash	Lack of support for homeless people and those stuck in Wuhan without a source of income during the crisis	Homeless people and those stuck in Wuhan without a source of income during the crisis
2/27/2020	Project to support elders living alone in Wuhan	Collected information on the needs of elders living alone in order to organize local Wuhan volunteers to send groceries to them	Lack of daily support for elders living alone during the crisis	Elders living alone in Wuhan
2/29/2020	Project to support farmers in Hubei	Collected and managed information regarding Hubei farmers who were unable to sell their products due to the lockdown or the stigmatization of products from Hubei; coordinated with e-commerce platforms, local governments in Hubei, and logistic corporations to help those farmers	Difficulties of Hubei farmers selling their products due to the lockdown or the stigmatization of Hubei products	Farmers in Hubei

Date	Project	Description	Problem/gap	Audience
3/7/2020	Global COVID-19 guideline project	Collaboratively created, translated, and promoted a grassroots guideline on COVID-19 in eight languages	Lack of translated records of the experiences of Chinese grassroots organizations and everyday Chinese in their fight against COVID-19	The public in other countries; grassroots organizations and NGOs in other countries that were responding to COVID-19
3/14/2020	Grassroots report on the COVID-19 situation in Italy	Created and published a grassroots report on the COVID-19 situation in Italy	Lack of independent reports and analysis of the COVID-19 crisis in Italy	The public and grassroots organizations in China
3/15/2020	Project to facilitate and coordinate PPE donations to and purchases from other countries	Created a real-time, verified, and reliable list of Chinese medical suppliers as well as a list of reliable international buyers of medical supplies from hospitals, government offices, and other institutions in other countries	Lack of communication and coordination between Chinese PPE makers and international buyers, including hospitals and other institutions in other countries	Frontline health workers in other countries
3/19/2020	The Global COVID-19 Support Platform	Collected, translated, and managed news of the COVID-19 crisis from other countries; provided support to overseas Chinese during the global COVID-19 crisis; provided guidelines for Chinese returning from other countries to help them prepare for traveling to and quarantining in China	Lack of support for overseas Chinese and returning Chinese during the crisis	Overseas Chinese and returning Chinese

[a] Infodemic refers to false news that "spreads faster and more easily than this virus," according to the WHO.
[b] Fangcang hospitals are "temporary hospitals built by converting public venues, such as stadiums and exhibition centers, into health-care facilities to isolate patients with mild to moderate symptoms of an infectious disease from their families and communities, while providing medical care, disease monitoring, food, shelter, and social activities" (Chen et al., 2020).

On January 25, Wang Jun, a trainee of the NGO 2.0 Project, initiated a grassroots organization, the Group for Medical Supply Donations to Hubei, in order to solicit and coordinate donations of medical supplies for frontline health workers in hospitals in Hubei. On January 28, Wang Jun and other volunteers in the newly formed group joined the NCP Life Support Network. Wang Jun became a core member of the Information Group of the network, focusing on medical supplies and the coordination and organization of related volunteers and activists. Knowledge of and expertise regarding PPE and other medical supplies, information regarding PPE needs and contacts in Hubei hospitals, and social networks assembled by the group were quickly employed in the NCP Life Support Network's response to the shortage of PPE and other medical supplies.

The decentralized structure of the network also enabled activists to quickly launch new groups and subnetworks to address new problems as they were identified during the COVID-19 crisis. Dolphin, an NGO activist in Beijing working on youth education and anti-bullying in schools, joined the network to support those infected with COVID-19 and their families. During her work with the network, she found that many pregnant women in Wuhan, including many with COVID-19, were seeking help online. In just two days (February 24–25), with the help of her friends and other volunteers in the network, she initiated and organized a new group, the Wuhan Pregnant Women Group, to help pregnant women during the lockdown.

The data in table 7.1 also indicates the significant capability of the network to adapt. It shows that the network was capable of launching new projects and adapting its existing projects to address new problems as they emerged in the rapidly evolving crisis. The network was launched to address Wuhan hospitals' lack of capacity to treat those infected with COVID-19. In its first recruitment announcement, the network stated:

> The health-care system in Wuhan has been depleted. All designated hospitals have been heavily overburdened. Many people who are "probably infected with COVID-19" cannot get timely and effective professional treatment [through hospitals].[3] Therefore, home treatment and quarantine have become the only options [for them]. Before health professionals and equipment from other parts of the country can arrive to aid the fight, they are in urgent need of professional medical advice [through the telehealth service]. (NCP Life Support Network, 2020a)

Therefore, the network launched the free telehealth service to serve those infected or probably infected with COVID-19, who "are unable to get treatment and be quarantined in hospitals and have to stay at home for self-treatment and self-quarantine," and their families. Yet within the first week of work, activists and volunteers already noticed many other urgent problems resulting from or closely related to the lack of hospital capacity to treat those with COVID-19. For example, due to the government policy to shift almost all hospital resources to treat COVID-19 patients, pregnant women were unable to get prenatal services they needed to ensure safe deliveries. The Wuhan government transformed many hospitals into COVID-19 designated hospitals to treat COVID-19 patients or patients with fevers. Due to lack of PPE and other medical supplies, most of the COVID-19 designated hospitals refused to accept pregnant women to avoid having those women and their newborns become infected with COVID-19 in the hospital. So pregnant women had enormous difficulties accessing obstetrical and prenatal services and labor and delivery care. Due to the lack of timely information about the availability of beds in the small number of hospitals that continued to accept pregnant women, the difficulty of securing beds for pregnant women worsened. Due to the suspension of all transportation during the lockdown, families were unable to drive pregnant women to hospitals on their own. To respond to the various problems that pregnant women faced, the network quickly launched the Wuhan Pregnant Women Group, led and coordinated by Dolphin. This new group recruited obstetricians/gynecologists to provide a telehealth service to pregnant women in Wuhan, recruited volunteers to assist the families in contacting hospitals to secure beds, and organized local community workers and volunteer drivers to drive pregnant women to hospitals. In collaboration with other grassroots organizations in the network, they maintained a verified and constantly updated list of available beds and other obstetrical services in Wuhan hospitals. They also created a checklist and detailed guidelines for pregnant women for registering at each hospital. (For an example of a list and guidelines, see table 7.2.) Through these services, assistance, and methods, the new grassroots group supported more than 1,200 pregnant women and 230 postpartum mothers between January 26 and March 15.

The network's telehealth and other assistance projects for those with COVID-19 is another indication of its adaptive capability. At the peak of the epidemic, the free telehealth service served more than nine hundred people with COVID-19. After mid-February, the network reported in its third situation report on COVID-19 in Hubei Province that the hospital capacity to treat those infected with COVID-19 had improved significantly in Wuhan due to new measures and efforts, such as the building of Fangcang hospitals and the arrival of tens of thousands of health workers from other place (Zhuoming Disaster Information Center, 2020a). Its own data also shows that from February 8 to February 17, the number of people seeking out the telehealth service dropped from 101 to 51 (see figure 7.1). At the same time, they noticed the rapid surge of people with other serious diseases desperately seeking help through all channels. On February 18, the network decided to shift the future focus of its

Table 7.2

Sample Record of the List of Available Beds and Other Obstetrical Services in Wuhan Hospitals

Wuhan Hanyang Hospital (**already verified** and updated on 2020-04-06 at 20:50:18)	027-84769966
Ordinary pregnant women	Admitted
Pregnant women presumably with COVID-19	**Not admitted**
Normal maternity checkup	Yes
Obstetric examination during pregnancy using ultrasound	Yes
...	
Noninvasive paternity test	**No**
Amniocentesis	**No**
Labor and delivery	Yes
RT-PCR (COVID-19 test)	Yes

Address of hospital: Wuhan Hanyang Qu Muoshui Lu 53 Hao

Special guidelines:

The clinic has resumed [operations]. You can go to the hospital directly. If you need to be hospitalized, you will need to pass a CT test and a blood test to exclude the possibility of COVID-19. If you have a fever or have had close contact with a confirmed COVID-19 case, you must go to a COVID-19 designated hospital. Department of OBGYN: 027-50100372 Clinic hours: 8:00–17:00

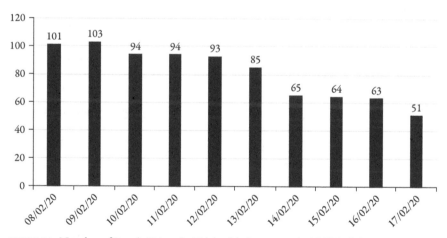

FIGURE 7.1 Number of People Using the Telehealth Service in the NCP Life Support Network

telehealth service and various assistant projects, such as providing one-on-one help to secure hospital beds to people with other severe diseases. The network announced on its Weibo: "Given the current situation of medical treatment of COVID-19 patients, the new government policy and efforts have effectively solved the lack of hospital capacity to treat those infected with COVID-19.

The focus of our telehealth service will shift to people with other diseases. We continue to have several hundred doctors from top hospitals serving our telehealth project. If you are an individual with another disease seeking medical help, please message us at this Weibo. Volunteers from our network will guide you to join the appropriate WeChat group for medical advice" (NCP Life Support Network, 2020e).

The data in table 7.1 also demonstrate the capacity of the network to attend to the suffering of a wide range of groups in the crisis and respond quickly and effectively. The numerous groups harmed physically and/or socially by COVID-19 or the pandemic crisis itself are included in the column "Beneficiary community" in the table, indicating the breadth of groups it sought to help through its actions. These groups included those infected with COVID-19 and their families, frontline health workers, and potential close contacts of COVID-19, who were the focus of government policy. They also included groups that were once ignored but came to be considered under the government's policy, such as pregnant women and non-COVID-19 patients with severe diseases. In addition, the network aimed to support vulnerable groups that state policy rarely considered in the crisis, such as those who had returned recently from Wuhan, homeless people in Wuhan, elders living alone in Wuhan, and victims of domestic violence and sexual harassment during the lockdown (see table 7.1). For example, during the lockdown, the government closed all grocery stores to individual buyers. Residents in Wuhan were required to buy groceries online and have special teams of social workers wearing PPE deliver groceries to them. Yet this policy completely overlooked elders living alone without access to the internet or without digital skills to do online shopping. On February 27, the network launched a project to collect information on the needs of elders living alone in order to organize local Wuhan volunteers to send groceries to them. On March 1, activist Brother En exposed on WeChat that roughly one thousand elders and disabled people in the Junweiyuan community were almost completely unable to get groceries during the lockdown. He posted that elders and disabled people in the community told him that "since the beginning of the lockdown, what they got from the government channels are only several radishes, potatoes, and cabbage. . . . Many of them had to rely on salty porridge for survival in the past month." Activist Linda, who worked in the group coordinating actions for helping elders living alone, took action that same day to follow up on his post. In the early morning of March 2, Linda reported in the network's WeChat group that she had verified the information and called local government offices and the hotline of the mayor of Wuhan repeatedly yet never received any response. Activist Rong replied to Linda volunteering to help distribute some grocery donations as a temporary remedy. Linda and Rong then worked with local volunteers in Wuhan to coordinate the delivery of the donations to the Junweiyuan community. On March 3, social worker Liu Hui reported the first distribution of grocery donations to Junweiyuan and posted the photos of the delivery in the

WeChat group of the network. In the afternoon of March 3, Liu Hui reported that he and other volunteers delivered a second batch of groceries to Junweiyuan. This example illustrates that the collaborations of activists and volunteers connected by ICTs enabled the network to quickly respond to the needs of elders living alone as well as other vulnerable groups in the COVID-19 crisis.

Channels and Technologies: Using ICTs for Social Good in a Quarantined City

This section addresses the communication channels and ICTs used by the NCP Life Support Network and how they were used to facilitate the network's response to COVID-19.

The Efficacy of ICTs in Responding to COVID-19

In considering the challenges in responding to the COVID-19 crisis effectively, Hao Nan found that the toughest was maintaining social distance while carrying out the projects and actions. He stated, "Unlike other disasters, we were unable to go to Wuhan under quarantine. We could only rely on local volunteers and do most of our work online. This significantly reduced the effectiveness of our actions. That was the biggest challenge" (N. Hao, 2020). This indicates the unique challenge grassroots organizations faced in their actions against COVID-19, yet it also indicates the power of ICTs in responding to this epidemic. When face-to-face communication was significantly constrained due to containment measures during the epidemic, ICT-mediated communication played a major role in the actions of grassroots organizations.

In its initial recruitment announcement published on January 23, 2020, the NCP Life Support Network had a special section called "Coordination Tools." It detailed the ICTs that volunteers were expected to be able to use in coordinating their actions. These tools are Weibo, WeChat, Shimo Docs, and Zoom. As in the case of the NGO 2.0 Project (see chapter 3), Weibo was used by the NCP Life Support Network as its major platform to communicate with the public and conduct social media advocacy. From January 23 to May 7, 2020, the Weibo of the network published 658 posts, attracted 28,040 followers, and followed 1,549 Weibo users. Being a relatively closed platform, WeChat is not the best tool for communication with the public, yet it was vital for the NCP Life Support Network as the major platform for coordinating its actions and interacting with volunteers and grassroots organizations. It was also the channel through which the network conveyed its actions to and interacted with various beneficiary communities, such as people infected with COVID-19 and non-COVID-19 patients. For example, WeChat groups served as an invaluable communication channel in the network's free telehealth service and various assistance services for people infected with COVID-19 and their families.

The case of the NGO 2.0 Project, in the age of Web 2.0, illustrates how grassroots organizations can rely on free Web 2.0 services to construct digital platforms to meet their needs rather than having to develop conventional websites that require significant programming skills. This is precisely what the NCP Life Support Network did to support its telehealth service. Within thirteen days, from January 23 to February 4, the network constructed a virtual hospital of four hundred health professionals exclusively using WeChat and other free Web 2.0 services (N. Hao, 2020; NCP Life Support Network, 2020b).

The network's virtual hospital simulated the service process of a real hospital (see figure 7.2). The service process entails three steps. First, the patient or the patient's family members would submit the patient's information. Second, a volunteer from the network's Little Angel Group would verify the patient's information with the patient or family member by telephone. The Medical Assistants Group was made up of graduate students in medical schools and residents in hospitals. They would manage the medical records of the patients, communicate with patients about their conditions, and triage patients to determine the severity of their conditions. Their conditions were ranked "mild," "severe," and "critical." Volunteers from the Medical Assistants Group would then invite the patient to join an appropriate virtual room for medical advice from doctors with significant experience in respiratory disease (NCP Life Support Network, 2020a; SEEDaBetterChina, 2020). Third, patients would join the designated virtual room. Each virtual room would have several doctors that would provide collaborative real-time medical advice on the condition of the patient. The volunteers in the Groups for Assistance and Accompanying [Patients] would provide patients with one-on-one services, such as communicating with hospitals to secure beds, providing mental health assistance, and accompanying services. In the first step, three of the entry points to submit patient's information would go on WeChat. The COVID-19 Patient Form hosted by Phoenix New Media is a WeChat mini-program. The Triage Group for Home Quarantine Patients and the Group for Supporting Critical Patients in Wuhan are two WeChat groups. In the second step, WeChat groups enabled communication and coordination among volunteers of the Little Angel Group. The Medical Assistants Group also relied on WeChat to communicate with patients and to maintain internal coordination and management. In the third step, each virtual room was housed by a WeChat group. The Groups for Assistance and Accompanying [Patients] also used WeChat groups to communicate with and provide support for patients and their families. By February 4, 2020, the network had eight WeChat groups for mild patients, four WeChat groups for severe patients, and one WeChat group for critical patients. In each WeChat group, the daily number of messages from patients hit several thousand. The Groups for Assistance and Accompanying [Patients] of the network also had over four WeChat groups provide assistance

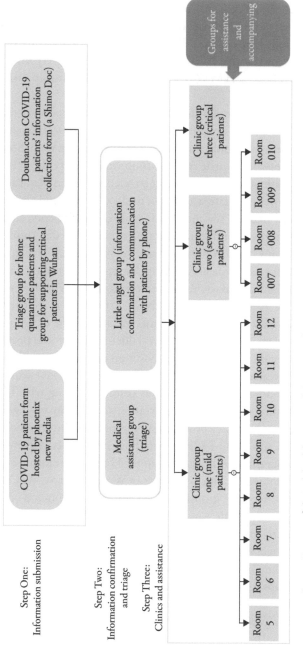

FIGURE 7.2 Service Process of the Telehealth Project of the NCP Life Support Network. Source: Adapted from the NCP Life Support Network's Weibo (February 4, 2020) and a post on SEEDaBetterChina (2020).

to COVID-19 patients and their families. Through these innovative uses of WeChat and the development of the corresponding service process, the network quickly constructed a virtual hospital that served more than nine hundred COVID-19 patients at the peak of the pandemic in Wuhan.

To increase the efficiency of communication in the virtual hospital, the telehealth project established community designed and implemented rules for its various WeChat groups. For example, the announcement of the Triage Group for Home Quarantine Patients stated: "To those who newly joined the group for medical advice, please read the group announcement carefully. Change your name in this WeChat group. Fill out the form for individuals with COVID-19 symptoms, https://shimo.im/forms/GokLVJMBnQhBF032/fill nCoV. After you fill out the form, our volunteers in the telehealth group or other groups will contact you." This announcement established the community rule requiring every individual joining the WeChat group to change their name immediately in order to "facilitate effective communications in the WeChat group." The community also established rules for names in the WeChat group. Anyone pursuing medical advice should name themselves "Your WeChat Name+Medical Advice." A doctor or social worker joining the WeChat group to offer help should name themselves "Your WeChat Name+Doctor or Social Worker+Your City." This naming rule enabled the members of the WeChat group to quickly and conveniently identify their roles and those of others in the WeChat group. This significantly improved the efficiency of communication in the group.

The community also required anyone seeking medical advice to fill out a form in order to collect immediate information on individuals with COVID-19 symptoms. To enforce these rules, anyone who failed to change their name or to fill out the form would be removed from the WeChat group every day at 10 P.M., as was stated in the WeChat group's announcement. To focus communication in the WeChat group on triage, activists in the WeChat group constantly posted messages to remind members to refrain from communicating on other issues. Other WeChat groups of the virtual hospital also established their own rules, designed and implemented to enhance communication and to protect the privacy of patients.

In Chinese internet parlance, the human flesh search is a massive collaboration among interested parties to search out information.[4] Much as in Tiger Gate (see chapter 4), activists in the NCP Life Support Network used human flesh search to generate collective knowledge, which in the latter case could be used to solve problems related to COVID-19. In Tiger Gate, ICT forum users spontaneously carried out the process of coordinating and verifying the human flesh search without any organizational direction. The NCP Life Support Network, however, used an enhanced human flesh search method wherein grassroots organizations intentionally coordinated and verified the search process. Moreover, the major ICTs used to support this type of massive human collaboration has shifted from forum/BBS to WeChat and Shimo Docs.[5]

Table 7.3

Quantity of Information Created by the Group for Medical Supply Donations to Hubei

PPE needs	PPE domestic shipping	Medical protective clothing	Other PPE	Other information
1,293	134	44	133	899

On January 23, using Shimo Docs, Wang Jun and other volunteers in the Group for Medical Supply Donations to Hubei created a platform to collect, organize, and present comprehensive, verified, and real-time updated information regarding PPE needs in Hubei hospitals, PPE makers, and PPE donations and related global shipping information. They collaborated with numerous grassroots organizations and thousands of individuals to create this collective knowledge to address PPE shortages in hospitals, which was one of the most serious problems in China's early response to COVID-19. The platform is made up of one master index and several separate documents focusing on different issues. The master index has four sections: PPE needs, domestic PPE suppliers, domestic shipping, and "global shipping: channels + needs". Each section contains the link to a separate document, with a brief description of that document's information and targeted readers. For example, the brief description of the information in the document for PPE needs is "PPE needs from hospitals and communities." The target readers for that document is "PPE suppliers, donors, and people working in logistics who want to coordinate the shipment of PPE." The platform's index enabled readers from different groups to find the right information they needed quickly. Its core team of seventy-three volunteers from different parts of the world would verify the information through various channels, including phone and face-to-face communication. Then the core team of the group would organize and post the information to the appropriate document and label the information as "verified" or "not verified" and provide special instructions or comments on the information, such as, "The information is at high risk of fraud! Use caution!" If a piece of published information had expired, they would strike through the text and label it "expired." Within the week between February 23 and February 29, the group had created thousands of pieces of information regarding PPE, more than 95 percent of which was verified by the group (see table 7.3). By January 29, over 2,300,000 people had visited this Shimo Docs–based PPE platform.

Whereas in Tiger Gate, ICTs provided the infrastructure and technological potential to activate an activist network that extended across geographical boundaries in China, in COVID-19 response, the activist network extended far beyond China. Activists and volunteers formed transnational networks to respond to the COVID-19 crisis. The new ICTs WeChat and Shimo Docs were the primary tools that provided the infrastructure and spaces for these transnational networks. These networks first focused on the COVID-19 crisis in Wuhan. In responding to the global pandemic after March 10, 2020, they extended their focus to support the Chinese diaspora, overseas Chinese students, and health professionals in other countries. In the Shimo Docs created by the Group for Medical Supply Donations to Hubei, the document "Global Shipping: Channels+Needs" contains the following information:

> Information on the needs for help of shipment from overseas Chinese who have PPE to donate
> Information on international shipment and customs clearance
> Information on channels for money donations in other countries

The target readers of the document were "overseas Chinese who have purchased PPE for donation but do not know of any means of transporting them and overseas Chinese who have a means of transporting PPE but lack the right amount of PPE." Within a week of January 23, the group had collected information regarding PPE donations from activists and volunteers in five continents, including Europe, North America, South America, and Africa. The following example is indicative of most of the information:

> Dubai, we are in urgent need of a team of more than 20 persons to bring back to China 20 boxes of N95 masks (10,000 in total) (published on January 25) https://www.douban.com/doubanapp/dispatch?uri=/status/2773177211/&dt_dapp=1
> Local phone at Dubai: 0502232981

This indicates that rather than relying on international shipping services using cargo flights, local activists in overseas Chinese communities sought out volunteer teams to hand deliver PPE to Wuhan using the earliest passenger flights. There were three reasons for this strategy: donors wanted to get PPE to hospitals as quickly as possible, circumvent the complex customs clearing process that could delay the arrival of PPE, and bypass any contact with the Red Cross—the government's gatekeeper for PPE donations—which activists and the media held responsible for significant mismanagement of donated PPE in the crisis.[6] This volunteer-coordinated transportation of PPE was a form of "human flesh transportation," a term derived from "human flesh search." In many cases, the donors of the PPE and the volunteers who actually "human fleshed the PPE back" (carried the PPE back) never knew each other. And neither knew the COVID-19 patients in Hubei personally. They were ordinary travelers who had prescheduled flights to China. Most of them would have seen the messages calling for help with human flesh transportation of PPE on global Chinese social media platforms like WeChat or Weibo. Others just

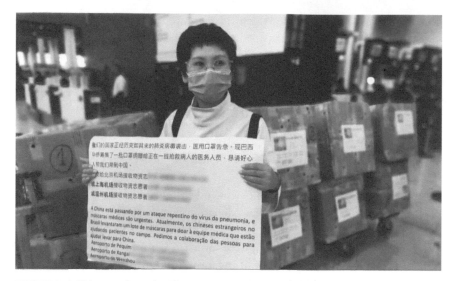

FIGURE 7.3 A Volunteer from the Chinese Diaspora in Brazil Recruiting Volunteers at an Airport to Carry Donated PPE to China

happened to see posters at airports calling for volunteers to provide this sort of help. Volunteer teams that agreed to take part would make contact with local volunteers in China to arrange a hand-off of the PPE at their destination airports in China. Giving their phone numbers to a coordinator or volunteer in that overseas Chinese community, they would then board their flights with a box of PPE (e.g., 500 masks) as their carry-on or checked luggage. The coordinator or the volunteers in overseas Chinese communities would then phone or WeChat the local volunteers in China with the flight times and names and phone numbers of the volunteer teams. The local volunteers in China would wait for the volunteer team of human flesh transportation to pick up the PPE at Chinese airports.

On January 31 at 14:35, A Xiasang, an activist in the NCP Life Support Network, posted a photo (see figure 7.3) and his or her WeChat history with a friend in the major WeChat group of the network. The WeChat history says, "Forwarded message, Chinese diaspora community in Brazil collected 20,000 N95 masks [for donation to hospitals]. From the 31st. they have been waiting at the airport, seeking out a volunteer team or individuals to take the masks back [to China]."

The WeChat messages in table 7.4 indicate that within four hours, five individual volunteers (A Xiasang, Prcht_Hefan, Wen Shaobuo, Little Monkey, and Violin) and one project coordinator of the network (the project coordinator in Hubei-Xiaoyue at Wuhan University) in the WeChat group made attempts to help the transnational PPE donation project of the Chinese diaspora community in Brazil. They collectively identified the location of the

Table 7.4

The Network's WeChat Messages Regarding PPE Donations from the Chinese Diaspora Community in Brazil

Message #	Activist's online ID	WeChat Message
1	A Xiasang	On January 31 at 14:35, A Xiasang posted a photo (see figure 7.3) and WeChat history with a friend: "Forwarded message, Chinese diaspora community in Brazil collected 20,000 N95 masks [for donation to hospitals]. From the 31st they have been waiting at the airport, seeking out a volunteer team or individuals to take the masks."
2	Prcht_Hefan	@A Xiasang Has anyone in the network followed up on the message regarding the N95 mask donation from Brazil? I could ask the community of tour leaders (if they could help).
3	Hubei-Xiaoyue Project Coordinator at Wuhan University (WHU)	To the volunteers in the message, please contact us. We have a way to bring these PPEs back to China. Thank you!
4	Hubei-Xiaoyue Project Coordinator at WHU	Folks, please contact us if you are the volunteers in the message or you know the direct contact of the volunteers in the message or photo. Please don't just forward the message to us again. Thank you!
5	Wen Shaobuo	Posted the photo again. The following is forwarded from the WeChat group Supporting Wuhan: "My friends in Brazil have collected 20,000 N95 masks. They wanted to circumvent the complex custom clearing process for PPE donations. So they have been waiting at the airport for 4 hours to seek kind individuals to 'human flesh' the PPEs back. We truly appreciate your help!" Wen Shaobuo then added, "The contact [info] of volunteers is on the signboard (in the photo)."
6	Prcht_Hefan	No mention of which airport in Brazil. How could we contact them?
7	Wen Shaobuo	The contact [info] of volunteers is on the signboard.
8	Prcht_HeFan	Those contacts are their volunteers in China. Chinese phone number. No contact [info] of volunteers in Brazil, not to mention the location of the airport.
		. . .
9	Hubei-Xiaoyue Project Coordinator at WHU	We have called the domestic volunteers (in China) in the Brazil project. The PPEs are in São Paulo. But the volunteers in Brazil probably got too many phone calls. So, we were unable to get in touch with them.

(continued)

Table 7.4 (Continued)

Message #	Activist's online ID	WeChat Message
10	LittleMonkey	São Paulo only has one international airport, GRU Airport. The other one is for domestic flights. @Hubei-Xiaoyue Project Coordinator at WHU
		. . .
11	Hubei-Xiaoyue Project Coordinator at WHU	Please continue to follow up on the event if you have any channels to help them. But their domestic volunteers said the PPEs must be delivered **directly** to hospitals. (They don't want to go through the Red Cross.)
		. . .
12	Hubei-Xiaoyue Project Coordinator at WHU	We have reached the volunteers in Shanghai on the PPE donations from Brazil. The PPEs in the photo were donated by overseas Chinese from Wenzhou for hospitals in Wenzhou. If you are from Wenzhou and could offer help, please continue to follow up on the event. They don't have a plan for donations to other regions.
13	LittleMonkey	I've contacted the Chinese diaspora community in Brazil. Do they have the specific dates for bringing these PPEs back?
14	Violin	@Hubei-Xiaoyue Project Coordinator at WHU The transportation of the masks from Beijing to Wenzhou has been solved. I'm in the WeChat group of this project. But the problem [of getting them] from São Paulo to Beijing has not been solved.
15	LittleMonkey	On January 31 around 16:30, LittleMonkey posted, "My friend has told me that he/she has reached the director of the Chamber of Commerce of Zhejiang in Brazil (for help with this donation)."[a]

[a] Wenzhou is a city in China's Zhejiang Province.

airport (Messages 9, 10), reached the domestic volunteers of the Brazil project (Messages 9, 12, and 14), and contacted the overseas Chinese community in Brazil for help (Messages 13 and 15). They effectively clarified the information (Message 12) and the status of the project (Message 14) as well as the donors' intention to have the PPE "delivered directly to hospitals" and to bypass the Red Cross (Message 11). Many more volunteers and activists have been involved in other WeChat groups, such as the Supporting Wuhan WeChat group to help support this transnational PPE donation. This example illustrates the role of WeChat in facilitating the emergence of a transnational volunteer network that extended across national boundaries in the COVID-19 crisis. Eventually, the donated PPE in the example were "human fleshed" back to Wenzhou by various volunteers on flights making connections in Madrid, Hong Kong, Shanghai, and cities in Japan, the United States, and elsewhere. The human flesh transportation of PPE for COVID-19—the strategy used by volunteers in the example—demonstrates an unconditional trust rarely seen among volunteers in other actions or projects for development and social change in China. Due to the Spring Festival and measures to contain the outbreak, most Chinese PPE makers suspended production at the early stage of the outbreak. For example, after factory workers returned to their hometowns for Spring Festival, they were unable to go back to the factories when transportation services were drastically reduced. At that time, donated PPE from overseas Chinese communities, coordinated by volunteers, provided badly needed support for frontline health workers in Hubei and other parts of the country, especially until Chinese PPE makers could resume and increase production.

On March 11, the WHO declared the COVID-19 outbreak a global pandemic. The shortage of PPE, ventilators, and other medical supplies became a worldwide problem in response to COVID-19 (e.g., Lintern, 2020; U.S. Department of Health and Human Services, 2020; WHO, 2020b). In mid-March, in the NCP Life Support Network's Information Center—the major WeChat group of the network—volunteers from various international sites (Belgium, Italy, the United States, and Southeast Asia) asked for help with information and channels to reach reliable Chinese PPE producers and dealers with the capacity and qualifications to export PPE and other medical supplies to their countries. On March 18, Boshu Yahui, a grassroots organization coordinating global donations of PPE and other medical supplies to Chinese hospitals, launched a new project in the NCP Life Support Network's Information Center, which aimed to create a reliable and verified list of Chinese medical supply producers and dealers updated in real time, as well as a list of trustworthy international buyers of medical supplies from overseas hospitals, government offices, and other institutions. In the WeChat message to announce the project, Boshu Yahui (2020) stated the following:

> We are seeking qualified PPE producers or dealers to openly publish information on and the price of their products. We will organize this information and send it to organizations and individuals who have need of PPE in the globe regularly. . . . It is very likely that public donations are not a stable source of PPE. Whereas PPE producers could provide stable supplies of PPE. . . . Yet we need to sharply reduce the risk of unqualified middlemen profiting from the sale of medical supplies at unreasonable prices. The behaviors [of those unqualified middlemen] harm people suffering from COVID-19 globally. Therefore, openly publishing the information and price of products of domestic PPE suppliers could effectively help international buyers acquire more transparent information and give them more choices of PPE products.

Regarding the targeted organizations they aimed to serve, the project announcement went on, "We hope to directly connect with organizations of the Chinese diaspora, alumni associations and student association of overseas Chinese, and volunteer organizations across the globe. We hope the following organizations contact us directly: purchasing department of foreign governments, embassies and consulates of other countries, hospitals fighting COVID-19, nursing homes, children's welfare homes, mental hospitals, prisons, and funeral service centers. We will help you to get the right information regarding your medical supply needs and assist you in contacting organizations that provide transportation services. We will also assist with translation in the whole process" (Boshu Yahui, 2020). This announcement indicates that Boshu Yahui's new project intended to help a wide range of organizations, institutions, and individuals outside China, including those of the Chinese diaspora, hospitals, NGOs, and government institutions. It also provided free services to assist logistic issues related to the transnational transportation of PPE and translation between different parties in these various efforts.

Boshu Yahui set up five working groups. The Group for Contacting Organizations collected real-time updated reliable needs for PPE and other medical supplies directly from volunteers, hospitals, and institutions in other countries. The Group for Contacting Producers and Dealers collected real-time updated, verified, and reliable information on medical supply producers and dealers in China. It required them to upload documentation of their qualifications and certifications. The volunteers of the group would verify whether the producers and dealers met all the required qualifications and had the certifications to export PPE and other medical supplies, and whether their products met the standards for imported medical supplies of the relevant country, according to the project announcement of the group. The group stated that doing so would "help suppliers avoid problems with quality and standards in exporting [PPE] and help buyers avoid buying unqualified products" (Boshu Yahui, 2020).

One challenge that the NCP Life Support Network and other volunteers encountered in organizing and coordinating global PPE donations to Chinese hospitals was the many different standards for PPE used by various countries. For example, when donors bought a face mask in the United States, they did not know if it complied with the standards for medical face masks in China. Donors, activists, and volunteers had very little knowledge of the compatibility of and differences between various masks, such as KN90, KN95, N95, FFP1, FFP2, and KF80. In many cases, the donated PPE from overseas Chinese were shipped to hospitals in Wuhan at a very high cost but could not be used by health workers because they did not satisfy China's medical supply standards (S. Feng, 2020). To solve this problem, the NCP Life Support Network, in collaboration with other grassroots organizations and health workers, collected and translated documentation on various standards of PPE used in China, Japan, the United States, the European Union, and South Korea. It examined whether specific models of products from major producers met the minimum requirements of medical-use PPE in China. On January 30, the network published its *Guidelines for Standards for the Purchase and Donation of Medical Supplies* on Weibo. These guidelines provided detailed information about the compatibility of various PPE standards and clear instructions on how to purchase PPE that meet Chinese standards. On January 31, the network completed and published *The Compatibility Table of Domestic Standards and Foreign Standards for Medical Supplies* and *The Summary of Requirements for Medical Supply Donations and Related Questions* to provide more detailed information and examples to solve compatibility problems. Based on the existing information and documentation created by the network, the Group on Medical Supply Purchase and Medical Supply Standards of Boshu Yahui further developed the collective knowledge of various PPE standards in different countries and shifted the focus to whether the products made by Chinese PPE producers complied with U.S., EU, and Japanese standards. It aimed to "help international friends get information regarding all qualified supplies and reduce the time spent on comparing the standards of different countries" (Boshu Yahui, 2020).

Boshu Yahui set up a Jielong in the WeChat group as the platform for its new project.[7] It required representatives of Chinese medical goods suppliers to post the types, quantities, and prices of their products as well as documentation proving that they are authorized representatives of that supplier. It also demanded that representatives upload documentation, including the business licenses of suppliers, production licenses of PPE manufacturers, product test reports, FDA certificates, and an EC certificate, and so on. Volunteers would evaluate whether suppliers had all the required qualifications and certifications to export their products to the United States or the European Union. If a supplier indeed had all of them, volunteers would identify that supplier as a "supplier with all of the qualifications and certificates" in the comments of the supplier's post. If some certificate was missing, the volunteers at Boshu Yahui would provide advice on what certificate was needed and how to get it. For example, when a supplier from Shenzhen posted its PPE products, product test reports, and related certifications in the Jielong, Boshu Yahui volunteer ella reviewed the documentation, posting the following comment: "The test reports of the products and the business license of the supplier are complete. . . . Yet the documentation shows that the registration number for FDA certification is 'waiting to be assigned.' Therefore, there is no proof that the supplier has received FDA certification." If crucial documentation were missing, such as a supplier's business license or proof of being an authorized representative, Boshu Yahui would give the supplier a day to provide documentation before removing the supplier from Jielong. For the information regarding the needs of PPE and other medical supplies, Boshu Yahui also required volunteers and staff in foreign organizations to post their documentation as authorized representatives of the organization. For example, a doctor in the Henry Ford Health System (HFHS) in Detroit posted his personal profile page on the website of the organization and an email with the HFHS supply chain management director as proof of his being an authorized representative. Using these strategies and processes, Boshu Yahui successfully created a platform to increase transparency between the supply side and the demand side of PPE and other medical supplies. This improved the efficiency of communication between the two parties. For example, Boshu Yahui volunteer alkane confirmed that a Chinese supplier in Jiangxi, China, was an authorized representative of Jiangxi Yuyue Medical. As the biggest manufacturer of ventilators in China, all its products met the required certification for export to the United States and the European Union. Several minutes after alkane's comment, demand-side representative Leno Fan posted their specific needs for ventilators in the comment section of the supplier's message. The supplier then immediately posted her cell phone number to further discuss the deal.

The Limitations of Online Communications and the Benefits of a Multichannel Perspective

ICT-mediated communication has been indispensable in actions to fight against COVID-19; yet it is not without its limitations or weaknesses. Hao Nan addressed three major challenges and difficulties that the NCP Life Support Network has encountered in its actions and projects (N. Hao, 2020). The worst of these was directly related to ICT-mediated communication: most network actions had to be conducted online, without direct face-to-face communication, due to the highly infectious nature of COVID-19 and containment measures. Hao asserted that this difficulty "largely reduced the effectiveness of our actions. The challenge is quite big. . . . To a big extent, it hindered all our work" (Hao, 2020). For example, Boshu Yahui has tried very hard to evaluate whether suppliers on its platform had the required qualifications and certifications to export products to the United States or the European Union. And it indeed helped to increase transparency between the supply side and the demand side of PPE and other medical supplies. Yet because it could not use other communication channels—especially face-to-face communication—to verify the information the suppliers uploaded online, such as proof of being an authorized representative, its evaluation could not be completed. Boshu Yahui recognized this limitation of ICT-mediated communication. In the announcement section of the platform, Boshu Yahui stated, "We want to reaffirm that we are unable to conduct further evaluation. Please strictly self-regulate your actions and make independent judgments on your own."

A Multichannel Perspective. Like the Tiger Gate and the Free Lunch Project cases in earlier chapters, a multichannel approach was important for the NCP Life Support Network's effective response to COVID-19. But unlike them, the telephone became crucial to many of the NCP Life Support Network's actions and projects, as direct face-to-face communication was heavily constrained by both government policies and the guidelines of grassroots organizations.

First, telephone communication functioned as a channel that could mitigate the limitations of online communication by verifying information published online. For example, the shortage of PPE and other medical supplies in hospitals was a severe problem in China's response to COVID-19 in Wuhan, especially in the early stages of the crisis. As early as January 20, many hospitals had run out of PPE. Information regarding urgent PPE needs at hospitals and messages calling for PPE donations to support frontline health workers went viral on the Chinese internet. Some of that information was published by hospitals, and some of it was posted by individual doctors. Wang Jun and other volunteers in the Group for Medical Supply Donations to Hubei and hundreds of other volunteers collaboratively created a platform to collect, organize, and present comprehensive and accurate information in real time regarding PPE needs in hospitals in Hubei. Through massive human collaboration online, they collected a large poll of PPE needs in hospitals. Yet like Boshu Yahui, they had difficulty verifying these PPE needs, which activists had assembled using the internet. Their solution was to establish a Verification Group, which would call the hospitals to confirm the PPE needs one by one. Using this strategy, 95 percent of the 1,293 pieces of information regarding PPE needs in hospitals had been verified by January 29.

More importantly, the telephone became a channel to get the most up-to-date information, which was crucial to the various vulnerable groups that the network aimed to help in the crisis. In many cases, it was the only channel for getting information that might affect the survival of members of the vulnerable groups, such as those infected with COVID-19, non-COVID-19 patients with severe health problems, and pregnant women. From about January 23 to February 11, it was extremely hard for those with COVID-19 to get beds in hospitals in Wuhan. In those hardest days of the crisis, individuals with COVID-19 flooded social media with desperate messages asking for help finding beds in hospitals. This was primarily due to the lack of hospital capacity to treat COVID-19 patients. Yet the problem was aggravated by the lack of real-time accurate information about the availability of beds in hospitals. In the early stage of the outbreak, neither the Wuhan government nor hospitals made real-time information about beds for COVID-19 patients available to the public. As a result of this lack of transparency of hospital resources, the already very limited hospital capacity was not fully utilized. On the one hand, those with COVID-19 and those exhibiting COVID-19 symptoms were desperately running from one hospital to another to secure a bed. On the other hand, because they did not have access to real-time information, beds in some hospitals were underused. This lack of information also resulted in imbalances within the health-care system. Hospitals at the center of the city and high-profile hospitals were overburdened with new patients that they were unable to admit or treat, while more remote and lower-profile hospitals remained underutilized. For example, on February 14, most of the COVID-19 designated hospitals had no beds, yet the Third Hospital of Wuhan Guanggu Guanshan Branch, which was newly designated, had 217 beds according to data collected by the NCP Life Support Network.

Telephones were the only channel that volunteers and grassroots organizations could use to get real-time availability of beds for COVID-19 patients. By systemically calling all COVID-19 designated hospitals in Wuhan directly, the BRIDGE Beds Group of the NCP Life Support Network created a real-time, verified, and comprehensive list of available beds for COVID-19 patients in Wuhan. The Beds Group developed a well-managed method of collecting and publishing this crucial information for those with COVID-19 and their families. Ms. Bed, the initiator and coordinator of the Group, stated, "We first create and organize the list of hospitals, their address, and their telephone numbers. Then, according to the number of telephone numbers, we will decide how many volunteers we need in order to call the hospitals. According to the level of urgency, we will set up the frequency for volunteers to call the hospitals. According to the needs of different types of patients, we will decide what information we need to verify during the phone call." The Beds Group published and updated the comprehensive list of available beds in a Shimo Doc in the NCP Life Support Network's Summary of Information Platforms of Domestic Grassroots Organizations against COVID-19. Yet providing information about available beds in hospitals was not enough to help a person with COVID-19 actually secure one of those beds. During the early stage of the crisis, admitting a new COVID-19 patient to a hospital was a complex process involving at least four parties: the patient, the designated COVID-19 hospital, the local community, and the community hospital.[8] The designated hospital would need available beds. The community would need to send the patient to the community hospital. And the community hospital would need to determine whether the patent is a severe patient needing hospitalization. If so, the community hospital would need to provide a referral. In the lockdown, COVID-19 patients could only be transported to hospitals by special vehicles from hospitals or local branches of the Center for Disease Control and Prevention (CDC). The community, hospitals and local branches of the CDC, and the patient need to coordinate the patient's transportation to the designated hospital. Dealing with all these issues was almost impossible for a family already overburdened with taking care of a family member with COVID-19 and protecting other family members from the highly infectious disease. The NCP Life Support Network's Groups for Assistance and Accompanying Patients provided badly needed one-on-one assistance to help those infected with COVID-19 go through this complex process and to secure a bed in a hospital. Volunteers in these groups communicated with all four of these parties and coordinated and assisted with all the processes. In this coordination, telephones were the most important channel. For example, because most hospitals did not have an official WeChat account, telephones were the only channel for reaching them. Community workers may have been without a WeChat account or without twenty-four-hour access to WeChat. The quickest channel to reach community social workers was cell phones. Volunteers may have had to make several hundred phone calls a day to help a person with COVID-19 gain admission to a hospital at the peak of the crisis (NCP Life Support Network, 2020f). In addition to these various projects and actions to help those with COVID-19, telephones also played an important role in the NCP Life Support Network's other projects and actions, such as collecting information regarding available beds for non-COVID-19 patients and providing one-on-one assistance to them and to pregnant women.

Like in the NGO 2.0 Project and the Free Lunch Project, the NCP Life Support Network made intentional use of a multichannel strategy to enhance the effectiveness of their projects and actions. For example, in the action of the Beds Group, the use of online channels and telephones interacted with and reinforced each other. Through online collaborations, volunteers first created a comprehensive list of hospitals, including addresses and telephone numbers related to bed information. They used collaborative online editing tools to create a Shimo Doc. Based on the collective knowledge of hospital bed information in the Shimo Doc, the group created the work schedule, assigned work tasks, and determined the frequency to place calls. Then volunteers, based on their work schedules and work tasks, acquired real-time bed information by calling all COVID-19 designated hospitals. Next, they generated verified bed information in the same Shimo Doc. Last, the link to the Shimo Doc was published and shared with the public through social media (see figure 7.4).

Direct offline face-to-face communication was constrained to a minimum due to the strict quarantine in Wuhan, yet offline actions and the work of offline volunteers contributed to the NCP Life Support Network's response to COVID-19. In fact, offline volunteers played a crucial role in filling the gap in the NCP Life Support Network's actions and projects to help vulnerable groups. For example, in the Wuhan Pregnant Women Group, offline volunteer work, such as driving pregnant women to hospitals, was critical to achieving the goal of the project. Due to the lockdown, family members were not allowed to drive pregnant women to hospitals even in the case of hospitals with available beds and services for pregnant women. Volunteer drivers who acquired permits from the local government were the only means for a family to send a pregnant woman to a hospital on time, unless by rare fortune they caught an ambulance. Yige, a small business owner turned volunteer, was the leader of a five-member volunteer driver team of the Wuhan Pregnant Women Group. The team provided a twenty-four-hour on-call service for pregnant women. Similarly, in the project to help elders living alone, offline volunteers served a crucial role in filling the logistic gap. In the Junwei-yuan community case discussed earlier, social worker Liu Hui and other offline volunteers made possible the timely delivery of groceries to elders living alone.

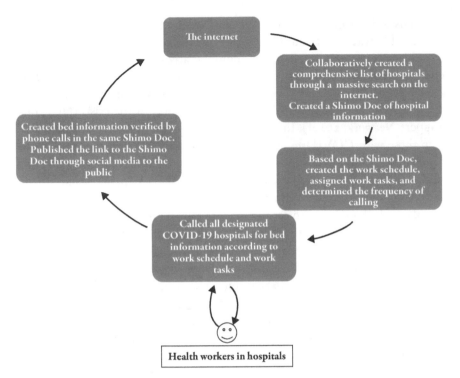

FIGURE 7.4 Interaction and Reinforcement of Telephones and Online Channels

The NCP Life Support Network's attentiveness to the recruitment of, collaboration with, and support of offline volunteers and organizations was an important factor in the success of its projects and actions. The network's second brief report summarizing its first four days of work noted that it had discussed collaboration with the directors of social worker organizations in Wuhan. The two sides agreed that the network would provide telehealth services on COVID-19 for the beneficiary communities of those organizations and medical training to their social workers. The volunteer driver team was organized on the same day that the Wuhan Pregnant Women Group was started. The project provided PPE, such as medical masks and protective suits, to volunteers. It also provided volunteers with medical training on how to handle medical emergencies, such as having a pregnant woman's water break while transporting her to the hospital.

Stakeholder Relationships

An effective response to a large-scale public health crisis requires the engagement of various stakeholders in society, as shown in previous research on communication for development (Airhihenbuwa et al., 2000; Lie, 2008; UNAIDS & Penn State University, 1999). Analyzing the relationship between different stakeholders is therefore very important to understand the NCP Life Support Network's actions and projects in the crisis.

Reciprocal Relationships between Activists and the Government

As in the NGO 2.0 Project and the Free Lunch Project, activists and grassroots organizations in the NCP Life Support Network saw the government as a stakeholder that should be engaged in their response to the COVID-19 crisis. This was first seen in the statements of leading activists and the mission statement of the network. For example, the initiator and coordinator of the network, Hao Nan, stated:

> We have also carried out a certain amount of policy advocacy. Because I found that no matter how hard we worked to scale our projects and actions, in order to effectively respond to such a big crisis, we must influence the government. We have to push the government to try their best in their response to the crisis. Therefore, since the first week, we have reached media and various government channels in order to convey the urgency, the distribution, and the trend of severe cases of COVID-19 that we learned from our telehealth project and the relevant recommendations to the policymaking system. We found this advocacy effective. (Hao, 2020)

In a long interview with a grassroots organization, Ms. Bed, the initiator of the Beds Group, stated, "The work of volunteers is not to compete with the government. Rather it is to fill the gaps that government policies were unable to address judiciously" (A2N COVID-19 Volunteer Group, 2020). On February 4, the official Weibo of the NCP Life Support Network published an important announcement titled "To Our Volunteers" to explain the mission of the network, who its members are, and the expectations of the network toward its volunteers. In the section "About Us," the network stated, "The NCP Life Support Network aims to use this kind of self-organized collaborative network to supplement what the government has done. We provide those patients and families who temporarily need medical help with clinically valid advice" (NCP Life Support Network, 2020b). Zhuoming Disaster Information Center, founded by Hao Nan, formed the backbone of the information group of the NCP Life Support Network. Its mission statement indicated that the center aimed to serve rescue teams, grassroots organizations, and the media, as well as the government.

The design of the NCP Life Support Network's information platform—Summary of Information Platforms of Domestic Grassroots Organizations against COVID-19—also indicated that the network saw the government as a major stakeholder that the network and other grassroots organizations could cooperate with in response to COVID-19. On February 16, the NCP Life Support Network launched this information project in order to "collect the links of information products and platforms of grassroots organizations against the

COVID-19 crisis" (Zhuoming Disaster Information Center, 2020b). As of April 11, the project had collected and organized 125 information products/platforms from eighty-one grassroots organizations and individual volunteers. The project categorized and presented these information products/platforms in twenty-three broad types that covered a wide range of issues and problems related to the COVID-19 crisis. These included information for those with COVID-19 and those with other illnesses, information on PPE and other medical supplies, information on agriculture products, independent situation reports on COVID-19 in China and other countries, information for frontline health workers, information for overseas Chinese, information on the experience of grassroots organizations in the crisis, and so on. The targeted audience of the information project was grassroots organizations, NGOs, activists and volunteers, and vulnerable groups in the crisis who were seeking help to address certain problems. The "Information Navigation" section of the Shimo Doc has functioned as the index of the information project. At the top of the section are two links categorized as "Authoritative Links" (circled in figure 7.5). The first link directs users to the WeChat mini-program on COVID-19 of the State Council. The second was linked to the WeChat mini-program on COVID-19 of the Hubei government. That these two links appear under the category of "Authoritative Links" indicates that the project thought these two platforms of the central government and the Hubei government would provide authoritative information regarding COVID-19. They were very important channels for grassroots organizations aiming to solve problems related to COVID-19 and for vulnerable groups seeking help in the crisis.

The way in which the network treated various government projects to collect patient information indicates that grassroots organizations in the network formed a reciprocal relationship with the government in response to the COVID-19 crisis. On January 31, as messages desperately asking for help securing hospital beds for those with COVID-19 in Wuhan flooded Chinese social media, the State Council at Beijing launched a new project in WeChat. Every WeChat user could use this new project to submit information regarding the COVID-19 crisis directly to the State Council. It was initially part of a project called "Internet + Supervision," which was initiated by the State Council on January 24:

> To implement the policies of the Central Committee and the State Council and to effectively contain and control COVID-19, the State Council launched the "Internet + Supervision" platform to collect information from the public regarding the inaction, incompetence, irresponsibility, and other problems of local governments in their responses to COVID-19, as well as related recommendations for improvement. The State Council will summarize and analyze the information and recommendations and will supervise local governments to respond to these problems and recommendations judiciously. The State Council will pay special attention to information regarding the cover-up of the

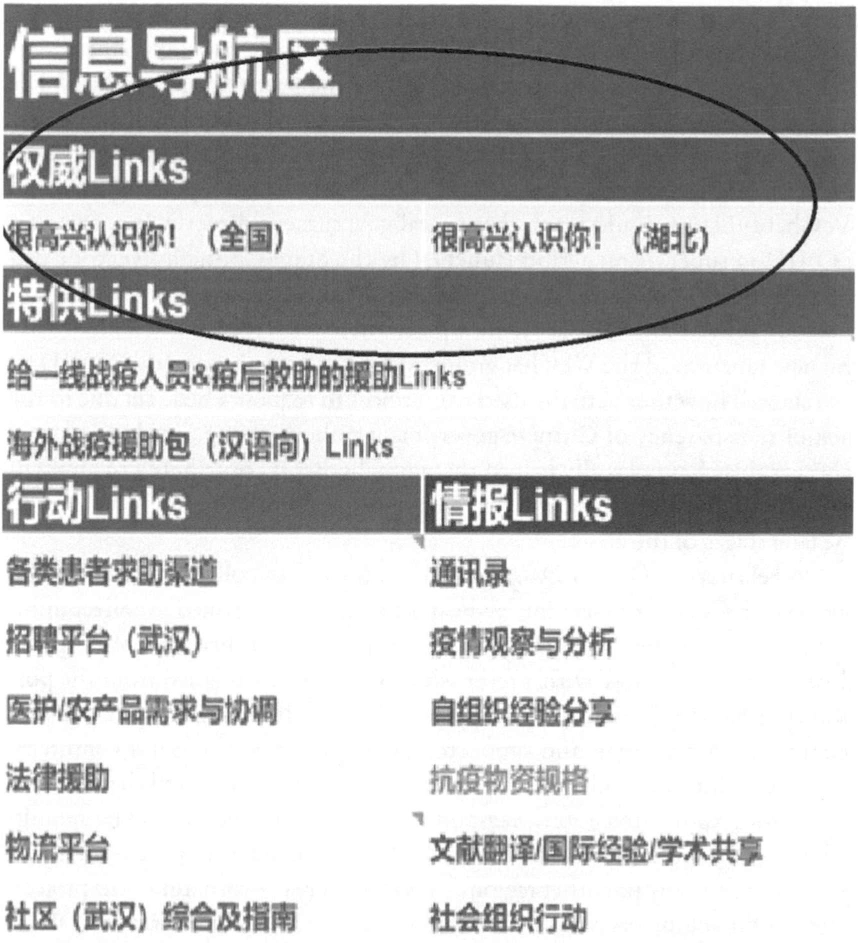

信息导航区

权威Links

很高兴认识你！（全国）　　　很高兴认识你！（湖北）

特供Links

给一线战疫人员&疫后救助的援助Links

海外战疫援助包（汉语向）Links

行动Links	情报Links
各类患者求助渠道	通讯录
招聘平台（武汉）	疫情观察与分析
医护/农产品需求与协调	自组织经验分享
法律援助	抗疫物资规格
物流平台	文献翻译/国际经验/学术共享
社区（武汉）综合及指南	社会组织行动

FIGURE 7.5. The Information Navigation Section of the NCP Life Support Network's Summary of Information Platforms of Domestic Grassroots Organizations against COVID-19

crisis, such as failing to report COVID-19 cases quickly, and to information on incompetence in response to the crisis. If such problems of local government caused serious consequences, such as the spread of COVID-19 in new communities, the State Council will directly send supervision teams to investigate the problems. If proven true, the local officials will be held accountable according to law and regulations. (State Council of the People's Republic of China, 2020)

Based on this statement, the project would collect "information . . . regarding the inaction, incompetence, irresponsibility, and other problems of local governments" for the public to hold them accountable. It is not a channel to help those with COVID-19 to secure beds. Yet many volunteers and internet users believed that by providing information regarding the inability of local government to find beds for those with COVID-19 to the State Council, the council's Supervision Team could pressure local government to solve the problem more quickly. For example, on January 31, five volunteers in the network's major WeChat group posted information regarding the platform separately and provided screenshots on how to use this new function in WeChat. Volunteer Xiaoya posted, "This new WeChat function could reach the central government directly. It is part of a COVID-19 supervision action launched by the State Council. Everyone can report to the State Council if your family member is unable to get a bed in hospital. Please disseminate." Xiaoya then posted detailed screenshots on how to use the new function in the WeChat group. Messages from those with COVID-19 also showed how they actually used this project to request a bed. Yet due to the lack of transparency of Chinese government policymaking, we do not know whether this channel really helped them or whether it contributed to any central government policy changes regarding people infected with COVID-19 in the later stages of the crisis.

On February 3, *People's Daily* launched a project to collect information on people with COVID-19 seeking medical help. The project aimed to collect information on four types of COVID-19 related persons: confirmed, presumptive, close contact, and those with a fever who could not be excluded from the possibility of having COVID-19. The project was coordinated and managed by a team in the party organ and supported by roughly two thousand volunteers recruited by internet and other channels. *People's Daily* submitted the collected information to "related government offices." The severe cases would be submitted directly to the Supervision Team on COVID-19 deployed by the central government to Wuhan and other regions.[9] Yaya, the core coordinator of the project, stated, "Our volunteers collected more than 40,000 pieces of information about people seeking help. . . . Our team aggregated and integrated the information to create a data set and submit it to related offices. The severe cases will be directly reported to the Supervision Team [on COVID-19] of the central government" (Xiao et al., 2020). She also revealed that at the peak of the pandemic, the project could only help around 8 to 10 percent of COVID-19 cases in severe and critical conditions to get beds in hospitals, making many volunteers in the project feel desperate and helpless. As Yaya said, "The first several days in February was the second peak of COVID-19. Many of the persons infected with COVID-19 who were unable to get timely treatment became severe and critical cases. The cases that needed to report to the Supervision Team [of the central government] surged to around 200 every day. We could only help around 8–10%. . . . Many of our volunteers felt desperate and helpless. I told them we have to hold on to help more people" (Xiao et al., 2020).

In mid-February, the difficulty of securing hospital beds for non-COVID-19 patients with severe disease became a new urgent problem in the crisis. Desperate messages asking for help generated a second wave flooding Chinese social media. On February 14, CCTV news, another major party organ, started a non-COVID-19 patient information collection project. Non-COVID-19 patients with severe disease could submit their personal information, needs, and three photos of their test results through CCTV's online platform. Using strategy similar to the NCP Life Support Network, the project first recruited volunteers to call patients to verify the information and then submit the verified information and needs from patients to local governments in Wuhan. By March 3, more than 100,000 users had visited the platform. Through its networks and information platforms, the NCP Life Support Network actively promoted the government's two information collection projects—on persons with COVID-19 and non-COVID-19 patients—to grassroots organizations, volunteers, persons with COVID-19, persons with other severe illnesses, and the public. On February 5, the network published the information and the link to the *People's Daily* project and encouraged those with COVID-19 to use it to submit their information for help. On February 9, its official Weibo published a post summarizing the most effective channels for getting a bed based on the firsthand experience of COVID-19 patients. The *People's Daily* project was among the two most effective channels. On February 14 and 15, the official Weibo of the network published two messages about the CCTV project and recommended this project to non-COVID-19 patients with cancer, cardiovascular diseases, chronic diseases, and other severe diseases. The Beds Group of the network added the two projects to the top of its collectively created document for those with COVID-19 and those with other illnesses who were seeking help.

The network also promoted information on the two projects through its one-on-one assistance project for those infected with COVID-19. It assigned volunteers to collect messages for help from those with COVID-19 and submit these messages to the *People Daily's* project. For example, volunteer Xiao Yu of the network worked with the *People's Daily* project on collecting and submitting information on those with COVID-19 to help them secure hospital beds. According to Xiao Yu, on February 9, the *People's Daily* project had helped more than a hundred people with COVID-19 secure beds in hospitals or Fangcang hospitals. This shows that the NCP Life Support Network and the government's two patient information collection projects formed a reciprocal relationship. By using and collaborating with the two projects, the NCP Life Support Network helped people with COVID-19 and those with other illnesses in its networks get timely treatment in hospitals. The two government projects significantly increased the number of patients they could reach through the NCP Life Support Network. Through working with volunteers from the network, the two projects also increased the accuracy of the data collected.

This reciprocal relationship between the NCP Life Support Network and the government is also notable in the network's influence on government policies through its advocacy. Like the Free Lunch Project and the NGO 2.0 Project, the network's advocacy is less confrontational than conventional advocacy communication in the West. In its advocacy, the network used mass media and internal channels within the government. For example, Hao Nan stated:

> We have also conducted a certain amount of policy advocacy. . . . Since the first week, we have reached out to media and various government channels in order to convey to the policymaking system the urgency, the distribution, and the trends in severe cases of COVID-19 that we have learned from our telehealth project. We also provided them with related recommendations. We found this advocacy to be effective. For example, several days ago, we communicated with an editor of Xinhua News Agency's Department of Internal Journals about the difficulties of non-COVID-19 patients with severe illness.[10] The next day, the Wuhan government made a series of announcements giving non-COVID-19 patients more opportunity to get timely treatment. It also broadened the dissemination of information. The problem that non-COVID-19 patients were unable to get timely treatment had by then been largely eased. (N. Hao, 2020)

The Network's Wuhan Pregnant Women Group contacted the Hubei Women's Federation, the government body tasked to protect women's right, to change the policy regarding pregnant women in the lockdown. On January 31, Dolphin, the project coordinator, posted on the network's WeChat group that she is reaching out to the Hubei Women's Federation to discuss the difficulties of pregnant women in getting adequate obstetrical services during the lockdown. The network's summary report published on January 31 stated the following:

8. We have organized sixty journalists to interview several pregnant women in order to expose the difficulties of pregnant women getting adequate obstetrical services.
9. We recruited ten volunteers to collect and compile information regarding obstetrical services that are available to pregnant women in every hospital in Wuhan.
10. We are summarizing and organizing the information we collected to propose policy recommendations to the Hubei Women's Federation.

On February 6, the Wuhan government published a list of forty-four hospitals that provided obstetrical services to serve the needs of pregnant women. Yet due to the lack of transparency in policymaking, we cannot be sure the network's advocacy actually contributed to these policy changes. Activists of the network believe that their advocacy work was somewhat effective in the crisis. Hao Nan stated, "We have tried to send the information regarding the difficulties of those with severe COVID-19 to the government through various channels. Yet we do not know whether this really has any impact. But I believe the information we provided may have had some influence on pushing the government to pay adequate attention to severe COVID-19 cases. It might have contributed to the policy change that made death rate reduction the most important goal in government's response to COVID-19" (N. Hau, 2020).

Contestation between Activists and the Government in New Media Actions against COVID-19

As I revealed when discussing the Free Lunch Project, the reciprocal relationship between NGOs and the central government—in this case between the NCP Life Support Network and the government—is only one dimension in the complex, multidimensional, and context-based relationship between activists and the government in the COVID-19 crisis. Activists and volunteers of the network also openly contested issues at various levels of government, even those that are politically very sensitive to the government. For example, the network posted the following message as a headline on its official Weibo:

> We used to believe that you have all been well treated and will soon be cured [of COVID-19], until thousands of test results and phone numbers appeared online in desperate calls for help. We recruited doctors attempting to explain to you the meaning of terminology such as "ground glass opacity." Regrettably, what we could do for you is extremely limited, as "the distance" between we and you is great and insurmountable. What we could do is to reduce our yearning to a minimum: getting a simple message that you have been admitted to the hospital. HOLD ON, DO NOT GIVE UP! (NCP Life Support Network, 2020c)

This message does not illustrate the success of China's response to COVID-19 but rather highlights the failures of the government's response and policy on COVID-19. The network used this headline as a vital part of the collective memory and knowledge of the network on the crisis. To reinforce this collective memory and knowledge, the network constantly posted Weibo messages that exposed problems in the government's response to COVID-19. For example, on February 7, the network reposted a message from an activist, the Intellectual, who questioned what happened in the first twenty days of the crisis and with the cover-up of, and delayed response to, the outbreak in Wuhan:

> On December 31, 2019, the Wuhan government first announced the outbreak of COVID-19 in the city. On January 20, 2020, Zhong Nanshan publicly confirmed the human-to-human spread of the virus.[11] For Wuhan, the 20 days between December 31 and January 20 is a crucial period. When we now look back at the outbreak, we can't help asking, in these critical 20 days that may determine the fate of Wuhan, whether we have any chance to change what has happened?

The network commented, "From the arrival of the first group of experts [from the Chinese Center for Disease Control and Prevention] to the lockdown, what has happened in those 20 days? What opportunity has been missed? Sooner or later, the headline news will shift away from COVID-19. Yet the history of the outbreak should never and will never be forgotten" (NCP Life Support Network, February 7, 2020).

The activist's message and the network's comment indicate that the network constructed a collective memory and knowledge of the crisis that exposed to its members and the public the problems and failures of the government's response. This could also be seen in the network's commemoration of the silenced whistle-blower, Dr. Li Wenliang, an iconic figure of resistance to the government's cover-up of the outbreak and censorship of this issue on many different Chinese internet platforms.

Dr. Li Wenliang, an eye doctor in the Wuhan Central Hospital, was the first whistleblower to draw attention to the outbreak.[12] According to interviews, on December 30 at 5:43 P.M., he posted on his private WeChat group of college classmates, "7 SARS cases have been identified in the Huanan Seafood Market" (M. Liu, 2020; Tan et al., 2020). He then posted one patient's lab test results on WeChat. At 6:42 P.M., he again posted on the WeChat group: "The most updated information is that it has been confirmed that they are coronavirus infections" (M. Liu, 2020). When Dr. Li's WeChat messages spread on the internet and went viral in Chinese social media, he was first summoned to talk with the supervision department at the Wuhan Central Hospital. Then on January 3, he was summoned to talk with local police in Wuhan and signed a Letter of Admonition for "spreading untrue information online that '7 SARS cases have been identified in the Huanan Seafood Market'" (M. Liu, 2020). The Letter of Admonition orchestrated by the Wuhan police stated that Dr. Li was "spreading untrue information" that "significantly threatened social stability" (M. Liu, 2020). In order to silence the whistleblowers and the voices from social media users questioning the veracity of Dr. Li's information, the local police in Wuhan summoned a total of eight individuals for talks about "spreading untrue information that '7 SARS cases have been identified in the Huanan Seafood Market'" (M. Liu, 2020; Tan et al., 2020). The silencing of the whistleblowers by the Wuhan police and the narrative of the Wuhan Health Commission that there was "no obvious evidence of human-to-human spreading, but the limited possibility of that spreading cannot be excluded" did not completely quiet the media and social media voices regarding the outbreak of a SARS-like disease in Wuhan. Yet according to an investigative report in *China Business News*, this significantly reduced the chances of warning the public and individuals of the outbreak so that they could take protective measures, such as wearing masks and social distancing in the very early stage of the outbreak (X. Ma, 2020). On January 20, 2020, Zhong Nanshan publicly confirmed human-to-human transmission of COVID-19. On January 23, a total lockdown was imposed on Wuhan and its eleven million people, which lasted seventy-six days. Yet twenty-three days had already passed since Dr. Li Wenliang first sounded the alarm.

At 2:58 A.M. on February 7, the Wuhan Central Hospital posted in Weibo that Dr. Li Wenliang "died of COVID-19 in the fight against the virus." The network's Weibo posted this comment at 10:30 the same day: "We are deeply indebted to you for . . . you have tried to save the earth."

On March 12, when many party organs were publishing articles praising the government's response to COVID-19, the network's Weibo posted an article by *Caixin Media* to expose the cover-up and mismanagement of the outbreak in Wuhan in general and in the Wuhan Central Hospital in particular. The network commented, "Li Wenliang, Jiang Xueqing, Mei Zhongming, and Zhu Heping, the four doctors all died of COVID-19 in their fight against the outbreak. Ai Fen, another doctor, became known by the public as a whistleblower of the outbreak. The five doctors are all from the Wuhan Central Hospital. According to the report from Caixin, more than 230 health workers in the hospital were infected by COVID-19, the largest number among all hospitals in Wuhan. What has happened in this hospital? Why did they have to pay such a bitter cost?" (NCP Life Support Network, 2020g).

Grassroots activists' statements of their own experience in actions against COVID-19 also reveal that resistance to the cover-up and the problems in the government's response are an important part of their memory and knowledge of the crisis. For example, Yige, the coordinator of the volunteer driver team of the Wuhan Pregnant Women Group, stated: "My dream for 2020 is not to find the one I love. It is for every pregnant woman in our WeChat group and every patient to survive [from the COVID-19 crisis] and keep healthy. Every day, I witnessed people around me die of COVID-19. Every minute and every second in our efforts against COVID-19 determine the life or death of those pregnant women and patients. We must hold on to win the fight against the virus. So that we won't let down those who have sacrificed their lives, for example Li Wenliang and He Hui!" (L. Yu, 2020).[13] Yige's statement indicates that she saw Li Wenliang as a hero who sacrificed his life in the fight against COVID-19. And she believed that Li Wenliang was one of the exemplars that mobilized her and other activists to continue their fight against the virus. The Wuhan police, in contrast, accused Li Wenliang of "spreading untrue information" that has "significantly threatened social stability" (M. Liu, 2020). This is evidence of open resistance among network activists to the narrative of the Wuhan police regarding the whistleblower.

Activist Kathy published a long reflection on her personal experience in the fight against COVID-19 on the WeChat public account of Zhuoming Disaster Information Center titled "A Reflection of My Experience as an Online Volunteer Born After 1995." Near the end of her account, she wrote:

True fighters dare face the sorrows of humanity and look unflinchingly at bloodshed.[14] I have witnessed this kind of sorrow in my own life in the past 46 days. They reside in stories related to the following names and events: for example the Wuhan government in January, the Wuhan Red Cross, the Wuhan Central Hospital, the Health Commission of Huanggang city . . . for example those censored media reports, those hospitals that were forced not to call for donations of PPE from the public, and those desperate messages calling for help to get a bed in a hospital. In addition, we must also remember forever those health workers who should not have died of the virus and those ordinary people who died of the virus in an unknown corner before even getting a test.

Kathy's inclusion of the quotation from Lu Xun's (1926) *In Memory of Miss Liu Hezhen*—"True fighters dare face the sorrows of humanity, and look unflinchingly at bloodshed"—indicates her desire to convey to fellow activists and the public the need to remember the bitter lesson of humanity's sorrows in the government's response to COVID-19. The "names and events" indicate iconic institutions, officials, and events that demonstrated various problems and failures with the government's response to COVID-19. For example, in January the Wuhan government was widely criticized by activists and the media for its cover-up of and delayed response to the outbreak. The Wuhan Red Cross was extensively criticized for its inefficiency, lack of transparency, and mismanagement of donated PPE from the public. The Health Commission at Huanggang, a city near Wuhan, is largely criticized for its inaction and inability in responding to COVID-19. By mentioning these institutions, officials, and events, the activist reminds the public to examine and remember the problems in the government's response to the crisis. In the next paragraph, Kathy wrote,

> Our parents got used to telling us, the generation born after 1995, "This is not what you should worry about. You should first take care of yourself. You aren't able to make a difference." Or, "you should not speak out or stand out." Or, "you should not voice your difference with the official discourse. You should not question." Yet I, and many of our generation, chose to stand out. We believed what Lu Xun said: "Youth in China should first change China into a country with a voice. Speak out boldly and march forward bravely."[15] More importantly, we chose to be the "new youth" who believe in "giving as much light as the heat can produce" (as expected by Lu Xun).[16]

The juxtaposition of what the post-1995 generation were told by their parents and what they chose to do on their own illustrates that young activists of Kathy's generation have a different view of the government than their parents ever had. They chose to act in response to the crisis rather than just protecting themselves to play it safe. They have the courage to question the government's policy and to voice differences with the dominant discourse of government. This can also be seen in the quotation from Lu Xun's *Silent China* (1927), in which he harshly criticizes the lack of courage and capacity among the Chinese of the 1920s to express themselves.[17] Kathy used *Silent China* to criticize the silencing of individuals and the dominance of state discourse regarding the crisis. The quotation "Youth in China should first change China into a country with a voice. Speak out boldly" demonstrates the determination of young activists to speak out about the various problems in the government's response to the crisis and to challenge the dominance of official discourse in the memory of the crisis. The last part of the quotation—"and march forward bravely"—and the statement "we chose to be the 'new youth' who believe in 'giving as much light as the heat can produce'" suggest that young activists in the NCP Life Support Network not only spoke out but also stood out. They voiced their difference with government discourse. More importantly, they took action to bring about change in the largest public health crisis in the past four decades.

At the end of her post, Kathy cheerfully claimed, "I'd like to pay tribute to all health workers, all community workers, and all volunteers who have participated in the fight. I'd like to pay tribute to every ordinary person who engaged in this fight. We are finally going to see the coming of a long-waited spring with flower blossoms." This cheerful ending indicates Kathy's belief that the bitter fight against COVID-19 will finally prevail, as of March 14. Yet in juxtaposition to the official discourse of party organs, she attributed this success not to the government but to the work of health workers, volunteers, and ordinary people who engaged in various efforts against COVID-19. It highlights the indispensable role of grassroots volunteers and ordinary people in responding to the COVID-19 outbreak in China.

The contentious relationship between activists of the network and government agencies could also be seen in activists' sharp criticism of the Wuhan Red Cross, the GONGO that controls the distribution of public donations of PPE and other resources to frontline hospital workers. On January 26, during the peak of the pandemic, the Ministry of Civil Affairs (MCA) announced a new regulation on the management of PPE and other supplies donated by the public to frontline hospitals. It required that all PPE and other donations go through the Red Cross and four other smaller GONGOs exclusively. The Hubei and Wuhan governments then announced that the Hubei and Wuhan Red Cross were the only channel for donated PPE and other medical supplies to hospitals in Hubei. They were granted a monopoly even though China's Red Cross has been at the center of round after round of nonprofit sector scandals over the past decade (Wang, 2019b). The Wuhan government stated that this designation was to "ensure [that] the use of PPE, money, and other donations could be documented judiciously and centrally managed to avoid bad guys from taking advantage of the chaos created by the crisis [by appropriating and reselling donations]" (M. Xu, 2020). Yet rather than serving as a gatekeeper to reduce chaos and increase transparency, the Red Cross became a source of chaos and opacity (e.g., Cui & Yang, 2020; Guo et al., 2020; Wu & Ma, 2020). The Wuhan Red Cross and the Hubei Red Cross were called "the black hole of donated PPEs" by media and activists (Guo et al., 2020). On January 30, the Wuhan Red Cross posted its

Table 7.5

Weibo Users' Comments on the Wuhan Red Cross's Weibo Message

Posted time	Activist number	WeChat message	Liked
13:29	Activist 1	Publish the detailed breakdown [of the distribution of donated PPE]!! Why on earth has the Wuhan Union Hospital run out of PPE?!!! You exposed frontline health workers to danger!!! We don't need your special report but a detailed breakdown!!! Is that so hard for you?!	274
13:30	Activist 2	Detailed breakdown of your expenditure, Detailed breakdown of your expenditure, Detailed breakdown of your expenditure!	373
13:35	Activist 3	If you can't publish your detailed breakdown of your expenditure, you are profiting from the country's crisis.	558
13:39	Activist 4	Please publish a detailed breakdown of your expenditure and the distribution of donated PPE.	841

special report for PPE donation solicitations in its official Weibo. The message received 5,890 comments and 667 forwards by users. Most of the comments were sharp criticism, harsh requests to improve transparency, and condemnations. For example, from 13:29 to 13:39, four users entered posts in the comment section of the Weibo message board (see table 7.5). The high number of likes indicates strong support among Weibo users for the demand for the Red Cross to provide a detailed breakdown of its expenditures and distribution of donated PPE. It also shows that online activists largely condemned the Red Cross for putting frontline health workers at risk and questioned the organization's apparent intentional discrimination against the Wuhan Union Hospital—a leading COVID-19 designated hospital on the front line. Comments on the Weibo message were so overwhelmingly negative that the Red Cross later closed and hid the comments section.

On January 31, in the NCP Life Support Network's major WeChat group, activist Autumn Shadow posted a summary of sharp criticisms to the Wuhan Red Cross that was largely censored on the Chinese internet. The following WeChat post is by activist SouthNorth, titled "Three Questions You Have to Answer! The Wuhan Red Cross!" SouthNorth charged that the low efficiency of the Wuhan Red Cross—the official gatekeeper and gateway for donated PPE to hospitals—caused the extreme shortage of PPE in frontline hospitals, while huge quantities of PPE and other donations sat in a warehouse of the Wuhan Red Cross: "According to the report, List of Distributed Donations, published by the Red Cross, they have made 17 distributions of donations worth 8,624,600 RMB in total. Yet as of January 30, the Red Cross has received donations of

379,054,900 in total." This means that, according to SouthNorth, the Wuhan Red Cross distributed only about 2 percent of the donations of PPE and other supplies to hospitals. SouthNorth then posed three questions to the Wuhan Red Cross regarding why it is so inefficient and how it plans to solve the problem that put the lives of tens of thousands of frontline health workers at risk. First, does it really have enough hands and enough warehouses to accept, manage, and distribute these donations? If not, how is it going to solve the problem? According to an activist who had interviewed Wuhan Red Cross volunteers, the organization had no computers, and all the records had to be done by hand. SouthNorth questioned why the Red Cross was so incompetent that it was unable to solve this very simple problem. Second, SouthNorth questioned the Red Cross's centrally controlled PPE allocation and distribution policy. During the peak of the crisis, the Red Cross stated that PPE donations were allocated and distributed by the Wuhan government and the Red Cross "according to the needs of hospitals and other institutions." Only the Wuhan government and the Red Cross could decide how much PPE a hospital could get. Hospitals were not allowed to get any PPE beyond their allocation from the Red Cross. As SouthNorth and other activists have pointed out, the so-called centrally controlled allocation policy was obviously a failure. There was a critical shortage of PPE in frontline hospitals, and a large number of frontline health workers were infected with COVID-19 due to the lack of PPE. Yet tons of PPE and other medical supplies that had been donated by the public remained in a Red Cross warehouse and could not be delivered to hospitals simply due to the incompetence of the organization that had been tasked with managing and allocating the PPE. SouthNorth posed this question: "Since the current central[ly] controlled allocation policy does not work on the ground, why not use other models? In this critical moment to save lives, why are hospitals only able to call on the public to have donations shipped directly to them [bypassing the Red Cross to get PPE on time] while there [is] actually enough PPE in Wuhan, in the warehouse of the Red Cross?!" Last, SouthNorth questioned the government's requirement that all PPEs and other donations go through the Red Cross: "If the government-appointed agency is unable to satisfy the PPE demands of hospitals on time, is the government willing to collaborate with grassroots forces to solve this problem?" SouthNorth warned that "currently, many donors are trying to circumvent the five official channels to transport donations themselves. Imposing restrictions on this will only further weaken the public's trust in the government. It is better that the government collaborate with those grassroots efforts to fight against COVID-19 together."

SouthNorth's post indicates that activists and grassroots organizations were questioning not just the inefficiency of the Red Cross but the government's policy to give low-efficient GONGOs such as the Red Cross monopoly control over PPE and other public donations in the COVID-19 crisis. They advocated giving grassroots organizations more rights to participate in the fight against COVID-19—for example, in the management and distribution of donated PPE.

One example of the problematic policy of "allocation" that angered network activists and other internet users was the discrimination against the Wuhan Union Hospital in the distribution and allocation of donated PPE. The messages in table 7.6 express activists' and volunteers' sharp criticisms and condemnations of the Red Cross for its problematic PPE "allocation policy." For example, activist Outreach Department of the Jianghan Oil Field Central Hospital posted a series of photos indicating that frontline health workers in the Wuhan Union Hospital have run out of PPE. These photos showed health workers using disposable raincoats and nurses having to make face masks for themselves (see figure 7.6). In MouseAndCat's message, the activist posted an article that criticized the "allocation policy" of the Red Cross. The article questioned why the Wuhan Union Hospital, a leading COVID-19 designated hospital, got only three thousand disposable medical masks, whereas a small private cosmetic hospital without any COVID-19 patients got sixteen thousand N95 masks. Then Li Jie-Volunteer of the Group to Support Patients Quarantined at Home posted that he or she had reliable information that the Wuhan Union Hospital went to the Red Cross and its warehouse many times hoping to get PPE, yet "they could only stand outside the warehouse watching others picking up PPE." Moreover, the messages in table 7.6 reveal that network activists not only exposed and criticized the misconduct of the Red Cross but have also taken action to build a network of activists, grassroots organizations, health professionals from frontline hospitals, and PPE donors to circumvent the Red Cross, the government's PPE donation gatekeeper in the crisis. In Message 15, "Li Jie-Volunteer of the Group to Support Patients Quarantined at Home" recommended that potential donors and grassroots organizations use designated donations that allow PPE to circumvent the Red Cross and be shipped directly to the hospitals. Messages 16 to 18 show that health professionals in other hospitals were using their own network to solicit PPE donations to help the Wuhan Union Hospital, which was discriminated against by the Red Cross. Messages 24 to 26 indicate that activists of the network were coordinating PPE donations that could circumvent the Red Cross. Messages 28 to 30 show that an alternative network of activists, NGOs, and health professionals for PPE donations was formed in the network's WeChat group. The messages in table 7.6 indicate the emergence of an alternative network of PPE donations that could circumvent the Red Cross. The messages in table 7.7 show the effectiveness of such a network coordinated by activists and volunteers of the NCP Life Support Network.

The messages in table 7.7 indicate that within several minutes, a transnational network of PPE donors in Dubai, health professionals in Wuhan's frontline hospitals, and activists on the internet was constructed in the WeChat group of the NCP Life Support Network. The transnational network created a new channel for PPE donations that circumvented the Red Cross. Compared with the inefficiency and poorly managed gatekeeper of donated PPE designated by the government, grassroots organizations and activists demonstrated their competence

Table 7.6

WeChat Messages on the Red Cross's Discrimination of the Wuhan Union Hospital in the Distribution of Donated PPE

Message ID	Activist ID	WeChat message
1	Outreach Department of the Jianghan Oil Field Central Hospital[a]	Posted a series of photos indicating that frontline health workers in the Wuhan Union Hospital have run out of PPE: health workers are using disposable raincoats, and nurses have to make their own face masks.
2	Outreach Department of the Jianghan Oil Field Central Hospital	Doctors in the Wuhan Union Hospital had to fight on the frontline in this manner [without any PPE].
3	MouseAndCat	Posted an article that criticized the so-called allocation policy of the Red Cross. The article questioned why the Wuhan Union Hospital received only three thousand disposable medical masks, whereas a small private cosmetic hospital without any COVID-19 patients received sixteen thousand N95 masks.
4	Li Jie-Volunteer of the Group to Support Patients Quarantined at Home	The Union Hospital staff have gone to the Red Cross many times. Yet the Red Cross refused to give them anything. They could only stand outside the warehouse watching others picking up PPE.
5	Outreach Department of the Jianghan Oil Field Central Hospital	@Li Jie-Volunteer of the Group to Support Patients Quarantined at Home How could they refuse to give PPE to the Union Hospital?!
6	Li Jie-Volunteer of the Group to Support Patients Quarantined at Home	Who knows!
7	Li Jie-Volunteer of the Group to Support Patients Quarantined at Home	The information is absolutely reliable. The Union Hospital was allocated none of the donated PPE stored in the International Expo Center.
8	ConSumma Te	The donations are supposed to be given to hospitals in Wuhan. Why was the Union Hospital allocated nothing?
9	Li Jie-Volunteer of the Group to Support Patients Quarantined at Home	Who knows this?
10	ConSumma Te	Didn't the Union Hospital fight on the front line to treat COVID-19 patients?
11	Outreach Department of the Jianghan Oil Field Central Hospital	Reposted three photos

(continued)

Table 7.6 (Continued)

Message ID	Activist ID	WeChat message
12	Outreach Department of the Jianghan Oil Field Central Hospital	@ConSummaTe Not fighting in the front line? Doctors in the Union Hospital are fighting on the front line in this manner [without any PPE].
13	LittleMonkey	Yes, the Union Hospital actually got nothing. I can confirm.
14	...	...
15	Li Jie–Volunteer of the Group to Support Patients Quarantined at Home	Please choose the Designated Donation if you want to donate next time!
16	Outreach Department of the Jianghan Oil Field Central Hospital	Folks, do you have the contact, specific PPE needs, and the address for delivery of the Union Hospital? We could help to forward the information to our network for donation solicitation.
17	Li Jie–Volunteer of the Group to Support Patients Quarantined at Home	@Outreach Department of the Jianghan Oil Field Central Hospital is the official information from the Union Hospital fine?
18	Outreach Department of the Jianghan Oil Field Central Hospital	Sure! Please send to me!
19	DaiTiantian	Posted a screenshot of his or her WeChat history with a doctor from the Union Hospital: "The 3,000 masks were shipped to us by a friend from Shaanxi. Yet the shipment was hijacked by the Red Cross in Wuhan. The Red Cross signed for receiving the shipment and claimed to have distributed it to us. But when our doctors went to the Red Cross, they didn't get any of the 3,000 masks. We were unable to get any PPE! (while fighting to treat COVID-19 patients): We got nothing from 'the allocation' and the donations directly shipped to us were hijacked."
20	DaiTiantian	The Union Hospital DID NOT get the 3,000 masks even.
21	Outreach Department of the Jianghan Oil Field Central Hospital	Fuck!! (icon)

22	Li Jie-Volunteer of the Group to Support Patients Quarantined at Home	Posted the donation agreement and the confirmed donation letter of intent from the Union Hospital.
23	Outreach Department of the Jianghan Oil Field Central Hospital	I'll send them out right now!
24	Telehealth Group-Jiang Nan	Help!! Compatibility Table for PPE standards in different countries! Did I make it clear? We have donors who want to bypass the Red Cross to donate PPEs~
25	Li Jie-Volunteer of the Group to Support Patients Quarantined at Home	@Telehealth Group-Jiang Nan is this one OK? Posted a list of PPE product codes that have proved qualified for medical donations in China, which was created collectively by the network.
26	prcht_HeFan	Posted a table of global PPE standards and examples of PPE products that are qualified for medical supply donations created by the Renming Hospital of Wuhan University. This one could be helpful.
27	…	
28	ZhaoXin-Volunteer from Shanghai NGO	Who could provide contact with the Union Hospital?
29	Li Jie-Volunteer of the Group to Support Patients Quarantined at Home	@ZhaoXin-Volunteer from Shanghai NGO I'll invite Union Hospital staff to the WeChat group very soon.
30	Li Jie-Volunteer of the Group to Support Patients Quarantined at Home	Please approve. I invited a staff in charge of medical supplies at the Union Hospital to this WeChat group.

a "Outreach Department of the Jianghan Oil Field Central Hospital" is the WeChat ID of a health worker and activist from the Outreach Department of the Jianghan Oil Field Central Hospital in Hubei.

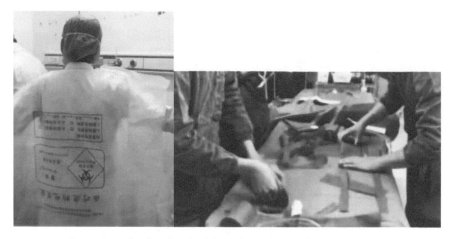

FIGURE 7.6 Photos show that frontline health workers in the Wuhan Union Hospital have run out of PPE

and high efficiency as an alternative channel for PPE donations during Wuhan's COVID-19 crisis.

As in the Free Lunch Project case, activists and grassroots organizations in the NCP Life Support Network illustrate the rise of a new activism in China's nonprofit sector that is distinct from conventional activism in the West. In this new activism, the relationship between activists/grassroots organizations and the government is very multidimensional and context based. Table 7.8 provides a specific example to illustrate that relationship.

On January 31, Zhi Guo posted on the NCP Life Support Network's WeChat group three photos of a warehouse with a large quantity of PPE and other medical supplies. He then posted, "Please help to disseminate: Section A of the International Expo Center now has a large number of medical supplies that need a hand to help with transportation. The medical supplies are already there, but we don't have enough hands for transportation and distribution. So the hospitals were unable to get them." Network activists quickly identified the warehouse as a major warehouse of the Red Cross. The messages from Wang Jun, prcht_HeFan, and Autumn Shadow in table 7.8 indicate that activists of the network view the urgent need to distribute PPE to frontline hospitals to be the most important. They were willing to help the Red Cross distribute PPE even though they believed the Red Cross should be condemned for misconduct and inefficiency in the management and distribution of donated PPE. The statement by prcht_HeFan in Message 8 helps explain why activists made this choice in the crisis. Their choice is not based on blind trust in the government or the Red Cross. It is from their firsthand knowledge of the urgent needs of vulnerable groups, specifically frontline health workers in "less profiled local hospitals" (see the bold text in Message 8 from prcht_HeFan). This choice was also based on the belief that less profiled local hospitals were crucial for achieving the primary mission of saving

Table 7.7

The Network's WeChat Messages on PPE Donations from Dubai

Message ID	Activist ID	WeChat message
1	Mr. Yue-Selling Qualified Protective Suits	Could anyone give me the contact of the Wuhan Union Hospital? I want to donate 300,000 masks [to them].
2	DaiTiantian	Posted the official donation solicitation letter with the contact and PPE needs of the Wuhan Union Hospital.
3	Mr. Yue-Selling Qualified Protective Suits	Could they accept donations from foreign counties? From Dubai?
4	Mr. Yue-Selling Qualified Protective Suits	Don't want go through the Red Cross.
5	Mr. Yue-Selling Qualified Protective Suits	Could any one of you give me the official donation agreement from the Union Hospital? Many thanks.
6	Outreach Department of the Jianghan Oil Field Central Hospital	Posted the donation agreement and the confirmed donation letter of intent from the Union Hospital
7	Mr. Yue-Selling Qualified Protective Suits	@Outreach Department of the Jianghan Oil Field Central Hospital Great! Thanks everyone in the group. I've contacted the Union Hospital.
8	Li Jie-Volunteer of the Group to Support Patients Quarantined at Home	A new official donation agreement with official seal [from the Union Hospital]
9	Mr. Yue-Selling Qualified Protective Suits	@Li Jie-Volunteer of the Group to Support Patients Quarantined at Home OK. Thank you very much.
10	Li Jie-Volunteer of the Group to Support Patients Quarantined at Home	Quote the message from Mr. Yue-Selling Qualified Protective Suits. "Could anyone give me the contact of the Wuhan Union Hospital? I want to donate 300,000 masks." A staff from the department of General Affairs at the Union Hospital is in our WeChat group.
11	Li Jie-Volunteer of the Group to Support Patients Quarantined at Home	@Union Hospital-Zhu Hongxing (Use @ function to connect Zhu Hongxing from the Union Hospital with Mr. Yue)

Table 7.8

The Network's WeChat Messages on Donated PPE in a Red Cross Warehouse

Message ID	Activist ID	WeChat Message
1	Zhi Guo	On January 31, posted in the WeChat group, the Information Center of the NCP Life Support Network, three photos of a warehouse with a large quantity of PPE and other medical supplies
2	Zhi Guo	Please help to disseminate: Section A of the International Expo Center now has a large number of medical supplies that need a hand to help with transportation. The medical supplies are already there, but we don't have enough hands for transportation and distribution. So the hospitals were unable to get them. For volunteers who would like to help, please call 18986279531 when you arrive there. For hospitals who are able to pick up medical supplies by yourselves, please tell your staff to go to the warehouse with an official letter and a valid photo ID. Please notice, you can now pick up the medical supplies by yourself! By yourself!
3	ShaoZi	@Zhi Guo Medical supplies from the Red Cross?
4	prcht_HeFan	Seems to be the Hubei Red Cross
5	Wang Jun	We may have to help distribute the medical supplies for them while scolding them for their low efficiency and misconduct. The Red Cross is recruiting volunteers to help with the transportation and distribution of medical supplies. Their current volunteers are working 24 hours and 4 shifts but still lack enough hands. The following is the recruitment message for the transportation and distribution of the medical supplies at the International Expo Center. Requirement: Have your own car. If you'd like to go to the International Expo Center to help, please call 18040548490, 18171303010, 18171313010, 19947601710, 18986279531. Please do disseminate. Increasing the speed of medical supply distribution will also help hospitals save lives.
6	ShaoZi	The Red Cross became willing to distribute the supplies they received?

| 7 | Zhi Guo | Several clarifications:

1 The A section of the International Expo Center is the warehouse where the Red Cross stored the donations they received.

2 The medical supplies in the photos are the donations that the Red Cross failed to distribute judiciously.

3 [For hospital staffs], to pick up the supplies, you need an official letter from your hospital. I have the template for the letter if you need it.

4 If your hospital has vehicles and hands for pick up, it could have its staff go to the warehouse with an official letter to have a try. Some hospitals have successfully received the PPE they need. But I can't guarantee. If the Red Cross is reliable, the badly needed medical supplies should have been distributed judiciously.

5 I've done what I can [to] help from my side. |

| 8 | prcht_HeFan | According to the information from various channels, the Red Cross clearly failed to distribute the donations of medical supplies judiciously. **The public and grassroots volunteers have not paid enough attention to the PPE needs of many less profiled local hospitals. [Those hospitals] have very limited channels to ask for help. They have to rely on local government, the Red Cross, or friends of their members to get donated PPE. The lack of hands at the Red Cross in repackaging and distributing the donations may worsen the difficulties of these local hospitals. The Red Cross made serious mistakes, such as mismanaging the priorities of various hospitals in their allocation of the donations. Yet, in this critical moment, what we can do is not curse the Red Cross online or tell the public not to donate [to the Red Cross] as this may cut off the only available channel through which those local hospitals can get donated PPE. What we can do in this hardest time is to work as volunteers to fill the last mile for the distribution. We should say "Yes I Can! Let me do it?"**

We have enough time after the COVID-19 crisis to hold the Red Cross accountable. In addition, if you have the contact of other reliable channels or foundations that can accept donated PPE, please do connect them with PPE makers as well as those less profiled local hospitals that are suffering from PPE shortages. The less profiled local hospitals may take up around 80% of all the hospitals fighting COVID-19. They are also an important battlefield for saving lives. |

| 9 | Autumn Shadow | @prcht_HeFan I agree very much with what you wrote above. |

lives in the crisis, because those hospitals "may take up around 80% of all the hospitals fighting COVID-19." Moreover, their having worked with the Red Cross to promote the distribution of PPE cannot be equated to mean that activists and volunteers stopped being critical of the Red Cross and related government policy or gave up on holding the Red Cross accountable. This can be seen in the messages of Wang Jun and prcht_HeFan, respectively: "We may have to help distribute the medical supplies for them while scolding them for their low efficiency and misconduct"; "We have enough time after the COVID-19 crisis to hold the Red Cross accountable." Nor does helping the Red Cross mean that they accept the government policy of granting the Red Cross a monopoly over donated PPE. prcht_HeFan's message ("If you have the contact of other reliable channels or foundations that can accept donated PPE, please do connect them with PPE makers as well as those less profiled local hospitals that are suffering from PPE shortages") indicates that network activists continue working to build an alternative network for donated PPE that could circumvent the Red Cross while helping it distribute PPE.

On January 31, the Hubei Red Cross issued a letter of apology on its official website for "problems in its management and distribution of donated PPE." On February 1, the Wuhan government announced that the largest logistics company in Wuhan's medical industry, Jointown Pharmaceutical Group, had taken over management of the warehouse of the Hubei and Wuhan Red Cross. The inefficient manual documentation system of the Red Cross was replaced by Jointown's warehouse management software. On February 4, under the constant pressure of the media and activists, the Hubei government announced that three officers of the Hubei Red Cross had been removed from their positions and punished disciplinarily for the incompetence, inaction, and lack of transparency in the Red Cross during the COVID-19 outbreak. Yet neither the Wuhan government nor the MCA made substantial changes to the problematic policy that gave the Red Cross a monopoly over donated PPE. This indicates that the government indeed responded to the criticism from activists and media by removing those officers who were responsible for mismanagement of donated PPE, yet, it was not willing to fundamentally change this policy by accommodating activist demands to have a greater role in the management and distribution of PPEs and other donated resources in the crisis.

The Dynamic Nature of Relations between Activists and the Government in New Media Actions against COVID-19

Like the case of the Free Lunch Project, the NCP Life Support Network reveals the dynamic nature of the relationship between activists and the government in new media interventions. It illustrates how this relationship and the attitudes of activists and grassroots organizations toward government policies changed as government policy response to COVID-19 changed and became more effective in addressing pressing problems in the crisis.

In the early stage of the outbreak, the silencing of whistleblowers, delayed response, and government mismanagement of donated PPE that occurred during the government's response to the crisis largely disappointed network activists. The headlined message in the network's Weibo is an example of such disappointment. Yet what made network activists desperate about the Wuhan government's response to the crisis was the ineffectiveness of that response as they saw it in their projects and actions on the ground.

For example, the most frequent keywords in Hao Nan's account of his experience and that of the network in early February were "desperate" and "hopeless":

> On February 2, when three patients in the same family that I was working with [in the telehealth service] called to say that they decided to give up treatment, I completely collapsed! . . . Three members of the family [a father, mother, and son] all got infected. The father is a severe case. The mother is a critical case. . . . They told me they will never go to a hospital again [after having failed to get a bed for weeks]. If they die, they would rather die together at home. In fact, the mother died three days after that call. Before that call, they had done everything they could do to survive. They had gone to hospitals every day [hoping to get a bed]. . . . This feeling of hopelessness has overwhelmed all of the network teams, including healthcare workers [in the telehealth service], volunteers in the Little Angel Group, and others. What we talked about most in our teams is hopelessness. We questioned why these tragedies happened? What could we do? It seemed we could hardly do anything. (N. Hao, 2020)

Activist Kathy of the telehealth group also documented this feeling of hopelessness and the desperation she felt in the face of the government's response. In a reflection of her personal experience in the fight against COVID-19, she stated:

> As a member of the telehealth group, I deeply felt the bitterness, sorrow, and fears that those infected with COVID-19 felt in their struggle for survival in Wuhan. Hospitals are overwhelmed with desperate patients. Communities are in a panic. Those infected cannot get a [hospital] bed. . . . This is the normal state of lives there. . . . "True fighters dare face the sorrows of humanity and look unflinchingly at bloodshed." I have witnessed this kind of sorrow in my own life in the past 46 days. They reside in stories related to the following names and events: for example, the Wuhan government in January, the Wuhan Red Cross, the Wuhan Central Hospital.

The feeling of hopelessness and the desperation to the government's response among activists and network volunteers directly affected the network's projects and actions. However hard they worked, these activists and volunteers knew that they could not help those with severe COVID-19 symptoms get hospital beds—given the limited capacity in Wuhan hospitals. So the network started a hospice care project for those critical cases and their families. Hao Nan stated, "[Given the current response measures,] thousands of people with severe COVID-19 won't be able to get a hospital bed. This means we are watching many of them die. On February 4, I was completely desperate. . . . So I reached out to other organizations working on hospice care. We wanted to provide an online service that could at least give individuals in critical condition and their families a little comfort as those individuals reached the end of life" (N. Hao, 2020).

According to medical experts and network activists alike, the most significant policy change in Wuhan's COVID-19 crisis was the construction of Fangcang hospitals and the arrival of tens of thousands of health-care workers from other parts of the country to aid the fight (Chen et al., 2020; "COVID-19 and China," 2020; Dickens et al., 2020; N. Hao, 2020; "Sustaining Containment of COVID-19 in China," 2020). Fangcang hospitals are "temporary hospitals built by converting public venues, such as stadiums and exhibition centers, into health-care facilities to isolate patients with mild to moderate symptoms of an infectious disease from their families and communities, while providing medical care, disease monitoring, food, shelter, and social activities" (Chen et. al., 2020). Since February 3 during the COVID-19 crisis, Wuhan built sixteen Fangcang hospitals with 13,467 beds in total (as of March 4). Another significant change in the government's response to the crisis was the dispatch of hundreds of teams of health-care workers from hospitals all over the country to hospitals in Wuhan and other cities in Hubei. These health-care worker teams joined the designated hospitals and Fangcang hospitals as functioning units, with team leaders, doctors, nurses, and medical equipment that significantly increased the health system's capacity to respond to COVID-19 in Hubei.

By March 1st, 344 teams of 42,322 health-care workers, including 11,416 doctors and 28,679 nurses from twenty-nine provinces, autonomous regions, and municipalities, had arrived in hospitals in Hubei (National Health Commission of PRC, 2020b). With the implementation of these new measures, the government's response to COVID-19 took a new track that focused on treating all COVID-19 related persons in hospitals, Fangcang hospitals, and isolation centers.[18] This included confirmed COVID-19 cases, presumptive positive cases of COVID-19, those having close contacts with COVID-19, those with fevers, and those with lung infections.

The implementation of these new measures changed perceptions of the government's response. Among activists of the NCP Life Support Network, attitudes toward the government's response became much more positive. For example, on February 13, the network published the following on its Weibo:

Yesterday, Cheng Yixin, the vice director of the Supervision Team from Beijing, stated in his inspection in Wuhan's COVID-19 Command Center:[19]

"We must clearly recognize the uncertainty of the crisis in Wuhan. We do not know the total number of people infected with COVID-19. The number of people that might be infected in the future is likely to be very large." Compared with what we were told before, this is a more trustworthy communication on the state of Wuhan's crisis for the public.

Activist accounts of their personal experiences in the crisis also revealed the change in their attitudes toward the government's response before and after the implementation of these new measures. For example, near the end of his long paragraph on the feeling of desperation and hopelessness of network activists in early February, Hao Nan stated: "On February 5, we heard about and saw the building of Fangcang hospitals. When I saw news of the construction of Fangcang hospitals, I literally cried. This measure should have been employed much earlier. Yet better late than never" (N. Hao, 2020). Two weeks later, based on firsthand personal experiences through projects/actions and information collected online, the network stated that "the new government policy and efforts have effectively solved the lack of hospital capacity to treat those infected with COVID-19" (NCP Life Support Network, 2020e).

Moreover, beginning on February 7, the network launched a series of projects and actions that complemented these new government measures, the most important of which were the Fangcang Hospital Project and the information project to support health-care workers coming from other parts of the country (see table 7.1). Around February 7, shortly after Fangcang hospitals first began operating, social media exposed the lack of adequate heating, showers, warm water, and other basic provisions in those hospitals. Rather than simply pointing out these problems online, the network collected information from patients and health-care workers in Fangchang hospitals to help Fangcang patients cope with these problems in order to support this new measure, which the network held to be important as an effective response to COVID-19. On February 7, this was posted on the network's Weibo: "Many patients and families told us that some Fangcang hospitals lack adequate basic provisions. Based on the information provided by frontline health-care workers, we created the guidelines and checklists of personal belongings needed for admission to Fangcang hospitals or makeshift quarantine camps. Patients and families can prepare needed personal belongings in advance to deal with a possible urgent situation." (See figure 7.7 for the specific guidelines and checklists.) Required personal belongings in the checklist included an original copy of test results, family contacts, a charged cell phone, and enough clothes for two weeks, as well as optional belongings such as food and water, books, and entertainment devices. To ease the fears and concerns in the public and among individuals with COVID-19, the network launched a new media campaign to build confidence in Fangcang hospitals by publishing grassroots video and posts by Fangcang patients. For example, on February 13, the Weibo of the network posted a video titled "3 A.M. in a Wuhan Fangcang

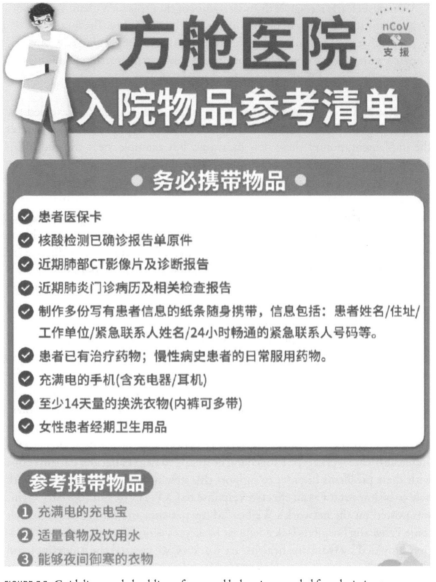

方舱医院 nCoV 支援

入院物品参考清单

● 务必携带物品 ●

- 患者医保卡
- 核酸检测已确诊报告单原件
- 近期肺部CT影像片及诊断报告
- 近期肺炎门诊病历及相关检查报告
- 制作多份写有患者信息的纸条随身携带，信息包括：患者姓名/住址/工作单位/紧急联系人姓名/24小时畅通的紧急联系人号码等。
- 患者已有治疗药物；慢性病史患者的日常服用药物。
- 充满电的手机(含充电器/耳机)
- 至少14天量的换洗衣物(内裤可多带)
- 女性患者经期卫生用品

参考携带物品

❶ 充满电的充电宝
❷ 适量食物及饮用水
❸ 能够夜间御寒的衣物

FIGURE 7.7 Guidelines and checklists of personal belongings needed for admission to a Fangcang hospital or a makeshift quarantine camp.

Hospital": "It's 3 A.M. at a Wuhan Fangcang hospital in Wuhan Keting, Dong-xihu District. The hospital is organized into small units of 50 beds. Every unit has four doctors and twelve nurses. These healthcare workers are night guard-ians of the Fangcang patients." On February 12, the network's Weibo posted a video titled "Dancing Time at a Wuhan Fangcang Hospital," in which a nurse in a protective suit and mask leads a group of masked patients in a dance for phys-ical exercise. The network stated: "Dancing time in a Wuhan Fangcang hospital: in this unprecedented crisis, ordinary people who did not know each other before are so closely connected in this space. Illness and recovery, hardship and happiness. This is an unusual time. This is the life of ordinary people."

These grassroots new media images from Fangcang patients, which were viewed hundreds of thousands of times, enabled the network to convey firsthand information to the public regarding the treatment and everyday life in Fangcang hospitals.

The attitudes of network activists toward the arrival of hundreds of health worker teams from other places was overly positive. On February 10, the National Health Commission of PRC (2020b) announced that nineteen provinces, autonomous regions, and municipalities would form partner assistance with the sixteen prefectures of Hubei Province in dispatching health-care worker teams to support the province's fight against COVID-19 outside Wuhan. The network's Weibo forwarded a CCTV depiction of this special partnership and cheerfully commented in red, "Quick! Come see which city your hometown has assisted." On February 27, the network's Weibo forwarded this message from Ruir, a nurse in a health-care worker team from Tianjing: "We have won our first battle. Health worker team from Tianjing has treated more than 200 patients, 110 of whom have recovered. . . . Today we handed over our work to a healthcare worker team from Guizhou and began our first recess. . . . Look, the Dawn is coming." The network then commented: "In the past two days, the first group of health-care teams coming to Wuhan have begun their first recess. We are deeply in debt to you! 'Are you not battle-dressed? Let's share a breast plate'; 'Let's make our armor shine! And march, your hand in mine!'"[20]

Besides posting messages to show support for health-care workers coming to Wuhan, the network launched projects to address the various difficulties of those health-care workers that the government structure did not address in time. On February 25, the network launched a portal with web links to projects and activities providing logistical support for those health-care workers. These projects and actions provided health-care workers with food, hotel rooms, in-city transportation, and other daily life needs. Network activists also conducted or coordinated hundreds of small actions to quickly respond to messages for help from health worker teams and individual health-care workers. These actions helped to solve problems directly related to health-care workers' fight against COVID-19, such as the shortage of PPE, the shortage of UV disinfection equipment, and the shortage of adult diapers. They also addressed the individual needs of health-care workers, such as food, transportation, clothes, and even computer and cell phone repairs. For example, on March 10, volunteer Ma Qin posted a message in the network's WeChat group: "Help: The laptop of a medical expert in Zhejiang Health Worker Team is broken. A local volunteer who has checked the laptop said it must be replaced: Lenovo ADLX45NCC3A. Could anyone in Wuhan who has that same model lend their computer to him? Thank you. Contact: 137 2013 2222 Dr. Qian." The message was immediately forwarded to several WeChat groups in the network, and the problem was solved within five minutes.

In the biggest public health crisis in China in the past four decades, the NCP Life Support Network supported numerous groups that are vulnerable to various health and/or social problems related to COVID-19, as I have shown in this chapter. It is one among the hundreds of grassroots organizations and NGOs that collectively played an important role in China's response to COVID-19. As of March 1, 2020, fifty-five grassroots organizations and NGOs in Hubei Province had participated in the response to COVID-19, according to the information collected by the NCP Life Support Network. Nationally, 387 grassroots organizations and NGOs took part in the response. Many more informal organizations, such as online communities and fan communities, were engaged in the response to COVID-19. These grassroots actions and projects targeted a wide range of issues related to COVID-19, from telehealth, support of patients, community support, PPE donations, women's rights, and animal rights, to communication and the dissemination of information. Like the NCP Life Support Network, some were networks of grassroots organizations focusing on various issues, such as the A2N Volunteers. Some were small organizations focusing on very specific issues in the crisis, such as the Stand by Her Action and the Gu Dian Team to Fight COVID-19. The Stand by Her Action was a grassroots organization initiated by Liang Yu Stacey in Weibo to support the physical health and well-being of frontline women health workers. It had fifty-one core volunteers (as of March 15). The action collected microdonations from the public to donate feminine care products, such as disposable underwear, pads, and period briefs, to frontline women health workers. It also collaboratively participated in advocating for women's rights in the fight against COVID-19. The Stand by Her Action donated and distributed 619,705 period briefs, 320,883 pairs of disposable underwear, and 144,216 pads to 83,600 women health workers in 199 hospitals (as of March 15) (Liang, 2020). The Gu Dian Team is a grassroots organization of sixty volunteers initiated by Gu Dian, a career coach in Beijing, to provide donated PPE to frontline health workers. Within twenty-five days (between January 24 and February 16), the team collected 11,230,000 yuan in donations. Using these donations, the team bought and shipped 213,480 N95 masks, 180,000 disposable medical masks, 70,160 protective suits, and other medical supplies from three continents. This PPE was delivered to 519 hospitals in twenty-eight provinces, autonomous regions, and municipalities in China.

Grassroots organizations and NGOs working on COVID-19 related issues emerged from every corner of Chinese society. Some of them were initiated by seasoned activists and volunteers such as the NCP Life Support Network. Others were initiated by first-time activists and volunteers, such as the Beds Group and the Gu Dian Team. Many of the participants of these grassroots organizations were not practitioners in the nonprofit sectors. They were small business owners like Wang Jun, Gu Dian, and Yige; college students like Kathy; health workers like those working in the telehealth project; IT professionals; and other ordinary Chinese. These grassroots organizations and NGOs demonstrated a strong capacity to promote ICT use, donation coordination, volunteer mobilization and organization, and project transparency and management. Compared with the inefficient and badly managed GONGOs, such as the Red Cross, they are much more efficient, competent, and adaptive in addressing various social and health problems related to COVID-19. They collectively formed an indispensable bottom-up force in China's fight against COVID-19. Their role and effects in China's response to COVID-19 have rarely been covered by the Western media. Their experience with issues connected to relationships with the government is very likely to be especially due to the particularity of China's sociopolitical context. Yet their experience on issues such as the role of grassroots organizations in transnational PPE donations will be helpful for grassroots organizations and NGOs in other parts of the world, as the shortage of PPE has become a major challenge for many other countries in their own responses to COVID-19 (e.g., Lintern, 2020; U.S. Department of Health and Human Services, 2020; WHO, 2020b). More broadly, the cases analyzed in this chapter call our attention to the role of grassroots organizations and actions in response to COVID-19 and other large-scale public health crises. Researchers, journalists, development workers, and policymakers need to give adequate attention to this bottom-up force in their coverage and investigation of COVID-19 responses in various parts of the world.

8

Conclusion

Drawing on the case studies in chapters 2 through 7, this chapter addresses the broader implications of these cases for Chinese internet studies as well as for communication for development research. It draws together all the cases that have been examined across the chapters and lays out what they tell us about the internet and development and social change in contemporary China under the rubrics of communication for development.

Development and Social Change

Communication for development, or development communication, is an interdisciplinary field with more than half a century of history (Kim, 2005; Servaes, 1999; Wilkins, 2015). Four works that use meta-research methods to assess the state of research in the field (Fair, 1989; Fair & Shah, 1997; Ogan et al., 2009; Shah, 2010) and various more general reviews of the field (e.g., Kim, 2005; Melkote & Steeves, 2015a; Servaes, 1999; Wilkins et al., 2014) provide a brief overview of the evolution of theoretical approaches in the field. They illustrate a shift away from adherence to a modernization paradigm to a participatory or multiplicity paradigm between the 1950s and 1990s. From the late 1950s to the 1960s, early scholars of the field (e.g., Lerner, 1958; Rogers, 1962; Rogers & Svenning 1969; Schramm, 1964) established modernization theory as the dominant paradigm in academic research and development practice. They generally defined development as the observable quantitative difference between rich and poor countries. Moreover, in the modernization paradigm, the most popular measures to determine the impact of communication initiatives were individual-level measures such as behavior change, knowledge gain, and frequency of media use (Shah, 2010). From the late 1980s to the 1990s, the rise of the participatory or multiplicity paradigm challenged the modernization paradigm and, since then, has completely transformed the field.[1] One significant feature of the theories in the participatory or multiplicity paradigm is the conceptual emphases on social change, meaning change of social structures, social relationships, or cultures in a given society, community, or context (Inagaki, 2007; Melkote & Steeves, 2015b; Servaes, 1999; Shah, 2010; Wilkins et al., 2014). Yet there has been a resurgence of the modernization paradigm in the new millennium (Ogan et al., 2009; Shah, 2010; Wei, 1998). The trend of research in communication for development was for modernization to have become the most used theoretical frame in the field from 1998 to 2007 (Ogan et al., 2009). Specifically, in the field of ICT4D, the modernization paradigm has almost become the dominant paradigm again: 44.7 percent of the research used modernization theories as their theoretical framework, whereas only 11.8 percent used participatory paradigm theories (Ogan et al., 2009). Ogan et al (2009) and Shah (2010) have argued that the resurgence of modernization theories is related to the new focus of the field on ICTs. Shah (2010) stated, "Technological innovations have rekindled confidence in the Lernerian version of communication and development. This renewed hope in Lerner's model is an old story: Each new technological innovation in the post-colonial world since 1958—television, satellites, microwave, computers . . . has been accompanied by determined hope that Lerner's modernization model will work" (p. 17).

Eschewing the dominant modernization approach in ICT4D, this book joins other scholarship in the participatory paradigm (e.g., Friedmann, 1992; Kleine, 2013; Lennie & Tacchi, 2013; Melkote & Steeves, 2001; Servaes, 1999; Servaes et al., 1996; Sparks, 2007) to promote incorporating discussions of social change into communication for development research. The case analyses in the early chapters illustrate that this approach offers effective investigations of broader forms of interventions and efforts to use communication and ICTs for socially beneficial goals. This does not mean that observable quantitative differences between the rich and the poor or between the privileged and the marginalized are not worth investigation in communication for development and ICT4D. Rather, they are generally important symptoms of deep-seated unequal social relationships that need to be changed, as presented in the case study of the Free Lunch Project. This new approach offers a broader and more complex way to conceptualize the problems that new media interventions aim to resolve, as presented in the case studies of the Free Lunch Project and the NCP Life Support Network. It may also extend the field of communication for development to address important issues in various societies, such as the empowerment of the grass-roots in the case of the NGO 2.0 Project and the lack of government accountability in the case study of Tiger Gate.

This book investigated five cases of new media interventions: the Connecting Every Village Project, the NGO 2.0 Project, Tiger Gate, the Free Lunch Project, and the NCP Life Support Network against COVID-19. The goals of the NGO 2.0 Project and Tiger Gate are both in line with social change initiatives of bringing about change in social structures or social relationships in a given society, community, or context. Specifically, the NGO 2.0 Project aimed to eliminate the inequality between grassroots NGOs and GONGOs vis-à-vis their respective relationships with the government, the mainstream media, foundations, and other institutions. It aimed to empower grassroots NGOs in China's nonprofit sector, in particular, and in Chinese society, in general, by challenging those relationships that privilege GONGOs. Through detailed analysis of the project's documents, such as its mission, vision, and value statements, as well as the director's statements, I show that the project has been committed to bringing about change in the inequality between grassroots NGOs and GONGOs over the past twelve years, especially in the realm of communications and information. At the same time, it gradually extended its efforts to target the overall inequality between grassroots NGOs and GONGOs through its programs (see chapter 3). For example, the first item in the mission statement ("Promoting information equality among NGOs") and the first and third items in its value statement ("Information equality" and "Empowerment of the grassroots") clearly reveal this commitment. The project's new focus on "the ecosphere of the nonprofit sector" shows how the project began to target various dimensions of the overall inequality between grassroots NGOs and GONGOs. For example, the second item in the project's 2018 mission statement ("Facilitating the equality and balance of the ecosphere of the nonprofit sector") illustrates this expansion of concerns. Jing Wang's 2019 interview further reveals this expansion. In her interview, she argued, "If we just pursue scaling-up [big] NGOs and their services, then medium and small NGOs will be unable to survive. I think that kind of nonprofit sector ecosphere is unbalanced. . . . The core value of the nonprofit sector is social justice and equality. We therefore should help and empower the most disadvantaged [NGOs]. . . . If we think of the nonprofit sector as a sea, it should have big fish, medium sized fish, as well as small fish" (Wang, 2019a).

In theories and practices with a conceptual emphasis on social change (e.g., Hamel, 2010; Jacobson, 2003; Melkote & Steeves, 2015a; U.N., 2012; United Nations Educational, Scientific and Cultural Organization, 2019), empowerment is an important approach for bringing about effective change. The case study of the NGO 2.0 Project reveals that from the launch of the project in 2009 to the present, the empowerment of the grassroots NGOs has consistently been a core value of the project. Empowerment first focused on communications and was then extended to other fields, such as resource distribution.

Tiger Gate is a nationwide grassroots new media action that aimed to increase government accountability in Chinese society, as discussed in chapter 4. Government accountability is an important dimension of the social relationships between activists/the public and the government/officials, according to its definition in the West and its understanding in China. Therefore, the action's goal is to change the social relationship between activists/the public and the government/officials in Chinese society. Tiger Gate contributed to the change in "slow-moving institutions" (Roland, 2004), such as culture, values, beliefs, and social norms, which shape notions of government accountability, although it has failed to change "fast-moving institutions," such as legal and political institutions in Chinese society.

The analysis of Tiger Gate shows that the activist community, including leading activists such as Fu Dezhi and Smallfish, and the most anonymous ordinary activists, all considered Tiger Gate to be about different aspects of government accountability, such as the punishment of officials for wrongdoing and the responsibility of officials for their behaviors, the answerability of the government to the public, and the transparency of government policymaking. These activists were mobilized to engage in online and offline actions due to their concern over various problems in Chinese society related to lack of government accountability. Smallfish (2008), for example, explained: "Why could so many people continue to engage in the action for eight months? The reason is very simple. The Tiger Gate incident involved all kinds of corruption in our government including illegal behavior, such as bribery, as well as malfeasance, such as disrespecting citizens' opinions. . . . The ultimate goal for citizens engaging in the anti-tiger action is to reduce these corrupt behaviors and . . . give honesty more space and a better environment to thrive." This indicates that they did advocate for increased government accountability in the whole society. Yet the immediate goal of most Tiger Gate activists was the punishment of local officials for their wrongdoing in this specific scandal, rather than institutional change or policy change in government accountability in the central government or in society as a whole, as chapter 4 shows. This is one of the reasons that this eight-month nationwide online action only brought about limited accountability at the local level.

Legal activists in Tiger Gate, notably Hao Jinsong, gave more attention to policy change or institutional reform of government accountability, as well as changes in people's values, experience, and beliefs that shape notions of government accountability in society as a whole. Hao's legal cases against the National Forestry Administration for inaction in Tiger Gate and his applications to the National Forestry Administration for publication of the information regarding Tiger Gate, according to the Regulations on Open Government Information, illustrate efforts of activists to increase government accountability using existing channels in China's current state institutions. Neither mainstream anti-tiger actions nor legal actions successfully brought about policy change or changes in political or legal institutions, as revealed in the case study. Yet for almost a year, these actions—involving hundreds of thousands of activists in different parts of the country, and the extensive media coverage these actions received—made issues related to government accountability headline news in mainstream media and the most read topic on internet portals, which were visited by millions of people. These actions have promoted awareness of government accountability and may contribute to change in the values, experience, beliefs, and cultures regarding government accountability among activists, in particular, and in Chinese society, in general.

The goals of the Connecting Every Village Project and the Free Lunch Project correspond with those of conventional development initiatives: reducing observable quantitative differences between rich and poor regions. The Connecting Every Village Project aimed to reduce the digital divide between urban and rural China. Informed by modernization theories, the Chinese government conceptualized the digital divide, as seen through the implementation of the ICT4D project, as the observable quantitative difference between rural and urban internet coverage. This grossly oversimplified the problem that the project aimed to solve. As it was, the Connecting Every Village Project was plagued with a lack of participation in rural communities and lack of consideration of skills access and motivational access, which indicate sustainability risks. To address these weaknesses, social change, such as fostering the participation of rural communities and NGOs in ICT policymaking and ICT policy implementation, must be considered (as I show in chapter 2).

In the case of the Free Lunch Project, the central government's National Nutrition Subsidies Policy defined the problem it targeted as an observable quantitative difference in nutritional intake among urban and rural children. As I show in chapter 5, at the early stage of the Free Lunch Project, activists conceptualized the problem much like the government did. Yet in later stages of the project, activists came to look at the problem in a new way: they envisioned the unjust social relationship between rural and urban people in contemporary China as an objective of the project. It was a problem of social justice, not just one of food and differences in quantitative nutritional intake. For example, Deng Fei stated that the real reason for hunger among rural children is "the longstanding policy employed by the Chinese state to sacrifice the rural population for development in big cities. State policies have systemically extracted resources, capital, and human capital from rural regions. The result of these unjust policies is that the 61 million children who were left behind [in rural China] have had to pay the price" (2014).

To effectively overcome the unjust social relationship between rural and urban sectors, activists believed that the Free Lunch Project had to address inequalities between rural and urban China in nutrition, health, education, economy, safety, and so on. They did this quickly by using their experiences from the Free Lunch Project, such as fostering multi-stakeholder collaborations, to start new projects that would promote change in other areas (see table 8.1 for details). Deng Fei stated that through all these efforts, the Free Lunch Project aimed to change Chinese society to provide safety, health, justice, and dignity to rural people, especially the sixty-one million children left behind (Deng, 2014). He wrote,

Table 8.1
Projects That Activists of the Free Lunch Project Initiated or Co-initiated

Project name	Focus of the project
E-Agriculture Project	Economic development in rural communities
Green Snail Project	Capacity development training for small rural NGOs
Protecting Girls Project	Training workshops on gender and sexual harassment for rural schoolgirls
Critical Illness Insurance for Rural Kids	Health of rural children
Warm Project	Education of rural children

"China is like a car running at full speed. Rural China is its chassis. If the chassis is not stable, the car will soon derail" (2014). Unlike conventional activism and state-led social change, the Free Lunch Project was seen as an experimental way of generating structural change in China, which could address the unequal and unjust relationship between rural and urban China before it derails China.

The last case is that of the NCP Life Support Network's response to the coronavirus pandemic, the largest public health crisis of the past four decades. Its goals were in line with conventional development initiatives focusing on crisis relief. Yet due to its broad approach to the pandemic, the network later incorporated social change initiatives into its projects and actions in response to wide-ranging social and/or health problems related to the crisis. Crises in conventional development encompass natural disasters such as earthquakes or health crises such as HIV/AIDS and other communicable diseases (Servaes & Lie, 2015; U.N., 2000; U.N., 2015). During the coronavirus crisis, the main goal of the government's response was to reduce the death rate and the daily new cases of COVID-19, the key quantitative indicators. The initiatives of the NCP Life Support Network have had much the same goals. This can be seen in the network's broad mission of saving lives, which is contained in the network's name and in its volunteer recruitment announcement (see chapter 7). Initially, it conceived its actions much like disaster relief projects focusing on health crises in the conventional field of development. This was clear in the first incarnation of the network, which was being called nCoV Relief. It can also be seen in the problems targeted by the network's major projects soon after it was launched (e.g., the telehealth project, the communication project, and the project to donate PPE and medical equipment to hospitals) (see table 7.1 in chapter 7). Yet by the later stages of the crisis, the responses of the government and the NCP Life Support Network represented two different definitions of health problems in communication for development, identified by Servaes and Malikhao (2010). The government's response corresponds with a narrow definition of a health problem that focuses almost exclusively on one specific disease—COVID-19 in this case. This is an old yet dominant approach that has been used extensively in conventional development projects in response to health crises such as HIV/AIDS and malaria (Lie, 2008; Servaes & Malikhao, 2010). The NCP Life Support Network's response corresponds with a broad definition of a health problem using a cross-cutting and transdisciplinary approach to addressing a wide range of social and/or health problems resulting from, or associated with, the disease (Lie, 2008; Servaes & Malikhao, 2010). A broad definition of a health problem generally engages in a rights-based approach that may incorporate gender relations and other socioeconomic aspects of health problems to effectively respond to such problems (Servaes & Malikhao, 2010). This broad definition of health problems is very much in line with new theories emphasizing social change in communication for development. The case analysis in chapter 7 shows that the NCP Life Support Network's broad definition of the COVID-19 crisis called for a more comprehensive and socially just response than the narrow definition employed by the government. This indicates that for health problems that affect all sectors of society, using a broad definition of a problem is more efficacious than using a narrow definition, which is consistent with Lie's (2008) research on rural HIV/AIDS intervention. The government's overwhelming focus on responding specifically to COVID-19 as a disease overlooked the needs and the well-being of many social groups who had not been infected with the virus. Rather than providing support to those social groups, the government's response to COVID-19 actually endangered the health and well-being of those groups, such as pregnant women in Wuhan.

During the lockdown, the Wuhan government appointed forty-eight hospitals, including all the top hospitals in the city, to be exclusively COVID-19 designated hospitals. These hospitals shifted all their resources to treat COVID-19 patients or patients with fever and suspended their obstetrical services. For many pregnant women, this sudden change in health-care structure during the lockdown virtually eliminated access to obstetrical services that were critically important for their health and that of their babies. Implementing a strict lockdown to slow the spread of COVID-19, the government suspended all transportation services. Families were prohibited from driving pregnant women to hospitals for tests or for labor and delivery. Instead, they had to contact hospitals or local governments to have an ambulance or a vehicle with a special permit take the pregnant women to the hospital. Yet the chances of getting such a vehicle on time were very limited because all the resources in the health-care system and the government were dedicated to the COVID-19 response. Moreover, during the lockdown, people and vehicles such as ambulances were not allowed to enter or leave communities without the permission of community workers managing those communities. This means that even if a family secured a vehicle to bring a pregnant woman to the hospital, they had to get permission from the local community workers to coordinate this whole process. This compromised the health and well-being of pregnant women and their babies. These problems

Table 8.2
The NCP Life Support Network's Projects That Addressed Social Inequality

Initiation of action	Project/Action	Problem targeted	Related inequality	Beneficiary community
2/21/2020	Anti–sexual harassment during the COVID-19 Crisis	Sexual harassment during the COVID-19 crisis, domestic violence in the lockdown	Gender inequality	Women such as female COVID-19 patients and female volunteers in Fangcang hospitals or quarantine camps; victims of domestic violence during the lockdown
2/26/2020	Project to support those stuck in Wuhan due to the lockdown	Lack of support for homeless people and those stuck in Wuhan without a source of income during the crisis	Economic inequality	Homeless people and those stuck in Wuhan without a source of income during the crisis
2/27/2020	Project to support elders living alone in Wuhan	Lack of daily support for elders living alone during the crisis	Digital inequality	Elders living alone in Wuhan

were related to COVID-19, but more precisely they resulted from the government's response to COVID-19, which was guided by a narrow definition of the crisis that focused exclusively on the specific disease. Pregnant women were not directly associated with COVID-19, unlike those infected with it. The government response to COVID-19 focused only on the health of those groups that were directly associated with COVID-19, such as those infected or presumptively infected with the virus, those who had close contact with COVID-19, and health workers fighting against COVID-19. Therefore, problems that might have threatened the health and well-being of pregnant women were overlooked in the government's response to the crisis. In contrast, the NCP Life Support Network's broad definition of the crisis enabled it to quickly identify the problems that pregnant women encountered during the lockdown and provide effective solutions, as presented in chapter 7.

The NCP Life Support Network's broad definition of the crisis enabled it to effectively tackle social problems that were completely overlooked by the government's response, which was based on a narrow definition of the crisis. Many of these problems are rooted in deep-seated social inequality, such as gender inequality, economic inequality, and digital inequality (see table 8.2). As with pregnant women, rather than providing help, the government's response to COVID-19 often worsened the disadvantaged position of groups suffering from social inequality. For example, elders living alone without digital skills or access to the internet were disadvantaged before the lockdown. In order to contain the spread of COVID-19 during the lockdown, the government closed off all brick-and-mortar stores to individual consumers and required that all groceries be ordered and purchased online. This policy worsened the situation for elders living alone, making it extremely difficult to get any groceries during the lockdown. Yet because this problem was not directly related to COVID-19, the government—based on its narrow definition of the crisis—was unable to respond to such problems with an effective remedy.

The Role of State Policy in Promoting Development and Social Change

Due to the priority given to broader political concerns in China, previous research on China's internet in connection with state policies has overwhelmingly focused on information control. State policies have been portrayed mainly as part of an apparatus to control and contain resistance and obstruct change. Thus, state policies that promote development and social change have rarely been examined. In contrast, my work (using a communication for development approach) advocates incorporating state policies for development and social change, as well as various other policies, in the analysis of how new media have been used to foster development and social change in China.

During the heyday of the modernization and dependency paradigms in communication for development, the state and state policies were an important focus of scholarly investigations, and the state was considered one of the most important stakeholders in development practice (Servaes, 1999). The more recent participatory paradigm challenged the dominant focus on the state and state policies (Huesca, 2001; Servaes, 1999; Wilkins & Mody, 2001). As a result, the field has become much more diverse, incorporating new topics such as empowerment, community participation, social movements, and direct action (Dagron & Tufte, 2006; Huesca, 2001, 2003; Wilkins, 2000; Wilkins & Mody, 2001). Besides formal development institutions, new stakeholders such as activists, grassroots organizations, and large and small NGOs have widely been considered actors that may engage in the "intentional use of communication technologies and processes to advance socially beneficial goals" (Wilkins & Mody, 2001). But this does not mean that the significant role of the state and state policies in promoting development and social change has diminished, or that scholarly research in the field has shifted away from the state and state policies. In communication for development, the state continues to be a key stakeholder in initiatives for development and social change (Kleine, 2013; Melkote & Steeves, 2015a; Servaes, 1999; Servaes et al., 2012). Melkote and Steeves (2015a), for example, assert that at the national level, the state and the civil society are the main agencies that "should share the primary responsibility of protecting and strengthening the welfare of their citizens." In conventional development studies, Pieterse (2010), for example, stressed the central and enduring significance of the state in economic and social development, especially in East Asian countries. Informed by all this research, my work analyzes state policies, NGO projects, and activist actions as three types of new media interventions that have intersected and interacted with each other. This provides a more complex, context-based, and comprehensive view of the role of state policy in development and social change in contemporary China.

The findings in the case analyses in the previous chapters illustrate first that in the current social and political context, state policies for development and social change had an important impact on deep-seated development problems and concerns in many communities in China. Although these policies have not been without problems and weaknesses, they have touched the lives of millions of people in China. This is not to deny the authoritarian nature of the Chinese state but to indicate that there is a component of development and social change in the state policies of the authoritarian government in China. As I have shown, the Connecting Every Village Project significantly improved internet infrastructure and extended telecommunication networks in vast rural regions of China, giving millions of rural people the opportunity to access the internet and phone services. I also exposed the weaknesses of the ICT4D policy, stemming from misguided modernization theories on which it rests. Using van Dijk's (2005) theory of the digital divide and previous findings on the sustainability of development projects in communication for development, I identified the sustainability risks of this state policy. The case study of the Free Lunch Project illustrates the lack of activist participation in policymaking and lack of government accountability and other problems of the Chinese government's National Nutrition Subsidies Policy. Yet it also shows that this state policy has helped alleviate hunger and malnutrition for twenty-six million rural schoolchildren.

The case study of the NCP Life Support Network exposes the inefficiency, lack of transparency, and other deficiencies in Chinese government's response to the COVID-19 crisis. Yet it also illustrates that the government's aggressive response to the crisis, especially in its later stages, brought about a drastic reduction of new cases in Wuhan—a city of eleven million people—from more than five thousand to nearly zero within three months (as of March 31, 2020).

Second, by accounting for state policies, NGO projects, and activist actions as three types of new media interventions that intersect and interact with each other, this analysis provides a unique view into the interactions between state policies for development and social change and new media interventions initiated by activists and NGOs. This aspect of using new media for development and social change has not been addressed in past research. The example of this in China not only enriches our knowledge of China's internet but may contribute to future research on communication for development in other countries. The case studies presented earlier show that state policies were indispensable in promoting new media and ICTs for development and social change in China.

Applying the INEXSK model of the UN and the digital divide model (van Dijk, 2005), I show how the NGO 2.0 Project and the Connecting Every Village Project cultivated different resources to promote the use of the internet among NGOs. The Connecting Every Village Project expanded the infrastructure for the NGO 2.0 Project that followed it, while the NGO 2.0 Project helped develop skills for NGOs that promoted the utilization of infrastructure in their use of the internet. The two projects became complementary, revealing different factors for NGO participation in various sectors of society through their use of the internet. For example, the data from the NGO ICT and communication capacity surveys conducted by the NGO 2.0 Project in 2012 and 2018 showed a considerable reduction in infrastructure-related impediments, skill-related impediments, and motivation-related impediments to internet use among NGOs (see chapter 3). The Connecting Every Village Project and related policies, which have significantly improved the internet infrastructure from 2012 to 2018, likely contributed to the reduction of infrastructure-related impediments such as "instability of the internet" (from 14% to 0.16%). The NGO 2.0 Project contributed to a significant reduction of skill-related impediments and motivation-related impediments. The project's efforts to improve the internet and communication capacity for Chinese NGOs, the strengthened infrastructure produced by state policies, and the growing popularity of the internet and social media in Chinese society coalesced to contribute to this change in internet use among Chinese NGOs.

In my analysis of the Free Lunch Project, I showed how the National Nutrition Subsidies Policy and the Free Lunch Project cooperated and joined with each other through their respective actions to resolve the same social problem: child hunger and malnutrition in China's less developed regions. The National Nutrition Subsidies Policy's capacity to take on hunger and malnutrition on a large scale significantly benefited the Free Lunch Project. In implementing and monitoring its free lunch programs in rural schools, the Free Lunch Project also benefited significantly from the rural telecommunication and internet networks that were built and extended under the Connecting Every Village Project.

Moreover, my findings help illustrate the complex and context-specific web of influence extending between state policies and actions and projects initiated by activists and NGOs. In the case of the NGO 2.0 Project, while grassroots NGOs may in fact have benefited from state policies pertaining to rural internet infrastructure, they were marginalized by state policies pertaining to NGO registration and fundraising. In the case of Tiger Gate, the so-called anti-tiger activists—who challenged the authenticity of the tiger photos on websites—were silenced by state internet control. The COVID-19 crisis presented an even more severe example of silencing activists. The first whistleblower of the outbreak, Dr. Li Wenliang, was silenced by the Wuhan government. The Wuhan police accused him of "spreading untrue information" on the internet that "significantly threatened social stability" (M. Liu, 2020).

Third, the overwhelming focus on state control of internet content in China seen in most research has tended to obscure our understanding of how activists and NGOs influence state policies in China. The recognition of that influence may indeed enrich our knowledge of China's internet. In their research on development in China from the 1950s to the 1980s, Nolan and White (1984) concluded that "in key areas of strategic choice, policies which are defensible . . . to promote economic efficiency, social equity and political democracy have been stifled or weakened by a state apparatus unable or unwilling to countenance change." They call this problem "state bias" in China's development strategy. My case study findings show that activists and NGOs have demonstrated the potential to address this "state bias" by influencing state policies, although that influence is limited and indirect, and requires long-term effort and commitment and accommodation by the government. For example, after almost a year of constant online actions and on- and offline investigations exposing significant evidence and generating nationwide mainstream media coverage, the Shaanxi Forestry Department was forced to announce that the South China tiger photos were fake, and the initiative to set up a South China tiger reserve in Shaanxi Province was canceled.

In the case of the Free Lunch Project, we saw how activists and participants in the project promoted the National Nutrition Subsidies Policy and shaped its implementation. For example, much of the media coverage portrayed the National Nutrition Subsidies Policy as a public policy guided and promoted by the grassroots actions of the Free Lunch Project. Under the constant scrutiny of activists and the media for its lack of accountability and transparency, the National Student Nutrition Commission initiated the use of Weibo to increase the transparency of the National Nutrition Subsidies Project. The costs and the lunch menus at every school were published to enhance the public's ability to monitor the implementation of the National Nutrition Project. Moreover, following the pronouncement of the National Nutrition Subsidies Policy, the Free Lunch Project issued a warning in various media outlets that the three yuan per student per lunch subsidy was an insufficient level of funding for rural schools to build their own kitchens and dining rooms. This insufficient funding might have also impeded the effective implementation of the National Nutrition Subsidies Policy and resulted in problems. In 2012, activists and media outlets exposed serious problems, including severe food poisoning, stemming from the lack of kitchens in the rural schools being supported by the National Nutrition Project. Then in January 2013, the Ministry of Education and the Ministry of Finance issued a joint policy notice to allocate special funds to support the construction of kitchens and dining rooms in all the rural schools that would be covered by the National Nutrition Subsidies Project. In other words, the state yielded to and even provided for community needs rather than assuming a combative posture toward NGOs and activists, as might be anticipated by conventional scholarship.

Table 8.3
Number of Hospitals for non-Covid-19 Patients

Service provided by hospital	Hospitals for cardiovascular patients, surgical disease patients, and other critical patients	Hospitals for hemodialysis patients	Hospitals for children, including newborn babies	Hospitals for pregnant women	Hospitals for cancer patients
Number of hospitals	14	9	9	9	9

In the case of the COVID-19 crisis, Life Support Network activists believed that their advocacy effectively changed, or at least contributed to the policy change in the government's response to COVID-19 in Wuhan (see chapter 7). Hao Nan held that the network's advocacy through mainstream media and internal government channels changed government policy on non-COVID-19 patients with serious illnesses. In the early stages of the crisis, the government's response was largely dominated by a narrow definition of the problem that overwhelmingly focused on the specific disease of COVID-19. Therefore, it overlooked the needs of non-COVID-19 patients and other health problems that a health-care system ought to respond to in a timely manner. For example, due to government policy during the lockdown, the COVID-19 designated hospitals, including all the top general hospitals in the city and the top specialty hospitals, suspended services for non-COVID-19 patients. Beginning in early February of the crisis, difficulty getting timely treatment for non-COVID-19 patients became an urgent problem. In the WeChat group of the NCP Life Support Network, activists posted numerous messages calling for help from people with other serious illnesses, such as renal failure, cardiovascular disease, cancer, and surgical disease. For example, in the network's major WeChat group, volunteer Uyea posted the following on February 10: "Do we have any information on how those with other serious illness could go to the hospital, such as those with hemorrhagic stroke and those with heart attack? Now even the Asia General Hospital [a hospital primarily focused on cardiovascular diseases] has refused to admit heart attack patients."

To respond to this new urgent problem, in addition to providing a telehealth service and real-time information on bed availability to non-COVID-19 patients, the network reached out to mainstream media and the Xinhua News Agency's Internal Journals to advocate changing the policy regarding non-COVID-19 patients in the crisis. On February 17, the Health Commission of Hubei published a list of hospitals that admitted non-COVID-19 patients, pregnant women, and children in Hubei (Health Commission of Wuhan, 2020) (see table 8.3). These hospitals included second-tier hospitals; top-tier general hospitals that resumed services for non-COVID-19 patients in wards that were isolated from the COVID-19 wards; and specialty hospitals for cancer, kidney disease, and women and children. For the numbers of each of these different hospitals, see table 8.3. On February 21, the Wuhan COVID-19 Prevention and Control Command Center stated that it had "made timely treatment of non-COVID-19 patients an important goal of the government's response to COVID-19 in Wuhan in order to try our best to reduce the death rate [of non-COVID-19 patients with serious illness] in the crisis" (Liao & Feng, 2020). The command center announced three new policies regarding non-COVID-19 patients. First, it established a new committee in the command center that would focus on the treatment of non-COVID-19 patients in the crisis. Second, it extended the scope of non-COVID-19 hospital services to cover diseases such as ENT facial diseases and burns. Third, it assigned ten designated pharmacy branches that could order two-month prescriptions for serious and chronic illnesses to reduce patient visits to pharmacies just for refills. This exemplifies how the NCP Life Support Network influenced government policy on COVID-19 in Wuhan. Due to the advocacy of grassroots organizations, the government's definition of the crisis was transformed to one more in line with the broad definition of the NCP Life Support Network. During the lockdown, the network also influenced the government's policy on pregnant women and may have also contributed to the policy change regarding those with severe COVID-19 symptoms, as presented in chapter 7. This indicates the many ways in which this grassroots organization guided government policy in response to COVID-19.

There is an increasing consensus among scholars and development agencies that adequate participation of activists and NGOs in policymaking and implementation of state policy for development and social change can significantly increase the effectiveness of those interventions (Ogan et al., 2009; Servaes, 2009; U.N., 2015; U.N. Educational, Scientific and Cultural Organization, 2005; World Bank, 2006). The findings from the case analyses in earlier chapters show that this consensus is applicable to the China case. The NCP Life Support Network's impact on the government's response to COVID-19, the successful effect of activists on the National Nutrition Subsidies Policy in the Free Lunch Project, and the eventual cancellation of a South China tiger reserve in Tiger Gate are all examples of the significant influence that activists and NGOs gained in public policymaking, especially in areas that are not politically sensitive for the government. This influence has indeed increased the effectiveness of state policies for development and social change in China.

Yet the findings in earlier chapters also indicate that the level of participation among activists and NGOs in state policy for development and social change is far from adequate. The authoritarian nature of the Chinese state makes it almost impossible for activists and NGOs to participate directly in state policymaking. Only by using mass media and public opinion to pressure or guide the government's policymaking have they been able to influence state policy. In other words, their influence on, and participation in, public policy is limited, indirect, and often inefficient. In the Tiger Gate incident, for example, when "anti-tiger" activists found the original source of the South China tiger photos in November 2007 and posted overwhelmingly incriminating evidence to establish that the tiger photos had been faked, they were unable to directly impact the policy regarding the new wild tiger reserve or to hold local government officials accountable for their involvement in the scandal. Instead, local officials continued to engage in a fierce online debate with activists to mislead and misinform the public. Local government agencies used provincial media outlets to defend their own claims, refuting reports by national media outlets, which supported the activists' stance. In the higher reaches of government, the National Forestry Administration coldly rebuffed the growing questions of the public and activists and refused to take responsibility for authenticating the tiger photos. After they proved the tiger photos were fake, the activists waited eight months for the Shaanxi government to announce the results of a so-called official reevaluation of the tiger photos.

The various actions by legal activist Hao Jinsong in Tiger Gate illustrate the persistent efforts of activists to use existing channels in a current institution to directly influence state policies and to hold government agencies accountable. Hao's four legal cases against the National Forestry Administration and the Shaanxi Forestry Department for their inaction and misconduct in Tiger Gate were rejected by four courts in Beijing and Shanxi. Hao's three applications to the National Forestry Administration and the Shaanxi Forestry Department requesting government information on Tiger Gate failed to force the two government agencies to provide more transparency on the so-called official investigations of the tiger photos. All of this serves to demonstrate the inability of activists in this instance to influence public policy and to enforce government accountability using existing channels. The various channels that the government claimed to increase citizen participation in public policy and government accountability fell short in Tiger Gate.

Similarly, in the Free Lunch Project, we see that activists are unable to directly participate in or influence public policy. For example, although the activists, the NGO, and the state think tank that were involved all independently established the hot meal mode to be cheaper, more nutritious, and much less prone to food poisoning than the Milk+X mode, online activists were unable to sway the National Nutrition Project to directly abandon Milk+X snacks and meals. Moreover, compared with corporations, business associations, local governments, and other such institutional entities, activists and NGOs have continued to face significant obstacles in influencing state policies. For example, the National People's Congress, the political body that is tasked with holding China's government accountable, is closed to activists because its members are not really elected. In contrast, elite CEOs of the dairy industry can easily assume positions as deputies of the National People's Congress to give policy advice within the body to directly pressure the Ministry of Education to promote policies that benefit the dairy industry year after year. Business associations such as the Dairy Association of China lobbied different levels of government to use the Milk+X mode in the National Nutrition Project by aggressively promoting its School Milk of China Project. The new provincial policies in Hebei and Shandong issued in 2017 to inject School Milk products into the National Nutrition Project indicate that the various efforts of the dairy industry to influence the provincial policies on the National Nutrition Project appeared successful, whereas activists and NGOs had little or no influence on provincial policymaking with regard to the implementation of the National Nutrition Project. The case also indicates that the lack of government accountability and the lack of activist participation in policy implementation led to waste in public funding. When the central government allocated 20 billion yuan—a very sizable public expense—for rural schools to build kitchens and dining rooms to implement the hot meal mode, provincial governments continued to use various forms of the Milk+X mode. They even required students to drink boxed milk in school dining rooms and kitchens, making it look like hot meals were constantly being served to fend off the central government. Provincial governments ignored constant criticisms of the Milk+X mode and support for the hot meal mode among activists. The emphasis on constructing substantial kitchens, which were not always used to make hot lunches, represented a huge waste of resources.

The lack of transparency and lack of activist participation in government policymaking was much more costly in the case of the COVID-19 crisis. The silencing of whistleblowers, the censorship of online information regarding the outbreak, and the government's delayed and inefficient response in the early stages of the outbreak have been extensively documented and criticized by the domestic Chinese media, activists and social media users in China, and the global media alike (Bao et al., 2020; Buckley, 2020; *Coronavirus: Macron Questions China's Handling of Outbreak*, 2020; "He Warned of Coronavirus," 2020; M. Liu, 2020; Tan et al., 2020). These are important issues in China's general response to COVID-19, yet a detailed analysis of them is beyond the scope of this conclusion.

The silencing of Dr. Li Wenliang and other whistleblowers indicated the inability of activists to participate in or influence the government's policymaking very early in the crisis, while media paid relatively little attention to the voices of activists. The case of the Red Cross shows the difficulty activists faced in influencing policymaking even with significant support from the media during the peak of the crisis. On January 26, the Ministry of Civil Affairs (MCA) limited the PPE supply line to just five GONGOs. Legally, only the five could receive PPE and other medical supplies donated to hospitals, among which the Wuhan and Hubei Red Cross was the most dominant. The various problems with managing donated PPE by the Wuhan and Hubei Red Cross were generally exposed and criticized by media, activists, and social media users. Yet neither the MAC nor the Wuhan government did anything to change the problematic monopoly that the Red Cross and four other GONGOs had been granted for all public donations. This left control over the distribution of PPE and other medical donations in the hands of the Red Cross and the Wuhan government. In fact, the two continually pointed fingers at each other over who should be blamed for the misconduct in PPE distribution, as in the discrimination against the Wuhan Union Hospital. However, the problematic policy regarding donated PPE was not strictly enforced. The government did not constrain or impose sanctions on so-called illegal donations that bypassed the Red Cross. The alternative network of activists, donors, and health-care workers continued to provide donated PPE and other badly needed medical supplies directly to frontline health-care workers in hospitals. This indicates the inability of activists to change the government's donation distribution policy even despite wide support from mainstream media. In the response to the COVID-19 outbreak, the disparity of influence between GONGOs and grassroots nonprofits was never rectified. The government blindly trusted a handful of GONGOs regardless of their capacity to manage the donations. They constantly overlooked the potentials of thousands of grassroots organizations in effectively coordinating donated PPE. This is the fundamental reason for the mismanagement of donated PPE during the crisis; frontline hospitals faced extreme PPE shortages, while large quantities of donated PPE sat in a Red Cross warehouse. This example also illustrates the inability of the government to impose policies that excluded grassroots organizations from such philanthropic endeavors due to the broad support they enjoyed from the public and the thousands of ordinary people who donated PPE to frontline health-care workers in the crisis. Also, grassroots organizations in China came to occupy substantially more space during the COVID-19 outbreak, space was not ceded to them by the government. Grassroots organizations like the NCP Life Support Network successfully claimed it for themselves through the efficiency of their actions and projects and through the support of thousands of devoted volunteers and hundreds of thousands of ordinary donors.

Overall, my findings clearly support the almost universal consensus that the lack of activist participation in state policymaking can significantly reduce the effectiveness of state policies for development and social change. Due to institutional obstacles, a significant weakness of state policies for development and social change in China is the lack of participation of activists and NGOs. More broadly, the ineffectiveness of China's state policies for development shown in the case studies should serve as a warning to policymakers around the world of the need to promote NGO and activist participation in state policies for development and social change. It also reinforces the need to make room for grassroots organizations, NGOs, and activists to participate in policymaking and implementation in practice and research in communication for development. At the same time, my findings on China's national policy for development caution against the standard argument in scholarly research and mainstream media that because the Chinese government system tends to silence different voices in society, its policies always lack adaptive capacity, irrespective of context. My case studies indicate the need to use a context-based approach. The lack of adaptive capacity in government policy is highlighted in Tiger Gate, the Red Cross monopoly on donated PPE, and the case of Dr. Li Wenliang. Yet the change in specific measures regarding pregnant women and non-COVID-19 patients in the COVID-19 crisis and the changes in the National Nutrition Policy regarding school kitchens indicate quick change by government agencies in response to the advocacy of activists and NGOs targeting specific policies. The announcement of the National Nutrition Policy and changes to broad policy responding to the COVID-19 crisis indicate that the government may indeed respond to the advocacy of activists and NGOs targeting national policies that are not politically sensitive. Yet due to the lack of transparency in China's policymaking, there is no way to verify this.

Stakeholder Relationships in Development and Social Change Initiatives

In communication for development and related fields, works by academics (e.g., Brinkerhoff & Brinkerhoff, 2002; Colle, 2008; Hemer & Tufte, 2005; Lie, 2008; Melkote & Steeves, 2015a; Servaes, 1999; Servaes, et al., 2012) and development practitioners (e.g., Food and Agriculture Organization, 2006; U.N. Development Programme, 2017) have both shown that analyzing how stakeholders engage in development initiatives and how those stakeholders are interrelated is crucial to understanding any given initiative.

Relations between Activists/NGOs and the Government

Previous research about China's internet that has looked at the relationship between the government and activists/NGOs has focused almost exclusively on political contentiousness or confrontation—as if it were a game of cat and mouse between the government and activists.[2] It ignores the many dimensions of this relationship other than contestation. By incorporating concerns related to development and social change, these case studies reveal this relationship to be much more context based, complex, multidimensional, and dynamic than how it was depicted in the dominant discourse on the Chinese internet.

Over the past ten years, activists and participants in the Free Lunch Project have successfully worked with different government agencies to address hunger and malnutrition problems cooperatively while challenging the government on Milk+X snacks and meals and the lack of government accountability in the National Nutrition Project. In the NGO 2.0 Project, NGOs benefited from the state policy to extend internet service to rural and less developed regions in China. Yet NGOs—especially grassroots NGOs—have also been marginalized by government rules on NGO registration and fundraising. NGO websites are also major targets of government policies on internet control. In response, NGOs have adopted new technologies, such as Web 2.0, to reduce the effectiveness of website registration regulations and other internet controls.

In the case of the NCP Life Support Network, network activists believed that the government was an important stakeholder that they and other grassroots organizations should engage to develop an effective response to COVID-19. In their projects and actions, network activists collaborated in the projects of the government when they shared the same goals (see Chapter 7). When they had problems with the government's response to COVID-19, they went beyond simply exposing the problem and criticizing the government. They took action "to fill the voids that government policies were unable to remediate judiciously," as it was put by Ms. Bed, the coordinator of the Beds Group (A2N COVID-19 Volunteer Group, 2020). Through advocacy, they made policy recommendations for improvement. In their advocacy campaign, they used both mainstream media and internal government channels to project their voices into the government's policymaking apparatus. To its credit, the government seems to have heard the voices of grassroots organizations and activists in the later stages of the crisis. In response to advocacy campaigns, it tackled, at least partially, the problems that those campaigns targeted and addressed the needs of the vulnerable groups in the crisis. For example, on January 31, the Wuhan Pregnant Women Group reached out to the media and the Hubei Women's Federation to expose the difficulties of pregnant women during the lockdown and to advocate for corresponding policy change (see chapter 7). On February 6, the Wuhan government published a comprehensive list of the forty-four hospitals providing obstetrical services, including labor and delivery services. While this policy change addressed a major concern of pregnant women in the lockdown, it still had many shortcomings, as was pointed out by Dolphin, the coordinator of the Wuhan Pregnant Women Group (L. Yu, 2020). For example, the government did not provide any information on the availability of various tests, such as a noninvasive paternity test and amniocentesis, at each hospital. It did not provide real-time information on the availability of beds for pregnant women at each hospital. Neither the government nor the hospitals published any information about the documents pregnant women should bring for admission to hospitals. On the one hand, network activists continually advocated for improvement. On the other hand, they indeed took actions to fill the gap in needs that government policies did not meet. For example, the Wuhan Pregnant Women Group collaborated with the Beds Group in creating real-time information regarding the availability of beds and other services in each hospital. They also created guidelines and a checklist for admitting pregnant women into each hospital. The Groups for Assistance and Accompanying [Patients] of the network offered one-on-one assistance to help pregnant women secure beds in hospitals. Although the government did not change its policy regarding the suspension of nonofficial forms of transportation, it gave volunteer driver teams special permits.

Pregnant women could therefore use a twenty-four-hour on-call service provided by those teams if they were unable to access a hospital or government vehicle in time.

The reciprocal relationship between the NCP Life Support Network and the government is only one of many dimensions in the relationship between activists and the government in the COVID-19 crisis. By contesting the government narrative in party organs touting the success of China's COVID-19 response, network activists created a collective memory and knowledge of the crisis, highlighting the importance of the failure and the bitter lesson of government's response to the crisis. The failed crackdown on whistleblowers and the delayed, inefficient response to the outbreak by the Wuhan government early in the crisis constitute indispensable components of the collective memory of the COVID-19 crisis created by network activists. This can be seen in the network's openly published commemoration of Dr. Li Wenliang's passing on its Weibo, network activists' heartbreaking comments about Dr. Li on the commemoration page, the headline on the network's Weibo, and personal reflections by activists about their personal experiences in the crisis. More importantly, network activists believed that this collective memory would extend beyond the activist community, to be part of the public memory of the crisis. This is why the network openly made these messages public on Weibo and WeChat and in media interviews. The network not only created this collective memory but also joined the voices from the mainstream and social media calling for an investigation into the crackdown on whistleblowers and other problems related to the government's response to the crisis. For example, on February 7, the network's Weibo re-posted an article by the activist the Intellectual who questioned what had happened in the first twenty days of the crisis. On March 12, the network's Weibo published an investigation by Caixin exposing the cover-up and mismanagement of the outbreak in the Wuhan Central Hospital. Upon identifying certain government policies as problematic, network activists not only aired their criticisms but took action against them in a grassroots response to the crisis. For example, network activists and other social media users severely criticized not only the misconduct of the Red Cross but also the government policy granting the Red Cross a monopoly on donated PPE in the crisis. While pointing out these problems online, the activists did not sit idle waiting for the government to change its policy. Rather, they built alternative networks for donated PPE. This supposedly "illegal" action was constantly important work for the NCP Life Support Network in the crisis. For example, the guidelines on PPE donations collaboratively created by the network provided detailed advice on how to circumvent the Red Cross. The network also used its WeChat groups extensively to coordinate so-called illegal donations, such as the donated PPE from Dubai and from Brazil.

Another example of the multidimensional and context-based relationship between activists and the government was the response from the activist community to the call for help from the Red Cross. Although network activists widely criticized and condemned the Red Cross, when the Red Cross actually reached out to the NCP Life Support Network for help with the distribution and transportation of PPEs, network activists chose to help rather than distance themselves from the Red Cross. Their choice was not based on trust in the government or the Red Cross; rather, it was based on their firsthand knowledge of the urgent need for PPE among frontline health-care workers in "less profiled local hospitals," which made up roughly 80 percent of all the hospitals fighting COVID-19. The inability of the Red Cross to distribute, repackage, and transport donated PPE in a timely manner served to endanger frontline health-care workers and COVID-19 patients in these local hospitals. Activists therefore stood up to help. By working with the Red Cross to help distribute PPE, however, activists did not relinquish their criticisms of the Red Cross or acquiesce to the government's policy of granting the Red Cross a monopoly on donated PPE. Network activists continued working to build an alternative network to supply donated PPE by circumventing the Red Cross, while simultaneously helping it distribute PPE.

Among the five cases examined in the book, Tiger Gate best exemplifies the contestation between activists and the government. By shutting down a major online forum for "anti-tiger" activists, the Shaanxi provincial government revealed its desperation with online actions. By resisting this crackdown, activists demonstrated their resilience. By demanding administrative reconsideration and by suing the National Forestry Administration, legal activists demonstrated their determination to confront the administration for its inaction in Tiger Gate. By rejecting the activists' application for administrative reconsideration, the administration revealed its unwillingness to be held accountable by activists and the public. By rejecting activists' legal cases against the National Forestry Administration, the courts sided with the National Forestry Administration, in the current climate of China's state institutions, and against activists' efforts to enforce government accountability. Yet even in the Tiger Gate case, relations between activists and the government were not purely contentious. For example, while the local government in Shaanxi tried to silence activists, party organs of the central government such as *People's Daily* published eleven official comments in support of the position of activists. Although legal activists' cases were rejected by the courts, they received positive coverage in party organs such as the *Procuratorate Daily*, CCTV, and Xinhua News Agency, as presented in chapter 4.

In line with previous research on the fragmented nature of the Chinese state, this book casts the Chinese government as a huge bureaucracy in which various government entities compete and interact with one another in policymaking and implementation processes. Accordingly, different government entities may have divergent policies on and attitudes toward development and social change initiatives. Activists' relations with those government entities may therefore vary significantly. The Free Lunch Project and activists who supported it entered into a reciprocal relationship with local government entities that wanted to supply hot meals to overcome the hunger and malnutrition problem for rural children. For example, to supply free hot lunches for rural students in Xinhua and Mashan Counties, the Free Lunch Project contributed two yuan per student per day while the local government provided one yuan per student per day. In Hefeng County, the Free Lunch Project not only collaborated with local government to provide free hot lunches for rural children but also introduced other projects, such as critical illness insurance for rural children in the county's less developed rural regions. However, when the Ministry of Education implemented the Milk+X mode through the National Nutrition Project, activists and the Free Lunch Project fiercely contested the ministry. For example, in response to an incident of a milk poisoning in Hunan Province, leading Free Lunch activist Deng Fei stated, "If the Ministry of Education does not stop providing [packaged] milk [in the National Nutrition Project] . . . I will call out the name of the Head of the Ministry of Education of China on Weibo every day [to remind the public who should be held accountable for this], until they shut down my Weibo account!" In the Tiger Gate case, activists fiercely contended with the local government in Shaanxi, but they got consistent support from party organs of the central government, such as *People's Daily* and CCTV. With the support of local media, the local government in Shaanxi, however, worked tirelessly to resist the pressures of activists, mainstream media, and, to some extent, the central government. In the NCP Life Support Network, network activists criticized and contested Wuhan government policies that overlooked the health needs of non-COVID-19 patients. Yet they approached and got the support of the central government's internal channels, such as the Xinhua News Agency's Department of Internal Journals regarding related policy change. It is likely that the central government supported this advocacy and, based on it, applied pressure that brought about the rapid change in policy in Wuhan.

These incidents show that relationships between activists and government entities are not always at odds but fluctuate over time, depending on the extent of mutual accommodation. Most activists and NGOs work with government entities that support their goals and selectively fight against those that oppose those goals, rather than oppose all those entities all the time and on every issue. Likewise, specific government entities may exercise some autonomy to be more accommodating in dealing with development and social change initiatives. Previous studies have overlooked this dynamic, focusing instead on activists opposing an authoritarian state or a rising working class set against the Communist Party.

My findings also illustrate the dynamic nature of relations between activists/ NGOs and the government in new media interventions. For example, before the announcement of the National Nutrition Subsidies Policy, the Free Lunch Project and activists tried to guide and promote state policy on hunger and malnutrition through "strategic philanthropy." Then, after the announcement of the National Nutrition Subsidies Policy, the Free Lunch Project collaborated with different government agencies that were willing to address the problem. Yet when the lack of accountability and the adoption of various Milk+X modes in the National Nutrition Project were exposed, activists and the Free Lunch Project became determined to challenge the government. They mobilized the public and media to pressure the government to change the policy regarding Milk+X snacks and meals, and they forced the government to adopt a policy that would improve the transparency of the National Nutrition Project and allocate funds to build kitchens in rural schools. When they met with significant pressure from the media, dairy corporations, and local governments to go along with the Milk+X modes, activists and Free Lunch Project organizers responded, "We will never make any concessions on it!"

Activists and NGOs are readily able to adapt their relationship with the government in actions for development and social change, which makes that relationship very dynamic. For example, after having fiercely contested the Department of Education of Hunan Province in the Milk+Bread incident in Fenghuang County, the Free Lunch Project became more accommodating when the department issued a notice of a new policy urging rural schools in the National Nutrition Project to abandon Milk+Bread meals and shift to hot lunches. The two parties then committed to launch pilot projects, collaborating to provide free hot lunches along the lines of the model developed by the Free Lunch Project in the province.

The case of the NCP Life Support Network is another example of the dynamic nature of the relationships between activists and the government in new media interventions. Chapter 7 shows that in the early stages of the crisis, from mid-January to early February, the silencing of whistleblowers and other problematic and ineffective measures made activists and grassroots organizations desperate about the government's response to the crisis in Wuhan. This feeling of desperation and hopelessness bitterly shattered their hope that their actions could save more lives in the crisis. This fueled the initiation of new projects by the network, such as the online hospice care service for those critical cases and their families in order to "at least give individuals in critical condition and their families a little comfort as those individuals reached the end of life" (N. Hao, 2020). In early February, facing tremendous pressure from the public, activists and grassroots organizations, the media, and health experts around the globe, the government was forced to make substantial changes to its response to this unprecedented public health crisis. The central government in Beijing removed the governor of Hubei Province, the mayor of Wuhan, and the directors of the Health Commission of Hubei. New measures, such as constructing Fangcang hospitals and dispatching teams of health-care workers from hospitals all over the country to hospitals in Wuhan and other cities in Hubei, were implemented by the new leadership in Hubei and Wuhan. Based on their firsthand experience in their projects/actions, the data they independently collected, and information collected online, network activists believed that the new measures largely increased the effectiveness of the government's response to the crisis. The messages posted in its official Weibo, the accounts of the activists' personal experience, and the network's situation report on COVID-19 all indicated that the attitudes of network activists toward the government's response turned much more positive after the implementation of the new measures, as presented in chapter 7. Moreover, in order to complement these new measures from the government, the network launched a series of projects/actions, such as the Fangcang hospital project and the information project to support health-care workers coming from other parts of the country. To help Fongcang patients cope with the temporary challenges they might encounter in Fangcang hospitals, such as the lack of adequate heating, the network created guidelines and checklists of personal belongings needed for admission to those hospitals. To build confidence in Fangcang hospitals among the public, the network collected and published Fangcang patients' grassroots videos on the treatment and everyday life in those hospitals. To support health-care workers from other places, the network launched a portal with web links to projects and activities providing various support for those health-care workers. In collaboration with other grassroots organizations and local volunteers, the network built a massive grassroots support network for health-care workers coming to Wuhan to aid the fight against COVID-19. This bottom-up support network effectively addressed various needs of those health workers, from institutional supply needs, such as PPE and UV disinfection equipment, to individual needs, such as food, transportation, clothes, and computer repairs.

As discussed earlier, in some cases the Chinese government did change its policies in response to activist and NGO advocacy or public and media pressure. And as government policy changed and became more effective, activists also changed their attitudes toward, and relationships with, the government. This attitudinal change was not unidirectionally positive, however. If changes in government policy were perceived to be less effective, activists for the most part used every option to contest what they perceived as negative change. For example, in the case of the Free Lunch Project, when the local government in Qinghai Province shifted its policy on the National Nutrition Project to a Milk+X mode, activists of the Free Lunch Project fiercely contested the new policy by negotiating directly with local officials and exposing it in the media. When all of this failed to deter the change, the Free Lunch Project required the five schools that were affected by the new policy to withdraw from the Free Lunch Project (see chapter 6).

The empirical data in the five cases concerning the relationships between activists/NGOs and the Chinese government in new media interventions revealed the following patterns: efforts to address conventional development issues such as hunger and malnutrition, poverty reduction, and disaster relief are more likely to engender cooperation, whereas those directed at social change issues such as government accountability and transparency in policymaking are more likely to engender confrontation. The goals of the Free Lunch Project and the NCP Life Support Network were largely in line with conventional development initiatives. In the Free Lunch Project and the NCP Life Support Network, cooperation is a prominent component in the relationships between activists/ NGOs and the government. The goals of the NGO 2.0 Project and Tiger Gate are in line with social change initiatives. For the NGO 2.0 Project, even though activists of the NGO made consistent efforts to nurture cooperation with the government over the past twelve years, the project had little success in generating direct cooperation with government entities such as the MCA to help eliminate inequality between grassroots NGOs and GONGOs in communication and resource distribution. Tiger Gate illustrates how confrontation became a major component in relations between activists and the government when activists sought to hold government entities accountable. In fact, we also see this pattern in the Free Lunch Project and the NCP Life Support Network. In the case of the Free Lunch Project—in both the Milk+Bread incident in Fenghuang County and the various incidents of food poisoning caused by the Milk+Bread mode in the National Nutrition Project—confrontation became a major component in the relationships between activists and the government when activists mobilized the public to hold government entities accountable for misconduct and wrongheaded policies. In the case of the NCP Life Support Network, when activists tried to hold the Wuhan Red Cross accountable for its mismanagement of donated PPE and lack of transparency in its distribution of donated PPE, relationships between activists and the Wuhan Red Cross—a GONGO headed by senior party officials—became largely confrontational. Other government entities, such as the Wuhan government and the MCA, responded coldly to activists advocating for changing the policy regarding donated PPE by upholding the failed policy of having the Red Cross maintain the monopoly over donated PPE and other medical supplies. It is important to stress here that activists' relationships with the government are multidimensional because of the fragmented nature of the Chinese government. Therefore, neither conflicts nor cooperation that activists have with certain government entities can define their relationships with other government entities.

The empirical data in the five case analyses also show how certain strategies and practices of activists/NGOs are more likely to engender cooperation with the government. First, a consensus among leading figures in the activist community and NGO leadership that the government is an important stakeholder with which they need to engage in their efforts to bring about positive change has been indispensable for cooperation between activists/NGOs and the government. Moreover, there is a need to formalize this consensus in the form of key policy documents of the NGO or the community. For example, in its strategy statement, the Free Lunch Project indicated that it sees the government as a potential stakeholder in eliminating hunger and malnutrition among children in less developed rural regions rather than an obstacle. The *Business Presentation* of the NGO 2.0 Project indicates its willingness to collaborate with the government in its efforts to change inequality in communication and resource distribution between grassroots NGOs and GONGOs. The *About Us* page of the NCP Life Support Network's online platform states that the network has aimed to supplement the government's work. This consensus on the role of the government in their efforts for development and social change and the related policy documents enabled NGOs/activists to foster collaborative projects with various government entities, as seen in the Free Lunch Project and the NCP Life Support Network's actions, and helped to develop a communication plan that clarified potential targets of NGO government-relations campaigns, as seen in the NGO 2.0 Project. Second, NGOs/activists have successfully fostered cooperation with various government entities through strategically taking full advantage of the fragmented nature of the Chinese government. NGOs/activists have been effective in efforts to bring about development and social change in the face of China's huge fragmented bureaucratic system by identifying entities that support their goals and strategically engaging with and even partnering with those entities.

An example of the effective use of such a strategy is the Free Lunch Project's partnership with the China Development Research Foundation (CDRF), the major state think tank advising the State Council on development issues such as hunger and malnutrition. As early as 2009, the CDRF conducted its pilot nutritional lunch project in rural schools in Guangxi and Qinghai, using the hot lunch mode that the Free Lunch Project employed later in its projects. Lu Mai, director of the CDRF, stated, "The mode we used was to buy food materials from local farmers. This could also increase the income of local farmers . . . and we emphasized that the schools needed to build their own kitchens and dining rooms" (Wang, 2012). In its early stages, the Free Lunch Project was inspired by the reports and research on children's hunger from the CDRF. For example, since 2012, the *About Us* page of the project's official website has used a 2011 CDRF report by Lu Mai to substantiate the severity of hunger among rural schoolchildren in China. The Free Lunch Project began directly collaborating with the CDRF in its actions regarding the Milk+Bread incident in Fenghuang County. Because the two parties have the same goal of eliminating hunger and malnutrition among rural children using the hot lunch mode, they later formed a strategic partnership that advocated for the hot lunch mode and against the Milk+X mode of the Ministry of Education's National Nutrition Project through media campaigns and lobbying activities (see chapter 6). This partnership largely increased cooperation between the Free Lunch Project and local governments, party organs like the CCTV, and other government entities. It also enabled those in the Free Lunch Project to project their voices more effectively into the policymaking apparatus, such as the Ministry of Education and the State Council.

Another example in the Free Lunch Project is the eleven-year collaboration between the Free Lunch Project and the local government in Hefeng County (see chapter 6). From 2011 to 2014, the Ministry of Education's policy made the Milk+X mode dominant in the National Nutrition Project in rural schools. Yet drawing on their firsthand project experience, those in the Free Lunch Project realized that they were able to persuade some county governments to use their mode to provide hot lunches collaboratively in the local implementation of the National Nutrition Project. For example, in December 2011, after months of communication and hard negotiation, the Free Lunch Project and the local government in Hefeng signed an agreement to collaboratively provide free hot lunches to students in rural Hefeng. This began eleven years of successful cooperation that benefited more than 110,000 students. Moreover, the Free Lunch Project viewed its successful collaboration with Hefeng as a model and worked to replicate it in other parts of the country.

We also see the effective use of this strategy in the actions and projects of the NCP Life Support Network. For example, in order to change a wrongheaded policy of the Wuhan government that threatened the health and lives of pregnant women during the COVID-19 lockdown, the NCP Life Support Network reached out to the Hubei Women's Federation—the government entity tasked with protecting women's rights. It held discussions over the difficulties pregnant women faced during the lockdown with the federation and collaboratively proposed policy recommendations to the Wuhan government.

The complex, dynamic, context-based, and multidimensional relationships between NGOs/activists and the government in new media interventions seen in the five case studies are not particular to contemporary China; rather, they are very much in line with universal patterns of government–nonprofit sector relations found in previous research (e.g., Brinkerhoff & Brinkerhoff, 2002; Najam, 2000; Young, 2000, 2006). Through a historical study of the United States, Young (2000) found that nonprofits have three types of relationships to government: supplementary, complementary, and adversarial. Moreover, these relationships must be understood as multilayered; overemphasizing one relationship over the others may create distortions in knowledge and public policy (2000). He then applied this model to three additional developed countries— Japan, Israel, and the United Kingdom—and found government-nonprofit relations to be multilayered in all these countries, as well as in the United States. In order to examine the increasing interactions between the nonprofit sectors and the government, "based on institutional interests and preferences for policy ends and means" of both governments and NGOs, Najam (2000) proposed a conceptual framework of NGO-government relations: the four-C's of NGO–government relations (see figure 8.1).

Najam (2000) asserts that a cooperative relationship is likely when government agencies and NGOs share similar goals and prefer similar strategies, and a confrontational relationship is likely when governmental agencies and NGOs

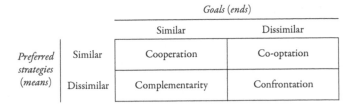

FIGURE 8.1 Najam's Four-C's of NGO-Government Relations

consider each other's goals and strategies to be antithetical to their own. Najam cautions that the government should not be viewed as monolithic within this framework. It is a huge bureaucracy with many agencies and various institutional interests and preferences. Thus, as I tried to show in the chapters herein, "On any given issue, different agencies and actors within the same government can nurture different types of relationships with a given NGO" (Najam, 2000, p. 391). Based on an empirical review of case studies on NGO projects around the world, he attempts to demonstrate the universal applicability of his framework in developing, as well as developed, countries.

My findings regarding the relationships between activists/NGOs and the government in new media interventions summarized in this chapter conform with Young's and Najam's two frameworks, which seem to be universal patterns. This indicates that even in authoritarian countries, the relationships between activists/NGOs and the government in new media interventions are very likely to be multilayered, multidimensional, and context based, incorporating a range of cooperative, complementary, and confrontational relationships. As Najam (2000) asserts, those relationships should be best explained through in-depth analyses of the specific goals of the NGOs/activists and the government agencies involved in the interventions, rather than "determined solely by isolated factors such as the nature of government (democratic or authoritarian), the state of development (advanced industrialized or agrarian), economic ideology (liberal market economy or controlled economy)" (p. 376). Najam's framework also helps explain how new media interventions into conventional development concerns such as hunger and disaster relief are more likely to engender cooperation, whereas actions targeting government accountability are more likely to engender confrontation. On issues such as hunger and malnutrition and disaster relief, government agencies and activists/NGOs in China are more likely to share similar goals in new media interventions. If they share similar means or strategies, their relationships will be cooperative, as seen in the relationship between the Free Lunch Project and the local government in Hefeng. Even if they do not share similar means or strategies, these relationships can be largely complementary, whereas in new media actions for government accountability, the activists/NGOs and the targeted government agencies consider the other's goals to be antithetical to their own. The activists aimed to hold the government agencies accountable for misconduct, and the governmental agencies persistently resisted being held accountable, as seen in Tiger Gate. Therefore, the relationships between the activists/NGOs and the targeted governmental agencies have been largely confrontational in those new media actions.

Relations between Activists/NGOs, the Government, and Corporations

When our analysis includes corporations and the private sector, the relationship between the three stakeholders in development and social change initiatives becomes even more complex and context based, as the case studies demonstrate. Under the modernization paradigm, a strong private sector was mainly understood to be a feature of "modern society" (Rogers, 1976). In development studies, due to the influence of neoliberalism, the rapid development of East Asian countries was largely attributed to the success of the private sector and deregulation, while other factors, such as the active role of the state and the unusual advantages offered by particular geographic and historical conditions, were largely overlooked (Pieterse, 2010). In contrast, supporters of the dependency paradigm believed that corporations, and especially Western transnational corporations, have contributed significantly to the dependency between developing and developed countries. The extractive properties of transnational corporations caused or exacerbated the underdevelopment of developing countries as well as various social and economic problems in poor communities in what was once called the Third World. Rather than a stakeholder that can contribute to the solutions to underdevelopment in developing countries, they were considered one of the causes of underdevelopment and the accompanying social problems.

In contrast to the modernization and dependency paradigms, research aligned with the participatory paradigm employed a context-based approach to look at the role of corporations in development and social change. They were considered important stakeholders in development and social change initiatives (e.g., Adu et al., 2014; Kleine, 2013; Servaes, 1999, 2007; Servaes et al., 2012; Tufte, 2005; Wilkins et al., 2014), whose role and impacts need to be examined in specific contexts. In Chinese internet studies, the role of corporations—especially private internet companies—in actions for political and social change were primarily analyzed within the framework of activists against an authoritarian state. They were thought to be contributing to the rise and diffusion of online contestation (G. Yang, 2009) or working with the government to censor online contention (MacKinnon, 2009). By employing a context-based approach aligned with the participatory paradigm, my work offers a more complex view of the role of corporations in development and social change initiatives in China.

In Tiger Gate, internet companies such as 163.com, Tianya.com, Baidu.com, xitek.com, and Tencent played an important role in fostering and sustaining the online actions that challenged official claims regarding the tiger photos and the policy of the new wild tiger reserve from the Shaanxi government. They provided activists with the spaces, channels, and tools to generate collective knowledge challenging the official claims, to coordinate their actions, and to mobilize the public, as demonstrated in chapter 4. Internet portals such as 163 .com and Tencent all created special topics on Tiger Gate on their websites. These special topics attracted huge numbers of visitors during the eight-month-long incident and played an important role in sustaining the public's attention on this incident. When local private internet companies such as Huashang.com censored online discussions on Tiger Gate and collaborated with the local government in Shaanxi to shut down activists' online forums on the South China tiger photos, private internet companies in other regions did not follow suit. Rather, Baidu .com and others offered new spaces for activists to regroup and to continue their online actions. This is consistent with Yang's (2009) findings from his research on online activism: private internet companies contributed to the rise and diffusion of contention. Yet in Tiger Gate, private internet companies, particularly 163 .com, went beyond their conventional role as platforms or channels of online actions, as they directly participated in the grassroots investigations of the tiger photos. And to some extent, they became part of the activist community.

On November 9, 2007, Ma Hongbin, director of the news department at 163 .com, arrived in Zhenping to negotiate with Zhou Zhenglong to buy all seventy-one of the South China tiger photos. Ma stated, "What we want to do is to expose the truth [of Tiger Gate] through making all the South China tiger photos available to public scrutiny. If the photos are authentic, we believe that Zhou Zhenglong should be rewarded. If not, this could help reveal the truth as early as possible" ("163.com Exposed How They Bought the Tiger Photos," 2007). After two weeks of negotiations and investigations at Zhenping, Ma failed to make a deal with Zhou Zhenglong due to Zhou's refusal to add the statement that he confirms that the tiger photos are authentic in a contract. Yet other members of Ma's team "surprisingly" bought the forty digital South China tiger photos from other people. Based on their communications with Zhou Zhenglong, Guanke, and other locals and officials involved in Tiger Gate as well as their investigations in Zhenping, Ma and his team concluded that Zhou Zhenglong was probably not the actual creator of the South China tiger photos. 163 .com published all forty South China tiger photos online, even though Zhou threatened to sue 163.com for violating his copyright of the tiger photos. Ma and his team reported the whole process of their negotiations and investigations in Zhenping and their judgment on Tiger Gate in their interviews with media.

The publication of all forty digital photos of the South China tiger online offered more ammunition for grassroots investigations of the photos. The reports on the investigation by 163.com in Zhenping and the revelation that Zhou is very likely not the real maker of the tiger photos further discredited the official claims regarding the tiger photos of the Shaanxi government. 163.com did not stop there. It went a step further to organize its own independent evaluations of the forty tiger photos, inviting six independent organizations and individuals to evaluate the photos: the Center for Digital Photo Evaluation of the China Photographers

Association, Beijing Huaxia Evidence Identification Center, wildlife expert Hu Huijian, American forensic scientist Henry Lee, vice director of the Forensic Science Association of China Liu Shiping, and professor of computer graphics at Sun Yat-sen University Lai Jianhuang. Using their respective forms of expertise, the organizations and experts involved in the evaluation independently concluded that the tiger photos were fake. This six-party independent evaluation from experts in various fields provided solid support to activists and enhanced the collective knowledge on the tiger photos that challenged the official claims. In sum, in Tiger Gate, corporations such as 163.com worked with activists and party organs such as *People's Daily* to pressure the Shaanxi government to reveal the fraud of the tiger photos. Local internet companies such as Huashang.net worked with the Shaanxi government and local media to defend local officials, silence activists, and misinform the public.

In the case study of the Free Lunch Project, corporations—especially those in the dairy industry—have been the major force opposing positive change. To sustain and increase the huge profits they receive from the National Nutrition Subsidies, the dairy industry mobilized against the hot meal mode, which has proved to be the most efficient mode to solve the hunger and malnutrition problem among twenty-six million rural children, as presented in chapter 6. The Ministry of Education—the agency of the central government that is in charge of the National Nutrition Project—has reiterated that the project must use the hot meal mode and the Milk+X mode must be replaced as soon as possible. Yet elite CEOs in the dairy industry have continuously used the National People's Congress to pressure and lobby the ministry to employ a policy that makes the Milk+X the primary, and even the only, mode in the National Nutrition Project. They demanded the ministry to ensure that boxed milk is required for each meal for every student covered by the National Nutrition Subsidies. The Dairy Association of China—the most powerful business association of the industry—paid mass media outlets to publish articles to misinform the public about the relationship between its School Milk of China Project and the National Nutrition Project and to advocate replacing hot lunches with Milk+X meals. They lobbied local governments to develop various forms of the Milk+X mode to infiltrate the "school kitchen" mode proposed by the central government and make the Milk+X a major part of the implementation of the National Nutrition Project at the local level. Due to the dairy lobby, local governments in provinces such as Hebei, Shangdong, and Qinghai took advantage of the loopholes in the central government's policy to force schools to replace hot meals with various forms of the Milk+X mode.

The case of the Free Lunch Project illustrates the complex relationship between activists, the central government, local governments, and corporations in interventions for development and social change. From the initial policy that gave the Milk+X mode almost 100 percent support, to the gradual shift away from the Milk+X mode, to the reiteration that the National

Nutrition Project must replace the Milk+X mode and use the hot meal mode, the central government—under constant pressure from activists, the media, and a state think tank—made positive change. However, dairy corporations, dairy business associations, and some local governments collaboratively obstructed this positive change and the effective implementation of the central government's policy. In pursuing social change and solving development problems, the most important ally of activists was the central government, whereas their biggest opponent was corporations.

Communication Channels and ICTs

Over the past half century, communication processes, communication technologies, and communication channels have risen to the forefront of research on communication for development. The meta-research of the state of the field shows that before 1986, mass media such as radio, TV, and newspapers were the dominant channels examined in communication for development (Fair, 1989). Between 1987 and 1996, new media were added to the mass media in scholarly investigations in the field (Fair & Shah, 1997). From 1997 to 2007, new media and ICTs became the dominant focus of the field (Ogan et al., 2009). James (2005) is critical of this new dominance of ICTs in the field. He stated that because of this dominant focus on ICTs in field research, considerations of traditional mass media have been abandoned. He argues that rather than abandoning mass media, ICT4D initiatives should incorporate both ICTs and mass media in their efforts to promote development in developing countries (2005). I join James and others (e.g., Costanza-Chock, 2014; Inagaki, 2007; Kleine, 2013; Servaes & Carpentier, 2006; Tacchi, 2007) to advocate using this multichannel perspective to examine and understand new media interventions in developing countries.

The Importance of ICTs in New Media Interventions

ICTs and the internet were vital tools in new media interventions that promoted development and social change, as shown by the findings on communication channels in the case studies. They played a vital role in collective knowledge construction by activists, mobilization of participants in new media interventions, empowerment of grassroots NGOs, social advocacy of activists and NGOs, and the enhancement of NGO project transparency and fundraising. The Tiger Gate case illustrates that ICTs such as forums/BBSs, blogs, and IM provided infrastructure and technological potentials for an activist network to emerge that cut across geographical barriers and disciplinary boundaries. The breadth, depth, and wealth of the collective knowledge of the activist community connected by ICTs extended beyond the mastery of any one expert. Furthermore, the ICT-facilitated creation of the collective knowledge of the tiger photos reveals a new form of knowledge construction in social change initiatives that aligns with the participatory model, in which knowledge of social change is considered to be constructed through the dialogue of all concerned, experts and ordinary people alike. Tiger Gate shows how ordinary internet users generated the most crucial part of the knowledge that questioned the authenticity of the tiger photos. They collectively discovered the original source of the South China tiger photos: the New Year's picture. In addition, the instantaneity of ICTs enabled activists to coordinate their knowledge construction in real time. For example, after anti-tiger activist Smallfish posted the New Year's picture and asked activists to help compare the New Year's picture and the South China tiger photos, more than five hundred people had responded to the post within three hours. Anti-tiger activists collectively developed various methods soundly proving that Zhou's photos were taken from the New Year's picture. The first response came out just two minutes after Smallfish's post, and the first method was posted in the forum just nine minutes after Smallfish's post. Without ICTs, such real-time coordinated knowledge creation would not have been possible.

The use of forums and IMs in Tiger Gate demonstrated the conventional use of ICTs in initiatives for social change, whereas the use of new technologies such as computer vision and 3D photography by grassroots activists in Tiger Gate elucidated the new power of ICTs in actions for social change. ICTs have surpassed their conventional role as pure communication tools and demonstrated their potential to be tools for grassroots investigations in the sense that activists no longer need to wait for the government to investigate such incidents for them. Rather, they can use new technologies to investigate incidents on their own, and use the collective knowledge and evidence created in grassroots investigations to lead public opinion and pressure the government to hold officials involved in such incidents accountable.

Analysis of the NGO 2.0 Project showed how Web 2.0 technologies have empowered Chinese grassroots NGOs and how the advocacy strategy of the project is quite different from the advocacy communication of communication for development in the West (Wallack, 1994; Wilkins, 2014; WHO, 1992). This strategy is based on the project's understanding of the marginalization of grassroots NGOs in the Chinese social media sphere, where users are constantly bombarded by content created by entertainment industries, corporations, celebrities, mainstream media, the government, and GONGOs. In the social media age, the empowerment of grassroots NGOs in communications is about ensuring not only that they can have a voice in cyberspace but also that their voices can be heard by the right audiences. In this highly commercialized social media context, the project held that grassroots NGOs needed to build communities that trust their organizations and have a desire to listen to their voices for effective advocacy and communications. Otherwise, the social media content created by grassroots NGOs would most likely be ignored by the target audience. The communication strategy of the NGO 2.0 Project's social media advocacy was therefore more like a dialogue. It emphasized listening to others, building communities, having interactions, generating mutual trust, and engaging in effective information and value dissemination (as revealed in chapter 3).

To implement this communication strategy, the project primarily used Weibo, WeChat group, and WeChat public account. Weibo was tasked with building a broad community of various stakeholders, interacting with those stakeholders, and disseminating information and values of the project. WeChat groups were used to foster NGO-to-NGO collaborations and to build and maintain a community of NGOs that participated in the project's training workshops. The project held that due to technical constraints, WeChat public account was not a good tool for community building and interactions. It "is more like a mini-media of the Web 1.0 age" (Xiao, 2016). Therefore, the project primarily used its WeChat public account to disseminate its information and values. The case of the NGO 2.0 Project also shows that the official website not only offered an official profile of the organization in cyberspace but also provided a platform to assemble the contents of the project compiled under various social media platforms in one place. Moreover, even in the social media age, its official website was still an important channel for disseminating its values and other information. The official website actually attracted nearly 4.6 times more visitors than did the WeChat public account. This means that for grassroots NGOs in China and other parts of the world, official websites are worthy of considerable attention and resources, even in an age when social media has become a hot topic in the nonprofit sector and makes headlines in the mainstream media.

The analysis of the NGO 2.0 Project also indicates that management and planning are indispensable for effective communications in new media for NGOs. NGOs in China and other places should pay equal attention to innovative use of ICTs as well as how such use of new media and ICTs should be managed and evaluated in their organizations. For example, to build and sustain its community in Weibo, the project held that providing timely responses to users' interactions is crucial. This cannot be achieved solely through technological measures; instead, it relies on the establishment of guidelines for people who manage the Weibo account. In its *Communication and Media Plan*, for example, the project stated that staff members who manage its Weibo should "forward and comment on popular Weibo messages [relevant to the field] at all times; reply to users' interactions quickly." To effectively disseminate information and values to audiences, the project specified the best time to post various forms of content in its *Communication and Media Plan* (see chapter 3). Communication plans should identify target audiences, new media channels and platforms to be used, and communication goals for each platform in order to achieve effective communication. The plan should also include how each platform should be managed and assign specific personnel to operate and manage the platforms. It should also include a benchmark to evaluate the performance of new media channels and how relevant data should be collected and analyzed to facilitate such evaluations. The NGO 2.0 Project underinvested in its official website in part because it failed to compare the performance of its social media platforms with its official website.

The Free Lunch Project illustrates how Weibo, online shopping platforms, and mobile payments were used to enhance its transparency and fundraising. The Free Lunch Project viewed transparency as the most important factor in its success over the past ten years. The analysis of the processes that are involved in the free lunch program at every rural school shows that Weibo was the major tool to enhance the transparency of the project's programs in those schools. During the publicity and visit process (see figure 5.1), all application materials from the schools, the verification of these materials by Free Lunch Project volunteers, and questions and answers regarding the applications were all published on Weibo for close public scrutiny. This enhanced the transparency of the programs in rural schools in their beginning stage. The most important and the longest process regarding transparency was, however, the implementation and monitoring process (see figure 5.1). As part of the monitoring process, schools were required to post estimated costs, real costs, balances, and the number of students who ate lunches on their Weibo every business day. To increase the transparency of their programs, many rural schools also posted detailed lunch menus and photos of the lunches on their Weibo posts (see figure 5.2). Thus, anyone with an interest has been able to monitor the program's implementation through the information published on Weibo. Weibo has two features that make it a perfect tool for the Free Lunch Project to increase the transparency of the program. Unlike friending someone in WeChat or other social network tools, following on Weibo is unidirectional and does not require approval. Weibo users need not be approved by a Weibo account to follow its posts. This means that any Weibo user who was interested in any school's free lunch program could monitor the program by following the school's Weibo account without the approval of the school. This opened the monitoring process to the public on Weibo. In contrast to conventional programs where monitoring would be conducted by several development workers, this method largely increased the transparency of the programs of the Free Lunch Project. It also increased the possibility of finding problems in the free lunch programs in rural schools, such as overpricing, because many more people could monitor the programs, including those living near the schools. The data from the Weibo accounts of the schools in the Free Lunch Project also show that people who monitored the free lunch programs through Weibo extended far beyond the Free Lunch Project team or core project volunteers. For example, the Weibo of Long Dong Primary School at Pingjiang County Yue Yang City showed 437 people followed its Weibo, over ten of whom were from the county or the province where the school is located. Another feature of Weibo is that users who follow a Weibo account automatically become subscribers to its Weibo messages. The updates of the Weibo account appear in their "home timeline" in real time. This enabled users to monitor the free lunch programs in rural schools instantaneously.

For this Weibo-mediated real-time monitoring to work, the Free Lunch Project believed that it needed to ensure that the schools publish true information regarding free lunches in a timely manner. To achieve this, the project used a formal agreement between the project and the schools that required rural schools to comply with requirements of transparency and the timely publication of true information about the free lunches. This was set out in the Free Lunch Project's application guidelines. The agreement established that if a school did not update its Weibo for a week, it would get a warning from the project. If a school did not update its Weibo for a month, its funding would be suspended.

To improve the accuracy of Weibo messages, the project provided detailed Weibo templates in its application guidelines. To ensure that the schools complied with these requirements, the schools had to undergo a one-month testing period. During this period, the project provided only one yuan per student per day for free eggs. If the schools' performance on transparency was satisfactory, the project would then provide the schools with funds for full free lunches. By using Weibo and related formal agreements with the schools, the Free Lunch Project was able to achieve real-time monitoring of its programs by the public and to enhance the transparency of its programs.

Analysis of the NCP Life Support Network reveals that ICTs such as WeChat, Weibo, and Shimo Docs were indispensable communication channels in the response of grassroots organizations to the COVID-19 crisis. Due to the infectiousness of the virus, ICT-mediated communication became the major communication channel for the actions and projects of the network. As in Tiger Gate, ICTs continued to be crucial for the creation of collective knowledge for activist communities. Yet the major ICTs used to support the creation of that knowledge have shifted forms: from forum/BBS and IM to WeChat and Shimo Docs. For example, the Group for Medical Supply Donations to Hubei used WeChat and Shimo Docs to create collective knowledge of PPE needs at frontline Wuhan hospitals. The Group for Medical Supply Donations to Hubei, Boshu Yahui, and other volunteers in the network used WeChat group in the creation of collective knowledge of PPE standards used by various countries. The example of PPE standards also shows that this collective knowledge could be enhanced, reused, and adapted by activist communities to solve new problems that emerged at different stages in the crisis. The collective knowledge on PPE standards was first created when the large quantity of donated PPE from various countries were shipped to hospitals in Wuhan but could not be used by health-care workers because they did not satisfy China's medical supply standards (Feng, 2020a). To overcome this problem, in January and early February, the Group for Medical Supply Donations to Hubei, other network volunteers, and health-care workers in frontline hospitals collected and translated documentation on the various PPE standards used in China, Japan, the United States, the European Union, and South Korea. They created and published the "Guidelines for Standards for Purchasing and Donating Medical Supplies" and "The Compatibility Table of

Domestic Standards and Foreign Standards for Medical Supplies" on Weibo to facilitate international donations of PPEs to Chinese hospitals.

As COVID-19 became a global pandemic, PPE shortages also became an international problem in the face of worldwide COVID-19 outbreaks. In mid-March, volunteers from various countries asked the network for help with information and channels to reach reliable Chinese PPE suppliers in order to access PPE and other medical supplies from China to import into their countries. Boshu Yahui volunteers aimed to help international buyers get information regarding all qualified products from Chinese PPE suppliers and "reduce the time spent on comparing the standards of different countries" (Boshu Yahui, 2020). Thus, Boshu Yahui volunteers reused the collective knowledge of PPE standards to assess which Chinese-made PPE met U.S., EU, and Japanese standards. Although technological determinists claim that ICTs drive the enhancement of collective knowledge (Levy, 1997), in the case of the NCP Life Support Network, the impulse to address various social and/or health problems drove the enhancement of collective knowledge within the activist community, facilitated in part by ICTs.

Much as in Tiger Gate, for the NCP Life Support Network, ICTs provided the infrastructure and technological potentials to activate an activist network that extended across geographical boundaries. In Tiger Gate, that network cut across different regions in China. In the NCP Life Support Network's response to COVID-19, that activist network extended far beyond China. Activists and volunteers formed transnational networks to respond to the crisis (see chapter 7). Unlike technological determinism, the use of new ICTs such as WeChat was not the major cause of the expansion of the activist network in response to COVID-19. It was more related to the problems that new media actions targeted and to the activists that engaged in those actions. Tiger Gate was primarily a domestic event whose activists lived mostly in China. COVID-19, however, was fundamentally a global pandemic and a global crisis. In the first phase of the crisis, overseas Chinese communities were mobilized to donate PPE to support frontline health-care workers in China. In order to facilitate and coordinate those transnational donations of PPE to Chinese hospitals, the network of activists, donors, and health-care workers were necessarily transnational. In the second phase of the crisis, PPE shortages became a worldwide problem. Boshu Yahui aimed to solve the lack of communication and coordination between Chinese PPE makers and international buyers in other countries. It also aimed to increase transparency between the PPE supply side and the demand side and to facilitate the communication between the two parties (see chapter 7). It also aided in the purchasing and transporting of PPE for those international buyers. Thus, Boshu Yahui's network had to be transnational.

The analysis of the NCP Life Support Network shows that innovative measures and procedures regarding the use of ICTs that were developed and implemented by activist communities should be an indispensable part of scholarly investigations into the use of ICTs for social change. These measures and procedures contribute directly to the success of new media interventions. For example, online fraud was a serious threat to the quality of information collected online regarding the solicitation of donations. Scammers frequently tried to trick donors by using fake donation solicitation letters. They copied donation solicitation letters published by hospitals and changed the contact information, such as phone number, delivery address, and the bank account where the money should be sent. They would then post the fake donation solicitation letter extensively on social media to trick the public into shipping medical supplies to them or transferring funds to their own accounts. To increase the quality of the information and avoid online fraud in the construction of the platform on PPE needs in Hubei hospitals, the Group for Medical Supply Donations to Hubei used a new feature in Shimo Docs that allowed users to create multiple documents and set sharing permissions for each document. Among the several documents the group created for the platform, the main document of verified PPE needs in hospitals was set as a read-only document to deter fraudulent changes. To utilize the power of ordinary internet users, the group granted everyone permission to edit another document called "Discussion Board for PPE Needs." The group's verification workgroup collected information from the discussion board, conducted verification, and then posted that verification in the main document. If they could not verify a PPE need, they labeled the message "Unverified" in red and added comments, such as, "The information is at high risk of fraud! Use caution!" Another challenge for the information collected online regarding donation solicitation was the rapidly changing needs for PPE in frontline hospitals, and the inability of hospitals to keep up with updating their donation solicitation letters, which were being disseminated to every corner of social media. Therefore, the PPE needs in a solicitation letter may have expired after the group had posted it in the main document for verified PPE needs. Rather than deleting such messages in the document, the group chose to strike through the text and label it "expired." This strategy helped inform readers of the document that those specific PPE needs had already expired.

The network's telehealth project is another example of the importance of innovative measures and procedures on ICT use that were developed by activists. WeChat simply provided the infrastructure for the activist community to construct the virtual hospital. The service process, which is the blueprint for a virtual hospital, was designed and implemented completely by the activist community (see chapter 7). To effectively provide services, activists established community rules to customize the functions of various WeChat groups. For example, as presented in the service process, the Triage Group for Patients Quarantined at Home collected information on and triaged individuals with COVID-19 symptoms who were quarantined at home (see chapter 7). The WeChat group required each participant to change their group name immediately according to the naming rule of the WeChat group. It also required anyone seeking medical advice to fill out a form in order to collect information on individuals with COVID-19 symptoms. To enforce these rules, anyone who failed to change their name or fill out the form would be removed from the WeChat group every day at 10 P.M. Other projects of the network, such as the Wuhan Pregnant Women Group, the Beds Group, and the NCP Life Support Network's Information Center, each established its own rules and procedures for communication and ICT use within their groups.

In contrast to the deterministic claim that technological innovation drives social change, the cases in this book demonstrate that technologies alone do not promote social change or solve social problems; they must be used with innovative measures and procedures developed and implemented by NGOs and activists when they engage in new media interventions. These measures and procedures may be used as plans or management tools for ICT use, as in the NGO 2.0 Project, or used as protocols to regulate the behaviors of various stakeholders involved in new media interventions, as in the Free Lunch Project, or used as rules on ICT use and communication designed and enforced by and for the community, as in the NCP Life Support Network. Thus, in order to understand the use of new media in development and social change, ICT4D and communication for development researchers need to investigate the effects of technological innovations as well as how innovative measures and procedures are developed. Moreover, the use of Weibo in the Free Lunch Project was very different from that in the NGO 2.0 Project. The NGO 2.0 Project used Weibo as a channel for building communities, interacting with others, and disseminating information to promote advocacy. The Free Lunch Project used Weibo as a platform for program monitoring and publicity to enhance the transparency of its programs in rural schools. In addition, an ICT such as WeChat group could be used very differently in different components of a single new media intervention. For example, the Triage Group for Patients Quarantined at Home used its WeChat group for triage and to collect patient information, thereby restricting communication on other issues. The network used the WeChat group the NCP Life Support Network's Information Center for information exchange, thereby encouraging open communication among its participations. This indicates that different activists and NGOs used the same ICT to achieve very different goals. And one organization or community could use the same ICT to achieve different goals in different components of a given project or action. How ICTs are or should be used in new media interventions depends on the context of their specific applications.

A Multichannel Approach

Mainstream research in ICT4D, especially those by scholars and practitioners outside communication studies, tend to focus exclusively on ICTs (Ogan et al., 2009). Interpersonal communication and mass media have rarely been considered in their investigations. My findings from the case studies, however, show that although ICTs are crucial tools to facilitate development and social change, their effects must be assessed in conjunction with various other communication channels, including the mass media and interpersonal communication, which coexist with—and are even interdependent with—ICTs. In new media interventions, ICTs and other communication channels are not mutually exclusive; they interact with and reinforce each other. An exclusive focus on ICTs may therefore reduce and limit the richness of ICT4D research. Future research in ICT4D and communication for development will benefit significantly by employing a multichannel perspective in understanding the use of new media and ICTs for development and social change.

My analysis of Tiger Gate illustrates how newspapers and other mainstream media platforms played a significant role in coordinating the construction of collective knowledge in real time, which challenged the authenticity of the tiger photos. Mainstream media also contributed to the effective mobilization of skills among ordinary people who were not part of online activist communities. Given that almost 80 percent of the population did not have access to the internet during the incident, coverage by mass media, such as newspapers and TV, significantly expanded the community that was mobilized to construct the collective knowledge to challenge the South China tiger photos. Mr. Xu's and Mr. Huang's involvement in Tiger Gate illustrate this expansion (see chapter 4).

The NGO 2.0 Project illustrates a strategy of using mass media communications to energize its new media advocacies and using new media to extend the impact and reach of its mass media communications. For example, the project used the launch of its book, *Internet Plus Social Good* (Wang, 2016), to enhance and energize its advocacy works in Weibo. The project used the crowdfunding campaign of this book primarily as a communications campaign to promote the book but also as a way to communicate the values of the project and to strengthen its communities of NGOs. At the same time, the new media campaigns surrounding the book extended the influence of the book and mobilized more people not only to buy and read the book but to share their comments on the book.

In the Free Lunch Project, activists and project representatives attested to the importance of mass media and the interactions between new media and conventional mass media in the Free Lunch Project's communication strategy. For example, leading Free Lunch Project activist Deng Fei stated, "When the free lunch issue is proposed, the first step of our action is to show the suffering of children [on Weibo]. The second step is to use the hot discussions of the suffering of children on Weibo to attract mass media to report this issue in depth. Then, we can further mobilize millions of urban residents" (Deng, 2011c). The Free Lunch Project also revealed how program monitoring conducted through Weibo and inspections relying on interpersonal communications complemented each other in enhancing the transparency of the free lunch programs in rural schools. The Weibo-mediated monitoring made real-time program monitoring by the public possible and enhanced the transparency of rural schools' free lunch programs. However, one limitation of this ICT-mediated program monitoring method was the inability to verify the information published by the schools on Weibo. Thus, the project used inspections to address the weaknesses of ICT-mediated program monitoring, incorporating another core method to enhance the transparency of free lunch programs in rural schools. Inspections provided a more accurate, reliable, and in-depth evaluation and monitoring of the programs in rural schools. Yet due to limited human and financial resources, the Free Lunch Project was unable to monitor the daily implementation of its programs in participating schools using inspections. Weibo and the procedures and agreement developed by the Free Lunch Project provided a real-time and low-cost method for the public to monitor the free lunch programs in participating schools.

The case of the NCP Life Support Network highlights the unique significance of ICTs in actions and projects responding to COVID-19. But it also shows how a multichannel approach contributed to the effectiveness of the network's response to COVID-19. A less profiled communication channel, the telephone, played an indispensable role in many of the network's actions because of social distancing needs. First, it functioned as a channel that mitigated the limitations of online communication in verifying information published online, as it did for the Group for Medical Supply Donations to Hubei. Second, telephone communication was the only channel to get the most up-to-date information to promote the survival of members of vulnerable groups, as it was in the case of the telehealth project, the Wuhan Pregnant Women Group, and the Beds Group.

Tiger Gate, the Free Lunch Project, and the NCP Life Support Network all illustrate how ICTs and other communication channels interact with and reinforce each other in new media interventions. For example, through analyzing the interactions between online communications in activist communities and mainstream media reports on the South China tiger photos, I revealed how new media and newspaper reports reinforce each other in the construction of the collective knowledge that challenged the authenticity of the tiger photos. Through examining the processes in each free lunch program, I demonstrated how ICT-based communication and interpersonal communication interact with and reinforce each other in the Free Lunch Project. In the analysis of the Milk+Bread incident, I illustrated that the interaction between new media and mass media was significant in facilitating real change and serving as a corrective vis-à-vis government policy. In the NCP Life Support Network, I showed that online channels and telephones interacted with and reinforced each other, as when the Beds Group acquired real-time updated information on the availability of hospital beds for those with COVID-19.

A Context-Based Approach to Technology

Following recent scholarship on communication for development (Bau et al., 2014; Servaes & Carpentier, 2006; Slater & Tacchi, 2004; Torero & von Braun,

2006), this book rejects the technological determinism of previous research on ICT4D (Ogan et al., 2009). However, this is not to say that technological advances and the technological characteristics of digital tools are irrelevant to the analysis of development and social change. Well-established research on the social impacts of technology has shown that the characteristics of technology merit significant consideration by scholars (e.g., Kleine, 2013; van Dijk, 2005; R. Williams & E. Williams, 2003). Kleine, for example, added technologies and innovations into the choice framework she developed for research on ICT4D (2013, p. 202). She argued that technologies "form an important part of social structure that individuals navigate while drawing on their resources" for development and social change (2013, p. 203). My findings in the case studies indicate that the characteristics of technological innovation remain an important component in research on the use of ICTs and new media for development and social change. In the case study of the NGO 2.0 Project, I identified two new characteristics of Web 2.0 technologies over Web 1.0: the web-as-free platform and lower technical barriers for ordinary internet users who lack the programming and coding expertise to create web content. These two new characteristics enable Web 2.0 technologies to empower grassroots NGOs by helping them to overcome the three major weaknesses of grassroots NGOs in their communications: lack of legal status, lack of money, and lack of human resources.

To examine the effects of Weibo in the Free Lunch Project, chapters 5 and 6 investigated how various features of Weibo—such as following and the @ method—have been used by activists, rural schoolteachers, and project participants to enhance the transparency of the free lunch programs and to conduct effective real-time program monitoring. Comparing rural schools' Weibo posts before and after the adoption of the internet and computer in the Free Lunch Project, computer and internet communications offered rural schools more capacity and more methods than text-message-based communications to enhance the transparency of their free lunch programs. After the adoption of the internet and computer, the schools' Weibo posts contained more detailed textual information about the lunches. The schools also began to frequently post high-resolution photos of the lunches. Moreover, each Weibo post published by computer began to use the @ method to inform the Free Lunch Project and the regional coordinator of the Free Lunch Project that the post for each lunch had been published. This indicates that the use of broadband internet and computers indeed increased the capacity of rural school communities to enhance the transparency of their free lunches and improved the efficiency of coordinating the Free Lunch Project. By comparing the donation process on online shopping platforms and mobile payment apps with bank transfers, the case study of the Free Lunch Project also showed that online shopping platforms and mobile payment apps effectively facilitated fundraising in that project.

My analysis of the NCP Life Support Network indicates that WeChat and Shimo Docs served as infrastructure for network activists and volunteers to build their own online platforms to carry out their actions and projects. With the new features of Shimo Docs, such as sharing permission settings, the Group for Medical Supply Donations to Hubei was able to build a platform in order to collect, organize, and present reliable, verified, and real-time updated information regarding PPE needs. The new feature of WeChat known as Jielong enabled Boshu Yahui to build its platform to increase transparency between the supply side and the demand side of PPE and other medical supplies. The various features of WeChat group allowed the network's telehealth project to build a virtual hospital within just thirteen days.

The findings of my case studies concur with Kleine's (2013) findings in Chile that technologies and innovations "form an important part of social structure" that significantly affect the efforts of individuals, activist communities, and NGOs for development and social change. Scholars in communication for development need to continue to engage in the investigations and debates on the effects of technological advances and the characteristics of new technologies on development and social change. Eschewing technological determinism, which tends to make sweeping arguments about the positive or negative effects of ICTs—irrespective of context—scholars and practitioners in communication for development should investigate the impacts of those innovations and characteristics on development and social change within specific sociopolitical and economic contexts.

The findings regarding specific ICT tools such as Weibo and WeChat discussed in this section are very particular to contemporary China due to the particularities of the technological and online environment of the Chinese internet, such as the lack of access to Google applications and other Western-based platforms, which are blocked by China's Great Firewall. Yet other findings presented in the section, such as the effectiveness of the multichannel approach, the significance of innovative measures and procedures developed and implemented by NGOs and activists when they engage in new media interventions, and the effectiveness of the context-based approach to technology, are universal across countries and cultures. They may be useful in research on and practice of using new media and ICTs for development and social change in other parts of the world.

As the International Telecommunication Union declared two decades ago, ICTs have diverse and far-reaching impacts on societies around the globe (1998). To expose and investigate these impacts, we need to employ diverse approaches to examine ICT use in various realms of social life. Yet mainstream discourse on the use of the internet and ICTs in China has long been dominated by two overemphasized storylines, critiqued at the beginning of this book. The problem lies not so much in research or media coverage of those two storylines but in the imbalance in existing research, which has obscured the diversity and richness of internet-related phenomenon in China. Eschewing the overemphasis on conventional political issues in Chinese internet studies, this book has employed a communication for development approach to examine the use of ICTs for development and social change. By so doing, it looked beyond the two dominant storylines in the West and offered a more comprehensive, deeper, and multidimensional understanding of the impact of the internet and ICTs in contemporary Chinese society.

Although communication for development has become a widely applied approach in studies of the internet and ICTs in various developing countries (e.g., Donner, 2015; James, 2005; Kleine, 2013; Ogan et al., 2009; Torero & von Braun, 2006; Unwin, 2009), it has rarely been deployed in studies of China's internet. China, the largest developing country with the biggest population and largest internet user base in the world, has not been given adequate attention in the field of communication for development. This book therefore also complements previous research on communication for development by providing an in-depth investigation into new media interventions in China. It is my hope that this examination of the dynamic and multidimensional relations between activists and the government in new media interventions, the role of state policies in development and social change, and ICTs and other communication channels promoting development and social change may offer new insights into the use of new media for development and social change in China. It aims to promote the practice of activists, NGOs, development agencies, local communities, and other change makers in China, as well as to enrich scholarly knowledge on communication for development.

The field of communication for development is transforming with the rapidly changing problems and crises societies now face. When I began writing the last chapter of this book, COVID-19 continued to be an epidemic and public health crisis in China. As I complete this conclusion of the book, it has become a global pandemic and global crisis affecting every corner of the globe. As of January 12, 2022, 312,173,462 confirmed cases were reported and 5,501,000 people had died from the virus worldwide (WHO, 2022). The COVID-19 crisis highlights long-standing inequalities and deep-seated development problems and social problems in various societies around the globe (Ahmed et al., 2020; Beaunoyer et al., 2020; Dorn et al., 2020; Tsai & Wilson, 2020; Wang & Tang, 2020; Wenham et al., 2020; Zhou et al., 2020). As a field that focuses on using communication theories and communication technologies to bring about development and social change, communication for development has unique strengths in addressing the social and/or health problems highlighted by the crisis. From this approach, this book may contribute to the ongoing discussions and debates on COVID-19 response and problems elsewhere in the world. Broadly speaking, the Chinese government's narrow definition of the COVID-19 crisis overlooked other health needs in society. However, the NCP Life Support Network demonstrated a broad definition of the crisis that may address various social and/or health problems in a society. The government's narrow approach contributed to the suffering and even deaths of people with other serious illnesses, including

HIV/AIDS, cancer, and hepatitis and kidney failure, as was documented by the international media and the domestic Chinese media alike (Feng, 2020b; Hu & Wang; 2020; Lei, 2020). Analysis of the two approaches and the ultimate cost of the Chinese government's approach will contribute to discussions of how government, the public, and NGOs in other parts of the world conceptualize and deal with the crisis. Specifically, chapter 7 shows how grassroots organizations and volunteers tackled the PPE shortages in frontline hospitals through an ICT-assisted transnational network, how grassroots organizations engaged in telehealth services to support individuals with COVID-19, and how grassroots organizations supported various vulnerable social groups, such as pregnant women and elders living alone. NGOs, development workers, activists, and volunteers in other parts of the world may benefit from the discussion in the chapter as they address similar problems and try to support those and other vulnerable groups in their response to the global pandemic.

If we examine the COVID-19 crisis with a broad-based approach, an approach that I have tried to advance in this book, we can see that the development problems and unequal social relationships I have discussed are also very evident in the crisis in other countries, such as the United States. For example, the COVID-19 crisis has fueled a surge in scholarship on and media coverage of the digital divide in the United States (Beaunoyer et al., 2020; Campos-Castillo & Laestadius, 2020; Lake & Makori, 2020; Strauss, 2020). In March 2020, almost all the universities, K–12 schools, and other schools in the United States suspended classroom teaching and moved all instruction online in response to the outbreak. In the age of online teaching and learning in the face of the COVID-19 crisis, educators, students, the public, and policymakers have all suddenly been forced to cope with the digital divide. At the public university where I teach in the United States, some of my American students could not watch Zoom videos during the crisis for lack of broadband internet access. In one of the two university classes I taught in spring 2020, 50 percent of the students reported having difficulties using digital skills in online learning. How should schools, educators, and policymakers come to grips with this new digital divide in the crisis? How should we make online classrooms digitally and socially inclusive? My analysis of the Connecting Every Village Project and its limitations may help illuminate discussion of these pressing questions in the United States.

Moreover, the crisis has compelled nonprofit organizations around the globe to move significant portions of their activities online, including fundraising activities. Should we be worrying about inequities of ICT capacity among different organizations in this context? If so, how can we address this inequity when the very survival of an organization relies on its ICT capacity? And how can we help small grassroots organizations enhance their ICT capacity? The examination of the NGO 2.0 Project in chapter 3 may contribute to discussions on these questions among nonprofit organizations, practitioners, development agencies, and other stakeholders in the nonprofit sector.

COVID-19 is one of many crises that communication for development scholars, nonprofit organizations, policymakers, and publics around the world will work together to address. At the U.N. World Summit on the Information Society in December 2003, leaders and representatives from 175 different countries reached the following consensus: ICTs are powerful tools for building "a people-centered, inclusive and development-oriented" society where individuals, communities and peoples can achieve "their full potential in promoting their sustainable development and improving their quality of life" (World Summit on the Information Society, 2003). It is my hope that the research on using new media for development and social change in contemporary China presented in this book may benefit not only those working to promote social change on the ground in China but also those engaged in social change actions, development practice, and ICT research in other parts of the world.

Acknowledgments

I would like to express my sincere gratitude for the support of the many people, organizations, and institutions that made this book possible. First, my passion for this research on using new media for development and social change in contemporary China was ignited by my work with researchers, activists, and NGOs at MIT's New Media Action Lab, led by Dr. Jing Wang. I am incredibly thankful to Dr. Jing Wang for her guidance and support. Over the past twelve years, our discussions, collaborations, and practices using new media for social change in rural and urban China have profoundly shaped my thinking about China and the internet. In the Department of Communication at the University of Massachusetts Amherst, the team of professors Jan Servaes, Briankle Chang, Jarice Hanson, and Enhua Zhang supervised the early stages of this research for my doctorate. They taught me how to be a scholar and educator in the field of communication and media. Dr. Servaes, in particular, has been a powerful intellectual ally, as well as a supportive mentor, in my research on communication for development.

During my time as a postdoctoral fellow at McGill University, I benefited from many inspiring discussions and productive collaborations with mentors and colleagues in the Department of East Asian Studies. I am deeply grateful for the support and advice of professors Grace Fong and Robin Yates, whose support and advice in China studies have been indispensable for the success of this book project.

More recently, I have been supported by colleagues at the University of Pittsburgh's School of Computing and Information, Kenneth P. Dietrich School of Arts and Sciences, Department of Communication, Department of East Asian Languages and Literatures, and Graduate School of Public and International Affairs, and Pitt Cyber, who inspired me through collaboration and aid for my career and research. I am thankful for my colleagues at this world-class university, particularly Kun Qian, Tim Huang, Kay Shimizu, Adam Lee, Mary K. Biagini, Calum Matheson, Michael Colaresi, Martin Weiss, Daqing He, and Ilia and Jennifer Brick Murtazashvili. In addition, I would like to thank Adam Leibovich, associate dean of the Dietrich School, for being so supportive of my research and career.

I deeply appreciate the work and influence of scholars in Chinese internet studies, communication for development studies, and media and communication studies: Jing Wang, Guobin Yang, Jack Linchuan Qiu, Florian Schneider, Yuezhi Zhao, Bingchun Meng, Cara Wallis, Shaohua Guo, David Kurt Herold, Gabriele de Seta, Jan Servaes, Karin Gwinn Wilkins, Srinivas Raj Melkote, Leslie Steeves, Christine Ogan, Jo Tacchi, Thomas Tufte, Dorothea Kleine, Jan van Dijk, and Colin Sparks. Their intellectual body of work has been invaluable to me throughout my research career.

I am grateful to my editor, Nicole Solano, at Rutgers University Press, for bringing this book to fruition. I would also like to thank the anonymous reviewers for their inspiring, insightful, and detailed comments and suggestions.

I am deeply indebted to the activists, friends, NGOs, and other research participants who have worked with me over the past twelve years. I would like to express my sincere gratitude to them for the time they spent with me, sharing their uses of new media in actions for social change. Particularly, I would like to thank the members of the NGO 2.0 Project for allowing me to participate in weekly meetings and the project's Web 2.0 training workshops over the past twelve years: Dr. Rongting Zhou, Dong Xie, Qiang Zhang, Qian Zhang, and Ruifeng Xiao. I would like to thank those who took part in the Web 2.0 workshops I ran in Guangzhou, Kunming, Xian, and Hefei. It was a great honor to be your instructor and friend. Thank you all for sharing your experience carrying out social change in China. I would also like to thank the members of the NCP Life Support Network for giving me the opportunity to work together on WeChat during the days and nights battling COVID-19 in Wuhan.

I could not have completed this book without the financial support of the Pitt Momentum Funds, the Thomas and Evelyn Rawski Faculty Research Award of the Asian Studies Center directed by Dr. Joseph S. Alter, the Kenneth P. Dietrich School of Arts and Sciences led by Dean Kathleen Blee, and the School of Computing and Information (SCI) led by Dean Bruce Childers at the University of Pittsburgh. I would like to thank Adam Lee, associate dean of the SCI, for being so supportive during my application for the Pitt Momentum Funds. Assistance was also provided by the Department of East Asian Studies at McGill University and the Department of Communication and the Graduate School at the University of Massachusetts Amherst.

Notes

Chapter 1   Introduction

1 The Chinese e-commerce giant Alibaba Group boasts the largest initial public offering on record, valued at $25 billion in September 2014. It owns the world's biggest business-to-business web portal, consumer-to-consumer e-commerce website, and online payment platform.

2 Singles' Day has spawned the world's biggest online shopping day, which occurs on November 11 each year in China (Davidson et al., 2016).

3 I will discuss this in detail later in the introduction.

4 Journalists and researchers have challenged the data published in Chinese sources regarding confirmed COVID-19 cases and deaths ("China's Data Reveal a Puzzling Link between Covid-19 cases and Political Events," 2020).

5 The NGO 2.0 Project is a nonprofit that has focused primarily on enhancing the capacity of grassroots organizations to use new media and ICTs in China. It will be discussed in more detail later in this book.

6 The Zhuoming Disaster Information Service Center is an internet-based volunteer organization initiated by activist disaster relief actions in response to the Yushu earthquake on April 14, 2010. Its mission has been to provide timely information services and bridge the information gap in disaster relief.

7 Social structure can be understood as "a persistent network of social relationships" or "persistent social roles, groups, organizations, institutions" (Harper & Leicht, 2015).

8 "Medium level of education" refers to junior high school or senior high school graduates, as well as those with equivalent education, such as graduates of technical and secondary vocational schools; "lower level of education" refers to people with no more than a primary school education; "high level of education" refers to people with two or more years of college education.

9 According to *Wikipedia*, the Great Firewall of China is the product of legislative and technological actions by the Chinese government to regulate the internet within China and is the primary means of internet censorship there.

10 Baidu, the most used search engine in China, is Google's Chinese counterpart; Renren.com is the most trafficked social networking site in China, but it is much

less popular than Facebook is in North America; Youku, the most popular video sharing website in China, is YouTube's counterpart in China; Weibo, the largest internet microblog site in China, is Twitter's counterpart in China.

11 "Instant messaging (IM) technology is a type of online chat allowing real-time text transmission over the Internet" ("Instant Messaging," 2023). The commonly used IM in the United States is Yahoo Messenger. The most used IM in China is Tencent QQ.

12 The basic function of mobile messaging apps is IM on smartphone. The most-used mobile messaging app in China is Tencent WeChat.

13 Scholars have debated the existence and definition of the Chinese internet studies field (Herold & de Seta, 2015). I use the term for convenience to refer to previous academic research focusing on the Chinese internet.

14 "The maker culture is a contemporary subculture representing a technology-based extension of DIY culture that intersects with hardware-oriented parts of hacker culture and revels in the creation of new devices as well as tinkering with existing ones" ("Maker Culture," 2023).

15 Research on political issues related to the internet and political impacts of the Chinese internet has been consistently categorized in the summary of research topics in five comprehensive reviews of the field of Chinese internet studies (Herold & de Seta, 2015; Hockx, 2005; Kluver & Yang, 2005; Qiu & Bu, 2013; Qiu & Chan, 2004). I have therefore adopted this categorization for this book. Among the prevalent issues are political participation, possibilities for political transformation, government control of the internet, confrontational activism, democratization, and cybernationalism.

16 Digital makers are a sector of maker culture that use technology for transformation and innovation.

17 For example, see Yang (2009), DeLisle et al. (2016), Roberts (2018), and Schneider (2018).

18 For example, see King et al. (2013), Roberts (2018), Endeshaw (2004), and Creemers (2016).

19 Ogan et al. (2009) embrace newer theories in communication for development, in which "development" is defined as social and political change, encompassing democracy and governance as well as economic growth.

20 According to *Wikipedia*, Web 2.0 refers to "websites that emphasize user-generated content, ease of use, participatory culture and interoperability . . . for end users" ("Web 2.0," 2023). Although the precise definition of Web 2.0 remains open to debate, some services and platforms have been widely accepted as typical Web 2.0 technologies, including social networking sites (Facebook), video sharing sites (YouTube), blogs (*Blogger*), wikis (*Wikipedia*), and so on. Due to censorship and Chinese government control, US-based Web 2.0 services are not accessible in China. However, China has counterparts for the primary U.S.-based Web 2.0 platforms. Thus, the NGO 2.0 Project workshops have mainly focused on Chinese Web 2.0 platforms.

Chapter 2 Connecting Every Village Project

1 The percentage of China's rural population declined from 80 percent in the 1980s to 43.9 percent in 2015. Yet as of December 2015, 603 million people, almost twice the U.S. population, continue to reside in rural China (National Bureau of Statistics of China, 2016).

2 *Xiang* is the township level administrative unit in China. It is the fourth-level administrative unit, whereas the administrative village is the fifth-level administrative unit.

3 An administrative village is generally made up of several natural villages.

4 Due to the impact of COVID-19, the data from 2020 may not represent the real trend.

5 Detailed examinations, reviews, and critiques of the concept of the digital divide have been presented in various substantial academic works by other scholars (e.g., DiMaggio & Hargittai, 2001; DiMaggio et al., 2004; Gunkel, 2003; Hargittai & Hinnant, 2008; Mossberger et al., 2007; Norris, 2001; Selwyn, 2004; TELEC & TIO, 1999; van Dijk, 2005, 2006; Warschauer, 2004). Offering yet another here would be redundant and lies beyond the scope of this chapter. The brief discussion here is to clarify what is meant by the term "the digital divide" in this chapter.

6 Five-Year Plans are a series of social and economic development plans proposed by the Chinese government to guide the country's overall social and economic development every five years.

7 Wireless telephone base stations transmit and receive signals to and from mobile or handheld phones.

8 "Dual society" is a key term used by policymakers in China to address the gap between urban and rural development. Yet while the features of the dual society in the development paradigm of the West have influenced Chinese perceptions of rural development and urban–rural difference, there is no indication that China's policymakers are reading (or directly borrowing from) the theories and practices of that development paradigm.

9 Due to transportation costs, the price of computers in rural areas is generally higher than it is in cities. ZOL (Zhong Guan Cun Zai Xian) is the largest Chinese shopping website focusing on IT products, including computers, cell phones, printers, and cameras.

10 I wish to thank the reviewer of an early version of this chapter for this critical observation.

11 Rural cultural centers were first established by the PRC's Ministry of Culture in *xiang* and administrative villages in the 1980s. They function as rural community centers and rural libraries as well as spaces to promote government policies. Between 2006 and 2010, the Chinese government invested a total of 6.4 billion yuan to build 26,700 new cultural centers. The government's goal is to have a cultural center in every *xiang* by 2010 (Ministry of Culture of PRC, 2009).

Chapter 3   The NGO 2.0 Project

1 The China Green Foundation was established in September 27, 1985. It is affiliated with the National Forestry Administration and chaired by retired CCP high-level officials.

2 Web 1.0 is a retronym that refers to the first stage in the evolution of the World Wide Web. In the Web 1.0 era, personal web pages or websites were the most common method to publish web content ("Web 1.0," 2023).

3 Internet content in China is heavily regulated. The basic idea of the agreement is to promise not to publish any forbidden content on a website. For more detailed information on China's internet regulations regarding forbidden content, please refer to Wacker (2003).

4 "A content management system (CMS) is computer software used to manage the creation and modification of digital content" ("Content Management System," 2023).

A website with a CMS enables users to change the contents of the webpages with an easy-to-use tool. To make any changes to webpages on a website without a CMS, users must have IT expertise in coding and web server configuration. Therefore, the initial cost for a website with a CMS is higher but the long-term update and maintenance costs are lower than for a website without a CMS.

5 Green-web.org or the Green-web is the first NGO to provide ICT training and IT support for NGOs and NPOs. I participated in its project in the late 1990s and early 2000s.

6 By "abandoning" their website, I mean these NGOs stopped updating and maintaining their websites.

7 According to techterms.com, "A static website contains static Web pages with fixed content. Each page is coded in HTML and displays the same information to every visitor. . . . The content of each page does not change unless it is updated manually by the webmaster" ("Static Website," 2009). "Maintaining large numbers of static web pages . . . can be impractical without automated tools" ("Static Web Page," 2023).

8 Although censorship in China is still a big problem that restricts online communications, especially communications that may generate collective actions and mobilizations (King et al., 2013), Web 2.0 technologies and Web 2.0 platforms provide more opportunities for Chinese NGOs to reach the public.

9 Please see chapter 2 for more detailed information regarding the model.

10 WordPress is a free software blog system that has been used by nearly sixty million people (WordPress, 2023). "WordPress.com is a platform for self-publishing that is popular for blogging. . . . It is run on a modified version of WordPress software . . . [and] provides free blog hosting for registered users" (WordPress.com, 2023).

11 For a more detailed discussion of the new characteristics and concepts of Web 2.0 illustrated by the NGO 2.0 Project, please see *Internet Plus Social Good* (Wang, 2016).

12 "YND (YiNongDai) is one of the largest online P2P (peer-to-peer) lending platforms in China. It allows people to lend directly to women in rural areas [to support poverty reduction efforts], especially in Northwest China. YND is a social enterprise based in Beijing. . . . It is supported mainly by individual lenders from the Internet" ("YiNongDai," 2021). "1KG (1kg.org) is a non-profit website platform based in China. It advocates 'hike + social responsibility,' whereby each hiker or backpacker is expected to take a kilogram of gifts (such as books) to rural locations . . . and share the gifts with the school kids in those areas" (changemakers.com, 2017).

13 Although material access has not been the focus of the NGO 2.0 Project, it did incorporate a component of material access to address the relative low computer ownership among NGOs. This issue will be discussed in the next section.

14 "RSS (RDF Site Summary or Really Simple Syndication) is a web feed that allows users . . . to access updates to websites in a standardized, computer-readable format" ("RSS," 2023). In the first four workshops, Google Maps was taught as a Web 2.0 tool. After Google quit China in 2010, Google services were blocked by the Chinese government and are not accessible to most NGOs in China. Therefore, the project replaced it with Baidu Maps.

15 In the first four workshops, Google Alter and Google search engine were used as example tools for listening. After 2010, when Google services were blocked by the Chinese government, the project began using Baidu and Baidu News Subscription as example tools for listening.

16 A hackathon is "an event where people engage in rapid and collaborative engineering over a relatively short period of time. . . . They are often run using agile software

development practices, such as sprint-like design wherein computer programmers and others involved in software development, including graphic designers, interface designers, product managers, project managers, domain experts, and others collaborate intensively on engineering projects, such as software engineering" ("Hackathon," 2023). "A . . . common approach to CSR is corporate philanthropy. This includes monetary donations and aid given to nonprofit organizations and communities" ("Corporate Social Responsibility," 2023). The core of the map platform was based on Baidu Maps.

17 This NGO 2.0 Project's one-on-one crowdfunding services are free. The contract is to show that the two sides have committed to work on the crowdfunding project together.

18 I provide a detailed discussion on the Group for Medical Supply Donations to Hubei in chapter 7.

19 The *Business Presentation* is a PowerPoint presentation collaboratively created by the core team of the project. It was used by members of the project to formally introduce and present the NGO 2.0 Project.

20 In its first ten years, the project thought it had not gained significant success to engage the government in the process to use ICTs to empower NGOs. In the section "Feasibility Analysis" in its *Business Presentation*, one of the weaknesses is government relation.

21 Yao Ming is a Chinese basketball executive and former professional basketball star who played for the Houston Rockets. He was named to the All-NBA Team five times ("Yao Ming," 2023). Yao Chen is a Chinese movie star and celebrity as well as an opinion leader in Chinese social media. Her Weibo had nearly 84 million followers as of 2019.

22 The project called this conventional understanding a "Web 1.0 understanding [of communication]."

23 As mobile internet and smartphone use have become increasingly popular among Chinese internet users, in 2017, the NGO 2.0 Project used Strikingly to upgrade its official website. Like WordPress, Strikingly is a website builder that allows a user with no development experience to create mobile-friendly websites. The change from WordPress to Strikingly has no effect on the analysis, as Strikingly shares the two characteristics of Web 2.0.

24 The process of embedding a video from a video sharing website into a web page or blog post does not require any coding or programming skills. The user just needs to copy the URL link generated by the video sharing website into that web page or blog post.

25 "Bounce rate" refers to the percentage of users who read only the home page of a website and leave, rather than visiting other pages.

26 A Weibo topic is similar to a hashtag in Twitter.

27 PRC China has thirty-one province-level divisions in total.

28 There are many debates on China's internet speed. The current data is published by the Chinese government and China's Broadband Development Alliance. Other sources, such as Akamai.com, put it much lower.

Chapter 4   Tiger Gate

1 China Central Television, aka Chinese Central Television, is the dominant state television broadcast network in China.

2 Emay.com.cn is an internet forum of botany launched by Fu and other researchers at the Institute of Botany.

3 The picture was originally produced by Yiwu WST Printing & Packing Corporation using Photoshop and standard printing technology. Panzhihua xydz, the activist who first found it, called it a "New Year's picture." Other activists and Chinese media continue to call it a "New Year's picture." It is similar to a poster that would be displayed in celebration of the Year of the Tiger.

4 The full online ID of Smallfish is "smallfish buo buo buo." Internet users and journalists in most news reports and online discussions referred to this activist as Smallfish.

5 Among digital technology fans, "PS" originally referred to Adobe Photoshop, the leading digital graphic editing tool. It later came to refer to all digital photography technologies, skills, and tools, and also came to be used as a verb. For example, the photo was PSed.

6 QQ is the most used IM tool in China.

7 Please refer to http://forum.xitek.com/thread-484393-1-1-2.html to see the photos of the New Year's picture posted by Smallfish.

8 No information about Panzhihua xydz, the netizen who sent the photos of the New Year's picture to Smallfish, has ever been disclosed.

9 *The Southern Metropolis Daily* is a mainstream media that played an important role in the coverage of Tiger Gate. I will discuss its role in Tiger Gate in more detail later in this chapter.

10 Matlab is a high-level computer programming language and interactive environment for numerical computation, visualization, and programming.

11 In computer vision, perspective transformation is the method of transferring one image to another image through linear algebra functions. Matlab provides methods to perform perspective transformations automatically.

12 An in-depth analysis of this method is beyond the scope of this research. For a detailed explanation of the method, please refer to Sancho's post (Sancho, 2007). For a more accurate explanation of the principles, please refer to Wren (1998) on computer vision.

13 Refer to http://i6.xitek.com/forum/200710/185/18505/18505_1193820638.jpg to see the image created by Sancho showing the result of his computer vision method, which challenged the authenticity of the South China tiger photos.

14 *Lian He ZaoBao* is a major Chinese newspaper in Singapore.

15 By the end of 2008, China's internet penetration rate had just reached 22 percent.

16 Severe acute respiratory syndrome (SARS) is a serious form of pneumonia. It is caused by a virus that was first identified in 2003 in South China.

17 *People's Daily* commentators are from the newspaper's editorial department. Their opinions generally represent the official voice of *People's Daily*.

18 This means that efforts to post any new information on the internet forum will be blocked temporarily, but the contents in the forum will still be available to readers.

19 Later, the forum registered under another domain name, http://bbs.qiuss.com.

20 FromPeasant is the online ID of the activist at bbs.hsw.cn.

21 Many anti-tiger activists argued that the majority of the pro-tiger users were in fact trolls, or 50-Cent Party members, who were hired by the Shaanxi government. "50-Cent Party" is the satirical name that Chinese internet users gave to online commentators hired by the Chinese government to manipulate online opinions.

22 Again, anti-tiger activists asserted that the majority of the pro-tiger bloggers were actually members of the 50-Cent Party.

23 The Supreme People's Procuratorate is the highest national level agency responsible for both prosecution and investigation in the People's Republic of China (see https://en.wikipedia.org/wiki/Supreme_People%27s_Procuratorate).

24 *New Youth* is a Chinese magazine that played a very important role in initiating the New Culture movement in the 1910s and 1920s.

Chapter 5   Free Lunches

1 The Free Lunch Project is also the name of the NGO that runs the project and the Free Lunch Fund. In this chapter, the specific projects of the Free Lunch Project in rural schools will be called free lunch programs.

2 The China Social Welfare Foundation is a government organized nongovernmental organization (GONGO) and a social welfare foundation that is legally able to accept donations from the public. It is illegal for individuals and grassroots NGOs to receive donations directly from the public under China's current political structure. Through its affiliation with the China Social Welfare Foundation, the Free Lunch Project qualified to legally receive donations from the public.

3 In March 2016, the project raised the level of its support to four yuan per lunch per child (Free Lunch Project, 2016a).

4 The National Nutrition Subsidies Project, aka the National Nutrition Project, launched by the central government, represents the implementation of its National Nutrition Subsidies Policy.

5 The China Development Research Foundation is a think tank and GONGO initiated by the Development Research Center of the State Council.

6 "Strategic philanthropy" is a term that leading activists of the Free Lunch Project used to describe the project. This concept will be addressed more specifically later in the chapter.

7 Liang Shuxin is a new media activist and practitioner at Tiany.com.

8 Left-behind children are children who are left behind in rural regions by their parents who migrated to urban regions to find jobs. Due to the unjust policies of the Chinese state, such as the inability of rural children to receive social welfare in urban areas, migrant workers have to leave their children in rural regions for free education and other forms of social welfare. According to the report on the National Nutrition Subsidies Project published by the China Development Research Foundation (2017), 83 percent of the children covered by the National Nutrition Subsidies Project are children who have been left behind by their parents.

9 Microblogs are a broadcast and blogging medium. Microblogs allow users to exchange small pieces of content. The most popular microblog service in the United States is Twitter. The most used microblog service in China is sina.com's Sina Weibo. Microblog posts have size limitations, much like Twitter's 280-character limit.

10 A multimedia messaging service, or MMS, is a standard way to send messages with photos, videos, and other multimedia content to and from mobile phones.

11 Please refer to http://help.sina.com.cn/i/203/r400_12.html for detailed instructions on how to send and receive Weibo through cell phone text messages from Sina.com.

12 Through a similar method, a cell phone can send and receive multimedia posts through MMS. For detailed information, please refer to Sina Weibo's user guide (Sina, 2022).

13 For a specific example of how this method was used to publish a detailed budget of the Free Lunch Project in Xiushui County, Jiangxi Province, see http://www.weibo.com/3061770487/z45qBkBNv?from=page_1002063061770487_profile&wvr=6&mod=weibotime&type=comment#_rnd1491845842572.

14 Taobao.com, Tmall.com, and Alipay (www.alipay.com) are three businesses all owned by Alibaba Group, the biggest e-business company in China. Taobao.com and Tmall.com are its online shopping platforms, and Alipay is its third-party online payment platform.

15 As of 2017, the current price of the virtual product is four yuan.

16 Bank transfers for donations made in the same city to a foundation may not incur service fees.

17 To see the online store of the Free Lunch Project on Taobao.com, go to https://mianfeiwucan.tmall.com/shop/view_shop.htm?prc=1.

18 QR codes are square bar codes. Smartphone users can install an app with a QR-code scanner that can read a displayed code. The app converts the code to a URL, which directs the smartphone's browser to the website of a company, store, or product with that code, where specific information can be found.

19 To see the QR code of the Free Lunch Project, go to http://www.mianfeiwucan.org/en/donate/donate1/.

20 51give is an online donation platform of the China Welfare Foundation. The "5" and "1" in 51give are homophones with "I" and "want"; thus, 51give is pronounced "I want to give," making it easy to remember.

Chapter 6   Contention and Reciprocity in the Free Lunch Project

1 According to haccpmentor.com, "The purpose of keeping retention samples is to support or verify the food products' shelf life period, quality, [and] microbiological, physical and chemical attributes. Retention samples may also be used as part of complaint investigations" or investigations of food safety problems ("What Is the Purpose of Keeping Retention Samples?" 2014).

2 Experimental pilot projects were underway at 699 schools under the National Nutrition Subsidies Project in 2012.

3 Several factors have contributed to the policy changes in the implementation of the National Nutrition Subsidies Project. I will continue my analysis of this issue in the next section.

4 Shaba Primary School is the first school that cooperated with the Free Lunch Project in Guizhou Province. Shaba is the name of the administrative unit where the school is located. The full name of the education bureau is the Education Bureau of Songtao Miao Autonomous County.

5 To see the Weibo post of Liang and the image of the small box of milk and toast, go to http://www.weibo.com/2825300304/z76K85q3F?refer_flag=1001030103_&type=comment#_rnd1491878935567.

6 According to media reports, the cost of packaging of a box of milk is three times higher than the profit of dairy companies (http://new.qq.com/cmsn/20140909046091, 2014). Note that one RMB dime is around 1.5 U.S. cents.

7 The Milk+X mode of the National Nutrition Project in some rural schools included various combinations of milk, bread, cookies, eggs, and sausage. This was served as breakfast (Milk+X breakfast), lunch (Milk+X lunch), or as a snack during recess (Milk+X snack).

8 For a detailed discussion on the definition and factors of government accountability, please refer to my analysis of the Tiger Gate incident in chapter 4.

9 The report compared the average height of schoolchildren in 2012 and 2016 and calculated the increase for each county. Then the counties were grouped by mode, and the average height gain was calculated for each group.

10 It should be noted that having school kitchens provide school lunches does not guarantee that they will serve hot meals. Later in the chapter, we will see how local governments required schools with kitchens to use the Milk+X mode.

11 "School Milk" products are dairy products registered as milk products for school-children through the Dairy Association of China, which will be discussed in detail later in the chapter.

12 New Hope Group's New Hope Dairy is a major producer of School Milk products.

13 The School Milk of China logo was issued by the Dairy Association of China.

14 On June 17, 2017, the Dairy Association of China announced the removal of this requirement, meaning that School Milk product prices very likely increased considerably since 2018. For example, an investigative report published in 2020 found that the price of School Milk products was from 2.08 yuan/box to nearly 4 yuan/box, higher than the market price (1.81 yuan/box) that consumers could get online (Cheng, 2020).

15 Mengniu Dairy is the second-largest dairy company in China.

16 Blue Media Solon is an NGO and online community of the most influential investigative journalists in China. Deng Fei is one of the founders of the organization.

17 In many schools that employ a Milk+X mode, school kitchens are not fully utilized. For example, they may be used only to boil eggs, while the meals consist mostly of packaged milk and cookies delivered by corporations, in which case the use of kitchens only superficially meets the Ministry of Education's requirement.

18 Wondersun Dairy is the third largest dairy company in China. Its CEO is Wang Jinghai, who regularly made proposals in the National People's Congress advocating for the inclusion of the Milk+X mode in the National Nutrition Project. New Hope Dairy is the dairy company of the biggest processed food and dairy company in China. Its CEO is Liu Yonghao, who co-proposed the policy advice with Wang Jinghai in 2015.

Chapter 7 NCP Life Support Network

1 Ground-glass opacity "is a descriptive term referring to an area of increased attenuation in the lung on computed tomography (CT) with preserved bronchial and vascular markings. It is a non-specific sign with a wide etiology including infection, chronic interstitial disease and acute alveolar disease" ("Ground-Glass Opacification," 2023).

2 In this book, non-COVID-19 patients refer to those without COVID-19 but who have other serious illnesses, such as renal failure, cancer, or cardiovascular diseases, and those who are in urgent need of medical treatment, such as surgery or burn treatment. Generally, they are in need of hospitalization but have not been hospitalized.

3 Due to lack of capacity for COVID-19 testing in the early stage of the outbreak in Wuhan, many people who were actually infected with COVID-19 were unable to get tested. These people were categorized as "people who are 'probably infected with COVID-19'" in government reports and media coverage. Many of them had severe COVID-19 symptoms.

4 Human flesh search is a Chinese internet phenomenon involving massive research, based on massive human collaboration, using online and offline skills and information to find the information that is of interest to a specific community or group of people.

5 Shimo Docs are the Chinese equivalent of Google Docs.

6 On January 26, while public donations of PPE to frontline health workers surged to unprecedented levels, the MCA determined that only five GONGOs could legally receive these donations. Of these five gatekeepers, the Red Cross was the most dominant. The problematic management of PPE donations by the Red Cross and how activists have bypassed the organization will be discussed later in the chapter.

7 Jielong is a WeChat mini-program that enables members of a WeChat group to form a subgroup and create a form-like app to run within the WeChat group.

8 During the Wuhan lockdown, the government used the community as the smallest unit to control the outbreak. Social workers in the community are generally public employees who manage and provide services to the community. During the lockdown, they were full-time workers in the local government.

9 The Supervision Team is the team from the central government that supervised the local government's response to COVID-19.

10 The Internal Journals of the Xinhua News Agency are journals that are only accessible to government and party officials. It is an internal channel within the government that provides information and analysis of sensitive and controversial issues in China and in-depth investigation of international affairs to government and party officials.

11 Zhong Nanshan is the top pulmonologist in China who first openly pointed out the human-to-human contagion of COVID-19. He was portrayed as the leading figure in China's response to COVID-19 and SARS by the Chinese media.

12 For more detailed information on Li Wenliang, see Green (2020) and "He Warned of Coronavirus. Here's What He Told Us Before" (2020).

13 He Hui, a volunteer driver, died of COVID-19 on February 3, 2020. His death shocked the community of volunteer drivers in Wuhan.

14 This is a quotation from *In Memory of Miss Liu Hezhen* by Lu Xun, published in 1926 (https://www.marxists.org/archive/lu-xun/1926/04/01.htm).

15 This is a quotation from *Silent China*, a talk given by Lu Xun in Hong Kong in 1927.

16 This is a quotation from Lun Xun's collection *Hot Air* published in 1919. The translation of the original sentences are as follows: "I hope all Chinese youth could get rid of the indifference and coldness. Just march forward regardless of the words from those despairing individuals. If you could do something, just do it. If you can voice something, just voice it. Give as much light as the heat can produce. Even if we are just fireflies, we should light in the darkness. No need to wait for a torch."

17 Lu Xun's focus in *Silent China* is a debate over the relationship between classical Chinese and vernacular Chinese in the 1920s. Kathy used Lu Xun's *Silent China* to address the relationship between individuals and the government in contemporary China.

18 On February 10, the governor of Hubei Province and the mayor of Wuhan were both removed from their positions. These measures were implemented by new leadership in Wuhan and Hubei.

19 The Wuhan COVID-19 Prevention and Control Command Center was the government body in charge of all issues regarding COVID-19 prevention and control in Wuhan. It made and implemented policies on COVID-19 in Wuhan. The head of the command center was the new mayor of Wuhan, Wang Zhonglin.

20 These two lines are from the poem "Comradeship" in the *Classic of Poetry*, also known as the *Book of Songs*, the oldest extant collection of Chinese poetry, dating from the eleventh to the seventh century B.C. (translated by Yang Xianyi and Gladys Yang). Japanese PPE donors printed these lines of the poem on the PPE boxes that

were donated to frontline hospitals in Wuhan. Chinese internet users then circulated the lines of the poem to show support and solidarity with frontline health-care workers.

Chapter 8 Conclusion

1 The differences between the modernization paradigm and the participatory or multiplicity paradigm have been extensively examined in previous research. See Melkote and Steeves (2015a), Servaes (1999), and Shah (2010).

2 Wang's new book on nonconfrontational activism is a rare exception in scholarship on the Chinese internet, as noted in chapter 1. It was published in December 2019, just before the COVID-19 outbreak.

References

Adserà, A., Boix, C., & Payne, M. (2003). Are you being served? Political accountability and quality of government. *Journal of Law, Economics, and Organization*, *19*(2), 445–490. https://doi.org/10.1093/jleo/ewg017

Adu, E. O., Adelabu, O., & Adjogri, S. J. (2014, June 3). *Information and communication technology (ICT): The implications for sustainable development in Nigeria* [Paper presentation]. EdMedia + Innovate Learning, Tampere, Finland.

The advice on "a cup of milk" attracted warm responses from deputies. (2015). *Economic Daily*. http://www.ce.cn/xwzx/gnsz/gdxw/201503/12/t20150312_4804653.shtml

Ahmed, F., Ahmed, N., Pissarides, C., & Stiglitz, J. (2020). Why inequality could spread COVID-19. *The Lancet Public Health*, *5*(5), e240. https://doi.org/10.1016/S2468-2667(20)30085-2

Airhihenbuwa, C.O., Makinwa, B., & Obregon, R. (2000). Toward a new communications framework for HIV/AIDS. *Journal of Health Communication*, *5*(Suppl.), 101–111.

Aker, J. C. (2011). Dial "A" for agriculture: a review of information and communication technologies for agricultural extension in developing countries. *Agricultural Economics*, *42*(6), 631–647.

Alibaba. (2020). *Alibaba Group announces September quarter 2020 results*. https://www.alibabagroup.com/cn/news/article?news=p201105

Alibaba Group & Recende. (2013). *Report on online donations in China*. http://www.alijijinhui.org/content/12381

Alibaba sees strong sales as Singles' Day beats record. (2019, November 11). BBC News. https://www.bbc.com/news/business-50370740

Alibaba's Singles' Day obliterates cyber Monday's sales total in less than two hours. (2016, November 10). *Fortune*. http://fortune.com/2016/11/10/alibaba-singles-day-sale-total/

Alipay. (2017). *Donate to the Free Lunch Project*. https://love.alipay.com/donate/itemDetail.htm?name=2014010616214122130

Almond, G. A., & Coleman, J. S. (1960). *The politics of the developing areas*. Princeton University Press.

Anti-tiger activists are voted to be the top 10 figures of the CCTV Rule of Law Award. (2008). Legal.people.com.cn. *Anti-tiger hero Hao Jinsong: I will fight for the rights of*

participation of netizens. (2008, July 9). Ifeng News. http://news.ifeng.com/society/5/200807/0709_2579_642969.shtml

Apter, D. E., & Rosberg, C. G. (1994). *Political development and the new realism in sub-Saharan Africa.* University of Virginia Press.

Associated Press. (2020, June 2). *How China blocked WHO and Chinese scientists early in coronavirus outbreak.* NBC News. https://www.nbcnews.com/health/health-news/how-china-blocked-who-chinese-scientists-early-coronavirus-outbreak-n1222246

A2N COVID-19 Volunteer Group. (2020, March 25). *What we could do is more than collecting beds information—The Beds Group.* https://mp.weixin.qq.com/s/Bxcu3DxPxngxzY-K6qMMtA

Bao, Z., Tan, J., Gao, Y., & Xiao, H. (2020). *Why the hospital where Dr. Li Wenliang worked has such a great number of health workers infected with COVID-19.* Caixin. https://new.qq.com/omn/TWF20200/TWF20200310036055oo.html

Bau, V., Brough, M., Hartley, J., Hommel, E., Jiang, Y., Lie, R., Ling, R., Malikhao, P., Morley, D., & Ogan, C. (2014). *Technological determinism and social change: Communication in a tech-mad world.* Lexington Books.

Beaubien, J. (2020, April 3). *China enters the next phase of its COVID-19 outbreak: Suppression.* NPR. https://www.npr.org/sections/goatsandsoda/2020/04/03/826140766/china-enters-the-next-phase-of-its-covid-19-outbreak-suppression

Beaunoyer, E., Dupéré, S., & Guitton, M. J. (2020). COVID-19 and digital inequalities: Reciprocal impacts and mitigation strategies. *Computers in Human Behavior, 111,* Article 106424.

Because of lack of profit, the School Milk of China project had little progress. (2005). *Economic Daily.* http://news.163.com/06/0913/05/2QSJFA7I0001124J_2.html

Beijing All in One Foundation. (2020). *About the Protecting Girls project.* https://all-in-one.org.cn/ntbhxmjs

Black, M. (2007). *The no-nonsense guide to international development.* New Internationalist.

Boshu Yahui. (2020, March 18). *Announcement of the new project.* WeChat.

Boeke, J. H. (1953). *Economics and economic policy of dual societies as exemplified by Indonesia.* AMS Press.

Branigan, T. (2009). Barack Obama criticises internet censorship at meeting in China. *The Guardian.* https://www.theguardian.com/world/2009/nov/16/barack-obama-criticises-internet-censorship-china

Brinkerhoff, J. M., & Brinkerhoff, D. W. (2002). Government–nonprofit relations in comparative perspective: evolution, themes and new directions. *Public Administration and Development: The International Journal of Management Research and Practice, 22*(1), 3–18.

Broadband Development Alliance. (2013). *China broadband speed report 2013.* http://www.chinabda.cn/article/251638

Broadband Development Alliance. (2018). *China broadband speed report 2018 Q1.* http://www.chinabda.cn/class/18

Brødsgaard, K. E. (Ed.). (2017). *Chinese politics as fragmented authoritarianism: Earthquakes, energy and environment.* Routledge.

Brookfield, H. (2012). *Interdependent development.* Routledge.

Buckley, C. (2020). Chinese doctor, silenced after warning of outbreak, dies from coronavirus. *New York Times.* https://www.nytimes.com/2020/02/06/world/asia/chinese-doctor-Li-Wenliang-coronavirus.html

BuYuGuiLiLuangSheng. (2007). *People's Daily: "Tiger Gate, another disappointing result?"* http://bbs.tianya.cn/post-free-1061487-1.shtml

Cadiz, M. C. H. (2005). Communication for empowerment: The practice of participatory communication in development. In Thomas Tufte & Oscar Hemer (Eds.), *Media and glocal change: Rethinking communication for development* (pp. 145–158). CLACSO.

Cammaerts, B. (2007). Activism and media. In B. Cammaerts & N. Charpentier (Eds.), *Reclaiming the media: Communication rights and democratic media roles* (pp. 217–224). Intellect Books.

Cammaerts, B. (2016). Overcoming net-centricity in the study of alternative and community media. *Journal of Alternative and Community Media, 1*, 1–3.

Campos-Castillo, C., & Laestadius, L. I. (2020). Racial and ethnic digital divides in posting COVID-19 content on social media among us adults: Secondary survey analysis. *Journal of Medical Internet Research, 22*(7), e20472.

Cantrill, J. G. (1993). Communication and our environment: Categorizing research in environmental advocacy. *Journal of applied communication research, 21*(1), 66–95.

Central government will provide 16 billion yuan to take up the torch from the Free Lunch Project. (2011). *Metropolitan Daily.* http://hzdaily.hangzhou.com.cn/dskb /html/2011-10/27/content_1158850.htm

changemakers.com. (2013). Entry for 1KG. https://www.changemakers.com/

Chase, M. S., & Mulvenon, J. C. (2002). *You've got dissent! Chinese dissident use of the internet and Beijing's counter-strategies.* Rand.

Chen, F. (2020). *The game behind a cup of school milk.* Finance & Economics. https:// finance.sina.cn/chanjing/gsxw/2020-10-19/detail-iiznctkc6467600.d.html

Chen, M., Liu, W., & Lu, D. (2016). Challenges and the way forward in China's new-type urbanization. *Land Use Policy, 55*, 334–339.

Chen, S., Zhang, Z., Yang, J., Wang, J., Zhai, X., Bärnighausen, T., & Wang, C. (2020). Fangcang shelter hospitals: A novel concept for responding to public health emergencies. *The Lancet, 395*, 1305–1314.

Cheng, H. (2008). Hao Jinsong: I wanted to foster the rule of law in China using this case. *New Legal Report.* http://jxfzb.jxnews.com.cn/system/2008/11/03/002873737 .shtml

Cheng, J. (2007). *It is time to tell the public the truth behind the Tiger Gate incident.* people.com.cn. http://opinion.people.com.cn/GB/6560343.html

Cheng, L. (2007, December 31). News on tiger cub skeleton is false. *Ta Kung Pao.* http://huasan2001.blog.163.com/blog/static/6168568020080166952897/

Cheng, M. (2012). *The smart phone users in China have reached 290 million.* 163.com. http://tech.163.com/12/0801/17/87RD251D000915BE.html

Cheung, C.-k., & Leung, K.-k. (2007). Enhancing life satisfaction by government accountability in China. *Social Indicators Research, 82*(3), 411–432. https://doi.org/10 .1007/s11205-006-9043-9

Chib, A. (2013). The promise and peril of mHealth in developing countries. *Mobile Media & Communication, 1*(1), 69–75.

Chib, A., van Velthoven, M. H., & Car, J. (2015). mHealth adoption in low-resource environments: A review of the use of mobile healthcare in developing countries. *Journal of Health Communication, 20*(1), 4–34.

Chien, S.-S. (2010). Economic freedom and political control in post-Mao China: A perspective of upward accountability and asymmetric decentralization. *Asian Journal of Political Science, 18*(1), 69–89. https://doi.org/10.1080/02185371003669379

Chimpanzee. (2007, October 30). *To prove the tiger is flat, we can use linear algebra.* Xitek.com. http://forum.xitek.com/forum-viewthread-tid-479467-extra—action -printable-page-2.html

China Development Research Foundation. (2013, May). An assessment report *of National Nutrition Improvement Plan*. https://tsf.cdrf.org.cn/yjcg/6261.htm

China Development Research Foundation. (2017, June). *China Development Research Foundation flagship report 2017: Progress of Nutrition Improvement Plan*. http://www.cdrf.org.cn/2017ztythbjbg/4163.jhtml

China Internet Network Information Center. (1997). *Statistical report on internet development in China*. https://www.cnnic.cn/NMediaFile/old_attach/P020120612485123735661.pdf

China Internet Network Information Center. (2007). *Statistical report on internet development in rural regions*. https://www.cnnic.cn/NMediaFile/2022/0909/MAIN1662703754929RCIUM46V2P.pdf

China Internet Network Information Center. (2008). *Statistical survey report on the internet development in China*. https://www.cnnic.cn/NMediaFile/2022/0830/MAIN1661848787213RHRPZ27GU2.pdf

China Internet Network Information Center. (2011). *The statistic report of the internet development in Guangdong Province*. https://www.cnnic.cn/n4/2022/0401/c125-917.html

China Internet Network Information Center. (2012, January). *The 29th statistical report on internet development in China*. https://www.com.cnnic.cn/IDR/ReportDownloads/201209/P020120904421720687608.pdf

China Internet Network Information Center. (2014, January). *The 33rd statistical report on internet development in China*. https://www.cnnic.com.cn/IDR/ReportDownloads/201404/U020140417607531610855.pdf

China Internet Network Information Center. (2016a, January). *The 37th statistical report on internet development in China*. https://www.cnnic.com.cn/IDR/ReportDownloads/201604/P020160419390562421055.pdf

China Internet Network Information Center. (2016b, July). *The 38th statistical report on internet development in rural regions*. https://www.cnnic.com.cn/IDR/ReportDownloads/201611/P020161114573409551742.pdf

China Internet Network Information Center. (2017a, January). *The 39th statistical report on internet development in China*. https://www.cnnic.com.cn/IDR/ReportDownloads/201706/P020170608523740585924.pdf

China Internet Network Information Center. (2017b, July). *The 40th statistical report on internet development in China*. https://www.cnnic.com.cn/IDR/ReportDownloads/201807/P020180711387563090220.pdf

China Internet Network Information Center. (2018a, January). *The 41st statistical report on internet development in China*. https://www.cnnic.com.cn/IDR/ReportDownloads/201807/P020180711391069195909.pdf

China Internet Network Information Center. (2018b, July). *The 42nd statistical report on internet development in China*. https://www.cnnic.com.cn/IDR/ReportDownloads/201911/P020191112538212107066.pdf

China Internet Network Information Center. (2019, August). *The 44th statistical report on internet development in China*. https://www.cnnic.com.cn/IDR/ReportDownloads/201911/P020191112539794960687.pdf

China Internet Network Information Center. (2020a, April). *The 45th statistical report on internet development in China*. https://www.cnnic.com.cn/IDR/ReportDownloads/202008/P020200827549953874912.pdf

China Internet Network Information Center. (2020b, September). *The 46th statistical report on internet development in China*. https://www.cnnic.com.cn/IDR/ReportDownloads/202012/P020201201530023411644.pdf

China Internet Network Information Center. (2022, August). *The 50th statistical report on China's internet development.* https://cnnic.com.cn/IDR/ReportDownloads /202212/P020221209344717199824.pdf

China invents the digital totalitarian state. (2016, December 17). *The Economist.* https://www.economist.com/news/briefing/21711902-worrying-implications-its -social-credit-project-china-invents-digital-totalitarian

China Mobile. (2011). *2010 report on sustainable development.* http://www.10086.cn /aboutus/res/2010csr_cn/index.shtml

China Mobile. (2012, February 6). *China Mobile took the responsibility to bridge the digital divide between rural regions and urban regions.* http://www.10086.cn/aboutus /news/GroupNews/201208/t20120815_35414.htm

China Rural Kids Care. (2017). *About us.* http://www.dbyb.org/77

China Rural Kids Care. (2018). *China Rural Kids Care project.* https://chudu.kuaizhan .com/56/16/p525459279sb0b4

China-Dolls Center for Rare Disorders. (2020). *Official website of China-Dolls Center for Rare Disorders.* http://chinadolls.org.cn/type/english

ChinaNews.com. (2020). *Hubei Red Cross responded to the question regarding the distribution of donated PPEs: We are deeply regretful.* http://www.chinanews.com/gn /2020/02-01/9075260.shtml

China's Alibaba breaks Singles Day record as sales surge. (2015, November 11). BBC. http://www.bbc.com/news/business-34773940

China's data reveal a puzzling link between COVID-19 cases and political events. (2014, April 07). *The Economist.* https://www.economist.com/graphic-detail/2020/04/07 /chinas-data-reveal-a-puzzling-link-between-covid-19-cases-and-political-events

Chu, J. (2018). Vindicating public environmental interest: Defining the role of environmental public interest litigation in China. *Ecology LQ, 45,* 485.

Clayton, R., Murdoch, S., & Watson, R. (2006). Ignoring the great firewall of China. In G. Danezis & G. Golle (Eds.), *Privacy enhancing technologies* (pp. 20–35). Springer.

Colle, R. D. (2008). Threads of development communication. In J. Servaes, (Ed.), *Communication for development and social change* (pp. 96–157). SAGE Publications.

Communication for Social Change Consortium. *What is CFSC.* https://www.cfsc.org /what-is-cfsc/

Congressional-Executive Commission on China. *Chinese civil society organizations.* Congressional-Executive Commission on China. http://www.cecc.gov/pages /virtualAcad/rol/ngosumm.php

Content management system. (2023, May 4). In *Wikipedia.* https://en.wikipedia.org /wiki/Content_management_system

Convention on the Rights of the Child, November 20, 1989. https://www.ohchr.org/en /professionalinterest/pages/crc.aspx

Coronavirus: Macron questions China's handling of outbreak. (2020, April 17). BBC. https://www.bbc.com/news/world-europe-52319462

Corporate social responsibility. (2023, June 19). In *Wikipedia.* https://en.wikipedia.org /wiki/Corporate_social_responsibility

Corporations are profiting from the National Nutrition Subsidies. (2013). Xinhuanet. http://edu.people.com.cn/n/2013/0525/c1006–21613309.html

Costa, P. (2012). The growing pains of community radio in Africa. *Nordicom Review, 33.* Special Issue, 135–148.

Costanza-Chock, S. (2014). *Out of the shadows, into the streets! Transmedia organizing and the immigrant rights movement.* MIT Press.

COVID-19 and China: Lessons and the way forward. (2020, July 25). *The Lancet, 396*(10246), 213. https://www.thelancet.com/journals/lancet/article/PIIS0140 -6736(20)31637-8/fulltext

Crazy Hao Jinsong talks about Tiger Gate (2008). Live.jcrb.com. http://live.jcrb.com /html/2008/258.htm

Creemers, R. (2016). Cultural products and the WTO: China's domestic censorship and media control policies. In P. D. Farah & E. Cima (Eds.), *China's influence on non-trade concerns in international economic law* (pp. 399–408). Routledge.

Cubism. (2007, November 23). *3D photography technologies and the debate over South China Tiger photos* http://bbs.dpnet.com.cn/bbs/Announce/Ann_1_1199034_0_0.html

Cui, H., & Yang, K. (2020, March 31). The review of what the Red Cross has done in its media crisis. *Southern Weekly.* http://news.southcn.com/nfzm/content/2020-04/18 /content_190765123.htm

Cui, L. (2007). Hao Jingsong applied to the National Forestry Administration for administrative reconsideration. *China Youth Daily.* http://society.people.com.cn/GB /6520815.html

Dagron, A. G. (2001). *Making waves: Stories of participatory communication for social change; A report to the Rockefeller Foundation.* Rockefeller Foundation.

Dagron, A. G., & Tufte, T. (2006). *Communication for social change anthology: Historical and contemporary readings.* CFSC Consortium, Inc.

Dairy Association of China. (2017). *White paper on promoting the School Milk of China Project in a new era.* http://paper.jyb.cn/zgjyb../images/2017-07/06/08/ZGJYB 2017070608.pdf

Dairy Association of China. (2020). *Five Years Plan (2020 to 2025).* http://i.ce.cn/ newwap/bwzg/202012/23/W020201223371156362519.pdf

Damm, J. (2007). The Internet and the Fragmentation of Chinese Society. *Critical Asian Studies, 39*(2), 273–294. https://doi.org/10.1080/14672710701339485

Davidson, L., Allen, E., & Armstrong, A. (2016). What is China's Singles Day and how does it compare to Black Friday? *The Telegraph.* http://www.telegraph.co.uk/black -friday/0/what-is-chinas-singles-day-and-how-does-it-compare-to-black-frid/

de Boer, D., & Whitehead, D. (2016). *The future of public interest litigation in China.* https://www.chinadialogue.net/article/show/single/en/9356-Opinion-The-future-of -public-interest-litigation-in-China

de Jong, M. W., Shaw, M., & Stammers, N. (2005). *Global activism, global media.* Pluto Press.

Delisle, J., Goldstein, A., & Yang, G. (2016). *The internet, social media, and a changing China.* University of Pennsylvania Press.

Deng, F. (2011a, March 24). *Deng Fei's Weibo.* http://www.weibo.com/1642326133 /wr4kA8vgHa#1356838968839

Deng, F. (2011b, November 1). *The future of the Free Lunch Project.* http://talk.weibo .com/ft/201111012378

Deng, F. (2011c, November 7). *Interview of Fei Deng.* http://xueye.ifeng.com/special /dengfei/

Deng, F. (2013a, April 25). *Deng Fei's Weibo on scandal regarding the National Nutrition Project in Fuyuan, Yunnan.* https://www.weibo.com/1642326133/ztPfbirRB?from =page_1035051642326133_profile&wvr=6&mod=weibotime&type=comment

Deng, F. (2013b, June 26). *Deng Fei's Weibo on milk poisoning incident at Xiandong Middle School in Lianyuan City.* https://www.weibo.com/1642326133/zDdEiEIRl ?from=page_1035051642326133_profile&wvr=6&mod=weibotime

Deng, F. (2014). *Free Lunch: Changing China through kindness.* Sino-Culture Press.

Deng, F. (2020). *Deng Fei's Weibo*. https://weibo.com/p/1035051642326133?profile_ftype=1&is_all=1#_0

Department of Education of Shandong Province. (2015). *Notice on the promotion of the School Milk of China Project*. http://www.schoolmilk.gov.cn/s/wxzl/wjgz/150922182833159107 26

Deputy Wang Jinghai: The Ministry of Education should require the National Nutrition Project to buy School Milk products. (2015a, March 4). Xinhuanet. http://www.xinhuanet.com/food/2015-03/04/c_1114516323.htm

Deputy Wang Jinghai stated: The Ministry of Education should take the responsibility to support the School Milk of China project. (2015b, May 12). Xinhuanet. http://news.xinhuanet.com/food/2015-05/12/c_127792818.htm

Diamond, L. (2003). The rule of law as transition to democracy in China. *Journal of Contemporary China, 12*(35), 319. http://search.ebscohost.com/login.aspx?direct=true&db=aph&AN=9303700&site=ehost-live&scope=site

Dickens, B. L., Koo, J. R., Wilder-Smith, A., & Cook, A. R. (2020). Institutional, not home-based, isolation could contain the COVID-19 outbreak. *The Lancet, 395*(10236), 1541–1542. https://doi.org/10.1016/S0140-6736(20)31016-3.

DiMaggio, P., & Hargittai, E. (2001). *From the "digital divide" to "digital inequality": Studying Internet use as penetration increases*. Center for Arts and Cultural Policy Studies, Woodrow Wilson School, Princeton University.

DiMaggio, P., Hargittai, E., Celeste, C., & Shafer, S. (2004). Digital inequality: From unequal access to differentiated use. In K. M. Neckerman (Ed.), *Social inequality* (pp. 355–400). Russell Sage.

Ding, J. (2007). *Experts argued: It is not suppressing that Zhou could take photos of South China tiger at Zheng Ping County*. Xinhuanet.com. http://city.finance.sina.com.cn/city/2007-10-18/91956.html

Donner, J. (2015). *After access: Inclusion, development, and a more mobile internet*. MIT Press.

Dorn, A. V., Cooney, R. E., & Sabin, M. L. (2020, April 18). COVID-19 exacerbating inequalities in the US. *The Lancet, 395*(10232), 1243–1244. https://doi.org/10.1016/S0140-6736(20)30893-X

Editorial Board. (2011). How to improve government accountability. *People's Daily*. http://news.ifeng.com/opinion/sixiangpinglun/detail_2011_05/29/6694149_1.shtml

Education Department of Hebei Province. (2019). *The guideline for the implementation of the National Nutrition Project in our province*. http://jyt.hebei.gov.cn/col/1595832726231/2019/09/30/1595832844346.html

Ekine, S. (2010). *SMS uprising: Mobile activism in Africa*. Fahamu/Pambazuka.

The 11th Singles' Day sale of Alibaba. (2019). Xinhua News Agency. http://www.xinhuanet.com/politics/2019-11/11/c_1125219000.htm

Endeshaw, A. (2004). Internet regulation in China: the never-ending cat and mouse game. *Information & Communications Technology Law, 13*(1), 41–57. https://doi.org/10.1080/1360083042000190634

Enghel, F. (2013). Communication, development, and social change: Future alternatives. In K. G. Wilkins, J. D. Straubhaar, & S. Kumar (Eds.), *Global communication* (pp. 129–151). Routledge.

Estrella, M. (2000). *Learning from change: Issues and experiences in participatory monitoring and evaluation*. IDRC.

Facing the Tiger Gate: What to do except wait? (2007, November 21). *The Southern Metropolis Daily*. http://news.sina.com.cn/o/2007-11-21/090114355275.shtml

Fair, J. E. (1989). 29 years of theory and research on media and development: The dominant paradigm impact. *Gazette*, *44*(2), 129–150.

Fair, J. E., & Shah, H. (1997). Continuities and discontinuities in communication and development research since 1958. *Journal of International Communication*, *4*(2), 3–23.

Fan, S. (2017). Supporting country-driven innovations and agrifood value chains for poverty and hunger reduction. In G. V. Barbosa-Cánovas, G. M. Pastore, & K. Candoğan (Eds.), *Global food security and wellness* (pp. 1–13). Springer.

Faulconbridge, G., & Holton, K. (2020). UK says China has questions to answer over coronavirus outbreak. *Reuters*. https://www.reuters.com/article/us-health -coronavirus-britain-china/uk-says-china-has-questions-to-answer-over-coronavirus -outbreak-idUSKBN22G0MF

Federal Communications Commission. (2010). *Connecting America: The National Broadband Plan*. http://www.broadband.gov/plan/

Feng, E. (2020b, February 22). *How COVID-19 has affected medical care for non-coronavirus patients*. NPR. https://www.npr.org/2020/02/22/808404816/how-covid -19-has-affected-medical-care-for-non-coronavirus-patients

Feng, S. (2020a, February 13). Why frontline health workers have run out of PPEs even though the public donated such a large number of PPE? *Ban Yue Tan*. http://yuqing .people.com.cn/n1/2020/0213/c209043–31585647.html

FirstImpression. (2007, October 17). *Wild tiger made from cardboard could pass the experts' evaluation but can't pass netizens' scrutiny*. http://www.tianya.cn/publicforum/content /free/1/1030532.shtml

FON. (2019). *Our public interest litigations*. https://www.fon.org.cn/action/way/cate/20

Food and Agriculture Organization. (2006). *Stakeholders analysis*. https://sarpn.org /documents/d0002793/Reporting_FS_info_FAO2006_Lesson1_annex1.pdf

Food and Agriculture Organization. (2011). *The state of food and agriculture, 2010–2011*. http://www.fao.org/docrep/013/i2050e/i2050e00.htm

Food and Agriculture Organization. (2012). *Food security indicators*. http://www.fao.org /publications/sofi/food-security-indicators/en/

Food and Agriculture Organization. (2015). *Regional overview of food insecurity—Asia and the Pacific 2015*. http://www.fao.org/publications/card/en/c/502a00e3-0334 -46ab-a73f-9192bc25f389/

Food and Agriculture Organization. (2017). *Global report on food crises 2017*. http:// www.fao.org/emergencies/resources/documents/resources-detail/en/c/876564/

Food and Agriculture Organization, UNICEF, World Food Program, & World Health Organization. (2019). *Asia and the Pacific regional overview of food security and nutrition 2019. Placing nutrition at the centre of social protection*. https://www.fao.org /policy-support/tools-and-publications/resources-details/en/c/1300308/

"Free Lunch" has become a new model for grassroots philanthropy projects. (2012). Xinhuanet. http://www.people.com.cn/24hour/n/2012/1030/c25408–19439550.html

Free Lunch Online Store. (2016). *About us*. http://mianfeiwucan.tmall.com/view_page -121451738.htm?spm=a1z10.1.3-4127047302.2.8CcWjf

Free Lunch Project. (2011). *Free Lunch Project inspection report: Xinhua Baiyun Primary School*. http://www.mianfeiwucan.org/fileadmin/user_upload/20130710137342686474 .pdf

Free Lunch Project. (2012a). *Annual financial statement 2011*. http://www.mianfeiwucan .org/infor/download/

Free Lunch Project. (2012b). *Feedback report on the inspection of the Haoyou Primary School in Fenghuang County, Hunan Province*. http://www.mianfeiwucan.org /fileadmin/user_upload/20130712137360123138.pdf

Free Lunch Project. (2012c). *Inquiry on donations*. http://www.mianfeiwucan.org/home/help/help3/

Free Lunch Project. (2012d). *Inspection report of the Haoyou Primary School in Fenghuang County, Hunan Province*. http://www.mianfeiwucan.org/fileadmin/user_upload/20130712137360123170.pdf

Free Lunch Project. (2013a, April). *Annual financial statement 2012*. http://www.mianfeiwucan.org/infor/download/

Free Lunch Project. (2013b, May). *Free Lunch Project monthly report April 2013*. http://www.mianfeiwucan.org/fileadmin/_migrated/content_uploads/%E5%85%8D%E8%B4%B9%E5%8D%88%E9%A4%90%E6%9C%88%E6%8A%A5__%E6%80%BB%E7%AC%AC7%E6%9C%9F_2013%E5%B9%B44%E6%9C%88%E5%88%8A.pdf

Free Lunch Project. (2014). *Annual financial statement 2013*. http://www.mianfeiwucan.org/infor/download/

Free Lunch Project. (2015a). *Annual financial statement 2014*. http://www.mianfeiwucan.org/infor/download/

Free Lunch Project. (2015b). *Free Lunch Project inspection report: Ganxi Village Primary School at Hunan Huaihua, Xinhuang County*. http://www.mianfeiwucan.org/fileadmin/user_upload/20150709143641109390.pdf

Free Lunch Project. (2016a, April). *The announcement of the rise of the standard of support of the Free Lunch programs*. http://www.mianfeiwucan.org/infor/detail3/post/1481/

Free Lunch Project. (2016b). *Annual financial statement 2015*. http://www.mianfeiwucan.org/infor/download/

Free Lunch Project. (2017a). *Annual financial statement 2016*. http://www.mianfeiwucan.org/infor/download/

Free Lunch Project. (2017b). *Free Lunch Project inspection report: Guangxi Guiling Longsheng County Mati Xiang Furong Primary School*. http://www.mianfeiwucan.org/fileadmin/user_upload/20131110138408427078.pdf

Free Lunch Project. (2017c). *School information*. http://www.mianfeiwucan.org/school/schoolinfo/

Free Lunch Project. (2017d). *Official Website*. http://www.mianfeiwucan.org/

Free Lunch Project. (2018a). *About us*. http://www.mianfeiwucan.org/index.php?id=9

Free Lunch Project. (2018b). *Annual financial statement 2017*. https://www.mianfeiwucan.org/infor/download/

Free Lunch Project. (2019a). *Annual financial statement 2018*. https://www.mianfeiwucan.org/infor/download/

Free Lunch Project. (2019b). *The Free Lunch Project application guidelines version 6.0*. http://www.mianfeiwucan.org/school/schoolapply/

Free Lunch Project. (2019c). *Official website of the Free Lunch Project*. http://www.mianfeiwucan.org/

Free Lunch Project. (2019d, June 3). *Free Lunch+???=???, how many possibilities could you think of?* http://www.mianfeiwucan.org/en/infor/detail3/post/2224/

Free Lunch Project. (2020a). *Annual financial statement 2019*. https://www.mianfeiwucan.org/infor/download/

Free Lunch Project. (2020b). *The Free Lunch Project application guidelines 8.0*. https://www.mianfeiwucan.org/school/schoolapply/

Free Lunch Project. (2020c). *Information publicity*. https://www.mianfeiwucan.org/school/schoolinfo/

Free Lunch Project. (2020d). *Inspection reports*. https://www.mianfeiwucan.org/school/jihe/

Free Lunch Project. (2022). *The official website of the Free Lunch Project.* http://www.mianfeiwucan.org/

Frey, L. R., Carragee, K. M., Crabtree, R. D., & Ford, L. A. (2006). *Communication activism: Vol. 1. Communication for social change.* Hampton.

Friedmann, J. (1992). *Empowerment: the politics of alternative development.* Blackwell.

Fu, D. (2007a). *The October 12th report from Xinhua News Agency is not reliable.* http://blog.sina.com.cn/s/blog_4ef9035a01000bh3.html

Fu, D. (2007b). *Tiger Gate fraud.* http://blog.sina.com.cn/s/blog_4ef9035a01000c2b.html

Fu, D. (2007c). *Tiger Gate: People's Daily is "surprisingly" 100% in line with the people.* Fu Dezhi's Sina blog.

Fu, D. (2007d). *My conversation with a high-level government official on Tiger Gate.* Fu Dezhi's post on emay.com.cn

Fu, D. (2008a). *On the shutting down of the South China tiger forum.* http://blog.sina.com.cn/s/blog_4ef9035a01008trk.html

Fu, D. (2008b). *Special report on Tiger Gate event to the Endangered Species Scientific Commission of China.* blog.sina.com.cn/s/blog_4ef9035a01008zg2.html

Fu, D. (2008c). *Tiger Gate event: Demonstrate the disproportion between the size of the tiger and the size of the leaves with figures.* http://blog.sina.com.cn/s/blog_4ef9035a01008a9o.html

Fu, D. (2008d). *To Professor Cai Dingjian.* http://blog.sina.com.cn/s/blog_4ef9035a01008wn1.html

Fu, D. (2008e). *About People's Daily report on Tiger Gate.* Fu Dezhi's blog.

Fu, H. (2012, July 14). *A concept and 16 million yuan.* Xinhua News Agency. http://www.gd.xinhuanet.com/newscenter/2012-07/14/c_112437805.htm

Furong Primary School. (2017, November 9). *Furong Primary School's Weibo.* https://m.weibo.cn/u/2816876825?luicode=10000011&lfid=100103type%3D1%26q%3D%E5%B9%BF%E8%A5%BF%E6%A1%82%E6%9E%97%E9%BE%99%E8%83%9C%E9%A9%AC%E5%A0%A4%E4%B9%A1%E8%8A%99%E8%93%89%E5%B0%8F%E5%AD%A6

Furong Primary School. (2020, June 30). *Furong Primary School's Weibo.* https://weibo.com/u/2816876825?is_all=1&stat_date=202006#_rnd1612620505785

Ge, S., & Ding, M. (2006). *The difficulty of the School Milk project: Schools are concerned for risks and corporations think profits.* Xinhua News Agency. http://news.sina.com.cn/o/2006-10-23/11231030387is.shtml

Government against public opinion, the Tiger Gate incident falls into stalemate again. (2007, November 20). *The Southern Metropolis Daily.* http://news.qq.com/a/20071121/001981.htm

Great Firewall. (2023, May 29). In *Wikipedia.* https://en.wikipedia.org/wiki/Great_Firewall

Green, A. (2020, February 18). Li Wenliang. *The Lancet, 395*(10225), 682. https://www.thelancet.com/journals/lancet/article/PIIS0140-6736(20)30382-2/fulltext

Ground-glass opacification. (2023, February 25). *Radiopaedia.* https://radiopaedia.org/articles/ground-glass-opacification-3?lang=us

Gu, B. (2016). Population living in poverty has reduced 90% since 1978 in China. *People's Daily.* http://f.china.com.cn/2016-12/28/content_39997859.htm

Gu, J. (2015). *Speech at the Third Student Nutrition and School Feeding Conference.* http://www.schoolmilk.gov.cn/s/wxzl/ldjh/15112309392612310120

Gu, L. (2015). *How should the Free Lunch Project move forward?* People Political Consultative Bao. http://epaper.rmzxb.com.cn/detail.aspx?id=361011

Guan, K. (2007a, October 28). *What changed a real tiger into a paper tiger.* http://blog.sina.com.cn/s/blog_4f100a001000db8.html

Guan, K. (2007b, November 30). *Tiger Gate is a war to protect human rights*. http://blog
.sina.com.cn/s/blog_4f100ac001000dof.html

Guan, K. (2008, April 20). *The astonishing false news in the Tiger Gate incident*.
http://blog.sina.com.cn/s/blog_4f100ac0010096i3.html

Gumucio-Dagron, A. (2001). *Making waves: Participatory communication for social
change: A report to the Rockefeller Foundation*. Rockefeller Foundation.

Gunkel, D. J. (2003). Second thoughts: toward a critique of the digital divide. *New
Media & Society, 5*(4), 499–522.

Guo, S. (2020). *The evolution of the Chinese internet: Creative visibility in the digital
public*. Stanford University Press.

Guo, S., Ye, Y., Deng, S., & Wang, Y. (2020). The missing masks and the Red Cross
Black Hole. *YiMagazine*. https://www.cbnweek.com/articles/normal/24357

Hackathon. (2023, May 18). In *Wikipedia*. https://en.wikipedia.org/wiki/Hackathon

Hall, B. L. (1992). From margins to center? The development and purpose of participatory research. *The American Sociologist, 23*(4), 15–28.

Hamel, J.-Y. (2010). *ICT4D and the human development and capabilities approach: The
potential of information and communication technology*. United Nations Human
Development Research Paper 37.

Hao, J. (2007). *Hao Jinsong formally sued Zhou Zhenglong*. Hao Jinsong's blog.
http://blog.sina.com.cn/haojinsong

Hao, J. (2008, September 28). Zhou Zhenglong is a scapegoat. *Beijing News*. http://news
.sina.com.cn/c/l/2008-09-28/031516373661.shtml

Hao, J. (2009). *My 115 minutes in Shanghai Minhang District People's Court*. http://blog
.sina.com.cn/s/blog_449d613do100gi6x.html

Hao, N. (2020, February 21). *The development of online and offline life support networks*.
https://mp.weixin.qq.com/s/5uCj6W3RPj1SHY9rQRbJ6A

*Hao Jinsong: Individuals could change the times; rights need to be acquired through
actions*. (2011). http://news.sohu.com/s2011/7685/s279676772/

Hao sued Zhou Zhenglong for making fake photos. (2007). *Beijing Times*. http://news
.sohu.com/20071108/n253120852.shtml

Hargittai, E., & Hinnant, A. (2008). Digital inequality: Differences in young adults' use
of the internet. *Communication research, 35*(5), 602–621.

Harper, C. L., & Leicht, K. T. (2015). *Exploring social change: America and the world*.
Routledge.

haw561. (2007). *Headline!!! Report from CCTV's news probe by Chai Jing on Tiger Gate*.
http://bbs.tianya.cn/post-free-1068273–1.shtml

Health Commission of Wuhan. (2020). *Announcement on the hospitals that admit
non-COVID-19 patients during the COVID-19 crisis*. http://wjw.hubei.gov.cn/fbjd
/tzgg/202002/t20200217_2040097.shtml

Hebei Province is expanding the National Nutrition Project. (2017). *Economic Daily*.
http://paper.ce.cn/jjrb/html/2017-09/09/content_343762.htm

Heeks, R. (2008). ICT4D 2.0: The next phase of applying ICT for international
development. *Computer, 41*(6).

Hemer, O., & Tufte, T. (Eds.) (2005). *Media and glocal change: Rethinking communication for development*. Nordicom.

Herold, D. K. (2014). Users, not netizens: Spaces and practices on the Chinese Internet.
In P. Marolt & D. K. Herold (Eds.), *China online: Locating society in online spaces*
(pp. 34–44). Routledge.

Herold, D. K., & de Seta, G. (2015). Through the looking glass: Twenty years of Chinese
internet research. *The Information Society, 31*(1), 68–82.

He warned of coronavirus. Here's what he told us before. (2020, February 7). *The New York Times*. https://www.nytimes.com/2020/02/07/world/asia/Li-Wenliang-china-coronavirus.html

Highlights of the decision on major issues concerning comprehensively deepening reforms. (2013). *China Daily*. http://www.chinadaily.com.cn/china/2013cpctps/2013-11/20/content_17119258.htm

Hockx, M. (2005). Virtual Chinese literature: A comparative case study of online poetry communities. *The China Quarterly*, *183*, 670–691. https://doi.org/10.1017/S030574100500041X

Holden, C. (2007). Rare-Tiger Photo Flap Makes Fur Fly in China. *Science*, *318*(9), 893. http://www.sciencemag.org/content/318/5852/r-samples.full.pdf

Horizon Research Consultancy Group (2014). *2014 Report on human resources in the non-profit sectors*. http://www.chinadevelopmentbrief.org.cn/news-16607.html

Howell, J. (2007). Civil society in China: Chipping away at the edges. *Development*, *50*(3), 17–17. http://www.palgrave-journals.com/development/journal/v50/n3/full/1100416a.html

Hsu, C., & Teets, J. (2016). Is China's new overseas NGO management law sounding the death knell for civil society? Maybe not. *The Asia-Pacific Journal*, *14*(4), 3.

Hu, J. (2007). Report to the Seventeenth National Congress of the Communist Party. *People's Daily*. http://cpc.people.com.cn/GB/104019/104099/6429414.html

Hu, J. (2017). The six anniversary of the Free Lunch Project: Hefeng model is replicating around the country. *Hubei Daily*. http://news.cnhubei.com/xw/hb/es/201705/t3838587.shtml

Hu, R. (2007). *Top anti-tiger heroes*. http://china.rednet.cn/c/2007/11/28/1383478.htm

Hu, T. & Wang, T. (2020). Wuhan people with other serious illness: Dying in the gap. *The Red Star News*. https://news.sina.com.cn/o/2020-03-15/doc-iimxyqwa0709938.shtml

Huang, Y. (2012). GONGOs got 60% of all the donations in China. *Beijing Times*. https://china.huanqiu.com/article/9CaKrnJu6s1

Hudson, H. E. (2013). *From rural village to global village: Telecommunications for development in the information age*. Routledge.

Huesca, R. (2001). Conceptual contributions of new social movements to development communication research. *Communication Theory*, *11*(4), 415–433.

Huesca, R. (2003). Participatory approaches to communication for development. In B. Mody (Ed.), *International and Development Communication: A 21st Century Perspective* (pp. 209–226). Sage Publications.

Hughes, C. R., & Wacker, G. (2003). *China and the Internet: politics of the digital leap forward* (Vol. 37). RoutledgeCurzon.

Inagaki, N. (2007). *Communicating the impact of communication for development: Recent trends in empirical research*. World Bank.

Instant messaging. (2023, May 30). In *Wikipedia*. https://en.wikipedia.org/wiki/Instant_messaging

International Covenant on Economic, Social and Cultural Rights, December 16, 1966. https://www.ohchr.org/en/instruments-mechanisms/instruments/international-covenant-economic-social-and-cultural-rights

International Telecommunication Union. (1998). *World telecommunication development report, 1998*. http://www.itu.int/ITU-D/ict/publications/wtdr_98/index.html

International Telecommunication Union. (2006). *Trends in telecommunication reform, 1999*. https://doi.org/https://doi.org/http://handle.itu.int/11.1002/pub/807b3d53-en

International Telecommunication Union. (2017). *Data explore*. http://www.itu.int/ITU-D/ict/statistics/explorer/index.html

International Telecommunication Union. (2022). *ITU statistics*. https://www.itu.int/en /ITU-D/Statistics/Pages/stat/default.aspx

Investigation to hold those officials involved in the Tiger Gate event accountable should be started. (2008). *Beijing News*. news.21cn.com/today/topic/2008/02/22/4374925.shtml

It is shameful to cover up or manipulate truth. (2007, November 16). *The Southern Metropolis Daily*. http://news.xinhuanet.com/comments/2007-11/18/content_7098023.htm

Jacobson, T. L. (2003). Participatory communication for social change: The relevance of the theory of communicative action. *Annals of the International Communication Association, 27*(1), 87–123.

James, J. (2005). Technological blending in the age of the internet: A developing country perspective. *Telecommunications Policy, 29*(4), 285–296. https://doi.org/10.1016/j .telpol.2004.11.010

Jenkins, H. (2006). *Convergence culture: Where old and new media collide*. New York University Press.

Jia, W. (2007, December 11). New progress in Tiger Gate: Lawyer Hao Jinsong sued the National Forestry Administration. *Procuratorate Daily*. http://society.people.com.cn /GB/1062/6637466.html

Jiang, Y. (2012). *Cyber-Nationalism in China Challenging Western media portrayals of internet censorship in China*. University of Adelaide Press.

Jiang, Y. (2017). *Social media and e-diplomacy in China: Scrutinizing the power of Weibo*. Palgrave Macmillan. http://search.ebscohost.com/login.aspx?direct=true&scope =site&db=nlebk&db=nlabk&AN=1363055

Jiaxin, Z. (2007). Top 10 internet events in 2007. *Nanfang Daily*. http://tech.sina.com .cn/i/2007-12-21/10541928518.shtml

Jing, W. (2014a). *About NGO2.0 China*. http://ngo2ochina.wikispaces.com/about

Jing, W. (2014b). *From Cambridge to Shenzheng: An Update of NGO2.0*. https://civic .mit.edu/blog/jing/from-cambridge-to-shenzhen-an-update-of-ngo2o

Jinsong, H. (2007). *Hao sued Zhou Zhenglong*. http://blog.sina.com.cn/s/blog _449d613d01000ceg.html

Johns Hopkins University. (2020). *COVID-19 dashboard*. https://coronavirus.jhu.edu /map.html

Johnson, L. (2020, March 13). China bought the West time with the coronavirus. The West squandered it. *The New York Times*. https://www.nytimes.com/2020/03/13 /opinion/china-response-china.html

Johnston, J. M., & Romzek, B. S. (1999). Contracting and accountability in state Medicaid reform: Rhetoric, theories, and reality. *Public administration review, 59*(5), 383–399. http://www.jstor.org/stable/977422

Jun, L. (2010). Anti-tiger netizens: Their targets are more than the tiger (the South China tiger photos). *Southern Weekly*. http://www.infzm.com/content/54107

Kanbur, R., & Zhang, X. (1999). Which regional inequality? The evolution of rural–urban and inland–coastal inequality in China from 1983 to 1995. *Journal of Comparative Economics, 27*(4), 686–701. https://doi.org/10.1006/jcec.1999.1612

Kellow, C. L., & Steeves, H. L. (1998). The role of radio in the Rwandan genocide. *Journal of Communication, 48*(3), 107–128.

Kharpal, A. (2019, November 11). *Alibaba breaks Singles Day record with more than $38 billion in sales*. CNBC. https://www.cnbc.com/2019/11/11/alibaba-singles-day-2019 -record-sales-on-biggest-shopping-day.html

Kharpal, A. (2021, November 11). *Alibaba, JD smash Singles Day record with $139 billion of sales and focus on "social responsibility."* CNBC. https://www.cnbc.com/2021/11/12 /china-singles-day-2021-alibaba-jd-hit-record-139-billio

Kim, Y. Y. (2005). Inquiry in intercultural and development communication. *Journal of Communication, 55*(3), 554–577.

King, G., Pan, J., & Roberts, M. E. (2013). How censorship in China allows government criticism but silences collective expression. *American Political Science Review, 107*(2), 326–343.

Kleine, D. (2013). *Technologies of choice? ICTs, development, and the capabilities approach.* MIT Press.

Kluver, R., & Yang, C. (2005). The internet in China: A meta-review of research. *The Information Society, 21*(4), 301–308.

Koesel, K., Bunce, V., & Weiss, J. (2020). *Citizens and the state in authoritarian regimes: Comparing China and Russia.* Oxford University Press.

Kostka, G., & Zhang, C. (2018). *Tightening the grip: Environmental governance under Xi Jinping.*

Kuai, L. (2009). Hao Jinsong, the citizen who disobeys. *The Southern People Weekly.* https://news.ifeng.com/society/5/200911/1110_2579_1429523_3.shtml

Kun, L. (2020). *Please also leave non-COVID-19 patients a path for survival.* Xinhua News Agency. http://www.xinhuanet.com/2020-02/17/c_1125583813.htm

Kwapong, O. (2007). Problems of policy formulation and implementation: The case of ICT use in rural women's empowerment in Ghana. *International Journal of Education and Development using ICT, 3*(2), 68–88.

Lake, R., & Makori, A. (2020). *The digital divide among students during COVID-19: Who has access? Who doesn't?* https://www.crpe.org/thelens/digital-divide-among -students-during-covid-19-who-has-access-who-doesnt

Langley, D., & van den Broek, T. (2010). *Exploring social media as a driver of sustainable behaviour: Case analysis and policy implications.* http://microsites.oii.ox.ac.uk /ipp2010/system/files/IPP2010_Langley_vandenBroek_Paper.pdf

Langziya. (2008). *The astonishing news of the shutting down of the South China Tiger forum.* http://blog.sina.com.cn/s/blog_539972480100 8ygo.html

Lao, B. (2007). *Questioning South China Tiger photos with scientific methods.* http:// forum.xitek.com/thread-479929-1-1-1.html

laoliu. (2007). *Is Tiger Gate a fraud?* http://www.wildchina.cn/bbs/thread-1657-2-1.html

Lavely, W. (2001). First impressions from the 2000 census of China. *Population and Development Review, 27*(4), 755–769.

Lee, L. O. F. (1987). *Voices from the iron house: A study of Lu Xun.* Indiana University Press.

Lei, K. (2020). *Please give non-COVID patients with other serious illnesses a path to survival.* XinhuaNet. http://www.rmzxb.com.cn/c/2020-02-17/2522380.shtml

Lei, Z. (2013, March 28). *Food poison incidents broke out frequently—Who actually benefited from the National Nutrition Project.* RedNet. http://views.ce.cn/view/ent /201305/28/t20130528_796770.shtml

Lennie, J., & Tacchi, J. (2013). *Evaluating communication for development: A framework for social change.* Routledge.

Lerner, D. (1958). *The passing of traditional society: Modernizing the Middle East.* Free Press. http://hollis.harvard.edu/?itemid=%7Clibrary/m/aleph%7C001060776

Lerner, D., & Schramm, W. L. (Eds.). (1967). *Communication and change in the developing countries.* East-West Center Press.

Lessig, L. (2005). *Creatives face a closed net.* http://www.ft.com/intl/cms/s/2/d55dfe52 -77d2-11da-9670-0000779e2340.html#axzz1h1y0FGiE

Lévy, P. (1997). *Collective intelligence: Mankind's emerging world in cyberspace.* Plenum Trade.

Li, H. (2018). *The reciprocal relation between foundations and grassroots NGOs*. Xinhuanet. http://www.xinhuanet.com/gongyi/2018-06/11/c_129891739.htm

Li, H., Ji, N., & Hou, Q. (2007). Shaanxi Forestry Department stated they have never questioned the authenticity of the South China tiger photos. *Three Qin Daily*. http://news.sina.com.cn/c/2007-10-31/065414201100.shtml

Li, J. (2016). Listen 2.0: Training materials for the Web 2.0 Workshop of the NGO 2.0 Project.

Li, K. (2007). Government should not be indifferent to the result of the grassroots investigation of the Tiger Gate event. *Information Times*. http://news.xinhuanet.com/newmedia/2007-12/04/content_7196303.htm

Li, L. (2012). Volunteer teacher exposed the suffering of the primary school students in Fenghuang Hunan province. *China Education Post*. http://edu.ifeng.com/news/detail_2012_11/29/19634540_0.shtml

Li, L. (2019). *Zoning China: Online Video, Popular Culture, and the State*. MIT Press.

Li, Y., Wang, X., Zhu, Q., & Zhao, H. (2014). Assessing the spatial and temporal differences in the impacts of factor allocation and urbanization on urban–rural income disparity in China, 2004–2010. *Habitat International*, *42*, 76–82. https://doi.org/https://doi.org/10.1016/j.habitatint.2013.10.009

Li, Z. (2017). Ye Dawei: Building a balanced ecosphere in the nonprofit sector. *China Philanthropist*. http://gongyi.sina.com.cn/gyzx/qt/2017-03-02/doc-ifycaafm4801926.shtml

Liang, Y. (2020, March 16). *Report from the Stand by Her Action*. https://zhuanlan.zhihu.com/p/113631506

Liao, J., & Feng, G. (2020). *The Wuhan government announced the list of hospitals that admit non-COVID-19 patients*. Xinhua News Agency. http://www.gov.cn/xinwen/2020-02/23/content_5482215.htm

Lie, R. (2008). Rural HIV/AIDS communication/intervention: From using models to using frameworks and common principles. *Communication for development and social change*, 279.

Lieberthal, K. G., & Lampton, D. M. (Eds.). (1992). *Bureaucracy, politics, and decision making in post-Mao China*. University of California Press.

Liebman, B. L. (2011). The Media and the Courts: Towards Competitive Supervision? *The China Quarterly*, *208*, 833–850. https://doi.org/10.1017/S0305741011001020

Lim, L. (2012). For China's "left-behind kids," a free lunch. *NPR*. http://www.npr.org/2012/01/24/145521090/for-chinas-left-behind-kids-a-free-lunch

Lin, C. (2006). *The transformation of Chinese socialism*. Duke University Press.

Lintern, S. (2020, March 30). Coronavirus: Italian doctors warn protective equipment vital to prevent healthcare system collapse. *Independent*. https://www.independent.co.uk/news/health/coronavirus-italy-doctors-nhs-hospitals-ppe-a9435891.html

Liu, D. (2008). *Could the South China tiger incident be selected for the top 10 news of 2008?* Enorth.com.cn. http://news.enorth.com.cn/system/2008/12/23/003836597.shtml

Liu, F. (2011). *Urban youth in China* (Vol. 10). Routledge.

Liu, J. (2016). Digital media, cycle of contention, and sustainability of environmental activism: The case of anti-PX protests in China. *Mass Communication and Society*, *19*(5), 604–625.

Liu, J., Yao, X., & Huang, X. (2012). The role switching of journalist Fei Deng. *Nanfang Daily*. http://news.xinhuanet.com/edu/2012-12/26/c_124147788.htm

Liu, L. (2014). *Speech in the spring 2014's coordinating meeting for the National Nutrition Project* [speech]. Coordinating Meeting for the National Nutrition Project. http://www.moe.gov.cn/jyb_xwfb/moe_176/201404/t20140411_167079.html

Liu, L. (2017, October). *The new era: The promotion of the School Milk of China Project* [speech]. China Students Nutrition Summit. http://www.sohu.com/a/204528166_162422

Liu, M. (2020, January 31). An interview with the so-called "rumor spreader" doctor: I am reminding the public to pay attention to the spread of COVID-19. *Beijing News.* http://www.bjnews.com.cn/feature/2020/01/31/682076.html

Liu, S., & Wu, Z. (2017). For rural children, how to grow healthy and strong. *Guangming Daily.* http://epaper.gmw.cn/gmrb/html/2017-01/12/nw.D110000gmrb_20170112_1 -14.htm

Liu, T. (2007). *In Tiger Gate, we need this kind of people who really take it serious.* http://opinion.people.com.cn/GB/8213/111733/111734/6582941.html

Liu, W. (2017). *Free Lunch Project brought about changes to hungry childhood.* Xinhua News Agency.

Li Wenliang: Coronavirus death of Wuhan doctor sparks anger. (2020, February 7). BBC. https://www.bbc.com/news/world-asia-china-51409801

Loges, W. E., & Jung, J.-Y. (2001). Exploring the digital divide: Internet connectedness and age. *Communication Research, 28*(4), 536–562.

Lu. C. (2015). *Gu Jicheng: School Mile is Indispensable in the National Nutrition Project. China Education Daily.* http://edu.people.com.cn/n/2015/0607/c1053 -27115051.html

Lu, M. (2009). *The origin and effects of the project to increase the nutrition status of boarding school students in rural area.* http://www.cdrf.org.cn/plus/list.php?tid=65

Lu, X. (1922). Preface to *Call to Arms.* https://www.marxists.org/archive/lu-xun/1922 /12/03.htm

Lu, X. (1926). *In Memory of Miss Liu Hezhen.* https://www.marxists.org/archive/lu-xun /1926/04/01.htm

Lu, X. (1927). *Silent China* [speech]. Hong Kong.

Lu, X. (2007a, November 30). Tiger Gate, another disappointing result? *People's Daily.* http://news.eastday.com/c/20071130/u1a3259615.html

Lu, X. (2007b, December 4). Tiger Gate event: From the debate over real and fake to the debate over the meaning of the event. *people.com.cn.* http://opinion.people.com .cn/GB/6611737.html

Lu, X. (2012). *Deputy Minister Lu Xin's speech on National Nutritional Project.* http:// old.moe.gov.cn//publicfiles/business/htmlfiles/moe/s6335/201209/142764.html

Ma, J. (2013). The NGO 2.0 Project: Facilitate the dreams of the grassroots. *Southern Metropolis Daily.* http://www.chinadevelopmentbrief.org.cn/news-6801.html

Ma, X. (2020, January 21). From "no obvious evidence of human-to-human spreading" to "human to human spreading": Review of the first 20 days of the COVID-19 crisis. *China Business News.* https://www.yicai.com/news/100476157.html

MacKinnon, R. (2008). Flatter world and thicker walls? Blogs, censorship and civic discourse in China. *Public Choice, 134*(1–2), 31–46.

MacKinnon, R. (2009). China's censorship 2.0: How companies censor bloggers. *First Monday, 14*(2).

Madanda, A., Kabonesa, C., & Bantebya-Kyomuhendo, G. (2007). Challenges to women's empowerment through ICTs: The case of Makerere University. *Agenda, 21*(71), 81–88.

Mailk, K. (2020, February 2). Locked-down Wuhan and why we always overplay the threat of the new. *The Guardian.* https://www.theguardian.com/commentisfree /2020/feb/02/coronavirus-wuhan-lockdown-breeding-ground-fear-stigma

Maker culture. (2023, March 16). In *Wikipedia.* https://en.wikipedia.org/wiki/Maker _culture

Mansell, R., & Wehn, U. (1998). *Knowledge societies: Information technology for sustainable development*. Oxford University Press.

Markus, M. L. (1987). Toward a "critical mass" theory of interactive media: Universal access, interdependence and diffusion. *Communication Research*, *14*(5), 491–511.

Martin, B. (2007). Activism, social and political. *Encyclopedia of activism and social justice*, *1*, 19–27.

McAnany, E. G. (2012). *Saving the world: A Brief history of communication for development and social change*. University of Illinois Press.

McConnell, S. (2000, May). A champion in our midst: Lessons Learned from the impacts of NGO's use of the internet. *Electronic Journal of Information Systems in Developing Countries*, *2*(1), 1–15. https://doi.org/10.1002/j.1681-4835.2000.tb00012.x

McDonald, T. (2016). *Social media in rural China*. UCL Press.

McKee, N., Manoncourt, E., Saik Yoon, C., & Carnegie, R. (2000). *Involving people, evolving behaviour*. Southbound and UNICEF.

McNeil Jr., D. G. (2020). Inside China's all-out war on the coronavirus. *The New York Times*. https://www.nytimes.com/2020/03/04/health/coronavirus-china-aylward.html

Melkote, S. R. (Ed.). (2012). *Development communication in directed social change: A reappraisal of theory and practice*. Asian Media Information and Communication Centre (AMIC) and Wee Kim Wee School of Communication and Information, Nanyang Technological University (WKWSCI-NTU).

Melkote, S. R., & Steeves, H. L. (2001). *Communication for development in the Third World: Theory and practice for empowerment*. SAGE Publications India.

Melkote, S. R., & Steeves, H. L. (2015a). *Communication for development: Theory and practice for empowerment and social justice*. SAGE Publications India.

Melkote, S. R., & Steeves, H. L. (2015b). Place and role of development communication in directed social change: A review of the field. *Journal of Multicultural Discourses*, *10*(3), 385–402.

Meng, B. (2010). Moving beyond democratization: A thought piece on the China internet research agenda. *International Journal of Communication*, *4*, 501–508.

Mertha, A. (2009a). "Fragmented authoritarianism 2.0": Political pluralization in the Chinese policy process. *The China Quarterly*, *200*, 995–1012.

Mertha, A. (2009b). Author's response: China's water warriors—Returning to the scene of battle. *Asia Policy*, *8*(1), 143–150.

Mertha, A., and Brødsgaard, K. E. (2017). In Brødsgaard, K. E. (Ed.), *Chinese Politics as Fragmented Authoritarianism: Earthquakes, energy and environment* (pp. 1–14). Routledge.

Miao, Y. (2017). *Interview with Miao Yu: Voice of ministers*. https://www.miit-icdc.org/info/1009/2019.htm

Mina, A. X. (2014). Batman, pandaman and the blind man: A case study in social change memes and internet censorship in China. *Journal of Visual Culture*, *13*(3), 359–375.

Ming, X. (2012). *The transparency of the Free Lunch Fund attracted increasing amount of donations*. Xinhuanet.com. http://www.people.com.cn/24hour/n/2012/1101/c25408-19461179.html

Ministry of Agriculture. (2013). Regarding the change of the management of the School Milk of China Project. http://www.moa.gov.cn/govpublic/NKJ/201309/t20130917_3607873.htm

Ministry of Civil Affairs of the PRC (2020). *Statistic report of 2019*. https://www.mca.gov.cn/n156/n189/index.html

Ministry of Culture of the PRC. (2009). *Rural Cultural Centers project.* https://zwgk .mct.gov.cn/zfxxgkml/ggfw/202012/t20201205_916520.html

Ministry of Education. (2016a, February 26). *Response to the No. 8952 advice from the Third Plenary Session of the 12th National People's Congress.* http://www.moe.gov.cn /jyb_xxgk/xxgk_jyta/jyta_ddb/201602/t20160226_230761.html

Ministry of Education. (2016b, June 29). *Report on the implementation of the National NutritionProject in Hebei Province in 2015.* http://www.moe.gov.cn/jyb_xwfb/xw_zt /moe_357/s6211/s6329/s6466/201606/t20160629_270102.html

Ministry of Education. (2017a, March 3). *Report on the implementation of the National Nutrition Project.* https://www.gov.cn/xinwen/2017-03/02/content_5172534.htm

Ministry of Education. (2017b, March 9). *Report on the implementation of the National Nutrition Project in Hebei Province in 2016.* http://www.moe.gov.cn/jyb_xwfb/xw _zt/moe_357/s6211/s6329/s6466/201703/t20170309_298857.html

Ministry of Education & Ministry of Agriculture. (2002). *Regarding the management of the School Milk of China Project.* http://www.gov.cn/gongbao/content/2003/content _62172.htm

Ministry of Education & Ministry of Finance. (2013, January 4). *Notice regarding enhancing the construction of the school kitchens and dining rooms in the National NutritionProject.* http://www.moe.gov.cn/srcsite/A05/s7052/201212/t20121213_181284.html

Ministry of Finance of the PRC. (2016). *Guideline for supporting the development of NGOs through purchasing services from NGOs.* http://www.mof.gov.cn/gp/xxgkml /zhs/201612/t20161229_2510301.html

Ministry of Finance of the PRC & Ministry of Industry and Information Technology. (2018). *Notice on the subsidy for the Universal Service Pilot Projects.* http://www.mof .gov.cn/mofhome/mof/zhengwuxinxi/caizhengwengao/wg201901/wg2019011 /20190A5/t20190506_3245936.html

Ministry of Foreign Affairs of PRC. (2015). *Report on China's implementation of the Millennium Development Goals (2000–2015).* http://www.cn.undp.org/content /china/en/home/library/mdg/mdgs-report-2015-.html

Ministry of Health of the People's Republic of China. (2012). *The report on the nutritional status of children under 6 in China.* http://www.camcn-cns.org/2-report-c.pdf

Ministry of Industry and Information Technology. (2004). *MIIT's policy regarding Connecting Every Village Project in 2004.* http://www.miit.gov.cn/n11293472 /n11293877/n11302021/n13046788/13047591.html

Ministry of Industry and Information Technology. (2008). *MIIT's policy in the 11th Five Year Plan of China.* http://www.miit.gov.cn/n11293472/n11293832/n11294072 /n11302465/11641609.html

Ministry of Industry and Information Technology. (2009). *2008 report of Connecting Every Village Project.* http://dzs.miit.gov.cn/n11293472/n11293877/n11302021 /n13046743/13047451.html

Ministry of Industry and Information Technology. (2011a). *All the goals for the Connecting Every Village Project in the 11th Five-Year Plan have been achieved.* http://www.miit.gov.cn/n11293472/n11293877/n11302021/n13735246/13735598.html

Ministry of Industry and Information Technology. (2011b). *Almost 100% of Xiang already have access to the internet.* http://www.miit.gov.cn/n11293472/n11293877 /n11302021/n13735246/13735577.html

Ministry of Industry and Information Technology. (2011c). *In the period of the 11th Five Year Plan, China has invested 50 billion yuan to connect every village with phones.* http://www.miit.gov.cn/n973401/n974219/n974221/c3787556/content.html

Ministry of Industry and Information Technology. (2011d). *Introduction of the Connecting Every Village Project.* http://www.miit.gov.cn/n11293472/n11293877/n11302021/13733363.html

Ministry of Industry and Information Technology. (2011e). *100% of administrative village have access to mobile phone or landline phone service.* http://www.miit.gov.cn/n11293472/n11293877/n11302021/n13735246/13735591.html

Ministry of Industry and Information Technology. (2011f). *Plenary assembly to summarize the Connecting Every Village Project in the 11th Five-Year Plan was held.* http://www.miit.gov.cn/n11293472/n11293877/n11302021/n13046758/13734203.html

Ministry of Industry and Information Technology. (2011g). *Serving the society and serving the development are the fundamental principles of the Connecting Every Village Project.* http://www.miit.gov.cn/n11293472/n11293877/n11302021/n13735261/13735690.html

Ministry of Industry and Information Technology. (2011h). *The strategy of the Connecting Every Village Project.* http://www.miit.gov.cn/n11293472/n11293877/n11302021/n13735261/13735676.html

Ministry of Industry and Information Technology. (2012). *The three phases of the Connecting Every Village Project and the goals for every phase.* http://www.miit.gov.cn/n11293472/n11293877/n11302021/index.html

Ministry of Industry and Information Technology. (2018a). *Guideline for the implementation of the Universal Service Pilot Projects in 2018.* http://www.miit.gov.cn/n1146295/n1652858/n1652930/n3757020/c6204576/part/6204606.doc

Ministry of Industry and Information Technology. (2018b). *MIIT video conference on the national Universal Service Pilot Projects.* http://www.gov.cn/xinwen/2018-07/07/content_5304390.htm

Ministry of Industry and Information Technology. (2019). Guideline for the implementation of the "Universal Service Pilot Projects." http://www.miit.gov.cn/n1146295/n1652858/n1652930/n3757020/c6791263/part/6791346.doc

Ministry of Industry and Information Technology. (2020). *Report on the telecommunication field in 2019.* http://www.miit.gov.cn/n1146312/n1146904/n1648372/c7696411/content.html

Ministry of Industry and Information Technology & Ministry of Finance. (2015). Announcement about the "Universal Service Pilot Projects." https://www.miit.gov.cn/jgsj/txs/wlfz/art/2020/art_41a4dfd7a5b34db39cd9d67f4eb21476.html

Ministry of Industry and Information Technology & Ministry of Finance. (2018). *Guidelines for the application for the universal service pilots projects in 2018.* https://www.miit.gov.cn/zwgk/zcwj/wjfb/txy/art/2020/art_b7fa6556547643ee9fff04fed63cd9f2.html

Morley, D. (2013). On living in a techno-globalised world: Questions of history and geography. *Telematics and Informatics, 30*(2), 61–65. https://doi.org/http://dx.doi.org/10.1016/j.tele.2012.08.001

Mossberger, K., Tolbert, C. J., & McNeal, R. S. (2007). *Digital citizenship: The Internet, society, and participation.* MIT Press.

The most updated nationwide data of COVID-19 as of January 31. (2020, January 31). *Huanqiu.* https://3w.huanqiu.com/a/c36dc8/9CaKrnKp7Oq?agt=8

The most updated report on COVID-19 on February 5. (2020, February 4). *Huanqiu.* https://china.huanqiu.com/article/9CaKrnKpcpz

Morris, N. (2003). A comparative analysis of the diffusion and participatory models in development communication. *Communication Theory, 13*(2), 225–248.

Mozur, P. (2017). China's internet censors play a tougher game of cat and mouse. *The New York Times*. https://www.nytimes.com/2017/08/03/business/china-internet-censorship.html

Mujahid, Y. H. (2002). Digital opportunity initiative for Pakistan. *The Electronic Journal of Information Systems in Developing Countries, 8*(1), 1–14.

Myers, M. (2008). Local radio: fostering community development or ethnic hatred? Donor dilemmas and perspectives from Rwanda, DR Congo and Kenya. Media and Development in Africa: CAMRI Conference, University of Westminster, London,

Najam, A. (2000). The four-C's of third sector–government relations. *Nonprofit management and leadership, 10*(4), 375–396.

National Bureau of Statistics of China. (2011). *China statistical yearbook (2010)*. China Statistics Press.

National Bureau of Statistics of China. (2016). *China statistical yearbook (2015)*. China Statistics Press.

National Health and Family Planning Commission & Ministry of Health of the People's Republic of China. (2015). *2015 nutrition and chronic disease report on Chinese residents*. http://www.nhfpc.gov.cn/

National Health Commission of PRC. (2020a). *National COVID-19 brief report*. http://www.gov.cn/xinwen/2020-02/06/content_5475116.htm

National Health Commission of PRC. (2020b). *On the dispatch of health worker teams to Hubei*. https://news.sina.cn/2020-03-03/detail-iimxxstf6071691.d.html

National Student Nutrition Commission. (2012a). *The National Student Nutrition Commission issued a notice to enhance the management and transparency of its project*. http://www.moe.gov.cn/publicfiles/business/htmlfiles/moe/s5987/201212/146094.html

National Student Nutrition Commission. (2012b). *The notice regarding opening Weibo account for the national nutritional project*. http://www.moe.edu.cn/publicfiles/business/htmlfiles/moe/s6366/201207/139500.html

NCP Life Support Network. (2020a, January 23). *Recruitment announcement of professional health workers for the telehealth project for COVID-19 patients*. https://shimo.im/forms/rqKXyh3GQjXkPp6h/fill

NCP Life Support Network. (2020b, February 4). *NCP Life Support Network's Weibo on its telehealth project*. https://www.weibo.com/6892480749/IsDX47CqN?type=comment#_rnd1593274505739

NCP Life Support Network. (2020c, February 5). *Headlined message of NCP Life Support Network's official Weibo*. https://www.weibo.com/6892480749/IsPOREkZK?type=repost#_rnd1593295810086

NCP Life Support Network. (2020d, February 7). *What has happened in the first 20 days of the crisis?* https://www.weibo.com/6892480749/It9iH4yNp?type=repost

NCP Life Support Network. (2020e, February 18). *The focus of our telehealth service will shift to people with other diseases*. https://weibo.com/6892480749/IuLEr3TRP?type=repost

NCP Life Support Network. (2020f, March 12). *The five volunteers of the Little Angel Group called thousands of times to Wuhan*. https://www.weibo.com/6892480749/IyeUllbi6?type=repost#_rnd1593359748039

NCP Life Support Network. (2020g, March 12). *What has happened in the Wuhan Central Hospital?* https://www.weibo.com/6892480749/IyhZObO38?type=repost#_rnd1593408052756

Netizens found that the origin of the South China tiger photos is a New Year picture. (2007). 163.com. http://news.163.com/07/1116/12/3TE1A6D50001124J.html

New Media Action Lab. (2009). *Project application to foundation, Beijing* (unpublished material).

New Media Action Lab. (2011). *Follow-up survey of the Web 2.0 workshops.* https://www .ngo20.cn/6Ng, J. (2013). *Blocked on Weibo: What gets suppressed on China's version of Twitter (and why).* The New Press.

NGO 2.0 Project. (2018a). *Business presentation.* NGO 2.0 Project.

NGO 2.0 Project. (2018b). *Communication and media plan.* NGO 2.0 Project.

NGO 2.0 Project. (2019). *About our projects.* http://www.ngo20.org/

NGO 2.0 Project. (2019). *2019 ICT for Good Summit.* http://www.ict4good.ngo20.org/

NGO 2.0 Project. (2021). *The picture of the NGO2.0 Project.* http://ngo20en.sxl.cn/

NGOCN. (2018). *Report on the policy environment of Chinese NGOs.* http://www .chinadevelopmentbrief.org.cn/news-21524.html

Nolan, P., & White, G. (1984). Urban bias, rural bias or state bias? Urban–rural relations in post-revolutionary China. *The Journal of Development Studies, 20*(3), 52–81.

Non-Profit Incubator, Swedish International Development Agency. (2011). *2011 report on funders and NGOs in China's nonprofit sector.* http://china.caixin.com/2011-03-07 /100233550.html

Norris, P. (2001). *Digital divide: Civic engagement, information poverty, and the internet worldwide.* Cambridge University Press.

North, D. C. (1990). *Institutions, institutional change, and economic performance.* Cambridge University Press. http://catdir.loc.gov/catdir/toc/cam025/90001673.html

NPO Development Center Shanghai. (2014). *Report on the development of Chinese NPOs.* http://www.naradafoundation.org/file/download/id/8afb7a4753f48fe06a553 767519e1796

Obregon, R., & Mosquera, M. (2005). Participatory and cultural challenges for research and practice in health communication. *Media & glocal change: Rethinking communication for development.* Clacso.

O'Brien, K. J., & Li, L. (2006). *Rightful resistance in rural China.* Cambridge University Press.

Officials from Shaanxi Forestry Department support the peasant who has taken the South China tiger photos. (2007, November 3). Sina.com.cn. http://news.sina.com.cn/c /2007-11-03/234914228446.shtml

Ogan, C. L., Bashir, M., Camaj, L., Luo, Y., Gaddie, B., Pennington, R., Rana, S., & Salih, M. (2009). Development communication: The state of research in an era of ICTs and globalization. *International Communication Gazette, 71*(8), 655–670.

163.com exposed how they bought the tiger photos. (2007). *Beijing Times.* http://society .people.com.cn/GB/6597155.html

Online anti-tiger activists. (2007). *Southern Metropolis Weekly.* http://past.nbweekly .com/Print/Article/3768_2.shtml

Optical brightener. (2022). In *Wikipedia.* https://en.wikipedia.org/wiki/Optical _brightener

Pan, C. (2007). Best anti-tiger activists. *Southern Metropolis Weekly, 172,* 19. http://past .nbweekly.com/Print/Article/3769_0.shtml

Pan, R. (2007a, November 28). Most Xian residents believe that the South China tiger photos are real. *Nianjing Morning Post.* http://news.sina.com.cn/c/2007-11-28 /094514404927.shtml

Pan, R. (2007b, December 30). Breaking news on the tiger from Zhenping: Tiger footprints and tiger cub skeleton are found. *Nianjing Morning Post.* http://blog.sina .com.cn/s/blog_47c509f801008kx9.html~type=v5_one&label=rela_prevarticle

Pan, R. (2008, January 4). Tiger Gate event: Cell phone log shows Zhou's neighbor lied to CCTV reporters. *Nianjing Morning Post.* http://finance.aweb.com.cn/2008/1/4 /2252008010423055721o.html

Pan, R., & Bian, N. (2007, December 2). Zhou Zhenglong is looking forward to searching for tigers after the first snow. *Nianjing Morning Post.* http://news.sina.com .cn/c/2007-12-02/074114431816.shtml

Pan, W. (2003). Toward a consultative rule of law regime in China. *Journal of Contemporary China, 12*(34), 3. http://search.ebscohost.com/login.aspx?direct=true&db =aph&AN=9040360&site=ehost-live&scope=site

Pan, X. (2017). Wang Jinghai advised to implement the Milk Drinking Project comprehensively to improve the physical health of the nation. *Takung Pao.* http:// finance.takungpao.com/gscy/q/2017/0305/3427317.html

Panzhihua xydz. (2007). *Reply to Smallfish's post—The origin photo of the South China tiger photos have been found.* http://bbs.tianya.cn/post-free-1044130-1.shtml

Pei, M. (1998). Chinese civic associations: An empirical analysis. *Modern China, 24*(3), 285–318. http://www.jstor.org/stable/189406

Peña-López, I. (2016). *World development report 2016: Digital dividends.* World Bank. https://documents1.worldbank.org/curated/en/896971468194972881/pdf/102725 -PUB-Replacement-PUBLIC.pdf

Pew Research Center. (2015). *Mobile messaging and social media 2015.* http://www .pewinternet.org/2015/08/19/mobile-messaging-and-social-media-2015/

Pham, S. (2019). *Singles Day sales for Alibaba top $38 billion, breaking last year's record.* https://www.cnn.com/2019/11/10/tech/singles-day-sales-alibaba/index.html

Pieterse, J. N. (2010). *Development theory.* Sage.

Primary school students poured milk from the National Nutrition Lunch Project into a street sewer. (2018, December 22). 163.com. https://www.163.com/dy/article /E3KOC8K105461JWC.html

Problematic school milk products in JiangSu. (2019, March 19). *China Youth Daily.* http://zqb.cyol.com/html/2019-03/19/nw.D110000zgqnb_20190319_5-01.htm

Proenza, F. J. (2015). *Public access ICT across cultures diversifying participation in the network society.* MIT Press. http://ieeexplore.ieee.org/servlet/opac?bknumber=7120884

Przeworski, A., Stokes, S. C., & Manin, B. (1999). *Democracy, accountability, and representation.* Cambridge University Press.

Qiang, C. Z.-W. (2007). *China's information revolution: Managing the economic and social transformation.* The World Bank.

Qiming, Q. (2018). *Stories from far away* (episode 2). Beijing, Qiu Qiming Studio. https://weibo.com/p/10080878339afbf2b6ceb457d440918a331e6d?k=%E8%BF%9C %E6%96%B9%E7%AC%AC%E4%BA%8C%E5%AD%A3%E4%B9%8B%E9%82%A 3%E4%BA%9B%E4%BA%BA&from=501&_from_=huati_topic

Qiu, J. L. (2009). *Working-class network society: Communication technology and the information have-less in urban China.* MIT Press.

Qiu, J. L., & Bu, W. (2013). China ICT studies: A review of the field, 1989–2012. *China Review, 13*(2), 123–152.

Qiu, J. L., & Chan, J. M. (2004). China Internet studies: A review of the field. *The academy and the Internet,* 275–307.

Race for China's $5.5tn mobile payment market hots up. (2017). *Financial Times.* https://www.ft.com/content/e3477778-2969-11e7-bc4b-5528796fe35c

Realtime national COVID-19 data. (2020). Ifeng News. Retrieved January 23, 2020, from http://news.ifeng.com/c/special/7tPlDSzDgVk

Report on Chinese dairy products. (2017). AskCI.com. http://top.askci.com/news/20170827/141804106353.shtml

Richardson, W. (2006). *Blogs, wikis, podcasts, and other powerful web tools for classrooms.* Corwin Press. http://hollis.harvard.edu/?itemid=%7Clibrary/m/aleph%7C0101o7654

Ridan, X., & Yingyan, X. (2008). *From the visa application refusal event to the South China tiger event: A new form of democracy is emerging in cyberspace.* http://media.people.com.cn/GB/7507640.html

Roberts, M. E. (2018). *Censored: Distraction and diversion inside China's Great Firewall.* Princeton University Press.

Rogers, E. M. (1962). *Diffusion of innovations.* Free Press.

Rogers, E. M. (1967). The passing of the dominant paradigm: Reflections on diffusion research. In D. Lerner & W. L. Schramm (Eds.), *Communication and change in the developing countries* (pp. 49–52). East-West Center Press.

Rogers, E. M. (1971). Social structure and social change. *American Behavioral Scientist, 14*(5), 767–782.

Rogers, E. M. (1976). *Communication and development: Critical perspectives.* Sage.

Rogers, E. M., & Shoemaker, F. (1983). Diffusion of innovation: A cross-cultural approach. *New York.*

Rogers, E. M., & Svenning, L. (1969). *Modernization among peasants: The impact of communication.* Holt, Rinehart and Winston, Inc.

Roland, G. (2004). Understanding institutional change: Fast-moving and slow-moving institutions. *Studies in Comparative International Development, 38*(4), 109–131.

Rostow, W. W. (1953). *The process of economic growth.* Clarendon Press.

RSS. (2023, May 30). In *Wikipedia.* https://en.wikipedia.org/wiki/RSS

Saich, T. (2000). Negotiating the state: The development of social organizations in China. *The China Quarterly* (161), 124–141.

Sancho. (2007, October 31). *Game over—Let's see who the real tiger is.* Xitek.com. http://forum.xitek.com/thread-479793-1-1-1.html

Sarfraz, M. (2014). *Computer vision and image processing in intelligent systems and multimedia technologies.* IGI Global.

Schlæger, J. (2013). *E-government in China: Technology, power and local government reform.* Routledge.

Schlæger, J., & Wang, Q. (2017). E-monitoring of public servants in China: Higher quality of government? *Journal of Chinese Governance, 2*(1), 1–19.

Schneider, F. (2018). *China's digital nationalism.* Oxford University Press. https://doi.org/10.1093/oso/9780190876791.001.0001

School Milk Project. (2015, August 5). *School Milk Project: What is the relation between the School Milk Project and the National Nutrition Project?* http://schoolmilk.cn/s/jhzx/13122716352255710022

Schramm, W. (1964). *Mass media and national development: The role of information in the developing countries.* Stanford University Press Stanford, CA.

Schwartz, J. (2004). Environmental NGOs in China: Roles and Limits. *Pacific Affairs, 77*(1), 28–49. http://www.jstor.org/stable/40022273

SeedaBetterChina. (2020, April 14). *How professional self-organized organizations have taken effective actions in the COVID-19 crisis—Using NCP Life Support Network as an example.* https://wemp.app/posts/783d3391-5221-47c2-b06b-c789fc1581d8

Selwyn, N. (2004). Reconsidering political and popular understandings of the digital divide. *New Media & Society, 6*(3), 341–362.

Servaes, J. (1999). *Communication for development: One world, multiple cultures.* Hampton Press.

Servaes, J. (2007). Harnessing the UN system into a common approach on communication for development. *International Communication Gazette, 69*(6), 483–507.

Servaes, J. (2008). *Communication for development and social change.* Sage Publications. http://hollis.harvard.edu/?itemid=%7Clibrary/m/aleph%7C011811852

Servaes, J. (2009). Communication policies, good governance and development journalism. *Communicatio: South African Journal for Communication Theory and Research, 35*(1), 50. http://www.informaworld.com/10.1080/02500160902906653

Servaes, J. (2011). *Social Change in Oxford Bibliographies.* http://www.oxfordbibliographies .com/view/document/obo-9780199756841/obo-9780199756841–0063.xml

Servaes, J. (2014). Introduction to the 3 A's. In Servaes (Ed.), *Technological determinism and social change: Communication in a tech-mad world.* Lexington Books.

Servaes, J., Carah, N., Hadlow, M., Louw, E., & Thomas, P. (2006). Communication for Development. Making a Difference—A WCCD Background Study. In *World Congress on Communication for Development: Lessons, Challenges and the Way Forward* (pp. 209–292). World Bank.

Servaes, J., & Carpentier, N. (Eds.). (2006). *Towards a sustainable information society: Deconstructing WSIS.* Intellect.

Servaes, J., Jacobson, T. L., & White, S. A. (1996). *Participatory communication for social change* (Vol. 24). Sage.

Servaes, J., & Lie, R. (2015). New challenges for communication for sustainable development and social change: A review essay. *Journal of Multicultural Discourses, 10*(1), 124–148. https://doi.org/10.1080/17447143.2014.982655

Servaes, J., & Liu, S. (Eds.) (2007). *Moving targets: Mapping the paths between communication, technology and social change in communities.* Southbound.

Servaes, J., & Malikhao, P. (2010). Advocacy strategies for health communication. *Public Relations Review, 36*(1), 42–49.

Servaes, J., & Malikhao, P. (2012). Advocacy communication for peacebuilding. *Development in Practice, 22*(2), 229–243.

Servaes, J., Polk, E., Shi, S., Reilly, D., & Yakupitijage, T. (2012). Towards a framework of sustainability indicators for 'communication for development and social change' projects. *International Communication Gazette, 74*(2), 99–123. https://doi.org/10 .1177/1748048511432598

Shaanxi Forestry Department showed the negative films of the South China tiger photos to CCTV reporters. (2007, October 30). *Hua Shang News.* http://news.sina .com.cn/c/p/2007-10-30/014112807634s.shtml

Shaanxi Forestry Department's announcement on the South China tiger photos. (2007, November 23). *ChongQing Morning Post.* https://news.cctv.com/society/20071123 /102062.shtml

Shah, H. (2010, December). Meta-research of development communication studies, 1997–2006. *Glocal Times* (15), 1–21.

Shapiro, A. L., & Richard, C. (1999). *The control revolution: How the Internet is putting individuals in charge and changing the world we know.* Perseus Books.

Shi, N. (2011). Government takes up the torch from the Free Lunch Project. *Qilu Evening Post.* http://edu.people.com.cn/GB/16083739.html

Shi, N. (2012). Delicious free lunch. *Guilin Daily.* http://www.gx.xinhuanet.com/dtzx /guilin/longsheng/2012-12/13/c_114017252.htm

Shi, S. (2013). The use of Web2.0 style technologies among Chinese civil society organizations. *Telematics and Informatics, 30*(4), 346–358.

Shieh, S. (2018). The Chinese state and overseas NGOs: From regulatory ambiguity to the overseas NGO law. *Nonprofit Policy Forum, 9*(1).

Shou Xi Ya Tou. (2007). *My criticism to the subjective reporting of Tiger Gate from the News Probe.* http://bbs.tianya.cn/post-free-1068515–1.shtml

Sina. (2020). *Help center.* http://help.sina.com.cn/comquestiondetail/view/959/

Sina. (2020). *How to update Weibo with MMS.* http://help.sina.com.cn/comquestiondetail/view/918/

65 primary school students were poisoned by milk from National Nutrition Project in Hunan. (2016). QQ.com. https://v.qq.com/x/page/w03274g33g6.html

Slater, D., & Tacchi, J. A. (2004). *Research on ICT innovations for poverty reduction.* UNESCO.

Smallfish. (2007a, November 9). *The original picture of the head of the tiger has been found.* Tianya. http://www.tianya.cn/publicforum/content/free/1/1044130.shtml

Smallfish. (2007b, November 16). *Result from human flesh search, origin of the tiger has been found!* Xitek.com. http://forum.xitek.com/thread-484393-1-1-2.html

Smallfish. (2007c, November 19). *I am tired of being coward, about the New Year picture.* Tianya. http://www.tianya.cn/publicforum/content/free/1/1052373.shtml

Smallfish. (2007d, November 21). *Apology from Smallfish.* Tianya. http://www.tianya.cn/publicforum/content/free/1/1054097.shtml

Smallfish. (2008, June 28). *Shaanxi can't solve the problem of the Tiger Gate scandal by itself.* Tianya. http://www.tianya.cn/publicforum/content/free/1/1324101.shtml

South China Tiger forum was shut down. (2008). *The Southern Metropolis Daily.* http://news.qq.com/a/20080309/000569.htm

Southcn.com. (2007). *Online anti-tiger activists.* http://news.qq.com/a/20071128/000977_3.htm

Sparks, C. (2007). *Globalization, development and the mass media.* Sage.

Standing Committee of the National People's Congress. (2005). *The provision on the advice from the deputies of the National People's Congress.* http://www.chinabaike.com/law/zy/xf/rm/1331022.html

State Administration of Radio, Film, and Television. (2008). *The plan for the Connecting Every Village with TV and Radio Project during the period of the 11th Five-Year Plan.* https://www.ndrc.gov.cn/fggz/fzzlgh/gjjzxgh/200804/P020191104623751015283.pdf

State Council of the People's Republic of China. (2000). *Regulation on internet information service.* http://www.gov.cn/gongbao/content/2000/content_60531.htm

State Council of the People's Republic of China. (2011). *Report of the State Council's meeting led by Primary Minister Wen.* http://www.gov.cn/zxft/ft218/content_2036423.htm

State Council of the People's Republic of China. (2013). *Notice on the implementation of the National Broadband Strategy.* http://www.gov.cn/zwgk/2013-08/17/content_2468348.htm

State Council of the People's Republic of China. (2016). *Special report on the National Nutrition Project 2016.* http://www.moe.gov.cn/jyb_xwfb/gzdt_gzdt/s5987/201609/t20160909_280612.html

State Council of the People's Republic of China. (2020). *About the Internet + Supervision platform: Collecting the information and advice for the response to the COVID-19 pandemic.* https://m.chinanews.com/wap/detail/chs/zw/9079740.shtml

Static web page. (2023, June 16). In Wikipedia. https://en.wikipedia.org/wiki/Static_web_page

Static website. (2009, June 12). In *TechTerms.* https://techterms.com/definition/staticwebsite

Strauss, V. (2020). Coronavirus pandemic shines light on deep digital divide in U.S. amid efforts to narrow it. *The Washington Post*. https://www.washingtonpost.com/education/2020/04/29/coronavirus-pandemic-shines-light-deep-digital-divide-us-amid-efforts-narrow-it/

Su, X. (2007). Who should feel shame for the Tiger Gate event. *People's Daily*. http://opinion.people.com.cn/GB/70240/6555058.html

Sullivan, J. (2012). A tale of two microblogs in China. *Media, Culture & Society, 34*(6), 773–783. https://doi.org/10.1177/0163443712448951

Supervision Center of the Free Lunch Project. (2017a, June 3). Supervision Center of the Free Lunch Project's Weibo message. https://weibo.com/u/6265182583?refer_flag=1005050010_

Supervision Center of the Free Lunch Project. (2017b, September 22). *Inspections and inspectors of the Free Lunch Project*. https://www.weibo.com/2058877932/FaIvJrqYe?type=repost#_0

Supervision Center of the Free Lunch Project. (2020, September 29). *Inspection report of Yun Nan Province Wen Shan Zhou Ma Guan County Di Fang Primary School*.

Surman, M. (2003). *Appropriating the internet for social change*. Social Science Research Council.

Sustaining containment of COVID-19 in China. (2020, April 18). *The Lancet, 395*(10232), 1230. https://doi.org/10.1016/S0140-6736(20)30864-3

Tacchi, J. (2007). Information, communication, poverty and voice. In J. Servaes (Ed.), *Moving Targets. Mapping the paths between communication, technology and social change in communities* (pp. 125–158). Southbound.

Tacchi, J., & Lennie, J. (2014). A participatory framework for researching and evaluating communication for development and social change. In K. Wilkins, T. Tufte, & R. Obregon (Eds.), *Handbook on development communication and social change* (pp. 298–320). Wiley Blackwell.

Tai, Z. (2006). *The Internet in China: Cyberspace and civil society*. Routledge.

Tan, J., & Eguavoen, I. (2017). Digital environmental governance in China: Information disclosure, pollution control, and environmental activism in the Yellow River Delta. *Water Alternatives, 10*(3), 910–929.

Tan, J., Gao, Y., Bao, Z., & Ding, G. (2020). *The whistleblower of COVID-19 Li Wenliang: Truth is the most important*. Caixin. http://china.caixin.com/2020-02-07/101509761.html

Tan, R. (2007). The origin of the South China tiger photos is a New Year picture. *The Southern Metropolis Daily*. http://news.sohu.com/20071116/n253297248.shtml

Tan, R. (2008, February 19). Shaanxi Forestry Department officials stated that they have no idea about whether the re-evaluation of the South China Tiger photos has begun or not. *Southern Metropolitan Daily*. http://news.xinhuanet.com/politics/2008-02/19/content_7629856.htm

Taobao.com. (2012). *Introduction of Taobao.com*. http://www.taobao.com/about/intro.php

TELEC, L., & TIO, A. (1999). *Falling through the Net: Defining the digital divide*. https://www.ntia.gov/legacy/ntiahome/fttn99/contents.html

Tenhunen, S. (2017). Digital ethnography of mobiles for development. In *The Routledge Companion to Digital Ethnography*. Routledge.

Terzis, G. (2002). Media and ethnopolitical conflict. In J. Servaes (Ed.), *Approaches to development communication* (pp. 501–526). UNESCO 4, 19.

Tiger Gate. (2008). China Central Television. http://news.cctv.com/special/C20076/01/

Thompson, J. (2008). Don't be afraid to explore Web 2.0. *Phi Delta Kappan, 89*(10), 711–778. http://search.ebscohost.com/login.aspx?direct=true&db=aph&AN =32537453&site=ehost-live&scope=site

Tian, G. (2015). Why could the Free Lunch Project get more than 100 million donations in four years? *China Youth Daily.* http://zqb.cyol.com/html/2015-04/29/nw .D110000zgqnb_20150429_1-08.htm

Ting, C. (2015). ICT4D in China and the capability approach: Do they mix? *International Journal of Information Communication Technologies and Human Development (IJICTHD), 7*(1), 58–72.

To clarify public's doubt on the Tiger Gate incident, government must face questions from the public. (2007, October 21). *The Southern Metropolis Daily.* http://nd.oeeee .com/sszt/tiger/

Torero, M., & von Braun, J. (Eds.) (2006). *Information and communication technologies for development and poverty reduction: The potential of telecommunications.* Johns Hopkins University Press.

Toutiao. (2023, April 20). In *Wikipedia.* https://en.wikipedia.org/wiki/Toutiao

Tsai, J., & Wilson, M. (2020). COVID-19: A potential public health problem for homeless populations. *The Lancet Public Health, 5*(4), e186–e187. https://doi.org/10 .1016/S2468-2667(20)30053-0

Tsai, L. L. (2007). *Accountability without democracy: Solidary groups and public goods provision in rural China.* Cambridge University Press.

Tufte, T. (2005). Entertainment-education in development communication: Between marketing behaviours and empowering people. In T. Tufte, & O. Hemer (Eds.), *Media and global change—Rethinking communication for development* (pp. 159–174). Nordicom.

UNAIDS & Penn State University. (1999). *Communications framework for HIV/AIDS: A new direction.* Penn State University. https://www.unaids.org/en/resources /documents/1999/19990922_jc335-commframew_en.pdf

UNICEF. (2011). *Communication rights.* https://www.unicef.org/cwc/cwc_58613.html

UNICEF. (2015). *United Nations hails China's progress towards the MDGs in final report.* https://www.unicef.cn/en/press-releases/united-nations-hails-china-progress -towards-mdgs-final-report

UNICEF. (2016). *Nutrition's lifelong impact.* https://www.unicef.org/nutrition/index _lifelong-impact.html

UNICEF. (2018). *China: Per capita disposable income, by urban-rural 1990–2017.* https://www.unicef.cn/en/figure-23-capita-disposable-income-urban-rural-19902017

United Nations. (2000). *Goal 6: Combat HIV/AIDS, malaria and other diseases.* Millennium Development Goals. https://www.un.org/millenniumgoals/aids.shtml

United Nations. (2011). *The millennium development goals report 2011.* https://www.un .org/millenniumgoals/pdf/(2011_E)%20MDG%20Report%202011_Book%20LR.pdf

United Nations. (2012). *Empowerment: What it means to you.* http://social.un.org /empowerment

United Nations. (2014). *Country classification.* http://www.un.org/en/development /desa/policy/wesp/wesp_current/2014wesp_country_classification.pdf

United Nations. (2015). *Transforming our world: The 2030 agenda for sustainable development.* https://sdgs.un.org/sites/default/files/publications/21252030%20 Agenda%20for%20Sustainable%20Development%20web.pdf

United Nations. (2016). *Sustainable Development Goal 2: End hunger, achieve food security and improved nutrition and promote sustainable agriculture.* https://unstats .un.org/sdgs/report/2016/goal-02/

United Nations Development Programme. (2001). *Human development report 2001: Making new technologies work for human development.* https://hdr.undp.org/system /files/documents/hdr2001enpdf.pdf

United Nations Development Programme. (2006). *Communication for empowerment: Developing media strategies in support of vulnerable groups (practical guidance note).* http://www.undp.org/oslocentre/docs06/Communicationforempowermentfinal.pdf

United Nations Development Programme. (2015). *Eradicate extreme hunger and poverty: Where we are.* http://www.cn.undp.org/content/china/en/home/post-2015 /mdgoverview/overview/mdg1.html

United Nations Development Programme. (2016). *What are the sustainable development goals?* https://www.undp.org/sustainable-development-goals

United Nations Development Programme. (2017). *Guidance note: UNDP social and environmental standards (SES); stakeholder engagement.* https://www .cvereferenceguide.org/sites/default/files/resources/Guidance%20Note%20 UNDP%20Social%20and%20Environmental%20Stand.pdf

United Nations Development Programme. (2019). *Human development report 2019: Beyond income, beyond averages, beyond today: Inequalities in human development in the 21st century.* https://hdr.undp.org/content/human-development-report-2019

United Nations Development Programme & Communication for Social Change Consortium. (2010, May). *Communication for empowerment: Global report.* http://archive.cfsc.org/pdfs/c4e-globalreport-june2010.pdf

United Nations Educational, Scientific and Cultural Organization. (2005). *Media and good governance.* http://www.unesco.org/new/en/communication-and-information /resources/publications-and-communication-materials/publications/full-list/media -and-good-governance/

United Nations Educational, Scientific and Cultural Organization. (2019). *From access to empowerment: UNESCO strategy for gender equality in and through education 2019–2025.* https://unesdoc.unesco.org/ark:/48223/pf0000369000

United Nations Millennium Declaration, September 8, 2000. https://www.ohchr.org /en/instruments-mechanisms/instruments/united-nations-millennium-declaration

Universal Declaration of Human Rights, December 10, 1948. https://www.un.org/en /about-us/universal-declaration-of-human-rights

Unwin, T. (2009). *ICT4D: Information and communication technology for development.* Cambridge University Press.

U.S. Census Bureau. (2011). *U.S. neighborhood income inequality in the 2005–2009 period.* https://www.census.gov/prod/2011pubs/acs-16.pdf

U.S. Department of Health and Human Services. (2020). *Hospital experiences responding to the COVID-19 pandemic: Results of a national pulse survey, March 23–27, 2020.* https://oig.hhs.gov/oei/reports/oei-06-20–00300.asp

U.S. Department of State. (2005). *Government accountability.* http://infousa.state.gov /government/overview/government_dem.html

van Dijk, J. (2000). Widening information gaps and policies of prevention. Digital democracy: Issues of theory and practice, 166–183.

van Dijk, J. (2005). *The deepening divide: Inequality in the information society.* Sage Publications.

van Dijk, J. A. (2006). Digital divide research, achievements and shortcomings. *Poetics, 34*(4–5), 221–235.

van Elsland, S. L., & O'Hare, R. (2020). *COVID-19: Imperial researchers model likely impact of public health measures.* http://www.imperial.ac.uk/news/196234/covid-19 -imperial-researchers-model-likely-impact/#authorbox

Verran, S. (2009). The role of the internet in state-society relations and the consequences for popular protests. *China Elections and Governance Review*(3), 16–27.

Vigdor, J. L., Ladd, H. F., & Martinez, E. (2014). Scaling the digital divide: Home computer technology and student achievement. *Economic inquiry, 52*(3), 1103–1119.

Wacker, G. (2003). The Internet and censorship in China. *China and the internet: Politics of the digital leap forward*, 58–82.

Waisbord, S. (2005). Five key ideas: coincidences and challenges in development communication. *Media and glocal change: Rethinking communication for development, 77*–90.

Wallack, L. (1994). Media advocacy: A strategy for empowering people and communities. *Journal of Public Health Policy, 15*(4), 420–436.

Wallis, C. (2013). *Technomobility in China: Young migrant women and mobile phones.* NYU Press.

Wang. B. (2020, October). The collaboration between the Free Lunch Project and Hefeng. *China Community Newspaper.* https://www.mca.gov.cn/n152/n166/c43882/content.html

Wang, C. & Bai, X. (2008). The South China tiger incident: ICT-supported investigation enables rational public discussion. *China Youth Daily.* http://zqb.cyol.com/content/2008-07/07/content_2252841.htm

Wang, F.-Y., Zeng, D., Hendler, J. A., Zhang, Q., Zhuo, F., Yanqing, G., Hui, W., & Guanpi, L. (2010). A study of the human flesh search engine: Crowd-powered expansion of online knowledge. *Computer, 43*(8), 45–53.

Wang, G. (2007). ZhengPing lost its "tiger," government lost its credibility, we can't lose justice again. *DongFang Daily.* http://opinion.people.com.cn/GB/6556051.html

Wang, J. (2007). Introduction: The politics and production of scales in China. In *Locating China: Space, place, and popular culture* (pp. 15–44). Routledge.

Wang, J. (2014). *From Cambridge to Shenzhen: An update of NGO2.0.* https://cms.mit.edu/update-on-ngo20/.

Wang, J. (2016). (Eds.). *Internet plus social good.* Publishing House of Electronics Industry.

Wang, J. (2019a). Interview with NGO 2.0 Founder Wang Jing. *China Philanthropy Times.* http://www.gongyishibao.com/newdzb/images/2019-09/17/16/GYSB16.pdf

Wang, J. (2019b). *The other digital China: Nonconfrontational activism on the social web.* Harvard University Press.

Wang, J., & Whitacre, A. (2013). *NGO 2.0: An interview with Jing Wang.* https://cmsw.mit.edu/ngo-2-0-interview-jing-wang/

Wang, J, (2020). The Free Lunch Project and the Hefeng Model. *China Society News.* https://www.mca.gov.cn/n152/n166/c43882/content.html

Wang, K. (2011). The free lunch project in Hebei Province is going to be launched in November. *Beijing News.* news.bjnews.com.cn/2011/1019/135751.shtml

Wang, S. (2012). *Mai Lu: Dining rooms and kitchens must be built to effectively implement the National Nutrition Project.* Caixin. http://china.caixin.com/2012-11-27/100465534.html

Wang, S. (2017). *Cyberdualism in China: The political implications of internet exposure of educated youth.* Routledge. https://search.ebscohost.com/login.aspx?direct=true&scope=site&db=nlebk&db=nlabk&AN=1512660

Wang, Y. (2007). *Mathematic methods could perfectly prove that the South China tiger photos are faked.* http://blog.sina.com.cn/s/blog_502d921d010083p7.html

Wang, Y., & Yang, X. (2006). Deputy minister of the Ministry of Information Industry: China will further narrow the digital divide between rural regions and urban regions. Xinhua News Agency. http://news.cctv.com/science/20061206/105793.shtml

Wang, Z., & Tang, K. (2020). Combating COVID-19: Health equity matters. *Nature medicine, 26*(4), 458–458.

Warkentin, C. (2001). *Reshaping world politics: NGOs, the Internet, and global civil society.* Rowman & Littlefield Publishers.

Warschauer, M. (2004). *Technology and social inclusion: Rethinking the digital divide.* MIT press.

Web 2.0. (2023, May 28). In *Wikipedia.* http://en.wikipedia.org/wiki/Web_2.0

Wei, W. (1998). Dominant or alternative paradigm? a meta-research of mass communication and development studies in Asia in the 1990s. *Journal of Development Communication, 9*(2), 31–44.

Weibo.com. (2020). *Text message and MMS version.* https://help.sina.com.cn/i/203/918 _12.html

Wen, M. (2019). Jing Wang: I prefer to stand at the margin observing the non-profit sector. *China Philanthropy Times.* http://www.gongyishibao.com/html/renwuzishu /17352.html

Wenham, C., Smith, J., & Morgan, R. (2020). COVID-19: The gendered impacts of the outbreak. *Lancet (London, England), 395*(10227), 846–848. https://doi.org/10.1016 /S0140-6736(20)30526-2

West, J. A., & West, M. L. (2009). *Using wikis for online collaboration: The power of the read-write web.* Jossey-Bass.

We wish XiaMen PX Project will become a milestone. (2008). News.qq.com. http://view .news.qq.com/zt/2007/xmpx/index.htm

What is the purpose of keeping retention samples? (2014, April 1). *HACCP Mentor.* https://haccpmentor.com/verification/keeping-retention-samples/

Why did a nutritional meal become a problematic meal? (2013). *Hubei Daily.* http:// news.cnhubei.com/ctdsb/ctdsbsgk/ctdsb29/201305/t2580370.shtml

Whyte, M. K. (2010). *One country, two societies: Rural–urban inequality in contemporary China* (Vol. 16). Harvard University Press.

Wikipedia. (2020). *Optical brightener.* http://en.wikipedia.org/wiki/Optical _brightener

Wilkins, K. G. (2000). *Redeveloping communication for social change: Theory, practice, and power.* Rowman & Littlefield.

Wilkins, K. G. (2005). Out of focus: gender visibilities in development. In O. Hemer & T. Tufte (Eds.), *Media and glocal change: Rethinking communication for development* (pp. 261–270), Nordicom.

Wilkins, K. G. (2009). What's in a name? Problematizing communication's shift from development to social change. *Glocal Times* (13).

Wilkins, K. G. (2014). Advocacy communication. In K. G. Wilkins, T. Tufte, & R. Obregon, *The handbook of development communication and social change,* (pp. 57–71). Wiley-Blackwell.

Wilkins, K. G. (2015). Development Communication. In *The International Encyclopedia of Communication.* American Cancer Society. https://doi.org/10.1002 /9781405186407.wbiecd020.pub2

Wilkins, K. G., & Mody, B. (2001). Reshaping development communication: Developing communication and communicating development. *Communication Theory 11*(4), 385–396.

Wilkins, K. G., Tufte, T., & Obregon, R. (2014). *The handbook of development communication and social change* (Vol. 4). Wiley Online Library.

Williams, I. (2017, September 6). *China's internet crackdown is another step toward "digital totalitarian state."* NBC News. https://www.nbcnews.com/news/china

/china-s-internet-crackdown-another-step-toward-digital-totalitarian-state
-n798001

Williams, R., & Williams, E. (2003). *Television: Technology and cultural form*. Psychology Press.

Wong, W., & Welch, E. (2004). Does e-government promote accountability? A comparative analysis of website openness and government accountability. *Governance*, *17*(2), 275–297. https://doi.org/10.1111/j.1468–0491.2004.00246.x

WordPress. (2013). Official website. https://wordpress.com/

WordPress.com. (2023, June 9). In *Wikipedia*. https://en.wikipedia.org/wiki/WordPress.com

World Bank. (2006). *Global monitoring report 2006: Millennium Development Goals—strengthening mutual accountability, aid, trade, and governance*. https://openknowledge.worldbank.org/server/api/core/bitstreams/6e88be2b-0d0a-5f8b-b2c2-8e11a74f6022/content

World Health Organization. (1992). *Advocacy strategies for health and development: Development communication in action*.

World Health Organization. (2015). *United Nations hails China's progress towards the Millennium Development Goals in final report*. http://www.wpro.who.int/china/mediacentre/releases/2015/20150724/en/

World Health Organization. (2020a). *Report of the WHO-China Joint Mission on Coronavirus Disease, 2019*. https://www.who.int/docs/default-source/coronaviruse/who-china-joint-mission-on-covid-19-final-report.pdf

World Health Organization. (2020b). *Shortage of personal protective equipment endangering health workers worldwide*. https://www.who.int/news-room/detail/03-03-2020-shortage-of-personal-protective-equipment-endangering-health-workers-worldwide

World Health Organization. (2022). *WHO COVID-19 Dashboard*. Retrieved January 12, 2022, from https://covid19.who.int/

World Summit on the Information Society. (2003). Declaration of principles: Building the information society: A global challenge in the new millennium. Geneva. https://www.itu.int/net/wsis/docs/geneva/official/dop.html

Wren, C. (1998). *Perspective transform estimation*. http://xenia.media.mit.edu/~cwren/interpolator/

Wu, F. (2002). New partners or old brothers? GONGOs in transnational environmental advocacy in China. *China Environment Series*, *5*, 45–58.

Wu, W., & Ma, J. (2020, February 1). Five questions to the Red Cross. *Beijing News*. http://www.bjnews.com.cn/news/2020/02/01/682834.html

Wu, X. (2007). *Chinese cyber nationalism: Evolution, characteristics, and implications*. Lexington Books.

Wu, X. (2012). Jingling Primary School's free lunch program is going to start. *Jiujiang Morning Post*. http://www.jjxw.cn/2012/1119/70179.shtml

Xi, J. (2013). *Equal modernization fruits for urban, rural residents: Xi*. http://english.cntv.cn/20131116/100750.shtml

Xiao, H., Wang, S., Zhao, N., & Ding, J. (2020, February 24). *Save Wuhan: How self-help networks were formed*. Caixin Weekly. http://weekly.caixin.com/2020-02-22/101518909.html

Xiao, R. (2016). WeChat public account. In J. Wang (Ed.), *Internet plus social good*. Publishing House of Electronics Industry.

Xie, Y., & Zhou, X. (2014). Income inequality in today's China. *Proceedings of the National Academy of Sciences of the United States of America*, *111*(19), 6928–6933. https://doi.org/10.1073/pnas.1403158111 [doi]

Xinxing, Z. (2011). Free lunches for rural students: From grassroots free lunch project to national nutritional subsidies. *Nanfang Daily*. http://finance.ifeng.com/news/macro /20111101/4967384.shtml

Xu, H. (2011). School Milk: Risk as high as drugs but profits as low as pickles. *China Business Journal*. http://biz.jrj.com.cn/2011/08/09130810684514.shtml

Xu, M. (2020, January 28). Secretary of Wuhan party committee: Donations must be centrally managed by the Red Cross. *Beijing News*. http://www.bjnews.com.cn /wevideo/2020/01/28/680848.html

Xu, X. (2008, June 29). *Zhu Julong was removed from his position*. https://news.sina.com .cn/c/2008-06-29/144215837893.shtml

Xue, J., & Gao, W. (2012). *How large is the urban-rural income gap in China?* http:// faculty.washington.edu/karyiu/confer/sea12/papers/SC12–110%20Xue_Guo.pdf

Yahoo.com. (2011). *Transparency is the life of the Free Lunch Project*. http://gongyi.cn .yahoo.com/ypen/20110806/512800.html

Yan, H., He, C., & Gao, L. (2017). The difficulty of grassroots practitioner in environmental NGOs. *China Environment Series* (9), 16.

Yang, C. (2012). The public service logic behind the Free Lunch bill. *The Southern Metropolis Daily*. http://big5.ifeng.com/gate/big5/news.ifeng.com/opinion/society /detail_2012_03/13/13154825_0.shtml

Yang, D. T. (1999). Urban-biased policies and rising income inequality in China. *The American Economic Review, 89*(2), 306–310.

Yang, G. (2003). The co-evolution of the internet and civil society in China. *Asian Survey, 43*(3), 405–422. http://www.jstor.org/stable/10.1525/as.2003.43.3.405

Yang, G. (2005). Environmental NGOs and institutional dynamics in China. *The China Quarterly, 181*, 46–66. https://doi.org/10.1017/S0305741005000032

Yang, G. (2009). *The power of the Internet in China: Citizen activism online*. Columbia University Press. http://discovery.lib.harvard.edu/?itemid=%7Clibrary/m /aleph%7C012029134

Yang, H., & Zhao, D. (2015). Performance legitimacy, state autonomy and China's economic miracle. *Journal of Contemporary China, 24*(91), 64–82.

Yang, L., & Sun, T. (2007, December 12). Wildlife in a camera. *Three Qin Daily*. http:// news.sina.com.cn/s/2007-12-12/073213063821s.shtml

Yang, Y. (2007). *The National Forestry Administration rejected Hao's application*. http:// news.sina.com.cn/c/2007-11-26/171114390386.shtml

Yao Ming. (2023, June 18). In *Wikipedia*. https://en.wikipedia.org/wiki/Yao_Ming

Ye, J. (2008). For China's web portals, controversy sells. *Wall Street Journal*. http:// online.wsj.com/article/SB120415879228098115.html

Ye, T. (2012). The public policy on rural education is getting back on the right track. *China Youth Daily*. http://zqb.cyol.com/html/2012-12/28/nw.D110000zgqnb _20121228_1-03.htm

Yi, A., & Chu, Y. (2012). Volunteer teacher exposed the problem of the national nutritional project. *Yangcheng Evening Post*. http://news.ycwb.com/2012-11/25 /content_4142451.htm

Yi Nong Dai. (2017). *2016 annual report*. http://www.yinongdai.com/annual/report/2016

Yi Nong Dai. (2020a). *About us*. http://www.yinongdai.com/aboutus/aboutUs

Yi Nong Dai. (2020b). *Empowering rural women*. http://www.yinongdai.com/aboutus /aboutUsValueLabel/valueLabelDetail?id=1000001

Yi Nong Dai. (2021). *Home page*. http://www.yinongdai.com/

Yibao. (2019). *The 2019 Survey report on the income and social security benefits of NGO practitioners in China*. http://www.chinadevelopmentbrief.org.cn/news-23666.html

YiNongDai. (2021, January 5). In *Wikipedia*. https://en.wikipedia.org/wiki/YiNongDai

YiTiaoBan Hanzi. (2007). *A critique to the Report on Tiger Gate from the News Probe*. http://blog.sina.com.cn/s/blog_499b1ee501007rjy.html

Young, D. R. (2000). Alternative models of government-nonprofit sector relations: Theoretical and international perspectives. *Nonprofit and Voluntary Sector Quarterly*, *29*(1), 149–172.

Young, D. R. (2006). Complementary, supplementary, or adversarial? Nonprofit-government relations. *Nonprofits and Government: Collaboration and Conflict*, *37*, 80.

Yu, H. (2017). *Networking China: The digital transformation of the Chinese economy*. University of Illinois Press.

Yu, J., & Guo, S. (2012). *Civil society and governance in China*. Springer.

Yu, K. (2002a). *The emerging of civil society and its significance to governance in reform China*. Social Science Academic Press.

Yu, K. (2002b). Toward an incremental democracy and governance: Chinese theories and assessment criteria. *New Political Science*, *24*(2), 181–199. https://doi.org/10.1080/07393140220145207

Yu, L. (2020). *Dare-to-die corps to fight for pregnant women in Wuhan*. https://gongyi.ifeng.com/c/7ttj4lMolBg

Zhang, F. (2012). The "safety" exploration of the Free Lunch Project. *Yunnan Information Post*. http://news.ynxxb.com/content/2012-3/6/N97543083296.aspx

Zhang, Q. (2019). Lecture in the Web 2.0 workshop of the NGO 2.0 Project at Kunshan.

Zhang, R. (2011). The Free Lunch project has raised more than 10 million yuan. *Jinghua Times*. http://news.xinhuanet.com/edu/2011-09/26/c_122085892_3.htm

Zhang, T. (2011). "Free Lunch": Passing the torch to the government. *People's Daily*. http://opinion.people.com.cn/GB/14602191.html

Zhang, Y. (2007). Shaanxi Forestry Department: Most of the South China tiger photos on the internet are not the original photos taken by Zhou. *ShangHai Morning Post*. http://news.sina.com.cn/c/2007-10-17/035714103137.shtml

Zhang San (2007). *Questioning the report on Tiger Gate from the News Probe*. http://blog.sina.com.cn/s/blog_490f766001007pa8.html

Zhao, J., & Wang, X. (2017). 2015 nutrition report on school children in rural areas in Shannxi. *Chinese Journal of School Health*, *7*, 035.

Zhao, X. (2011). Nutrition subsidies for children in poverty: From a grassroots action to the National Nutrition Subsidies policy. *Nanfang Daily*. https://www.chinanews.com.cn/edu/2011/11-01/3429001.shtml

Zhao, Y. (2003). Transnational capital, the Chinese state, and China's communication industries in a fractured society. *Javnost—The Public*, *10*(4), 53–74.

Zhao, Y. (2008). *Communication in China: political economy, power, and conflict*. Rowman & Littlefield.

Zhao, Y. (2009). Rethinking Chinese media studies. *Internationalizing media studies*, 175.

Zheng, Y. (2007). *Technological empowerment: The Internet, state, and society in China*. Stanford University Press.

Zhong, G. (2017). The implementation of the national nutritional project for rural students in the past five years. *China Youth Daily*. http://zqb.cyol.com/html/2017-06/02/nw.D110000zgqnb_20170602_6-01.htm

Zhou, F., Yu, T., Du, R., Fan, G., Liu, Y., Liu, Z., Xiang, J., Wang, Y., Song, B., & Gu, X. (2020). Clinical course and risk factors for mortality of adult inpatients with COVID-19 in Wuhan, China: A retrospective cohort study. *The Lancet*.

Zhou, Y. (2006). *Historicizing online politics: Telegraphy, the internet, and political participation in China*. Stanford University Press.

Zhu, G.-L., & Zhou, W. (2011). Improving government's capacity of attaining public trust in the process of transforming government functions. *Journal of Renmin University of China*, *14*(03), 120. http://xsqks.ruc.edu.cn/Jweb_rdxb/EN/abstract/article_8409.shtml

Zhu, H. (2009). *Canonical examples of new and old media holding government accountable*. http://opinion.people.com.cn/GB/159301/10256012.html

Zhu, J. (2004). The grassroots NGO and the development of civil society in China. *Open Times*, *6*(special issue), 36–74.

Zhu, Y. (2011). "Performance legitimacy" and China's political adaptation strategy. *Journal of Chinese Political Science*, *16*(2), 123–140.

Zhuang, Q., & Liu, D. (2012). Grassroots activists advocated that the national nutritional lunch should switch to formal meal. *China Youth Daily*, 03. http://zqb.cyol.com/html/2012-12/01/nw.D110000zgqnb_20121201_4-03.htm

Zhuoming Disaster Information Center. (2020a). *The third situation report on COVID-19 in Hubei Province*. http://shimo.

Zhuoming Disaster Information Center. (2020b). *Update history*. Summary of information platforms of domestic grassroots organizations against covid-19,https://shimo.im/sheets/onq7MwYMb6i4FjA9/MODOC

Zittrain, J. (2008). *The future of the internet and how to stop it*. Yale University Press. http://hollis.harvard.edu/?itemid=%7Clibrary/m/aleph%7C011421173

Zittrain, J., & Edelman, B. (2003). *Empirical analysis of internet filtering in China*. https://cyber.harvard.edu/filtering/china/

ZOL Center for Internet Consumption Research. (2011). *China desktop market report 2010 to 2011*. http://zdc.zol.com.cn/211/2112527.html

Index

About the Author

SONG SHI is a teaching assistant professor in the School of Computing and Information and the School of Arts and Sciences at the University of Pittsburgh. He has been engaged in internet research over the last fifteen years, with intimate ties to many of the activists and NGOs analyzed in this book. Since 2010, he has been the associate director of the New Media Action Lab at MIT.